# BAHISHTI ZEWAR
### (Virtues to Earn Allah's Pleasure)

*By*
Late Maulana Ashraf Ali Thanvi

*English Version by*
Muhammad Masroor Khan Saroha
M.A., LL.B. (Alig.)

**Islamic Publications Ltd.**
13 - E, SHAH ALAM MARKET
LAHORE - PAKISTAN

*All Rights Reserved*

First Edition : August, 1982—2,100

Published by
Ashfaq Mirza, Managing Director
Islamic Publications Limited
13-E, Shah Alam Market, Lahore
Printed by
Syed Afzal-ul-Haq Quddusi,
Quddusi Printers, Nasir Park,
Bilal Gunj, Lahore.

# CONTENTS

|  | Page |
|---|---|
| Publisher's Note | xiv |
| Foreword | xv |
| True Beliefs ('Aqaed) | 9 |
| Misguiding Acts and Beliefs | 17 |
| Heresy, Innovation (Bid'ah) and Wrong Customs | 19 |
| Grave Sins—which have been seriously warned against | 22 |
| Material Loss by Sins | 23 |
| Material Gains by Devotion and Good Deeds | 24 |
| Ablution – (Wudu) | 26 |
| Obligatory and Sunna Acts of Wudu | 27 |
| Breaches of Wudu | 30 |
| Bath—(Ghusul) | 35 |
| Suitable and Unsuitable Water for Bath and Ablution | 39 |
| The Well—Clean and Unclean | 42 |
| The Leavings of Animals | 45 |
| Tayammum | 47 |
| Masah of Leather Hoses | 53 |
| Obligatory Bath | 56 |
| Additional Instructions about Wudu | 58 |
| Injunctions for being without Wudu | 59 |
| Bath—when obligatory | 60 |
| Sunna Bath | 61 |
| Appreciable Bath | 61 |
| Instructions about Use of Water | 63 |
| Injunctions for Minor Impurities | 65 |
| Additional Instructions about Tayammum | 66 |
| Some Typical Problems of Pollution | 68 |
| Things Unsuitable for Istanja | 72 |
| Purification from Pollution | 74 |
| Istanja (Cleaning by Earth Clod) | 79 |
| The Prayers (Namaz) | 82 |

(iii)

(iv)

| | Page |
|---|---|
| **Times of Prayers** | 83 |
| 1. Morning Prayer (Fajr) | 83 |
| 2. Mid-day Prayer (Zuhr) | 83 |
| 3. Afternoon Prayer ('Asr) | 83 |
| 4. After Sunset Prayer (Maghrib) | 83 |
| 5. Night Prayer (Isha) | 83 |
| **Instructions for Prayer** | 86 |
| **Conditions of Prayer** | 88 |
| Intent for Prayer | 90 |
| To face Ka'aba while Praying | 92 |
| Method of Offering Fard Prayer | 93 |
| Some Requisites of Fard Prayer | 100 |
| Difference in Postures of Men and Women in Prayer | 102 |
| **Things or Acts which Disrupt Namaz** | 104 |
| **Execrables of Prayers** | 106 |
| Breaches in Prayers | 109 |
| Conditions when break in Prayers is proper | 112 |
| **The Sunnah and Nafl Prayers** | 114 |
| Method of its Performance | 116 |
| Witr Prayer | 118 |
| **Prayer for Guidance (Namaz-e-Istikhara)** | 121 |
| Prayer for Repentance (Namaz Tauba) | 122 |
| **Offering of Missed Prayers (Qada Namaz)** | 123 |
| **Prostration for Correction (Sajda-e-Sahav)** | 127 |
| **Prostration of Recitation (Sajda-e-Tilawat)** | 134 |
| **Patients Prayer (Namaz)** | 139 |
| **Prayer of a Traveller** | 142 |
| **Recitation of the Holy Quran** | 148 |
| **Calling for Adhan and Iqamat** | 150 |
| Injunctions for Adhan and Iqamat | 151 |
| Appreciables of Adhan and Iqamat | 153 |
| About Moadhdhin | 153 |
| About Adhan and Iqamat | 154 |
| Injunctions | 155 |
| **Prayer on Entering the Mosque (Tahiyatul Masjid)** | 156 |

|  | Page |
|---|---|
| **Tarawih Prayer of Ramadan** | ... 157 |
| **Prayer for Rain (Namaze Istasqa)** | ... 159 |
| **Prayer during Eclipses** | ... 160 |
| **Some Obligatory and Essential Problems of Namaz** | ... 162 |
| **Offering of Prayer in Congregation (Namaz-e-Imamat)** | ... 164 |
|    Value of Congregation | ... 164 |
|    Ahadith | ... 164 |
|    Conditions of Proper Congregation | ... 165 |
|    Injunctions | ... 166 |
|    Example | ... 168 |
|    Excuses for Congregation | ... 171 |
|    Injunctions for Congregation | ... 172 |
|    Warning | ... 174 |
|    About the Imam and the Followers | ... 174 |
|    Example | ... 179 |
|    Example | ... 180 |
|    On Missing of Congregation | ... 181 |
|    Things or Acts which Spoil the Namaz | ... 183 |
| **About Death, Funeral and Shroud (Death)** | ... 186 |
|    Bath of the Dead | ... 187 |
|    Method of Bath | ... 188 |
|    Shrouding | ... 190 |
|    Method of Shrouding | ... 191 |
| **The Funeral Prayer** | ... 194 |
| **Burial (Dafn) of the Dead** | ... 201 |
|    Instructions for proper Funeral | ... 204 |
|    About Shaheed (Martyr) | ... 206 |
|    Injunctions about Martyrdom | ... 208 |
| **The Mosque-Injunctions** | ... 210 |
|    Offering of Prayer Inside Ka'aba | ... 211 |
| **Juma (Friday) Prayer** | ... 213 |
|    Virtues of Friday | ... 214 |
|    Respect and Reverence of Friday | ... 216 |
|    Importance of Friday Prayer | ... 217 |
|    Conditions for Juma Prayer to be Wajib | ... 219 |

|  | Page |
|---|---|
| Conditions for Juma Prayer to be correct | 220 |
| Khutba (Sermon) of Juma and Juma Prayer | 221 |
| Injunctions for Juma Sermon | 223 |
| **Eid Prayers** | 225 |
| Eidul Fitr and Eidul-Azha | 225 |
| Method of Eid Prayer | 226 |
| **The Fast** | 230 |
| Instructions about Ramadan Fast | 231 |
| Visibility of Moon | 233 |
| Breaches of Fast | 235 |
| Missed Fast | 237 |
| Vowed of Fasts | 238 |
| Nafl Fasts | 239 |
| When a Compensatory or Recompensatory Fast becomes Due | 240 |
| About Sehri and Iftar | 244 |
| Kaffara-Recompensation of Fast | 245 |
| When Breaking of Fast is Permissible | 247 |
| Conditions for not Keeping Fasts | 247 |
| Fidiya—Recompensation Cash or Kind | 250 |
| Aitikaf or Seclusion | 251 |
| **Zakat** | 256 |
| Zakat on Produce of Land (Ushr) | 262 |
| Who is Entitled to Receive Zakat | 263 |
| **Sadqa-e-Fitr** | 267 |
| **Sacrifice (Qurbani)** | 269 |
| Injunctions | 270 |
| **Aqeeqa—Removal of Hair of New-born Child** | 276 |
| **Haj Pilgrimage** | 278 |
| Visit to Madina Munawwara | 280 |
| Traditions about Masjid Nabawi | 281 |
| **Nikah (Marriage)** | 282 |
| Prohibited Matrimonials | 283 |
| Wali—Guardian | 286 |
| Mehr—Dowry | 290 |

| | Page |
|---|---|
| Family or Model Dowry | 294 |
| Marriage of New Converts to Islam | 294 |
| Equality among Wives | 294 |
| Considerations in Nikah | 295 |
| Divorce (Talaq) | 296 |
| Divorce before Joining after Nikah | 299 |
| Talaq-e-Moghallaza (Three Talaqs) | 300 |
| Conditional Divorce | 301 |
| Divorce by Patient | 302 |
| Rejoining in Revocable Divorce | 303 |
| Oath not to Go to Wife (Eila) | 305 |
| Release from Marriage (Khula') | 306 |
| Declare Wife equal to Mother | 309 |
| Recompensation for Zihar | 310 |
| Allegation of Adultery (Li'aan) | 311 |
| Absconding of Husband | 311 |
| Wife's Confinement on Husband's Death or Divorce (Iddat) | 312 |
| Mourning for the Dead | 314 |
| Maintenance of Wife | 315 |
| Residence | 316 |
| Legitimate Issues | 317 |
| Right of Fostering a Child | 318 |
| Mother's Milk – Sucking and Suckling | 318 |
| **Oath—Vow and Pledge (Mannat)** | 322 |
| Recompensation (Kaffarah) of Oath | 326 |
| **Apostasy** | 328 |
| **Slaughtering of Animal (Dhabiha)** | 330 |
| Permissible and Prohibited Things | 331 |
| Intoxicants | 331 |
| **Clothes and Purdah** | 333 |
| **Miscellaneous Instructions** | 336 |
| **Salutation (Salaam)** | 339 |
| **Waqf-Endowment** | 340 |
| About Dreams | 341 |

|   | Page |
|---|---|
| **Rights and Duties** | 342 |
| Parents | 342 |
| Relatives | 343 |
| In-Laws | 343 |
| General Muslims | 343 |
| Neighbours | 343 |
| Orphans and Poor | 344 |
| All Human Beings | 344 |
| Animals | 344 |
| **About Will** | 345 |
| **Gift—Hiba** | 347 |
| Gift to Children | 348 |
| To Take Back the Gift | 348 |
| Rent and Wages | 349 |
| **Transactions on Interest** | 350 |
| **Sale Through Advance Money** | 352 |
| Transaction on Loan | 353 |
| **To be Surety—Zamanat** | 354 |
| To Appoint Agent or Representative | 354 |
| To Join Together in Business—Mudarbat | 355 |
| Keeping Deposit—*Amanat* | 355 |
| Articles Taken on Loan | 357 |
| Bad Contracts | 357 |
| Partnership | 358 |
| Compensation of Loss—Ta'wan | 359 |
| Cancellation of Contract | 360 |
| Taking anything without Permission | 360 |
| Sharing Joint Property | 361 |
| Mortgage | 361 |
| **Bad and Non-Permissible Hobbies** | 363 |
| Dance | 363 |
| Pet Dogs and Photographs | 364 |
| Fireworks | 365 |
| Playing Cards and Chess | 365 |
| **Some Usages, Customs and Ceremonies** | 366 |

|   | Page |
|---|---|
| Child Birth | 366 |
| Aqiqa Ceremony | 368 |
| Circumcision (Khatna) | 369 |
| Bismillah Ceremony | 370 |
| Participation in Ceremonies | 370 |
| Engagement—Mangni | 371 |
| Marriage Customs | 371 |
| Excessive Mehr | 376 |
| Prayer for the Dead | 376 |
| After Death Ceremonies | 378 |
| Ceremonies of Ramadan | 380 |
| Eid Ceremony | 380 |
| Sermon and Ceremonies of Rabi-ul-Awwal | 381 |
| Shab-e-Barat and Muharram | 381 |
| Ziarat of Sacred Relics | 383 |
| **Etiquettes of Devotional Practices** | 385 |
| Ablution and Cleanliness | 385 |
| Prayers | 385 |
| Zakat—Charity—Fasts | 386 |
| Recitation of Holy Quran | 387 |
| Some Prayers (Dua) | 387 |
| **Correct Dealings** | 391 |
| Eating and Drinking | 392 |
| Safeguard of Tongue and Good Manners | 393 |
| Talkativeness | 394 |
| Envy | 395 |
| Love of Worldly Wealth | 396 |
| Miserliness | 397 |
| The Desire for Name and Fame | 397 |
| Pride and Boastfulness | 398 |
| Conceit | 399 |
| Hypocrisy or Pretence in Good Acts | 399 |
| Repentance | 400 |
| Fear of Allah | 400 |
| Hope from Allah | 400 |

|  | Page |
|---|---|
| Patience | 400 |
| Thankfulness | 401 |
| **Rules for Guidance of Muslims** | 403 |
| **Reward and Punishment—Some Holy Traditions** | 406 |
| Purity of Motive | 406 |
| Fame and Show | 406 |
| To Follow the Holy Quran and Traditions | 406 |
| To Initiate Virtue or Evil | 406 |
| Religious Knowledge | 407 |
| Concealing of Religious Knowledge | 407 |
| Precaution against Urine | 407 |
| About Ablution and Bath | 407 |
| Place of Prayer for Women | 408 |
| Punctuality in Prayers | 408 |
| Praying in Early Period | 408 |
| Careless Offering of Prayers | 409 |
| Debt and Debtor | 409 |
| Recitation of the Holy Quran | 410 |
| To Curse Oneself | 410 |
| Ill-gotten Income | 410 |
| Cheating | 410 |
| To Borrow | 410 |
| To Defer the Due | 411 |
| Interest | 411 |
| Unlawful Possession of Land | 411 |
| Prompt Payment of Labour | 411 |
| About the Death of Children | 411 |
| Women's Use of Perfume and Fine Clothes | 411 |
| Injustice | 412 |
| To be Kind and Merciful | 412 |
| Propagation of Virtue | 412 |
| Covering of Faults | 413 |
| To be Pleased on Someone's Loss | 413 |
| Taunting on One's Sins | 413 |
| Committing of Minor Sins | 413 |

| | Page |
|---|---|
| Parents' Pleasure | 413 |
| Ill-Treatment with Relatives | 413 |
| To Look after Orphans | 413 |
| Treatment with Neighbours | 414 |
| Helping a Muslim | 414 |
| Modesty and Immodesty | 414 |
| Politeness and Impoliteness | 414 |
| Mildness and Rudeness | 414 |
| To Peep in One's House | 415 |
| Eaves-Dropping | 415 |
| Anger | 415 |
| To Stop Talking | 415 |
| To Curse and Call Unbeliever | 415 |
| To Frighten a Muslim | 415 |
| To Accept a Muslim's Apology | 416 |
| Back-Biting | 416 |
| Slander | 416 |
| To Talk Less | 416 |
| Humility | 416 |
| Pride | 416 |
| Truth and Falsehood | 417 |
| Double Facedness | 417 |
| Swearing | 417 |
| To Remove Offensive Things from the Path | 417 |
| Promise and Trust | 417 |
| Sooth-Saying | 417 |
| Pet Dogs and Pictures | 418 |
| Lying on the Belly | 418 |
| Omen and Charms | 418 |
| Greed of the World | 418 |
| To Remember Death | 418 |
| Value of Time and Patience in Trouble | 418 |
| Visiting a Sick | 419 |
| About Dead | 419 |
| Crying with Lamentation | 419 |

| | Page |
|---|---|
| Orphan's Property | 419 |
| Qiyamat or Dooms Day | 419 |
| To Remember Paradise and Hell | 420 |
| **Qayamat or Dooms-Day** | 421 |
| Some Signs | 421 |
| Actual Day of Judgment | 426 |
| Paradise and the Hell | 428 |
| Hell | 429 |
| **Requisites of Iman (Faith)** | 430 |
| Seven things related to the Tongue | 431 |
| Forty Matters are related to our Body | 431 |
| Ills of 'Self' (Nafs) | 433 |
| Self-Treatment | 433 |
| **Nikah of the Consorts and Daughters of the Holy Prophet (SAW)** | 436 |
| Nikah of Hadrat Fatima | 436 |
| Dowry (Mehr) of the Consorts of the Holy Prophet | 438 |
| About Women | 438 |
| Defects of Women | 442 |
| **For Pleasant Life** | 444 |
| Behaviour with the Masses | 444 |
| Fear of Allah and Cleanliness of Heart | 446 |
| **Remembering Death** | 448 |
| **A'amal-e-Qurani** | 449 |
| For Head and Tooth-Ache | 449 |
| For all Kinds of Pains | 449 |
| For Weakness of Mind | 449 |
| For Weak Eye-Sight | 449 |
| For Stammering | 450 |
| For Depression of Heart | 450 |
| For Stomach Pain | 450 |
| For Cholera and Plague | 450 |
| For Spleen | 450 |
| For Fever | 450 |
| For Boils and Ulcers | 451 |

(xiii)

| | Page |
|---|---|
| For Snake and Wasp Bite | ... 451 |
| For Dog Bite | ... 451 |
| For a Son | ... 451 |
| For Small-Pox | ... 451 |
| For Removal of Poverty | ... 452 |
| For Removal of Difficulties | ... 452 |
| God's Help for Good Acts | ... 452 |
| To Get Pleasure of Allah | ... 452 |
| To Get Rid of Difficulties | ... 452 |

## Publisher's Note

"Bahishti Zewar" originally written in Urdu by the late Maulana Ashraf Ali Thanvi needs no introduction. Originally it was written for the guidance of Muslim women in the Indian sub-continent in their day to day life and to help them know the teachings of Islam in every aspect and sphere of domestic living.

We are presenting its English version by the courtesy and cooperation of the learned translator who has taken great pains in translating this voluminous work in an abridged form.

It is in fact a work of Fiqh made easy for those who have no real access and understanding of the original sources of Islamic Law i e. Quran and Sunnah and fall an easy prey to false customs and traditions prevalent in the decaying Muslim Society deeply influenced by the dominance of Non-Muslims around them.

We hope it shall prove quite helpful to Muslims abroad looking forward for Islamic guidance in their daily chores of life and pray Allah to accept this humble contribution to project and propagate Islamic teachings all the world over.

بِسْمِ اللَّهِ الرَّحْمَٰنِ الرَّحِيمِ

# Foreword

Hakim-ul-Ummat Hadrat Maulana Ashraf Ali Thanvi, the renowned philosopher and scholar of Islamic Jurisprudence, was grieved to see the degeneration of Muslim women in matters of Islam and its instructions. He found them surrounded and engaged in anti-Islamic activities, customs, rites and ceremonies which are detrimental not only from the worldly point of view but from religious view also. These were spreading like a contagious disease. The learned Maulana (may his soul rest in peace) pondered over it very seriously and as its remedy he compiled a voluminous book in Urdu language entitled "BAHISHTI ZEWAR" meaning Heavenly Ornaments, covering all the aspects of life from birth to death. He accomplished this onerous task with a view to bring about an improvement in their daily lives in the light of religion, Sunna and the Traditions.

This book is an encyclopaedia of Islam dealing in a very simple way with the tenets and principles of Islam as they are practised in day to day life. It is ready reference to our religious problems which we come across in our normal life. The esteemed book is so popular in India and Pakistan that it is given to daughters by their parents at the time of their marriage as a necessary part of their dowry.

Seeing the utility of the book and in order to make it useful universally, it was thought proper to translate it into English language so that our sisters and brothers-in-Islam of other countries who do not know Urdu, may also be benefited.

Hence the present book is in your hands. It is a translation of that valuable book in an abridged form. The portions which are peculiar to India and the chapters dealing with treatment of certain diseases with Unani medicines, have been omitted.

If one studies the book minutely, it is rightly believed that such a person can never be led astray in matters of religion. Keeping this point in view the translation has been done in such a way that it is equally good for men and women.

So far as the use of Arabic technical terms is concerned the equivalents of all of them are not easily available in English language. Hence certain Arabic technical terms have been used, but they have been explained so that the reader may easily comprehend their meanings and aims.

In its translation I have been immensely benefited by the famous translation of the Holy Quran by Mr. Marmaduke Pickthall and the dictionary compiled by Dr. Abdul Haq.

May Allah accept this humble effort of the Publishers and myself. Ameen.

Muhammad Masroor Khan Saroha
M.A., LL.B. (Alig.)

## In the Name of Allah, the Merciful, the Compassionate

بِسْمِ اللهِ الرَّحْمٰنِ الرَّحِيْمِ

اَلْحَمْدُ لِلّٰهِ الَّذِىْ قَالَ فِىْ كِتَابِهٖ يٰاَيُّهَا الَّذِيْنَ اٰمَنُوْا قُوْۤا اَنْفُسَكُمْ وَاَهْلِيْكُمْ نَارًا وَّقُوْدُهَا النَّاسُ وَالْحِجَارَةُ وَقَالَ اللهُ تَعَالٰى وَاذْكُرْنَ مَا يُتْلٰى فِىْ بُيُوْتِكُنَّ مِنْ اٰيَاتِ اللهِ وَالْحِكْمَةِ ط وَالصَّلٰوةُ وَالسَّلَامُ عَلٰى رَسُوْلِهٖ مُحَمَّدٍ صَفْوَةِ الْاَنْبِيَاءِ الَّذِىْ قَالَ فِىْ خِطَابِهٖ كُلُّكُمْ رَاعٍ وَّكُلُّكُمْ مَسْئُوْلٌ عَنْ رَعِيَّتِهٖ وَقَالَ عَلَيْهِ السَّلَامُ طَلَبُ الْعِلْمِ فَرِيْضَةٌ عَلٰى كُلِّ مُسْلِمٍ وَّمُسْلِمَةٍ وَّعَلٰى اٰلِهٖ وَاَصْحَابِهِ الْمُهْتَدِيْنَ وَالْمُؤَدَّبِيْنَ بِاٰدَابِهٖ

This humble Ashraf Ali Thanvi, Hanafi, takes this opportunity of expressing his grief and feelings over the degeneration of Indian Muslim women in matters of religion, faith and instructions of Islam. This pained me much and I was always anxious to find a remedy for the same. The concern was more because the degeneration was not limited to religion only but it had creeped into their world also—from their person to their children and husbands even. The speed with which it was spreading showed that if not checked and remedied immediately, the disease may become irremediable.

The root cause of all this, through the Mercy of Allah, experience, facts and self-knowledge, proved to be that our women are ignorant of religious knowledge. This ignorance has spoiled their beliefs (Aqa'ed), actions (A'mal), their moral, dealings and way of life so much so that their faith (Iman) is not being spared because certain of their actions and words amount to kufr (disbelief). Our generations are reared in their laps and as such their words and actions are impressed upon the hearts of the children which spoil their (childrens') Deen (religion) and at the same time their world also becomes tasteless.

This state of affairs create ill-beliefs which in turn give birth to immorality. Immorality leads to bad actions, bad actions to bad dealings which is the root of disturbed life. If the husband is also like her, then the collection of the evil-doers enhances the evil and destroys the world hereafter. Sometimes this evil results in personal dissensions which spoil the world also. If the husband has some sense, the poor chap's life turns into life-imprisonment Every action of the wife is a constant torture for him and advice of husband is nauseating for the wife. If patience is lost, the result is divorce and separation. If borne, life becomes miserable. For example talking ill about someone creates enmity with him which may result in some loss. For the sake of mere fame and name, money was spent lavishly on worldly ceremonies and customs and it turned into poverty. The husband may be displeased and turn her cut. Undue love and affection of children may deprive them of education or any other training and thus their lives may remain incomplete. The greed for wealth and ornaments increased and if the same could not be obtained. then whole life is spent miserably in solving this insatiable problem. In this way contagious and necessary-evils are due to ignorance.

Cure needs an antidote, hence the remedy of all these evils is the knowledge of religion. With this aim in view, I was obsessed with the idea of providing the knowledge of religion. Under the obligation of this necessity all the Urdu magazines and books were studied. But they were not found sufficient for the purpose. Some of those were not proper or authentic.

## IN THE NAME OF ALLAH

There are some authentic books but their language is not simple and easy to be grasped by women. Moreover these contain such topics which are not meant for women. So it was resolved that a special book for women be compiled in a very simple language.

Now by the Grace of Allah, this book has come into being which not only covers all the requisites of Deen (religion) but also economic necessities to such an extent that if anyone studies it with care and understanding, that in knowledge of religion he can be equal to an average scholar. Two kinds of doctrines and instructions have been discussed in this book. Firstly those which are common to men and women and secondly those which are meant for women particularly. In those particular problems, too, arrangement has been made to make them useful for men also to avoid mis-understanding.

Hence, just after finishing the study of the Holy Qur'an, the beginning of reading this book is advised. This book according to the taste of women has been entitled "BAHISHTI ZEWAR", because they are fond of ornaments. But the real ornaments are the teachings and achievements in religion and in Heaven they shall be adorned with these genuine ornaments in exchange of religious actions and values.

Before discussing the main problems it is advisable to describe some true stories for the sake of learning some moral from them.

### FIRST STORY

The Holy Prophet (peace be upon him) once said that a person was in a forest. Suddenly he heard a voice in the cloud above him ordering the cloud to go and water the garden of a certain person. The piece of cloud moved forward and at a stony place rained heavily. The water collected in a drain and flowed forward. This man followed the water. At some distance this man saw a person watering his garden with this water. This man asked the name of the owner of garden. In reply he gave the same name which the man has heard in the cloud. The owner of the garden asked him as to why he was asking his name. The man told him whatever he had heard in the cloud and then asked the owner of the garden as to what good deeds he did that he had become so dear to Allah. The owner of the garden replied, "When you have asked, I will tell you. When I collect the proceeds of this garden, one-third of it I give in alms, the other one-third I keep for myself and my family and the rest I re-invest in the garden."

**Moral :**

Allah be praised for His benevolence. One who obeys Him, his needs are fulfilled in such a way that no one knows about them. No doubt if one submits himself to Allah, He comes near Him.

## SECOND STORY

The Holy Prophet (peace be upon him) once said that there were three men of Banu Israel. One of them was a leper, the other bald and the third deaf. God, in order to test them, sent an angel to them. First of all the angel came to the leper and asked him what he desired most. The leper said that he wanted fair colour, beautiful skin and that he may be relieved from that disease due to which people did not allow him to sit with them, and hate him. The angel passed his hand over the body of the leper and immediately the disease disappeared and fair colour and beautiful skin appeared. The angel asked him which wealth he liked most. He named camel. So the angel gave him a pregnant she-camel and prayed to Allah to bless his wealth.

Then the angel came to the bald person and asked him what he liked ? The bald man said that he wanted good hair and cure from baldness. The angel passed his hand over the head of the bald and immediately good hair cropped up. Then the angel asked him as to which wealth he desired. The man asked for a cow. The angel gave him a pregnant cow and also blessed him wealth.

In the end the angel came to the blind man and asked him as to what he wanted. The man said that he wished God to cure his blindness so that he may see other persons. The angel passed his hand over his eyes and his eye-sight was cured by God. The angel asked him which wealth he liked. The man desired for a goat. The angel gave him a goat. The animals of these three persons gave birth to new issues in such a large number that their respective parts of the forest were full of them.

The angel again came to them after some time under orders of Allah. First he went to the ex-leper and told him that he was a traveller and that all of his provisions meant for the journey have exhausted and left with nothing to reach his home. He asked in the name of Allah, who had cured him of leprosy, a camel to reach his destination. The ex-leper scolded and snubbed him coldly and said that he had other responsibilities and cannot spare a camel for him.

The angel reminded him that formerly he was a leper from which Allah cured him and blessed him with all the wealth. The man said that he had inherited the wealth from his forefathers. Thereupon the angel cursed him that if he was a liar he may revert to his previous position.

The angel came to the ex-bald and asked him the same questions. The man replied in the same manner as the leper had done. The angel cursed him also.

In the end the angel came to the ex-blind man and relating his misfortune begged him for a goat. The man said, "No doubt I was blind. God blessed me with eye-sight. Take as many goats as you like. By God I will not refuse." The angel said he may keep his goats with him and prosper. He only wanted to test them. God is pleased with him and displeased with the other two.

*Moral* :—

Due to their thankiessness and ungratefulness the first two were deprived of the blessings of Allah and were reduced to their former positions and were cursed in this world and Hereafter.

## THIRD STORY

Once Hadrat Umme Salma received some meat from somewhere. The Holy Prophet (peace be upon him) liked meat very much, so she directed the maid to keep it for him. In the meantime a beggar came to the door and asked for something in alms. Hadrat Umme-Salma asked blessings for him which meant that there was nothing to give. The beggar went away. When the Holy Prophet (peace be upon him) came and asked Hadrat Umme-Salma for something to eat. She asked the maid to bring the meat. When the maid went to take the meat, it was not there and in its place a stone was found there. The Holy Prophet (peace be upon him) said that because she had refused to give it to the beggar hence the meat has turned into stone.

*Moral* :—

The shape of the meat changed because it was not given in the name of Allah to a needy person. Those who refuse to give to needy and enjoy themselves are eating stones and their hardheartedness grows day by day. It was shown to the Holy Prophet (peace be upon him) so that he may learn lesson from it.

### FOURTH STORY

It was the noble routine of the Holy Prophet (peace be upon him) that after Fajr (morning) prayer he used to ask his companions if anyone of them had seen any dream. If anyone did, the Holy Prophet (peace be upon him) used to interpret the same. Once the Holy Prophet (peace be upon him) asked the same question but none of them had seen any dream. The Holy Prophet (peace be upon him) then said that he himself had seen a dream last night and described that two men came to him and holding his hand led him to a sacred place. On their way he saw a man sitting and another man standing with a pincer in his hand with which he was tearing the cheek of the sitting man to the extent of his neck. Then he would do the same with the other cheek and in the meantime the first cheek would become normal. The other man started the same operation once again and this continued. The Holy Prophet (peace be upon him) asked the men accompanying him as to what was that. But they asked him to proceed further. Then they passed by a man lying and near his head another man was standing with a heavy stone in his hand and with which he was crushing the head of the lying man. Whenever he struck the stone it rolled down to some distance. The man goes to fetch the stone and in the meantime the head of the lying man becomes normal. He again crushes the head and the process continued. The Prophet (peace be upon him) asked about it. But they again asked him to go ahead.

Accompanied by the two men the Holy Prophet (peace be upon him) came to an oven-like cave which was narrow at the mouth and broad at the bottom. Huge fire was burning in it and it was full of naked men and women. When the flames of the fire rose the naked persons also rose up so high that they were about to come out but when the flames receded, they also went down with it. On the Prophet's (peace be upon him) asking about it he was again asked to move further.

Then they came to a canal full of blood and saw a man standing in its centre and another standing on the bank with a pile of stones before him. The man in the canal tries to reach the bank and come out of the canal. The man on the bank strikes his face with the stone with such force that the man is pushed back to the centre of the canal. The action is repeated again and again. The Holy Prophet (peace be upon him) again asks about it but the men accompanying him take him further on.

In the end they reach a green garden where under a large tree he saw an old man sitting with many infants. Near the tree another man was sitting with burning fire before him and he was blowing it. Then the companions of the Holy Prophet (peace be upon him) took him over the tree into a beautiful house as he had never seen before. In this house there were many men, women—young and old and children. Then they took him further up into another house which was more beautiful than the former. In this house there were many men and women—young and old.

The Holy Prophet (peace be upon him) asked the two men that they had spent the whole night in taking him round to different places and asked them to explain the mysteries. Then one of them explained that the first man whose cheeks were being torn was a liar. He used to tell a lie and it spared in the world. He will be treated like this till the Day of Judgment.

The man whose head was being crushed was blessed by Allah with the knowledge of Holy Quran. But he became careless about it and did not act according to it during his days and nights. He will suffer this fate till the Day of Judgment.

The naked men and women in the cave of fire were adulterers, while the man in the canal of blood was a usurer. The old man under the tree was Hadrat Ibrahim (Prophet Abraham) and the children were minor children of other men. The man blowing the fire was the Guardian of Hell. The first house in which he entered was the abode of Muslims in general and the other of martyrs. One of those accompanying him, was angel Gabriel and the other Michael. Then he asked the Holy Prophet (peace be upon him) to look above, where he saw a white piece of cloud and the angels told him that it was his house. The Prophet (peace be upon him) asked them to let him go into his house but the angels said that he has not yet completed his age. Had he completed it he could go into the house immediately.

*Moral* :—

Let us remember that the dreams of the prophets are revelations and inspirations and are always true. The above facts are true and point out many things. Firstly the punishment of lying, secondly the fate of a Scholar (*'Alim*) without action (*'Amal*) thirdly the doom of adulterers and fourthly the usurers. May Allah save us all from these evils and sins. Aameen.

## TRUE BELIEFS

### (AQĀED)

1—There was no Universe in the beginning. It came into being by order of Allah.

2—Allah is one. He is not subordinate to or dependent upon any one. He has neither given birth to anyone nor has been born of someone. He has no consort nor anyone is equal to him.

3—He is eternal. He has been from eternity and shall remain till eternity.

4—There is nothing like Him. He is unique.

5—He is alive. He has command over everything and there is nothing without His knowledge. He sees and hears everything. He talks but His speech is not like us. He does whatever He likes according to His will and there is no one to check Him. He alone is worthy of being worshipped. He has no partner. He is merciful to His creatures. He is the Lord of all, free from all blemishes. He is the Creator of all things and Forgiver of sins. He is Almighty. He bestows respect or reduces to disgrace. He is the Just. He has the greatest tolerance and forbearance. He values worship and devotion. He accepts prayers. He saves his creatures from all calamities. He is the Creator of all and will bring all to life again on the Day of Judgment.

6—He gives life and death. His signs and qualities are known to all but no one can know the mystery of His existence. He forgives sins and punishes those who deserve it. He guides and all that happens in this world is under His orders. Even a leaf cannot move without His order.

7—He neither sleeps nor dozes and is never tired of controlling the affairs of the world. He sustains everything and all good qualities are His. He alone possesses the knowledge of the things to be.

8—All of His qualities are eternal and none of them shall ever diminish.

9—He is free from human qualities and whatever is said in the Holy Quran about it, its meaning should be left to Him as He alone knows its significance and we believe it all without being inquisitive and have faith in it. Whatever it means is true and just. This is the best way or we may give meaning to it according to our better understanding in order to make it comprehensible

10—Whatever good or bad happens in this world has ever been in His knowledge long before its happening and He lets it happen according to His knowledge. This is called destiny or fate and there are mysteries in the creation of evils which every one cannot comprehend.

11—Allah has blessed the human beings with understanding and intent and according to their discretion they do good or evil but no one has the power to create anything. Allah is displeased with sinful deeds and pleased with good acts.

12—Allah has not commanded His creatures to do anything beyond their capacity.

13—Allah is not bound by anything. Any kindness that He does is on account of His Mercifulness.

14—Lot of Messengers (Prophets) have been sent by Allah to the world for the guidance of the human beings and all of them are free from blemishes and sins Their actual number is known to Allah alone. To establish their truthfulness, Allah made such supernatural events happen through them which ordinary men cannot afford to do. Such acts or events are called miracles.

The first of those Messengers was Hadrat Adam and the last is Prophet Muhammad (peace be upon him) and the rest were in between. Some of these are very famous *i. e.* Prophet Noah, Hadrat Ibrahim, Hadrat Ishaq, Hadrat Ismail, Hadrat Yaqub, Hadrat Yusuf, Hadrat Daud, Hadrat Sulaiman, Hadrat Ayyub, Hadrat Musa, Hadrat Haroon, Hadrat Zakariya, Hadrat Yahyah, Hadrat Isa, Hadrat Ilyas, Hadrat Al'yasa, Hadrat

Yunus, Hadrat Lut, Hadrat Idris, Hadrat Zul'kifl, Hadrat Saleh, Hadrat Shu'aib (peace be upon all of them).

15—Allah has not revealed the number of the prophets to anyone, our belief should be to have faith in all of the Prophets those who are known or whom we do not know.

16—Out of the Prophets the position of some is more exalted than others and the most exalted is our Holy Prophet Muhammad (peace be upon him). No new Prophet shall come after him and he is the Prophet of all those to be born till the Day of Judgment.

17—While awake our Holy Prophet (peace be upon him) was taken by Allah with his material body from Mecca to Bait-ul-Maqdis (Jerusalem) and from there through the seven Heavens upto where Allah wished. Then he was brought back to Mecca. This is called Me'raj (ascension).

18—Allah has created some of His creatures from light (*Noor*) and they are not visible to us. They are called angels. They have been entrusted with many tasks and errands. They never disobey Allah. Four of these angels are well-known—Hadrat Jibrael, Hadrat Michail, Hadrat Israfil and Hadrat 'Izra'il.

19—Allah has created some creatures with fire also and they, too are not visible to us. They are called jinns (genii). Amongst them are good as well as bad. They have progenies also. The most well-known devil among them is Iblis or Satan.

20—When a Muslim devotes himself to good and abstains from sins and does not love this world and whole-heartedly obeys the Holy Prophet (peace be upon him) he becomes friendly and dear to Allah. Such a person is called 'Wali' (Saint). Sometimes such persons perform such things which others cannot do. These are called 'Karamat' (inspiration or super-natural acts).

21—However exalted a Wali may become, but he can never be equal to the Prophet.

22—However dear a Wali may be to Allah, so long as he retains his senses, obedience of Shariah, religious instructions and practices is incumbent upon him. He cannot be excused the observance of prayers, fast and other obligations. Sinful acts are not permissible for him in any case.

23—Anyone who does not follow the Shariah cannot be friendly to Allah. If any extraordinary or surprising act is done by him, it is either magic or satanic. No one should have faith in him or his acts.

24—Sometimes the Aulia (plural of Wali) get knowledge of something mysterious in their sleep or while awake. These are called 'Kashf or Ilham' (revelations or inspirations). If they are in conformity with the Shariah they are acceptable otherwise not.

25—All religious matters, acts and practices etc have been explained by Allah through the Holy Quran and the Traditions of the Holy Prophet (peace be upon him). To create and introduce new things in religion is not proper. Such a new thing is called Bid'ah (innovation or bad practice). Bid'ah is a major sin.

26—Allah has revealed many big and small books to Prophets through the angel Jibrael so that they may guide, teach and explain religious problems to their respective Ummahs (communities). Of all these four books are very famous. Taurah was given to Prophet Musa (Moses), Zabur (Psalms) to Prophet Daud (David), Injeel (Bible) to Isa (Jesus) and the Holy Quran to our Holy Prophet Muhammad (peace be on all of them) which is the last revealed book. No other book shall now be revealed and the instructions of the Holy Quran shall rule till the Day of Judgment. Some aberrated persons have intentionally interpolated in other books but the preservation of the Holy Quran has been promised by Allah. No one can change it in any way.

27—All those Muslims who had the fortune and privilege of seeing our Holy Prophet are called As'hab (companions) of the Holy Prophet (peace be upon him). High qualities have been attributed to them. We should have affection and good opinion for all of them. If any differences are known among them, they should be treated as omissions and they should not be degraded on that account and none should speak ill of them.

The most exalted amongst these are four companions, that is, Hadrat Abu Bakr Siddique who succeeded the Holy Prophet (peace be upon him) as his Caliph and regulated the religious affairs. He was succeeded by Hadrat Umar Faruque, the Second Caliph. Then Hadrat 'Usman Ghani, the third Caliph and Hadrat Ali, fourth Caliph.

28—The status and position of the Companions of the Holy Prophet is so high and exalted that even a greatest Wali (saint) cannot be equal to the humblest of them.

29—All the wives and children of the Holy Prophet (peace be upon him) are worthy of great respect. The most honoured among his progeny is Hadrat Fatima (daughter) and among the consorts, Ummul Mominin (mother of the believers) Hadrat Khadija and Ummul Mominin Hadrat Aiyesha Siddiqa are the most honoured.

30—One's Faith (Iman) is complete when everything from Allah and the Holy Prophet (peace be upon him) is admitted and believed to be true. To doubt Allah or the Holy Prophet (peace be upon him) in anything or to contradict or to find fault with or to ridicule them disrupts the Faith (Iman).

31—Not to admit and believe the clear meanings of the Holy Quran or Hadith (Traditions) or to twist their meaning according ones own choice, is anti-religion and against the Faith (Iman).

32—To think a sin to be permissible extinguishes the Faith.

33—However major a sin may be, but so long as it is believed to be bad, it will not disrupt the Faith (Iman) and will only weaken it.

34—To lose fear of Allah or to lose hope in Him amounts to (disbelief).

35—It also amounts to disbelief to ask someone about things to be or matters of mystery and to believe in them.

36—No one, except Allah, knows about the unknown. But Prophets through revelations, Aulia (saints) by inspirations and common men through certain signs may know about them.

37—To call a person disbeliver by name or to curse him is a major sin. Of course we can say that the tyrants and the liars be cursed. But it is not a sin to curse those persons who have been cursed by Allah or the Holy Prophet (peace be upon him) as doomed and disbelievers by their names.

38—When a person is dead, then after his burial and if not buried then in whatever condition and manner the dead body has been disposed of, two angels come to him. One of them is called Munkar and the other Nakir. They enquire from the dead as to who is his Creator (Allah), what was his religion and who is Prophet Muhammad (peace be upon him). If the deceased has been a faithful believer, his replies are correct and proper and he gets peace and amenities of all kinds. They open a window in his grave towards the Heaven and the cool, sweet and fragrant air of the Heaven enters his grave and the dead sleeps peacefully.

But if the dead was not a faithful believer or had no Faith (Iman), in reply to all the questions of the angels he says that he knows nothing. Then such a person is subjected to great hardships and punishment till the Day of Judgment. Some are exempted from this test by Allah, but only the dead knows about it. We are not aware of it in the same way as a sleeping man sees a dream but the man sitting by his side remains unaware about it.

39—After death every person is shown his permanent abode in the world-hereafter every morning and evening. Blessed person is given the tidings by showing him his abode in Heaven and the one condemned to Hell is made more despondent by showing him his abode in Hell.

40—Any prayer or act of charity done for the dead increases his credit and is very beneficial for him.

41—All the signs of the Last Day as fore-told by Allah and the Holy Prophet (peace be upon him) shall come into being. Imam Mehdi shall appear and would rule with justice. The one-eyed devil Dajjal will appear and shall create great mischief on the earth. The Prophet Isa (Jesus) shall descend from Heaven to destroy him. Yajuj and Majuj (Gog and Magog) who are a mighty people, will spread all over the earth and shall create much mischief and in the end will be destroyed by the wrath of Allah.

An abnormal and unusual type of animal would come out of earth and would talk with human beings. Sun will rise in the West. The Holy Quran shall be lifted and within a short time all Muslims will die and the world will be filled with pagans and non-believers. There are such other signs and things which will happen.

42—When all the fore-told signs and things would have happened, preparations for the Last Day would begin. Hadrat Israfil (angel) shall, by order of Allah, blow the SOOR (clarion) which is of the shape of a large horn and with its blowing the whole of the earth and the skies shall rent asunder and torn into pieces. All creatures shall die and the souls of those already dead will go into a swoon. But those whom Allah wishes shall remain as they are. A long period shall pass in this condition.

43—Again when Allah would like the entire world to be reborn, the SOOR shall be sounded again. Hearing its sound the whole universe shall come into being again. The dead shall become alive and shall gather in the vast arena of the Day of Resurrection and being embarassed with the hardships of that place they shall approach the Prophets for recommendations. In the end our Holy Prophet (peace be upon him) shall recommend. The Scales shall be raised and good and bad deeds shall be weighed and accounted for. A statement of the same shall be prepared. Some will be sent to Heaven by Allah without any statement of deeds. The good and pious ones will be given their character rolls in their right hands and the sinners in their left hands. Our Holy Prophet (peace be upon him) shall offer the sweet water of *Kausar* (tank) to his followers which shall be whiter than milk and sweeter than honey.

All shall have to cross the *Pul Sirat* (bridge). The good and pious shall cross over it into Heaven and the sinners shall fall from it into the Hell.

44—Hell has been created. There are snakes, scorpions and other different kinds of awful dooms in it. Out of the dwellers of the Hell those who have the slightest Faith will be sent to Heaven after completing their punishment and upon the recommendations for the Prophets. But the unbelievers who rejected the faith and pagans shall remain there for ever and will never die.

45—Heaven has also been into being. There are different kinds of amenities and blessings of Allah in it. The dwellers of Heaven shall have no fear or dread. They shall live there for ever. They shall neither come out of it nor shall they die even.

46—It is the discretion of Allah that He may punish for a minor sin or may forgive a major one.

47—The sins of Kufr (disbelief) and Shirk (paganism) shall not be excused by Allah and with this exception only other major or minor sins may be pardoned by Allah at His sweet will.

48—With the exception of those who have been declared by Allah and the Holy Prophet (peace be upon him) by names to be entitled to go to Heaven, none else can be declared by anyone else to go to Heaven. Seeing good signs and deeds we can only be optimistic and hopeful of the blessings of Allah.

49—The greatest blessing of Heaven shall be the vision of Allah by dwellers and its pleasure would be so immense that other pleasures would appear minions before it.

50—No one has even seen Allah with his eyes in this world nor can anyone see Him.

51—However good or bad a person may have been in his life, but he is rewarded or punished according to his condition at the time of his end (death).

52—Whenever a person deprecates or begs for pardon or becomes a Muslim in his life, it is acceptable to Allah. But just at the time of death when the breath is not regular and the angels of doom are visible, no deprecation or regret or Faith is accepted by Allah.

## MISGUIDING ACTS AND BELIEFS

It deems proper at this stage that some wrong beliefs, rites and major sins which pollute our Faith, should be described and explained so that they may be avoided and not practised. Some of these are sheer disbelief or Shirk (paganism). Some of them amount to disbelief or Shirk. Some are Bid'ah (innovations) and deflection from the right path.

Then the harms of sin and benefits of submission in worldly matters will be described because generally human beings attach great importance to the world. It is possible that they may do good deeds and avoid sins from worldly point of view.

**Kufr and Shirk**
(Disbelief in Allah and attributing of partners to Him)

The following deeds and acts are forbidden in Islam and their practice is Kufr and Shirk :—

1. To like disbelief and to appreciate acts of disbelief or to make someone else to commit an act of disbelief.

2. To repent own Faith on account of any reason and to think that had he not been a Muslim he could get such and such privileges or benefits.

3. To wail and cry at the death of a child or other relative and to say that this was the only being left for Allah to kill and there was none else in the world or to say that Allah should not have done this or that no one commits such outrage as Allah has done.

4. To think ill of or to criticise adversely any act, order or instructions of Allah or that of the Holy Prophet (peace be upon him) and to find fault with them.

5. To insult, defame or disgrace any prophet or to find fault with them.

6. To believe that any saint or holy man is aware of our state.

7. To ask about unknown matters from an astrologer or a person under the influence of a Jinn and believe in it.

8. To take omen from the writings of a holy man and believe it.

9. To call a person from a great distance and think that he has heard it.

10. To think someone to be the controller of the affairs of harm and benefit.

11. To beseech someone for the fulfilment of one's desires, livelihood or childhood.

12. To keep fast in the name of someone other than Allah. To bow before anyone, to release an animal in anyone's name or to make an offering in anyone's name.

13. To make a pledge in the name of someone to do certain act or offering upon the fulfilment of the beseeched desire, to circumambulate the grave or house of someone.

14. To give priority to other things, customs or rites over the orders of Allah or to bow before anyone or to stand motionless like a statue before anyone.

15. To make an offering of goat etc. to a Jinn, to sacrifice an animal in anyone's name or to offer something to be relieved from ghosts or to worship the navel cord for the life of the child. To call anyone for justice.

16. To respect any place equal to Ka'ba.

17. To prick the ears or nose of the child in the name of anyone and to let them wear ear or nose rings in his name.

18. To tie a coin on the arm in the name of someone or wear a string in the neck in anyone's name.

19. To tie bridal chaplet to the children or to keep lock of hair over their heads or to make them beggars of someone or to give them such names as Ali Bakhsh (given by Ali), Hussain Bakhsh (given by Hussain) or Abdul Nabi.

20. To offer an animal in any saint's name to honour it.

21. To believe that the affairs of the world are under influence of stars.

22. To take omens and to enquire about auspicious or inauspicious days and dates. To consider and believe any month or date as inauspicious.

23. To recite any saint's name as remembrance or to swear by someone's head or to keep photos particularly of some saint and to respect it.

24. To say that if Allah and His Holy Prophet (peace be upon him) wished such and such thing will be done.

All of the above acts and beliefs are anti-religion and Muslims should avoid them.

**Heresy, Innovation (Bid'ah) and Wrong Customs**

1. To organize and hold grand fairs on tombs, to light lamps, to cover them with sheets and visiting them by women.

2. To construct pucca tombs over the graves and to respect them extremely with a view to win pleasure of the Saint lying in the grave.

3. To kiss the graves or Tazia (model of someone's grave), to rub its dust on face, to circumambulate them or to bow before them, to offer prayers facing the graves, to make offering of sweets, rice on the graves.

4. To keep Tazia or flag (an emblem) and to offer porridge and sweets etc on them, to salute them and to consider them sacred.

5. Not to chew betel leaves during the month of Muharram or refrain from using myrtle, lip paint and the company of husband. Also not to wear red clothes during this month and prevent men from eating out of the dish named after Hadrat Fatima, daughter of the Holy Prophet.

6. To observe the Soyam (third day) and Chehlum (fortieth day) as compulsory after-death ceremonies.

7. To regard re-marriage as improper.

8. To perform different ceremonies, in spite of lack of means, on occasions of marriage, circumcision, Bismillah (beginning of education) etc arranging music and dance and borrowing money for such ceremonies.

9. To observe the festivals of pagans like Holi and Diwali.

10. Instead of greeting with Assalam-o-alaikum to greet in

any other way or just bow by keeping the arm on the fore-head.

11. For women to appear unveiled without bashfulness before brother-in-law and other cousins or any other stranger.

12. To bring water pitcher singing from the river, to listen music or play musical instruments or to make dancing-girls dance and to give them rewards.

13. To be boastful of one's family and to consider family relation with any saint as sufficient for salvation.

14. To taunt someone and look down upon him on account of his humbler pedigree and to regard any profession as low.

15. To praise anyone with exaggeration.

16. To spend extravagantly in marriages and other useless ceremonies. To make the bridegroom wear such clothes which are forbidden under Islamic law, to adorn him with floral chaplet, wristlets and apply myrtle paste to his hand and feet, to arrange fire-works and make unnecessary decorations.

17. To bring bridegroom among the women and to come unveiled before him to joke with him.

18. To try to peep and eavesdrop in the privacy of bride and the bridegroom and, if heard something, to spread it.

19. To make the bride sit and remain in strict seclusion to the extent that even the prayers are missed.

20. To fix exorbitant Mehr (dowry) just in boastfulness.

21. To weep aloud at the death of someone and to wail beating face and chest.

22. To break the pitchers in use at the time of death or to get clothes washed which touched the body of the dead.

23. Not to prepare pickles etc. in the house of mourning or any other function for about a year and to revive the mourning on certain fixed and particular days.

24. To indulge in excessive make-up and decoration of the body to appear beautiful and to look down upon simple dress.

25. To hang pictures and photos in the house.

26. To use golden or silver utensils or to wear very thin clothes and jingling ornaments.

27. To go (for women) in gatherings of men such as Tazia processions or fairs etc.

## MISGUIDING ACTS AND BELIEFS

28. To wear the dress of the opposite sex and adopt its manners.

29. To get the body tatooed, to do witch-craft etc.

30. To embrace and hug prohibited persons at the time of departure or coming back from the journey.

31. To get the nose or ear pricked of a male child as an omen for long life and to make him wear nose or ear ring, silk or saffron dyed clothes and neck, feet or wrist ornaments.

32. To give opium to the children to keep them quiet and asleep.

33. To treat an ailment of the child with the milk or meat of a lion.

These are some of the undersirable deeds and acts described above. Muslims should avoid them as they have been prohibited by Allah and His Holy Prophet (peace be upon him).

# GRAVE SINS—WHICH HAVE BEEN SEVERELY WARNED AGAINST

1. To assign partners to Allah.
2. To kill anyone unjustly without proper cause.
3. Practising of witch-craft and charms by childless women during the confinement of another woman so that the child of that woman may die and she may have a child. This also amounts to murder.
4. To tease the parents and to put them to inconvenience.
5. To indulge in adultery.
6. To misappropriate the property of orphans, to deprive the daughters of their share in the legacy.
7. To accuse a woman of adultery even on slightest doubt.
8. To oppress someone, to speak ill of someone and backbite.
9. To be disappointed of Allah's mercy and blessings.
10. Not to fulfil a promise or to misappropriate a trust.
11. To abandon wilfully any of the duties enjoined by Allah such as prayers (namaz), fast, Haj and Zakat ; to forget the Holy Quran after memorising it.
12. To tell a lie and particularly to take a false oath.
13. To swear by the name of anyone other than Allah.
14. To swear in such words that he or she be deprived of Kalima at the time of death or may die with want of Iman (Faith).
15. To prostrate before anyone other than Allah.
16. To miss Prayers without legitimate cause.
17. To call any Muslim a non-believer or dishonest, or to call Allah's curse upon anyone or to call anyone as enemy of Allah.

18. To complain against anyone or to hear such complaint.
19. To steal or to indulge in usury ; or to express joy on dearness of food grains ; to compel on lowering of price after settling the bargain.
20. To sit in seclusion with prohibited persons—male or female.
21. To gamble. Some women and men play certain games with stakes on them, this is also a kind of gambling.
22. To like and appreciate the customs of infidels.
23. To find fault with food or with other persons.
24. To enjoy dance and music.
25. In spite of being in a position, not to advise others.
26. To ridicule others with a view to humiliate them.
27. To find defects in others.

These are some of the grave and major sins which negate Faith (Iman). May Allah save all of us from these. Aameen.

**Material Loss by Sins**

Human beings are always in loss on account of sins committed by them. Due to them they suffer here and hereafter. Sins manifest themselves in worldly affairs also. A person engaged in sins :—

(a) is deprived of learning and knowledge.
(b) faces decrease in sustenance and living.
(c) dreads the remembrance of Allah.
(d) fears men, particularly good and pious men.
(e) meets difficulties in most of his affairs.
(f) loses purity of heart.
(g) feels weakness of heart and body.
(h) is debarred from submission and devotion.
(i) his life is shortened.
(j) is deprived of capability of repentance.
(k) loses the weight and abhorrence of sins after some time.
(l) is humiliated in the sight of Allah.
(m) loses his brain and wisdom.
(n) is cursed by the Holy Prophet (peace be upon him).
(o) is deprived of the good wishes of the angels.
(p) faces shortage in crops.

- (q) loses modesty and sense of self-respect.
- (r) loses the sense of the exaltedness of Allah.
- (s) loses the blessings and benefiction of Allah.
- (t) is surrounded by difficulties and calamities.
- (u) Satans are deputed over him.
- (v) loses the peace of mind and heart.
- (w) is deprived of the capability of reciting Kalima at the time of death.
- (x) loses hope in the Mercy of Allah and dies without repentance.

These are some of the examples of material losses incurred on account of sins. Muslims should not indulge in such activities and sins.

## Material Gains by Devotion and Good Deeds

1. Sustenance is increased.
2. Receives blessings and all kinds of abundance.
3. Removal of difficulties and harassment.
4. Easy accomplishment of all legitimate desires.
5. Life becomes a pleasure.
6. There are plenty of rains and all evils are warded off.
7. Allah becomes very kind and helpful.
8. The angels are ordered to keep the heart of such a person ever strong.
9. Gets true respect and honour.
10. His status is raised and becomes very popular.
11. The Holy Quran becomes a source of deliverance in favour of such a person.
12. Gets better compensation for any loss.
13. Experiences day by day increase in the blessings of Allah and increase in his wealth.
14. Experiences comfort and peace in heart.
15. The benefits pass on to next generations.
16. Hears mysterious tidings in life.
17. Angels give good tidings at the time of death.
18. Increase in the span of life.

19. Remains immune to poverty and starvation.
20. Experiences abundance in things which are in small quantity.
21. Removal and cooling of Allah's anger.

These are some of the gains which a true believer gets on of account devotion and submission to Allah.

## WUDU—ABLUTION
### (Pre-requisite of Prayers)

While making ablution one should sit on some raised place facing Ka'ba (Mecca) and begin with *Bismillah-ir-Rahmanir-Rahim* (In the name of Allah the most Merciful and most Compassionate). First of all both the hands should be washed upto wrists thrice ; clean and rinse the inner mouth three times and rub the teeth with a Miswak or a brush. If Miswak or brush is not available, teeth should be rubbed clean with the help of hand or some rough cloth and should gargle properly. While fasting gargle is not allowed.

Then inner part of the nose should be washed and cleaned with left hand, but while fasting water should not be pushed above the soft bone of the nose.

Then wash the face three times wetting the fore-head from the hair of the head to the lower portion of the ears. No portion of the face should remain dry.

Then both the arms should be washed thrice each beginning from the right arm upto and including the elbows. Pass fingers of one hand between the fingers of the other hand. If wearing a ring, it should be moved freely to allow the water to pass under it. Then perform the *Masah*, that is, wet hands should be passed all over the head and the first fingers of right and left hands should be moved in the right and left ears respectively and in the same operation thumbs should be passed around the ears and pass the backs of the hands over the hind part of the neck only. Hand should not be passed around the fore-neck as it is prohibited. Fresh water need not be taken for performing the *Masah* of ears.

Then wash the feet beginning with the right feet upto and including both the ankles three times each. The little finger of the left hand should be passed between the fingers of both the feet beginning from the little finger of the right foot and ending with little finger of the left foot.

This is the method of *Wudu* as prescribed by *Sunna*.

**Obligatory and Sunna Acts of Wudu**

Some of the items of ablution as described above, are *Fard* (obligatory), some *Sunna* (Tradition—as done by the Holy Prophet peace be upon him) and the rest are *Mustahab* (appreciable).

1—The obligatory items of *Wudu* are four only *viz.* washing the face once, washing once both the arms including the elbows, performing *Masah* of one-fourth of the head and washing both the feet once upto and including the ankels.

If any of these obligatory items is missed or even the slightest part of any limb is left dry, then ablution will not be complete.

2—To wash both hands upto wrists, reciting Bismillah, rinsing the inner mouth, washing the inner part of nose, passing wet hands over the whole head and around ears, passing of fingers between the fingers of hands and feet, brushing the teeth and washing each limb thrice are *Sunna* and the rest of the items are *Mustahab* appreciable.

3—With the washing of the four prescribed limbs ablution will be performed whether it has been intended or not. Just as any one flows water over his body without doing *Wudu* or falls into a cistern, or stands in the open while it is raining and thus the prescribed four limbs are washed, then ablution will be complete. But such a person shall not get any reward or credit of ablution.

4—It is proper and *Sunna* to perform *Wudu* as described above, but if anyone alters or reverses its procedure so as to wash the feet first, then perform *Masah* and then washes the arms etc. ablution will be complete but shall not be in conformity with the *Sunna* and there is apprehension of sin also.

5—In the same way if the left feet is washed first, ablution will be done but it is not appreciable.

6—There should not be so much delay between washing two

limbs that the former is dried up. The next limb should be washed immediately. If the first limb dries before the next is washed, no doubt the ablution would be complete, but it is against the *Sunna*.

7—While washing a limb it is also *Sunna* to pass hand over it so that no part of it may remain dry. Men should pass their fingers between the hair of their beards thrice.

8—It is appreciable to prepare for prayer and perform ablution well before time.

9—Unless checked by some legitimate cause, ablution should be performed by oneself and should not ask anyone else to pour water. While doing ablution one should not engage himself in worldly talk, but should recite Bismillah and Kalima while washing the limbs. The water may be abundant in quantity or the person may be sitting on the bank of a river, only so much water should be used as is necessary, nor the water should be used so sparingly that the limbs may not be washed properly. No part should be washed for more than three times. While washing the face, water should not be sprinkled forcefully nor the water should be blown to sprinkle about. The eyes and mouth should not be closed tightly. These practices are *Makrooh* (execrable) and undesirable because if any part of the eyes or the lips is left dry, the ablution will not be complete.

10—If a woman's ornaments like rings, bangles or wristlets are so loose that water can pass under them freely, even then it is appreciable to move them. If the ornaments are so tight that water cannot pass under them, then it is obligatory to move them properly to let the water reach under them. The same should be done for the nose pin.

11—If the flour sticking over the nails dries up and the water did not reach under it, then ablution will not be complete. Whenever recollected the flour should be removed and water poured over the nails. If some prayer has already been offered, it should be repeated after pouring of water.

12—If someone has applied decorative paint over the forehead and flows water over it, the ablution will not be complete. It should be removed before ablution.

WUDU—ABLUTION 29

13—After performing the ablution *Sura Qadr* (97) and the following prayer should be recited :

اَللّٰهُمَّ اجْعَلْنِىْ مِنَ التَّوَّابِيْنَ وَاجْعَلْنِىْ مِنَ الْمُتَطَهِّرِيْنَ
وَاجْعَلْنِىْ مِنْ عِبَادِكَ الصَّالِحِيْنَ وَاجْعَلْنِىْ مِنَ الَّذِيْنَ لَا
خَوْفٌ عَلَيْهِمْ وَلَا هُمْ يَحْزَنُوْنَ ط

(O' Allah include me among the repentants, the purified and Thy virtuous devoters and among those who shall have no fear or sorrow).

14—After performing ablution two *Raka'at* prayers should be offered. This is called '*Tahiyatul Wudu*' (complimentary to *Wudu*), which according to Traditions has much credit.

15—If ablution was done for one prayer but it remained intact then the other prayer may be offered with this ablution. But a fresh ablution for each prayer has much credit.

16—When an ablution has been performed and it is yet intact, it is prohibitory and detestable to perform another ablution unless some prayer has been offered with it. If ablution was performed at the time of bath, then prayer should be offered with it.

17—If any one's skin of hands or feet is cracked and some wax or ointment has been applied over the same and it is injurious to remove the medicine or to wash the injured part, then it is enough to flow water over the affected part to complete the ablution.

18—While doing *Wudu* if the heel or some other part could not be washed and it is recollected after completion of *Wudu*, then that part should be washed and it would not be enough to pass wet hand over it.

19—If there is an abscess in hand or feet or is suffering from such a disease that washing with water is injurious, then water should not be flowed over that part, but the passing of wet hand over it would be sufficient. This is called *Masah*. Even if this may increase the illness, then the affected limb may be left dry.

20—If a wound is bandaged and it is harmful to wash it or pass wet hand over it, or the opening of the bandage is painful, then a wet hand may be passed over the bandage. If it is not so, then wet hand should be passed over the wound after removing the bandage.

21—If the wound is not under the entire bandage, then after removing the bandage the portion of the limb, other than the wound, should be washed. If the bandage cannot be removed then wet hand should be passed over the entire bandage.

22—In case of a fracture where splints and pads are applied, the above directions would apply and unless the splints are removed, it is enough to pass wet hand over them. The same is true in case of bleeding (*fasd*).

23—In case of splints, pad or bandage it is appreciable to pass wet hand over the entire covering. It is also permissible to pass wet hand over more than half of the covering. But it is not permissible to pass wet hand over less than half or just half of the covering.

24—If after performing *Masah*, the bandage, pad or the splint fall and the wound has not healed yet, it may be tied again and the previous *Masah* is sufficient. But if the wound has healed and it requires no further bandaging, then the limb should be washed and prayer offered. There is no need for fresh ablution.

25—It is obligatory for men to pass the fingers of hands through the hair of their beards.

26—If the hair of beard, brow or moustache are very thick and the skin below them is not visible, then only those portion of the hair should be washed which are within the limits of the face.

27—To perform ablution on the floor of the Mosque is not proper and desirable.

**Breaches of Wudu (Ablution)**

The happening of any one of the following would breach the *Wudu*:

1—Passing of stool, urine or gases breaches the ablution. If some worm like earth-worm or stone comes out from behind

## WUDU—ABLUTION

or front organ, then ablution is breached.

2—If a worm comes out of a wound, ear or a piece of flesh falls from a wound and there is bleeding also, then *Wudu* is breached otherwise not.

3—If someone has been bled (*fasd*) or has nose-bleeding or got injured with bleeding or blood or pus flows out of a wound then ablution is breached. If the blood or pus remains upto the mouth of the wound and does not flow out, then *Wudu* is not breached. If flows even a little beyond the affected part, the ablution is breached.

4—If anyone sneezes and some piece of dried up blood comes out, then ablution is not breached. It is breached only if the blood is thin and flows. If some one passed his finger in the nose and blood stain was found on it, but it is not more than a stain and neither flowed, the *Wudu* is intact.

5—If an abscess in the eye opens and its water or pus remains just inside the eye, then ablution is not breached. But if it flows out of the eye, then ablution is breached.

In the same way if an abscess of the ear opens and pus or blood remains upto the part which is not compulsorily washed in ablution or bath, then ablution is not breached. But if it flows out upto the part of the ear which is washed in ablution or bath, then the ablution is breached.

6—If anyone scratches his wound and blood or pus comes out but does not flow, then ablution is not breached. If it flows out then ablution is lost.

7—If an abscess or wound is very deep but the blood or pus remains inside and does not flow out, ablution is not lost.

8—If blood or pus is pressed out of a wound and it flows, then ablution is breached.

9—If blood trickles out of a wound and it is wiped off every time or covered with dust, should be guessed and judged whether it would have flowed if not wiped off the *Wudu* is breached. If it seems that it would not have flowed, then the ablution is not lost.

10—If blood is discovered in the saliva of someone and its

colour is whitish or yellowish, then ablution is not lost. But if the bleed is equal or more in quantity of the spitting or its colour is reddish, then *Wudu* is breached.

11—If anything is bitten with teeth and a blood spot is found on that thing ; or while using a tooth-pick, redness of blood is found on it but there is no blood in the saliva, then ablution is not breached.

12—If any one gets stung by a leech and it sucks so much blood that on cutting the leech the blood flows, then *Wudu* is lost.

13—If on account of pain in the ear water flows out of it, then such water is filthy and desecrated. Though there may be no abscess but mere flowing of water would breach the *Wudu*.

14—Similarly the flowing of water from the nose with pain, will breach the ablution.

15—Water coming out of breast with pain is also filthy and will breach the *Wudu*. If it is not accompanied with pain, then ablution will not be breached.

16—If vomit is mouthful, then ablution is breached. If one vomits several times in small quantity and they together become equal to one mouthful, then ablution is breached. But if the vomits are caused at intervals, the *Wudu* is not lost.

17—If one sleeps while lying or with the support of some thing without which he could fall, then ablution is breached. If one sleeps during the prayer while standing or sitting, then ablution is not breached. But if he sleeps while prostrate (in Sajda) then ablution is lost.

18—If someone sleeps, while not in prayer, pressing the buttock with heels and does not take help of a wall etc. ablution is not breached.

19—If there is a sudden attack of sleep while sitting and it makes one fall, then if he rises immediately after falling, ablution is not breached. But if rose after some time, then ablution is lost. In the same way if he continues to drowse while sitting, ablution is not breached.

20—If anyone faints or loses sense in insanity, ablution is lost even though the faintness or the insanity was momentary.

## WUDU—ABLUTION

Similarly if some intoxicant is consumed and it makes one to lose balance while walking and steps are unsteady, then ablution is lost.

21—If one laughs so loudly in the prayer that its sound is heard by the laugher and those near him, then *Wudu* and prayer both are lost. But if the sound is heard by one's own-self and not by others, then prayer alone shall be lost, not the ablution. While in a laugh only the teeth are visible and there is no sound of the laugh, then neither the prayer nor the ablution is lost.

22—On being touched by the opposite sex or just by thinking liquid comes out of the front organ, ablution is breached.

23—If sticky or glutinous liquid comes out from front organ of a woman due to some illness, then it is unclean and the ablution is lost.

24—If a drop of urine or liquid (Mizi) comes out of the urinary passage and remains within the covering skin of the organ, even then the ablution is breached.

25—If a man's organ touches woman's private part and no cloth etc. intervenes, ablution is breached. Similarly if two women join their private organs, ablution is lost.

26—If nails are clipped or dead skin of a wound is scratched after making ablution, then ablution is not breached.

27—If after performing ablution one sees by chance the private part of another which is compulsory to be covered ; or took bath in nakedness and performed ablution in the same condition, then ablution is complete and there is no need for a fresh ablution. But it is detestable to expose one's private part or to see another's intentionally.

28—The matter or liquid whose discharge causes breach of *Wudu* is unclean and desecrated, whereas the matter, whose discharge does not cause breach of ablution, is not unclean. So if a little blood comes out and does not flow and vomit is not mouthful, then the blood or the vomit is not unclean and if those fall on the clothes or body their washing is not obligatory. But if the vomit is mouthful or the blood has flown then it is unclean and it is necessary to wash it.

If after mouthful vomit mouth is cleaned with the water

contained in a tumbler or any vessel and it is touched by the mouth then that vessel also becomes unclean. So it is advisable to take the water by the palm of the hand.

29—A small child's vomit-milk is also covered by the above instructions. If it is mouthful, then it is unclean and if not mouthful then it is clean. When the child's vomit is mouthful and the mother offers her prayers with it on her clothes, then prayer would not be in order. She should repeat the prayer after washing the clothes.

30—If one remembers that ablution has been performed but does not remember whether it has been breached or not, then prayer without fresh ablution is proper. But it is better to make a fresh ablution.

31—If one is in doubt whether certain limb has been washed in ablution or not, then that part should be washed. If the doubt crops up after completing ablution, then ablution is complete and need not worry. But if convinced that a certain item of ablution has been left, then that item should be completed.

32—It is not proper and permissible to touch the Holy Quran without ablution. But it can be touched with a cloth which the person is not wearing. To touch it with the end or lapel of the shirt which is on body is not proper or permissible. If the Holy Quran is being read by a person without touching it, then it is permissible. In the same way touching an amulet or a plate on which the verses of the Holy Quran are written or inscribed, is not permissible.

## BATH : GHUSUL

Islam had laid great stress upon cleanliness of mind and body. So the method of taking a bath has also been described through Traditions and the same are being discussed as under :—

1—One who takes a bath should first of all wash both the hands upto and including the wrists. Then wash the private parts and remove dirt or filth from the body. Then make ablution. If sitting on a stool or stone, while bathing, feet should also be washed along with ablution. But if sitting in a muddy place, feet should not be washed while making ablution.

After ablution water should be poured over the head three times so that it flows all over the body. Then pour water over both the shoulders three times each and then move to a clean spot and wash the feet if not washed in ablution.

2—Hands should be passed all over the body when water is poured so that no part of the body is left dry.

3—The above method of bath is according to *Sunna* (Tradition). Some of the items explained above are obligatory without which bath cannot be complete and the person remains unclean; while some items are Traditional (*Sunna*). Their observation is creditable. The obligatory items are three only :

(a) To gargle and wash the mouth in such a way that water reaches everywhere inside the mouth.

(b) To wash and clean the inner nose upto its soft part.

(c) To flow water all over the body.

4—While bathing one should not sit facing the Ka'ba (Mecca) and should neither use more water than what is necessary nor it should be so insufficient that the bath may not be done properly. Bath should be taken at such a place where no one can see the bather. One should not talk while bathing. The body should be wiped with some clean cloth or towel after bath and the body should be covered quickly without delay.

5—If the bathing-place is secure and private where no one can see, then it is permissible to bathe naked—whether standing or sitting but it is appreciable to bathe sitting. To expose the body from the navel to below the knee before anyone is sin. Some women bathe naked in presence of other women, it is very shameful.

6—When water has flown all over the body, mouth has been rinsed and the inner nose cleaned, then bath is complete whether it was intended or not. In the same way as if one stands in the rain or falls in a tank and the whole body is wetted, the mouth and the inner nose has also been washed, the bath is complete. Kalima, Holy Quran or any other prayer should not be recited during the bath.

7—If any part of the body, even to the extent of hair's width, is left dry, the bath shall not be complete. In the same way the bath will not be complete if the mouth is not rinsed or the inner nose not cleaned and washed.

8—If after bath it is recollected that a certain part has been left dry, then only that part should be washed, and it is not necessary to bathe again. But the portion in question should be washed and mere passing of wet hand over it would not be proper. If washing of mouth or inner nose is missed the same should be washed afterwards.

9—If on account of some illness, it is injurious to pour water over the head, then all other requirements should be completed leaving the head and the bath would be complete. When the sickness or ailment is cured, only the head should be washed.

10—It is obligatory in a bath to wash the front skin of the uninary organ. The bath shall not be complete if it is left.

11—It is compulsory to get all the hair wet and water should reach their roots. If a single hair is left dry or water does not reach the roots of the hair, the bath would not be complete,

## BATH : GHUSUL

But if the hair (of women) are gathered and tied, the washing of the hair is not necessary but water should reach their roots. If it cannot reach then the hair should be untied and washed. Not a single hair should be left dry.

12—A woman should move all of her nose, ear and finger rings while bathing so that water may reach to every hole. If she is not wearing any such ring even then water should be passed through all the holes. Then bath would not be complete if any hole is left dry.

13—If flour sticking to the nails dried and while bathing water has not reached under the flour, the bath is faulty. When remembered the flour should be removed and the nails washed. If any prayer has been offered without doing this, it should be repeated.

14—If the skin of the hands or feet is cracked and some wax or ointment has been applied over it, then mere flowing of water over the portion should be sufficient to complete the bath.

15—Care should be taken that water reaches ear and the nose failing which bath shall not be complete.

16—If mouth was not washed while bathing but only a mouthful of water was taken so that it reached every where inside the mouth, then the bath is complete. But if the water is taken in such a way that it does not reach every where, then it is not enough and the mouth should be washed properly.

17—If the hair, hand or feet have been oiled before bath and while bathing water passes off without wetting those parts, then there is no fault and the bath is complete.

18—If a piece of betel nut has stuck between the teeth, it must be removed with the help of a tooth-pick. If water did not reach to all the parts of teeth due to this piece, then the bath shall not be complete.

19—If someone has made decorative designs on the fore-head or has applied gum etc. to the hair to the extent that the hair cannot be wet or water cannot reach the skin of the forehead, then the gum etc. should be removed before the bath without which the bath would not be complete.

20—If someone has applied lip-stick or other thing over the lips excessively, it should be removed before taking a bath.

21—If anyone has eye-sore or conjunctivitis and a lot of matter comes out of the eyes and dries at the corners, it is necessary to remove the same and wash the portion in bath and ablution as neither would be complete without removing and washing the same.

## SUITABLE AND UNSUITABLE WATER FOR BATH & ABLUTION

1—Ablution or bath is permissible with water of rain, brook, spring or pond—whether it is sweet or sour.

2—To make ablution or bathe with juice of fruits or leaves is not proper and permissible. In the same way the water of a water-melon or sugarcane juice cannot be used for the purposes of ablution or bath.

3—If something is mixed or boiled in water in such a way that it can no longer be called water but something like syrup, soup, vinegar, rose-water etc. then it is not permissible for ablution or bath.

4—If any clean thing is mixed in water and it has changed its colour, or smell also, but it has not been cooked or boiled in the water nor it has changed the density of water i.e. sand mixed in running water or some soap or saffron is mixed and has slightly changed its colour, then ablution and bath with such water are permissible.

5—If anything has been cooked or boiled in water and it has changed its taste, colour etc. then ablution or bath with such water is not permissible. But if any such thing is boiled in water which purifies it and has not made it thicker, then ablution or bath with such water is permissible. For example berry leaves are boiled in water to bathe a dead person but if the leaves are boiled in such large quantity that the water becomes thick then ablution or bath with such water is not permissible.

6 – Water in which saffron or some other colour has been mixed for dying a cloth is not fit for bath or ablution.

7—If milk is mixed in water and its colour is dominant, then the water is not suitable for ablution or bath. But if the milk is in such quantity as does not give its colour to the water, then such water can be used for bath or ablution.

8—While in a jungle if insufficient quantity of water is found, then so long as its filthiness is not established, it can be used for ablution. It should not be discarded on mere doubt. In the presence of such water the doing of *Tayammum* is not proper.

9—Leaves of tree falling in a well or pond have changed its taste or colour and have also given it bad smell, such water is fit for ablution so long as the density of water is not changed.

10—If water is polluted with filth, whether in small or large quantity, bath and ablution with such water are nor allowed— Flowing water is not polluted with filth unless it changes its colour, taste or smell. Water which carries away grass, leaves, pebbles etc. along with it is a running water whether its flow is slow or quick.

11—A large tank measuring about $5 \times 5$ meters and is so deep that when a handful of water is taken from it its bed is not visible, is also treated as running water. If some filth falls into such tank and is not visible i.e. urine, blood, wine etc. its water is permissible for ablution from all of its sides. If, however, the filth is visible then water should be used from the side where filth has not fallen.

But even in such a tank if the fallen filth changes its colour, taste or smell then its water becomes polluted and is not suitable for ablution etc.

12—The water of a tank measuring about $10 \times 2/1\text{-}2$ meter or $12\text{-}1/2 \times 2$ meter is also treated as running water.

13—If filth is lying on a roof and it rains and the water comes down the spout, so if half or more than half of the roof is covered with filth the water is polluted otherwise not.

14—If the flow of the water is slow, one should not make haste in performing ablution as there is apprehension of the used water coming back into the hands again.

15—If from a tank measuring about $5 \times 5$ meters, water is taken from the side where filth has fallen then there is no harm.

16—Water is not polluted if a non-believer or a child puts his hands into it. If, however, it is found that his hands were filthy, the water would be polluted. But because children cannot be trusted such water should not be used for ablution or bath as a precaution.

17—If a living creature whose blood does not flow such as a fly, mosquito, gnat, scorpion, bee etc. dies in water or falls into it after dying, the water is not polluted.

18—The acquatic beings i.e. fish, frog, turtle, crab etc. if die in the water then water is not polluted. Rule is the same for water or land frog, that is, their dead bodies do not pollute the water.

19—Creatures which live in water but are not born in water (such as ducks) if die in water, then it becomes polluted.

20—If a frog or turtle dies in water and its body is dissolved in it, then the water is fit for ablution. But it should not be used for drinking or cooking purposes.

21—Water heated or burnt in the sun should not be used for bath or ablution as it is likely to cause leprosy (white spots).

22—The skin of dead animal when dried or treated chemically becomes clean and purified and it may be used for offering prayers on it or can be used for making water bags with it. But the skin of a swine can never be clean. To use a human being's skin in any way is a major sin.

23—The skins of dogs, monkeys, cats etc. become clean after curing them chemically. They will also be clean if these animals are killed by reciting Bismillah, whether the skins are cured or not. But their flesh is not clean and should not be consumed.

24—The hair, horn, bone and teeth of dead animals are clean and they will not pollute the water if they fall into it. If these things have some fat of the dead animal upon them, then they are unclean and their falling into water would pollute it.

25—The bones and hair of human beings are also clean but their use in any way is prohibited. These should be buried in the ground with respect.

## THE WELL—CLEAN AND UNCLEAN

1—If some filth falls into a well, it becomes polluted ; but by drawing out its water it becomes clean. The quantity of the filth may be large or small but the entire water of the well should be drawn out to make it clean. There is no need to wash the walls and gravel of the well. All these will be automatically cleaned and in the same way the rope and bucket with which water has been drawn will become clean when the well has been cleaned and its entire water has been drawn out.

Drawing out of the entire water means that the well becomes empty to such an extent that even half a bucket cannot be filled with its water.

2—The well is not polluted if the excretion of a pigeon or a sparrow falls in it ; but the excretion of a hen or a duck would pollute it and entire water should be drawn out to clean.

3—If a goat, dog, cat or human being passes urine into a well or some other filth falls into it, the whole water of the well should be drawn out.

4—If a human being, dog, cat or goat or some such other animal falls into a well and dies in it, then entire water of the well should be drawn out. If any such living being dies outside and then falls into the well, the same rule applies—whole water should be drawn out.

5—If a living being, big or small, dies in a well and its body is decomposed or burst, then entire water should be drawn.

6—If a rat or sparrow or any other being of their size falls into a well and dies in it but its body is not decomposed or burst, then drawing out twenty buckets of water is sufficient. But drawing out 30 buckets is appreciable. Before drawing out water the dead being should be taken out first.

## THE WELL—CLEAN AND UNCLEAN

7—The above rule applies to a lizard which has liquid blood. But the being whose blood is not liquid does not pollute the water.

8—If a pigeon, hen or cat or an animal of their size falls into a well and dies but its body does not burst or decompose, then forty buckets of water should be drawn out and drawing out sixty buckets is better.

9—The count of buckets is according to the bucket which is normally used in that well. If a bucket larger than the one in use, is used for drawing out the water, then proportion should be taken according to its size—whether the larger bucket is equal to two or four buckets of the one in use normally.

10—If the fount of the well is so large that the entire water cannot be drawn out as water continues to come out of the fount, then in such case the water in the well at the time of drawing out should be estimated as to how many buckets of water are in it and then drawn out accordingly. If the estimate is not possible then 300 buckets should be drawn out to clean it.

11—If a dead mouse or any other creature was discovered dead in a well and it had not yet decomposed or burst and also the duration of its falling into the well could not be ascertained, then those who have offered their prayers after ablution with the water of this well should repeat their prayers of one day and night and the clothes washed with this water should be washed again. But if the body has burst or decomposed, then prayers for three days and nights should be repeated.

12—If anyone for whom bath has become obligatory goes down a well to search the bucket and there is no filth upon his body or clothes, then the well would not be polluted. In the same way if an unbeliever enters a well and his body and clothes are clean, the well shall not be polluted. But if there is filth on the bodies or clothes of both the persons, then the water of the well shall be pollute and its entire water should be drawn out.

13—If a goat or a rat falls into a well and comes out alive, its water is clean and there is no need to draw out any water.

14—If a rat is caught and wounded by a cat with its teeth

and blood comes out and in this condition the rat falls into a well, then entire water of the well should be drawn out.

15—If a rat comes out of an out-let and its body is covered with filth and then falls into a well, the entire water of the well should be drawn out whether the rat dies in the well or is taken out alive.

16—If the slashed tail of a rat falls into a well, its entire water should be drawn out. The same rule applies for the bleeding tail of a lizard.

17—If the thing which has polluted the well cannot be traced in spite of best efforts, then the nature of the thing should be judged. If it is observed that the object in itself is clean but has become polluted by being soiled i.e. filthy cloth, ball or shoe, then taking out the object is excused. But if the thing is unclean in itself like a dead creature, then so long as it is not proved that it has rotten and turned into mud, the well shall remain unclean. When it is reduced to mud, then all the water should be drawn out.

18—The quantity of water which is to be drawn out may be drawn at a stretch or little by little, the well shall become clean in every case.

## THE LEAVINGS OF ANIMALS

1—The leavings of human beings are clean whether the person is an infidel or unclean. So a woman's leavings are also clean whether she is in her monthly course or after-birth discharge. In the same way the sweat of all these is clean.

2—The leavings of a dog are unclean. If a dog puts its mouth in a utensil it would become filthy and it should be washed three times whether it is an earthen or copper vessel. But it is better to wash it seven times and rinse with earth.

3—Leavings of pig is filthy and so is that of lion, wolf, jackal, monkey and all other ferocious animals.

4—Leavings of a cat, though clean, is detestable. If the cat puts mouth in the water and if other water is available, then this should not be used for ablution. If other water is not available then this water may be used.

5—If a cat puts its mouth into milk or curry etc. then a man with enough means should not consume it, but a poor man may use it—there is no harm or sin in it neither it is execrable.

6—If a cat immediately after eating a rat puts its mouth in an utensil, then it shall become polluted. But if it does so after some time, after having licked its mouth, then the pot shall not be unclean but execrable only.

7—A roaming hen which eats filth and dirty things, its leavings are execrable. But if the hen is kept as a pet and fed properly, its leavings are clean.

8—The leavings of hunting birds like falcon, hawk etc. are execrable. But if these are pet birds and do not eat dead animals and their beaks are not filthy, then their leavings are clean.

9—Leavings of *Halal* animals (slaughtered) according to Islamic law i. e. ram, sheep, goat, cow, buffalo, antelope etc.

and birds like maina, dove, pigeon, parrot, sparrow etc. are clean. The leavings of a horse are also clean.

10—The leavings of creatures which live in house like snake, scorpion, mouse, lizard etc. are execrable and detestable.

11—If a rat nibbles a bread then it is advisable to cut off the nibbled part and eat the rest.

12—The water left over by a donkey or mule is clean but its use for ablution should be avoided. But if no other water is available except that one, then one should perform ablution and *Tayammum* both.

13—Animals whose leavings are unclean, their sweat is also unclean. Those whose leaving is execrable their sweat is also execrable. But the sweat of a donkey or mule is clean and if it soils a cloth, it is not necessary to wash it but washing is better.

14—If a pet cat while sitting with its owner licks his hands etc. then it should be washed and the saliva should not be allowed to remain. If not washed then it is bad and execrable.

15—For a woman it is detestable to eat or drink food or water left by an unrelated person. If she is unaware that the food etc. has been left by some stranger, then it is not execrable.

## TAYAMMUM

#### (Making ablution or bath with clod of earth)

When water is not available, under conditions explained below, ablution or bath may be done with earth. It is called *Tayammum*. Its method is :—

Selecting a clean piece of ground. First of all the palms of both the hands should be dusted on the ground and then passed over both the arms upto and including the elbows. Woman should be careful to rub under their ornaments of fingers, ears, nose or wrists. If the least space is left out *Tayammum* will not be complete. Fingers should also be passed through the fingers of hands. In the same way bath through *Tayammum* is allowed.

1—If anyone is in a jungle and is not aware where water can be found, nor is there anyone to guide to get water, then *Tayammum* be performed as explained.

If a person is found and he pointed out water within a legal mile or one can himself guess that within a legal mile water would definitely be available, then in such circumstances search for water is essential. To make *Tayammum* without searching water is prohibited. If it is definite that water is available within a legal mile then it is compulsory to bring water from there for ablution or bath.

A legal mile according to *Sunna* is equal to nine furlongs or about 1-1/4 Kilometer.

2—If water is available but it is at a distance of more than a legal mile, then it is not essential to bring water from there and *Tayammum* should be done.

3—If a person is at a distance of one mile from the population and no water is available within a mile, then *Tayammum* is permissible whether the person is in journey or not.

4 – If a well happens to be on the way but there is no rope or bucket to draw water, then *Tayammum* is permissible.

5—If water is available but it is so little in quantity that it can scarcely be sufficient to wash face, both hands and feet once only, then *Tayammum* is not permissible. These parts should be washed once and wet hands be passed over the head. But if the water is not sufficient even for washing once, then *Tayammum* is permissible.

6—If due to some illness water is harmful or ablution or bath may aggravate or delay its healing, then *Tayammum* is allowed. If cold water is injurious then ablution or bath should be performed with warm water. If warm water is not available then *Tayammum* may be performed.

7—If water is available within a mile, it is not permissible for woman not to go there merely on account of shyness or purdah and perform *Tayammum*. Purdah which obstructs the performance of religious duty is not permissible. They should go covering themselves with a sheet or veil. They should not do *wudu* in the presence of man sitting before them.

8—So long as water is not available for ablution or bath, one should continue to perform *Tayammum* and let no doubt or misgiving creep in mind even if it continues for several days. The same cleanliness is obtained from *Tayammum* as from bath or ablution.

9—If water is sold and one has no money to purchase it, then *Tayammum* may be performed. But if one has the means and can spare then it is essential to purchase the water. But if the price of water is exorbitant then there is no need to buy it and *Tayammum* is permissible.

10—If somewhere the climate is so cold that bathing may be fatal or cause sickness nor there is any quilt or blanket to cover the body after bath, then *Tayammum* is permissible.

11—If one has wounds over more than half of the body or is suffering from small-pox, then bath is not essential for him. Only *Tayammum* would suffice.

## TAYAMMUM

12—If in some open field or large expanse of land one had offered prayers with *Tayammum* without knowledge of water being near, then *Tayammum* and prayer both are in order and need not repeat.

13—While in a journey if some one else has water, then it is not proper to do *Tayammum* instead of asking for the water from him. If there is an apprehension that the other person will not give water, then *Tayammum* is permissible. If under this impression prayer has been offered with *Tayammum* and after the prayer the water is got for asking, then prayer offered should be repeated after doing ablution.

14—If Zamzam water is available in cans, then *Tayammum* is not permissible. Zamzam cans be opened and *wudu* or bath be done.

15—In a journey water is with the person but there is an apprehension that more water may not be available during the rest of the journey and there is fear of death or illness on account of thirst, then the water may not be used for *wudu*. *Tayammum* is sufficient in such case.

16—If bath and not ablution is injurious for health then *Tayammum* be done for bath and ablution be made with water. *Tayammum* for ablution in such case is not permissible.

17—After dusting palms on the ground the excessive dust should be blown or wiped off so that it may not stick to the face and make one ugly looking.

18—Besides earth *Tayammum* may also be done by anything else possessing earthen qualities i.e. common earth, sand, stone, lime, surma, geru, etc. But things which do not possess earthen qualities like gold, silver, antimony, wheat, wood, cloth etc. *Tayammum* is not permissible with them. But if any of these things is covered with sufficient dust, then *Tayammum* is permissible with that dust.

19—Matter which does not burn in fire or rot, possesses earthen quality and *Tayammum* is permissible with that. But anything which is reduced to ash after burning or rots, *Tayammum* is not allowed with it. So also *Tayammum* is not permissible with ash.

20. *Tayammum* is not permissible with copper vessels, quilt, pillows or cloth. But if these are covered with sufficient dust which rises when struck with the palms of hands and also smears them, then *Tayammum* is allowed with that dust. *Tayammum* is also permitted with earthen pitcher or pot whether empty or filled with water. But if it is painted *Tayammum* is not allowed.

21—*Tayammum* is permissible with a stone even if it is not covered with dust or has been washed clean. Similarly *Tayammum* is permitted with a burnt brick.

22—*Tayammum* with mud is permitted but not desirable. If there is an apprehension of missing a prayer, then *Tayammum* may be done with wet or dry mud.

23—If there was urine or other filth on the ground and it has dried up to the extent that even its odour has gone, then the ground has become clean and prayer can be offered upon it but *Tayammum* is not permitted with it.

24—Just as *Tayammum* can be done for ablution in the same way it is also permitted for bath.

25—A woman who has just completed her monthly course or afterbirth discharge in such case she can perform *Tayammum*. There is no difference between the *Tayammum* of ablution and bath.

26—If *Tayammum* was performed just to show it anyone else as to how it is done but with no intent, then *Tayammum* would not be complete. Intent to perform *Tayammum* is necessary without which it cannot be complete.

27—While intending for *Tayammum* it is sufficient to say within oneself that *Tayammum* is being done to be purified or to offer prayer. This intent would suffice.

28—If a *Tayammum* is made for the purpose of reciting the Holy Quran, then prayer cannot be offered with it. If it is made to offer prayer of one time, the next prayer can also be offered with it and the touching to the Holy Quran is also permissible with the same *Tayammum*.

29—If one is in need of ablution and bath, then only one

## TAYAMMUM

*Tayammum* would be sufficient for both. There is no need for separate *Tayammums* for them.

30—If one has offered prayer with *Tayammum* and water becomes available thereafter and there is time even for the prayer also even then repeating of the prayer is not necessary. The prayer has been offered properly and there is no defect in it.

31—If water is available within a legal mile but time is short and there is apprehension that if one goes to fetch water prayer time may pass, even then *Tayammum* is not permissible. One should go to fetch water, make ablution and offer the prayer as delayed (*qada*) prayer.

32—If water is available then it is not permissible to make *Tayammum* for touching the Holy Quran.

33—While in a journey there is hope of getting water and it is also the time of a prayer, then it is preferable not to offer the prayer in its early time but should wait for the water. But prayer should not be delayed so much that it may become execrable.

34—While in a train, if water is available nearby but there is a fear of missing the train, then *Tayammum* is permissible. In the same way if there is a snake or any other dangerous animal near the water and water cannot be obtained, then *Tayammum* is permissible in that condition.

35—If water was put in the luggage but was forgotten and prayer was offered with *Tayammum* and later on it is remembered, then there is no need to repeat the prayer.

36—Causes which breach ablution also breach *Tayammum*. It is also breached when water is available. Thus if anyone after doing *Tayammum* proceeds in his journey and reaches a place where water is available within a legal mile, then *Tayammum* is gone.

37—If *Tayammum* was done for ablution and then so much water becomes available which is sufficient for ablution, then the *Tayammum* would be finished. In the same way if it was done for bath and then water is available to be sufficient for a bath, then *Tayammum* shall break.

38—Water happened to be on the way in a journey but one could not learn about it, then the *Tayammum* shall remain. So water is available and known but it is not possible to come down from the train, even then the *Tayammum* will remain.

39—If *Tayammum* was done on account of illness and after recovery when ablution or bath is not harmful then *Tayammum* is gone. Now ablution and bath are compulsory.

40—If *Tayammum* was done for lack of water and then fell ill in which water is harmful and water is available during the illness, then the *Tayammum* is finished because it was done due to lack of water. Fresh *Tayammum* should be done.

41—If one is taking an obligatory bath and the water exhausts and some parts of the body remain dry, then purification is incomplete. Such a person should make a *Tayammum* and whenever water is available these parts should be washed.

42—If someone's body and clothes are dirty and unclean and he needs ablution also and the water at disposal is not enough for all purposes. Then such a person should wash his body and clothes with the water and do *Tayammum* for ablution.

## MASAH OF LEATHER HOSES
### (Passing of wet hands over leather hoses)

1—If leather hoses are put on after making ablution and in due course ablution is breached, then while performing the next ablution it is allowed to do *Masah* over the hoses instead of removing them and washing the feet - that is merely hand should be passed over the hoses. But it is better to wash the feet after removing the hoses.

2—If hoses are so small that ankles are visible then doing *Masah* over the hoses is not permissible. Similarly if hoses are put on without making ablution then *Masah* over them is not allowed. They should be removed and the feet washed.

3—While in a journey it is permissible to do *Masah* for three days and nights and if not in a journey then for one day and one night only. The day and night shall be counted from the time ablution was breached and not from the time when the hoses were put on. For example if anyone puts on hoses after making ablution for Zuhr prayer and ablution was breached at sunset, then it would be proper to do *Masah* over the hoses till sunset of the next day or while travelling till sunset of the third day. After sunset of the permitted period *Masah* would not be proper.

4—If circumstances demand an obligatory bath, then bath should be performed after removing the hoses. Bathing with hoses is not permissible.

5—While doing *Masah* hands should be passed over the upper side of the hoses and not under the heels.

6—The method of doing *Masah* is that after wetting all the fingers of the hands they should be placed on the front side of the hoses keeping the palms apart and then the fingers be

53

drawn towards the ankle. If palms are also placed upon hoses and drawn with the fingers, it is also permitted.

7—If anyone reverses the method of *Masah* i.e. starts from the ankle and ends at the fingers, it is also allowed but is against the appreciable method. Or passes the fingers on the breadth of the fingers, it is also permitted but not appreciable.

8—Passing of fingers on the sides of heels or corners of the hoses is against the rules and the *Masah* shall not be complete.

9—If full length of the fingers is not placed upon the hose and only the tips are used and the rest of the fingers are kept standing then *Masah* shall not be in order.

10—It is appreciable in *Masah* if it is done with the sides of the palms and it is also permissible to do it with the upper side of the palm.

11—If one has not performed *Masah* over the hoses and came out when it is raining or walked upon wet grass and thus the hoses were drenched, then *Masah* will be complete.

12—It is necessary to pass full three fingers over the hoses while performing *Masah*. Less than that would make *Masah* defective, that is width equal to three fingers should be covered.

13—The things or acts which breach ablution also breach *Masah* and it is also breached by removing the hoses. For example, if anyone's ablution has not been breached but he has removed the hoses then *Masah* is breached and he should wash his feet. In such case fresh ablution is not necessary.

14—If one hose has been removed then the other should also be removed and both feet should be washed.

15—If the specific period of *Masah* (as explained above) has expired, *Masah* is breached. But if ablution has not been breached then only both the feet should be washed. If ablution is breached then both the hoses should be removed and a fresh ablution be made.

16—If the foot of a person who has made *Masah* falls into water and the hose being loose the whole or more than half of foot is drenched, then *Masah* is breached. Both the hoses should be removed and feet washed.

17—If a hose is torn and the foot equal to the measure of three fingers is visible, then *Masah* is not permissible upon such hose.

18—If the opening in one hose is equal to two fingers and in the other equal to one finger, then *Masah* is permissible. But if the hose is torn at several places and the total opening is equal to three fingers in the same hose, then *Masah* is not allowed otherwise permissible.

19—If one has made *Masah* over the hoses and before the expiry of one day and night limit he goes on a journey, then he may continue to do *Masah* for three days and nights.

20—If *Masah* was done by someone during his journey but he came back to home, then if one day and night have passed, he should remove the hoses—new *Masah* upon them is not permissible.

21—If hoses are worn upon socks, *Masah* is allowed upon the hoses.

22—*Masah* upon socks is not permissible. But if they are covered with leather or they are not fully covered with leather but are in the shape of a male shoe or the socks are so hard and thick that they can stay on without being tied and one can walk with them a distance of three or four miles, then in all these cases *Masah* on socks is permissible.

23—*Masah* on Burqa (covering) or hand-gloves is not permissible.

## OBLIGATORY BATH
Things or acts which make bath obligatory :

1—If semen is discharged with excitement while asleep or awake, bath becomes obligatory in whatever way it may discharge whether by touching of the opposite sex or by mere thinking.

2—If upon waking semen is found on clothes or the body, bath becomes obligatory whether there has been a wet dream or not. But the discharge of *Mizi* does not make bath obligatory. *Mizi* : At the time of excitement a liquid other than semen comes out. It is called *Mizi*. It increases the excitement. It is thin while the semen is thick.

3—When the top of male organ (penis) has entered the vagina and is not visible, bath becomes obligatory whether there has been the discharge of semen or not. The insertion of penis from front or back makes bath obligatory. But it is a major sin to insert the penis in the back side.

4—When monthly course or the after-birth discharge ends bath becomes obligatory for women. Briefly bath is obligatory in four conditions :—(1) On discharge of semen with excitement. (2) Entry of the top of the penis into vagina. (3) On stopping of monthly course and (4) on stopping of after birth discharge.

5—If someone has sexual intercourse with a minor girl, then bath is not obligatory for her. But in order to make her used to bath she may be required to take a bath.

6—If wet dream has occurred during sleep with excitement, but on waking up no sign of seminal discharge is found on clothes or body, the bath is not obligatory. But if there is definite discharge of semen bath becomes obligatory. When

## OBLIGATORY BATH

some part of clothes is found wet and it is presumed to be *Mizi* even then bath is obligatory.

7—If small quantity of semen came out and took bath and if after bath more semen came out, bath becomes obligatory. If a woman has bathed and afterwards husband's semen came out which was in the vagina then fresh bath is not obligatory.

8—If due to some illness, weakness or any other causes semen is discharged without excitement or desire then bath is not obligatory—only ablution is breached.

9—If husband and wife were sleeping on the same bed and on waking up found certain stains of semen on clothes but neither the man nor the woman remembers to have seen a wet dream, caution requires that both should take bath.

11—One who bathes a dead man, it is appreciable for him to take a bath afterwards.

12—If one for whom bath is obligatory, wants to eat or drink something, he should first wash his hands, face and the mouth.

13—Those for whom bath is obligatory, it is prohibited for them to touch the Holy Quran, to enter mosque. To take the name of Allah and to recite Kalima or Darood Sharif is allowed.

## ADDITIONAL INSTRUCTIONS ABOUT WUDU

1—Men should pass their fingers in their beards after washing the face. Face should not be washed for more than three times.

2—The space between the cheeks and the ears should be washed. It is obligatory whether the beard has appeared or not.

3—It is essential to wash the part of the lips which remains visible after closing the mouth.

4—Ablution is breached if some part of the body of excretion hole comes out whether it goes back of its own or is pushed back with the help of some cloth etc.

5—If anyone loses sense and it does not amount to insanity or unconsciousness, then ablution will not be breached.

6—Ablution will not be breached if one, whether major or minor, laughs in a funeral prayer or while reciting the Holy Quran.

### About Masah

1—*Masah* on boots is permissible provided that they cover the whole feet including the ankles and their laces are so tied that the skin of the feet is not visible to the extent upon which *Masah* is not permitted.

2—If any one puts on hoses after *Tayammum* then *Masah* cannot be performed over them while making ablution as *Tayammum* is not complete purification.

3—*Masah* is not permissible for one who is bathing whether the bath is obligatory or *sunna*.

4—Just as the ablution of an incapacitated person is breached after the time of the prayer, in the same way *Masah*

## ADDITIONAL INSTRUCTIONS ABOUT WUDU

is also breached and removing of both the hoses and washing of feet becomes essential.

5—If the major portion of the feet is washed or drenched in any way, then both the hoses should be removed and feet washed.

### Injunction for being without Ablution

1—It is highly execrable and prohibitive to touch the Holy Quran—any part of it written or unwritten paper—without ablution. If it is not complete Quran but a verse of it is written on any cloth or skin etc. then it is allowed to touch the blank part of it but not the written part.

2—It is not execrable to write the Holy Quran without ablution provided the written part is not touched by hand. It is also not execrable to quote a part of a verse in a book, but writing only a part of the verse of the Holy Quran is not permissible.

3—It is not execrable for minor children to touch the Holy Quran while they are in need of ablution or bath.

4—It is execrable to touch the written part of other revealed books such as Bible etc. without ablution. But even the blank part of the Holy Quran cannot be touched without ablution.

5—It is also execrable to touch the books of Tafseer (commentary) without ablution or bath.

6—It is not permissible to read the Holy Quran without ablution, but verbal recitation is allowed.

# BATH—WHEN OBLIGATORY AND NON-OBLIGATORY

1—If any man's circumcision has not been performed and his semen comes out of the organ and sticks in the superfluous skin which is cut off in circumcision, then bath will become obligatory.

2—If a man, covering his penis with a cloth or anything else, enters it into the vagina of a woman, then if the warmth of the body is felt bath becomes obligatory. But caution demands that bath should be considered obligatory whether warmth has been felt or not.

3—If semen is discharged without excitement, then bath is not obligatory i.e. a man lifts some heavy weight or falls down from a height and as a result semen is discharged, then bath will not be obligatory.

4—If a man indulges in sexual intercourse with a minor girl, bath will not be obligatory if there is no seminal discharge and also there be an apprehension of both the private organs of the girl being connected during the intercourse.

5—Bath will also not be obligatory if a man enters his penis lesser than its front portion.

6—Bath is not obligatory in non-seminal discharge.

7—Bath is not obligatory in the discharge of blood.

8—If any one is suffering from spermation and semen continues to come out, then it will not make bath obligatory.

9—If a man inserts his penis into the navel of a man or woman and there is no seminal discharge, then bath will not be obligatory.

**Essential Bath**

1—If a non-believer accepts Islam and before that he had an occasion making bath obligatory for him and had not bathed or the bath was not correct according to religious code, then it is essential for him to bathe after accepting Islam.

2—If any person has matured before the age of 15 years and has a wet-dream for the first time, caution demands that such a person should essentially bathe. Wet-dream after the age of 15 years' make bath obligatory.

3—To give bath to the dead body of a Muslim is the collective duty of the Muslim.

**Sunna Bath**

1—Bath is *Sunna* for those for whom Friday prayer is essential during the period from *Fajr* to Friday prayer.

2—To bathe on Eid day after *Fajr* prayer is *Sunna* for those on whom Eid prayer is essential.

3—Bath is *Sunna* before wearing *Ahram* of Haj or Umra.

4—It is *Sunna* to take a bath after mid-day on the day of Arafat for those who are performing Haj.

**Appreciable Bath**

1—It is appreciable for one to bathe before accepting Islam provided that before that he was not in need of an obligatory bath.

2—If a man or woman completes 15 years of age and signs of maturity are not visible in them, if he or she takes a bath it is appreciable.

3—After the removal of insanity or unconsciousness etc. it is appreciable to take a bath.

4—After giving bath to a dead it is appreciable to bath for those who had given bath to the dead.

5—It is appreciable to bathe on *Shab-e-Barat* i.e. on the night of 15th of Sha'ban.

6—It is appreciable to bathe in *Laila-tul-Qadar* (Night of Excellence) for one who has the fortune of seeing it.

7—It is appreciable to bathe before entering Madina.

8—It is appreciable to bathe on the 10th of Zilhijja after sun-rise at Muzdalefa.

9—It is appreciable to bathe for *Tawaf* and visiting Ka'aba.

10—It is appreciable to bathe for performing **Rami** (throwing of pellets).

11—It is appreciable to bathe for the prayer of eclipses and want of rain.

12—It is appreciable to bathe before offering prayer to seek forgiveness of a sin.

13—It is appreciable to bathe before offering prayer of fear and trouble.

14—It is appreciable to bathe after returning home from a journey.

15—It is appreciable to take a bath before going to attend a common meeting and before putting on new clothes.

16—It is appreciable to take a bath for the person who is to be killed.

# INSTRUCTION ABOUT USE OF WATER

1—If the water's three qualities *i.e.* taste, colour and smell have been changed by some pollution, it is not fit and permissible to be used for any purpose and it should also not be given to the animals. The making of mud with the help of such water is also not permissible. If all the three qualities of the water have not been changed, then giving it to the animals or making mud with it or sprinkling it in the house is permissible.

2—River, stream or a pond which is not in anyone's land or a well which has been donated by the builder for public use, their water may be used by every one and no one has a right to check anyone from using them or adopting such methods which may be harmful to others i.e. if anyone digs a canal from a pond which may drain and dry it or there is fear of some land or village being submerged in the canal, then it is not a proper way of using water and every one has a right to prevent such action.

3 – If a well, spring or a pond happens to be in someone's property, then he cannot prevent other persons from taking water from it or giving water to their animals or for ablution or bath or for washing clothes or taking it into pitchers for domestic use as this water is public property and everyone has a right in it. But if there is risk of the whole water being spent or the stream being spoiled by a large number of animals, then the owner has right to prevent others, but it will have to be seen whether other person's need can be met from somewhere else, for example there is another well within one religious mile. If there is no such facility and others may suffer for non-availability of water, then the owner of the well or the stream etc. will be required to allow the use of water on the condition that the well or the canal shall not be demolished

by the animals etc. or the owner himself will arrange for the water according to the need of others to be drawn and given to them. But it is not permissible for others to take water without the permission of the owner to irrigate their fields or garden. The same is true for the common grass without trunks. It is the property of all. But plants having trunks are the property of the owners of the land.

4 – If anyone takes water from the well of another person to irrigate his fields and the owner demands its price, it is controversial whether demanding price by the owner is permissible or not. Scholars of Balakh have decreed in favour of price taken.

5—If anyone brings water from a well or stream in a pitcher or bucket, it becomes his property and no one else can use it without his permission. But in case of severe thirst it is permissible even to snatch the water forcefully, but in such case the loss shall have to be made good.

6—It is not permissible to make ablution or bath with such drinking water which has been kept for public use. But if its quantity is sufficient then there is no harm. It is permissible to drink from the water kept for ablution.

7—If one or two bits of a goat's excretion fall into a well and is taken out whole without being dissolved, the well is not polluted whether it is in population or in a jungle and whether it is covered or not.

# INJUNCTIONS FOR MINOR IMPURITIES

1—One, on whom an obligatory bath is due is prohibited from entering a mosque. However, in case of urgent need it is permissible with *Tayammum* i.e. the door of anyone's house opens in a mosque and has no other way or there is a well in the mosque only and no where else.

2—It is permissible for such a person to enter Eidgah. Madrasa or Khanqah.

3—To look at the navel or thigh of a woman in her menses or after-birth discharge or to rub once's body with her without a cloth in between or to indulge in sexual intercourse with her is unlawful according to religious code.

4—It is not prohibited to kiss a woman in her menses or after-birth discharge or to drink her left over water or to sleep with her, or embrace her. To contact one's body with her at navel or above it or with her thigh without any cloth in between, while between the navel and thigh with some cloth intervening, it is all permissible. But it is execrable to avoid such a woman or to sleep away from her and not to mix with her on account of her menses or after-birth discharge.

## SOME ADDITIONAL INSTRUCTIONS ABOUT TAYAMMUM

1—If there are no means to draw water from the well, or there is water in a pitcher but there is nothing by which to take it out nor it can be taken out by bending the vessel or hands are unclean and there is no one else to take out water or get his hands washed, then in such cases *Tayammum* is permitted.

2—If the inability due to which *Tayammum* was done was caused due to someone's action, then as soon as the inability is removed all the prayers offered with *Tayammum* should be repeated. For instance a man is in prison and the Jail wardens do not give him water for ablution or if he is threatened to be killed if he dares to make ablution, then *Tayammum* can be made and prayers offered with *Tayammum* should be repeated on coming out of Jail.

3—It is permissible for several persons to make *Tayammum* with the same clod or spot one by one.

4—If one is unable to use either water or earth because they are not available or on account of sickness, then such a person should offer prayer without ablution and should repeat them when clean. For example a person is travelling by train and the time of prayer is approaching but no water, earth or dust is available and the time also has become narrow, then he should offer prayer without ablution or *Tayammum* and should repeat them when he can clean himself and make ablution.

5—If one is certain or has a strong hope of getting water upto the last time of prayer, then it is appreciable for him to wait for the last time. For instance there is nothing to draw out water from the well and he is certain to get it upto the last time or one is travelling by train and he is sure or has strong hope that the train will stop at a station upto the last time of

# SOME ADDITIONAL INSTRUCTIONS ABOUT TAYAMMUM

prayer and water would be available there, then it is appreciable for him to wait in such cases.

6—If anyone travelling by train had performed *Tayammum* in the absence of water and during the journey he sees water ponds or well etc. from the train, then his *Tayammum* shall not be breached as that water is beyond the reach of that person as the train cannot stop there and he cannot get down of a running train.

## SOME TYPICAL PROBLEMS OF POLLUTION

1—If a bull passes urine over the grain when crushing it, then it is excusable on account of necessity and the grain will not be polluted. But if the bull passes urine over the grain at any other time it will be polluted.

2—The eatables prepared by non-believers or their utensils or clothes should not be treated as unclean unless it is proved by some reason or probability.

3—Some people use fat of lion thinking it to be clean, it is wrong. But if a qualified and pious physician prescribes it and says that there is no other treatment for the disease except it, then according to some scholars it is permissible. But it is necessary for such a person to be clean at the time of offering prayer and the fat should be removed and cleaned at that time.

4—The mud and dirty water of the path is excusable provided it leaves no mark of it on the clothes. But one should take the precaution of cleaning his body and clothes whether the effect of pollution is visible or not.

5—If pollution or dirt is burnt its smoke is clean.

6—The dust resting over pollution is clean provided the wetness of the pollution has not affected it.

7—Gases rising from dirt are not unclean. Moths and insects of flowers are clean their eating is not allowed. Moths of berries and other fruits are governed by the same rule.

8—Edibles when stale or stinking do not become unclean i.e. meat etc. but eating them is not proper from health's point of view.

9—Mushk and its sack are clean and in the same way Amber etc.

10—The water that comes out of one's mouth while asleep is clean.

## SOME TYPICAL PROBLEMS OF POLLUTION 69

11—Rotten egg of a permitted bird is clean provided that it is not broken.

12—The crut of a snake is clean, but its skin is unclean.

13—Water in which some polluted object has been washed is unclean.

14—Water with which dead body has been bathed is unclean.

15—Saliva of a dead person is polluted.

16—If upon a cloth some filth falls and it penetrates to the other side and is within the permissible size, but on passing to the other side the total polluted part exceeds that limit, even then it will be treated as less and will be excusable. But if the cloth has two folds and the part polluted exceeds the limit, it will not be excusable.

17—While milking a cow or goat etc. if one or two bits of the animal's excretion or dung equal to those bits fall in the milk, it is excusable provided it is taken out immediately.

18—If a child of four or five years of age does not know the method of ablution or an insane person makes ablution then that water is not usable.

19—Water with which clean clothes or utensils etc. have been washed may be used for ablution and bath provided that two of the three qualities of water remain unchanged and unaffected. But if two qualities are changed, then it is not permissible.

20—It is execrable to drink or make food with used water and ablution or bath is also not permissible with it. But cleaning of pollution with it is permissible.

21—One without ablution should not make ablution with Zamzam water and also one in need of a bath should not take bath with it. Washing dirty articles with it or performing Istanja (cleaning after urination) is execrable. But in case of urgency when necessary cleanliness cannot be had with any other means, then it is permissible with Zamzam water.

22—Men should not make ablution or bath with the water left after bath or ablution by a woman.

23—The places where some nation has been cursed by Allah as the nations of Thamood and A'ad, the water of those places should not be used for making ablution or bath. But this problem is controversial and it is also governed by the same rules as that of Zamzam water.

24—A polluted oven will be purified by burning fire in it provided that no trace of it is left after heating.

25—If filthy ground is covered with earth in such a way that even its odour disappears, then the surface of the soil is clean.

26—Soap prepared with polluted oil or fat is clean.

27—If any part of the body is polluted with blood by injury or pus etc. and use of water is injurious, then it is enough to wipe the part with a wet cloth and it is also not necessary to wash it after recovery.

28—If polluted colour falls on the clothes or body or hair coloured with such colour, then so much washing is sufficient that washed water remains clean even if the colour is not removed.

29—If a broken tooth is again fixed at its place either with a clean or unclean substance and in the same way if a broken bone is replaced with a clean or unclean bone or a wound is stuffed with some unclean medicine, then it should not be taken out after healing as all these will become clean automatically after being healed.

30—If an unclean stuff such as oil, butter or fat of a dead animal sticks to anything, then it should be washed so much that clean water starts to flow—then it would become clean though the grease of the same may not be removed.

31—If a polluted object falls in water and it splashes over some one, then it is not unclean provided the effect of pollution is not in the splashed water.

32—A cloth having two folds or stuffed with cotton becomes polluted on one side then the whole would be treated as unclean. Offering of prayer on it is not proper. If both the folds of cloth are not sewn together then the other fold will not become unclean and offering of prayer on the clean fold would be in order provided that the pollution or its colour or stink of the other fold does not penetrate to it.

33—If a fowl or any other bird is boiled in water without

## SOME TYPICAL PROBLEMS OF POLLUTION

opening and cleaning its stomach, it would not be clean.

34—Facing the moon or sun or keeping back towards them while passing urine or easing oneself is execrable.

35—It is also execrable to do so on the banks of a canal or pond though the pollution (urine etc.) may not fall in them.

36—It is highly execrable to pass urine or ease oneself under shady trees where people rest or trees bear in flowers or fruits or places where men sit in sun during winter season or in the middle of cattle or so near a mosque or Eidgah that its stink may cause inconvenience to the *Namazees*, or in a graveyard at such places where people make ablution or in the path or towards the flow of air or near a caravan or some gathering. In short at all such places which are used by human beings in any way.

## THINGS UNSUITABLE FOR ISTANJA
### (Cleaning After Urination)

Cleaning after urination with the following is execrable:—
- (a) Bones, eatables, dung, all polluted things and clod of earth which has once been used for cleaning.
- (b) Solid brick, broken pieces of earthen ware, glass, coal, lime and iron.
- (c) Things which do not clean filth like vinegar etc.
- (d) Things which animals eat like grass, husk etc.
- (e) Things which have a price—much or meagre—like cloth or herbal water.
- (f) All human parts like hair, bone, flesh etc.
- (g) The mat of a mosque or dirt or broom, leaves of trees, paper written or unwritten and Zamzam water.
- (h) With the property of another person without his permission whether it is water, cloth or anything else.
- (i) Cotton and all such things which are of benefit to human beings and animals.

**Suitable for Cleaning**

Water, earth clod, stone, cloth having no price and all such things which are clean and are capable of cleaning provided that they are not property and respectable.

**Acts to be Avoided in Urination**

While passing urine the following acts should be avoided :—
- (a) Talking or coughing unnecessarily.
- (b) To recite any verse of the Holy Quran or a Tradition or any other sacred Text.
- (c) To keep any such thing with him upon which the names of Allah or the Holy Prophet (peace be upon him) or of an angel or a verse of the Holy Quran or a Tradition

# THINGS UNSUITABLE FOR ISTANJA

or any prayer is written. If, however, it is in pocket or wrapped in anything, then it is permissible.

(d) Passing of urine in standing position or lying down without any genuine cause or doing it being completely naked.

(e) To perform *Istanja* with right hand.

All of the above acts are execrable and should be avoided.

# PURIFICATION FROM POLLUTION

1—Pollution is of two kinds—One which is very thick or strong and even a slightest touch of the same makes washing obligatory. This is called strong (*Ghaleeza*) pollution. The other is milder in nature and is called weaker or lesser (*Khafifa*) pollution.

2—Blood, urine, human excretion, semen, wine; the urine of dogs, cats; meat, hair, bone and every thing of pig; excretion of horse, donkey, mule, cow, bull, buffalo, goat, sheep, in short excretion of all animals, hen, duck, wild hen and other prohibited animals are strong or thick pollutions.

3—Urine and stool of suckling baby are also strong pollutions.

4—The excretion of all prohibited birds and urine of permitted animals such as goat, cow, bufallo etc. and of horse are milder pollutions.

5—With the exception of hen, duck or fowl the excretion of other permitted birds such as pigeon, sparrow, maina etc. are not pollution. The excretion and urine of bat is also not pollution.

6—If liquid or fluid portion of strong pollution touches the body or clothes and is not more than the size of a rupee coin or less than that, then it is excusable. But not to wash the same and continue to offer prayer with it is execrable.

But if the spot is more than a rupee coin in size, it is not excusable and offering of prayer without washing the same is not proper and in order.

In the same way if the stronger pollution sticks to body or clothes and its weight is not more than 5 grammes, offering of prayer without washing the same would be in order. But if it is more than that, the prayer shall not be in order.

## PURIFICATION FROM POLLUTION

7—If milder pollution sticks to body or clothes and covers less than one-fourth of that part of body or clothe, it is excusable. But if it covers just one-fourth or more, then it is not excusable and washing is essential i.e. if it sticks to the hand, then if it is less than one-fourth of the hand or if it is on the sleeve and is less than one-fourth of the sleeve, then it is excusable. But if it is just one-fourth or more of the hand of sleeve, then it is not excusable and prayer shall not be in order unless washed properly.

8—If strong pollution falls into water, then it will also become strongly polluted. In the same way if milder pollution falls into water, it shall pollute the water mildly. In both the cases the consideration of quantity of pollution is immaterial—it may be large or small.

9—If cloth is smeared with polluted oil and has spread in a day or two and is less than the depth of palm or the size of a rupee coin, then it is excusable. But if it exceeds that size then it is not excusable and washing becomes essential and without washing prayer shall not be in order.

10—The blood of fish is not pollution and there is no harm if it falls on body or clothes. In the same way the blood of fly, bugs and mosquitoes is not pollution.

11— A small drop of urine of the size of a needle's point falls on body or clothes and is also not visible, then it does not matter. Washing such a drop is not essential.

12—If substantial pollution such as blood or excretion falls on the body or clothes, it should be washed till it is removed properly and no stain of it is left. It should be washed as many times as it takes to be removed. When it is removed, the body or the cloth will become clean. If it is removed in the first washing, then it should be washed twice more. Washing for three times is essential.

13—If the pollution is such that by washing several times it is removed but its odour or some stain of it is left, even then the clothe will become clean. It is not necessary to remove the stain or the bad smell with soap or any other such material,

14—If pollution is like urine and is not substantial, then it should be washed and squeezed for three times and after the third wash it should be squeezed with full force. If it is not squeezed with full force, the cloth will not be clean.

15—If the pollution has stuck to such an article which cannot be squeezed i.e. wooden seat, mat, ornaments, pots or shoes, then the method of cleaning them is to wash them once and wait till the droppings of water stop. Repeat this process three times and then the article would become clean.

16—Washing with a clean liquid like rose water etc. is also permissible, but with oil, butter, milk etc. containing fat is not permissible.

17—If semen has stuck to clothes and dried, then mere scratching and rubbing would be sufficient to make the cloth clean. If it is wet, then washing is essential.

18—If a substantial pollution such as excretion, blood etc. sticks to shoe or leather hose, then it should be rubbed hard against the ground till the pollution is completely removed and the shoe or hose would become clean. This rule applies to wet and dried pollution.

19—If a liquid pollution like urine, which is not substantial in nature, falls on the shoe or leather hose, it will not be clean unless washed.

20—Body and clothes are cleaned by washing only. It does not matter whether the pollution is substantial or not.

21—Polluted mirror, knife, gold and silver ornaments, articles of copper, brass, iron, gilt etc. can be purified by rubbing them properly or by rinsing with dust. But engraved articles shall have to be washed for their purification.

22—If pollution falls on the ground and has dried up in such a way that no trace or smell of it is left, then the ground has become clean. But *Tayammum* with it is not premissible. Prayer may be offered on it. The same rule applies to bricks or stones which have been so laid with cement, lime or mud that they cannot be pulled out without digging. They become clean if the pollution upon them has dired up and no trace of it or its smell is left.

## PURIFICATION FROM POLLUTION

23—Bricks which have only been spread on the ground and no type of mortar has been used to fix them, they will not become clean by mere drying of the pollution. They will have to be washed to clean them.

24—Grass growing on the ground also becomes clean when the pollution has dried up and no trace of it or its smell is left. But the grass which has been cut will not be clean without washing.

25—Knife, earthen or copper vessels should be cleaned and purified by putting them in burning fire.

26—If pollution on hand is licked three times by some one with tongue, hand would become clean. But such licking is prohibited.

27—Earthen pots made by a potter with unclean clay shall not be clean unless heated in fire.

28—If an unused earthen pot is polluted and it has sucked the pollution also, then it would not be purified with washing only. It should be filled with water and when the water takes the pollution, it should be emptied. This process should be repeated till the pollution, its trace, colour or smell comes in the water and when it is removed the pot would become clean.

29—If honey, molasses, butter or oil is polluted, then it should be mixed with equal or more quantity of water and boiled till all the water is evaporated. This should be repeated three times to clean the article.

30—Cloth dyed with polluted colour should be washed till clear water comes. The cloth would be clean whether the colour is washed away or not.

31—The ash of dung cakes and of other polluted things like excretion of animals and smoke of these cakes is clean. There is no harm even if the ash touches the breads.

32—If one corner of bed is polluted and the rest is clean, then offering of prayer on the clean part is in order.

33—Ground plastered with cow dung is polluted and offering of prayer upon it is not permissible without spreading a clean cloth over it.

34—If the dung plaster over the ground has dried up then

offering of prayer on it is permissible even if a wet cloth is spread over the ground. But the cloth should not be so wet that some earth sticks to it.

35—If after washing feet one walks over polluted ground and foot marks are impressed on it, then the feet would not be polluted. But if the earth under the feet becomes so wet that some of it sticks to the feet, then the feet would become unclean.

36—If one sleeps on a polluted bed and it becomes wet with sweat, then neither the body nor the clothes of the person would be polluted. But if the clothes are so wet that some pollution of the bed also sticks to them or the body, then the clothes or the body would become unclean.

37—If polluted myrtle is pasted on the hands and feet, they should be washed three times to be clean. Removing of colour is not essential.

38—If polluted *Surma* (lead) or *Kajal* (eye-black) is applied to the eyes, then wiping or washing it is not necessary. But if it has come out of the eyes then washing is essential.

39—If polluted oil has been in the hair or rubbed on the body, then it should be washed thrice. It is not necessary to remove it with soap etc.

40—If a dog puts its mouth in flour or a monkey has eaten some of it, then if the flour is kneaded the polluted part should be thrown away and the rest is fit for consumption. If the flour is dry then only such part of it should be removed where the saliva of the animal is found.

41—The saliva of a dog is pollution and unclean but its body is not. Mere touching the body of a wet or dry dog does not pollute. But if the body of the dog bears some pollution then the clothes or body touching it would be polluted.

42—If gases pass through the wet middle part of the trousers then the trouser is not polluted.

43—If a clean cloth is wrapped with a polluted and wet cloth and the clean cloth absorbs some wetness of the polluted cloth and no colour or odour of the polluted cloth is transferred to it, then the clean cloth will not be polluted. But if the clean cloth becomes so wet that by squeezing it some drops come out then it will become polluted.

44—If a wooden plank is polluted on one side and the other side is clean and it is so thick that it can be sawed into whole pieces, then offering of prayer on the clean side is permissible. But if it is not thick enough, then it is not permissible.

45—If a cloth is double folded and one of the folds is polluted, and if both the folds are not sewn together, then offering of prayer upon the clean fold is permissible.

## Istanja (Cleaning by earth clod)

1—On getting up from sleep one should not put his hands into water without washing them upto wrists whether they are clean or unclean. If the water is in a small pot like jug or tumbler, then it should be picked up by the left hand and the right hand be washed thrice. Then the pot be taken into the right hand and the left hand be washed like-wise. If the water is in a large container, then it should be taken out by a tumbler but the fingers should not touch the water while taking it out. If no tumbler etc. is available then water may be taken out by handful provided that they are not polluted.

2—It is *Sunna* [according to Tradition of the Holy Prophet (peace be upon him)] to clean thoroughly the front and back private organs from which pollution—urine or excreta—has come out.

3—If pollution does not stick to the sides of the organ and without using water it can be removed with the help of a clean clod of earth or stone, then it is permissible if the parts are cleaned in such a way that no trace of it is left. But such practice is against the taste of cleanliness and should only be done when water is not available.

4—There is no specific method of performing *Istanja*. Only care should be taken that pollution does not spread and the parts are cleaned properly.

5—After *Istanja* it is *Sunna* to wash with water. But if the pollution is more than the size of a rupee coin, then washing is essential and without washing prayer would not be proper.

6—While cleaning with water both hands should first be washed upto wrists and then going to a lonely place one should sit with relaxed body and wash properly till satisfied that the part has become quite clean.

7—If no lonely place is found then it is not proper to bare the private parts in the presense of others—men or women. In such circumstances prayer can be offered without Istanja or washing. Disclosing of one's private organs before others is a major sin.

8—It is improper and not permissible to clean (perform Instanja) with a bone or unclean stuff like dung, coal, pebbles, glass, burnt bricks, eatables or paper and with right hand. No doubt if one does, the body would be clean but it should be avoided.

9—Passing urine while standing is prohibited.

10—To sit facing Ka'aba while passing urine or easing oneself or to sit with back towards Ka'aba is prohibited.

11—It is execrable and prohibited to keep the face or back of a minor child towards Ka'aba while making him to pass urine or stool.

12—To perform ablution with the water left after *Istanja* or to perform *Istanja* with the water left after ablution, is permissible but it should be avoided.

13—While going to pass urine or ease one should say *Bismillah* outside the door of the latrine and the following prayer should be recited before entering the closet :

اَللّٰهُمَّ اِنِّىْ اَعُوْذُبِكَ مِنَ الْخُبْثِ وَ الْخَبَائِثِ

One should not enter the latrine bare headed. If the name of Allah or the Holy Prophet (peace be upon him) is engraved upon a ring, it should be left out. One should enter the latrine with left foot and the name of Allah should not be called inside the latrine. Neither one should talk inside it.

**14**—If one has to sneeze then *Alhamdolillah* should be said within himself and should not utter it. While coming out of the latrine right foot should be put out and the following prayer should be recited after coming out :—

غُفْرَانَكَ الْحَمْدُ لِلّٰهِ الَّذِىْ اَذْهَبَ عَنِّى الْاَذٰى وَعَافَانِىْ

**15**—After performing *Istanja* wash and rub the left hand properly.

# THE PRAYER—NAMAZ

Allah holds *Namaz* in great esteem. No other prayer and devotion is dearer to Allah than *Namaz*. Five times' prayer has been prescribed by Allah for his servants (human beings). The offering of prayer is virtue and its omission a major sin.

The Holy Prophet (peace be upon him) in his Traditions has said that anyone who performed ablution properly and offered prayers with deep sincerity, all of his minor sins shall be pardoned by Almighty Allah on the Day of Judgement. The Holy Prophet (peace be upon him) has said that *Namaz* (prayer) is the pillar of Faith (*Iman*) and one who performed prayer properly, kept the Faith and one who demolished this pillar (did not offer prayer) destroyed the Faith.

The Holy Prophet (peace be upon him) has said that the first question that would be asked on the Day of Judgement would be about *Namaz*. Those who have offered their *Namaz* properly and punctually, their faces, legs and hands shall shine like the sun. Those who have intentionally omitted *Namaz* shall be deprived of this blessing.

The Holy Prophet (peace be upon him) said that the end of the *Namazees* (those who offered *Namaz*) shall be with the Prophets, martyrs and the pious, while those who have neglected the prayers shall be treated like the non-believers.

Offering of prayer is not obligatory for a lunatic, small girl or boy who have not matured and is obligatory for the rest.

It is obligatory for parents to make their children offer prayer when they attain the age of seven years. They should be punished at the age of ten years for not offering *Namaz*. The omission of *Namaz* at any time is not allowed.

# TIMES OF PRAYERS
## AUQUAT-E-NAMAZ

**1—Morning Prayer** (*Fajr*)

In the last part of the night when it is nearing dawn and in the east wherefrom the sun rises some whiteness is visible in the length of the sky and after some time it appears at the corner of the sky in its breadth and spreads quickly and very soon it lits up everywhere. So from the moment this broad whiteness appears the time of *Fajr* prayer begins and it lasts till the rising of the sun As soon as a small corner of the sun appears the time of *Fajr* prayer ends. It is preferable to offer *Fajr* prayer in its early time.

**2—Mid-day Prayer** (*Zuhr*)

The time of *Zuhr* prayer begins at the decline of noon. As the sun rises in the sky the shade of every thing decreases and when this lessening stops it is exact noon. Then again the shades begin to increase and the shade moves slowly from the West towards North and then towards East. At this stage it means that noon has declined and the time of *Zuhr* begins from this moment. Its time will end when the shade of a stick spreads two cubits and four fingers. For example the shade of a stick, which is of one arm length (one cubit), is equal to four fingers at noon, then so long as its shade does not spread to two arm lengths (two cubits) and four fingers *Zuhr* time shall remain.

**3—Afternoon Prayer** (*Asr*)

When the shade of a stick spreads to two cubits and four fingers, it is afternoon and the time of *Namaz-e-Asr* begins and lasts till sun-set.

When the colour of the sun changes and the sunshine

turns pale, the offering of *Asr* prayer at this time is execrable. But if the prayer was delayed due to some unavoidable reason, then it may be offered and should not be postponed or put off. No other prayer is permissible at this time except that of *Asr*.

### 4—After Sun-set Prayer (*Maghrib*)

When the sun has set, the time of *Maghrib* prayer begins and lasts till the redness on the corner of the sky remains in the West. But the *Maghrib* prayer should not be delayed so much that stars may begin to twinkle. Such delay is execrable.

### 5—Night Prayer (*Isha*)

When the redness of the sky in the West disappears the time of *Isha* prayer begins and lasts till morning. But offering of *Isha* prayer after mid-night is execrable and its virtue decreases. So it should not be delayed till after mid-night. It is preferable to offer the *Isha* prayer before one-third of the night passes away.

# INSTRUCTIONS FOR PRAYER

1—There should be no haste in offering *Zuhr* prayer during summer and it is appreciable to offer *Zuhr* prayer when the mid-day heat has decreased while during winter the offering of *Zuhr* prayer in its early time is appreciable.

2—It is better to delay the *Asr* prayer a bit so that *Nafl* (voluntary) prayers may be offered becaus *Nafl* prayers are not permissible after *Asr* prayer. The rule for *Asr* prayer is the same whether in winter or summer. But this delay should not be so much that the colour of the sun changes and turns pale.

3—It is appreciable to make haste in offering *Maghrib* prayer just after sun-set.

4—One who is used to offer *Tahajjud* (special after midnight prayer) and is confident to wake up at that time, then it is better for such a person to offer *Witr* prayer after *Tahajjud* prayer. But if one is not sure to wake up for *Tahajjud* in time then he should offer *Witr* prayer after *Isha* prayer before going to bed for sleep.

5—It is preferable to offer *Zuhr* and *Maghrib* prayers with some delay on cloudy days but one should not make haste in offering *Asr* prayer on such days.

6—No type of prayer is in order at the time of rising of the sun, noon and sun-set. But *Asr* prayer if not offered yet may be offered when the sun is setting. During these three times it is execrable to offer *Sajda-e-Talawat* (prostration of recitation).

7—The offering of *Nafl* prayers after *Fajr* prayer before rising of the sun is execrabe, but offering of postponed prayers is proper before sunrise. But when the sun has risen the offering of postponed prayer is also not permissible till night.

In the same way *Nafl* prayer is not permissible, but postponed *Asr* prayer and prostration of recitation of Quranic verses are permitted. But when the sun light becomes dim even these are not allowed.

8—Being late and for fear that sun may rise one has hurriedly offered only *Fard* prayer of *Fajr*, then *Sunna* prayer should be offered after sun rise and not before that.

9—In the morning when it is *Fajr* prayer, no other *Nafl* prayer is permissible but is execrable except two *Raka'at* of *Fard* and two *Raka'at* of *Sunna* But offering of postponed prayer and prostration of Quranic verse is permissible.

10—While offering *Fajr* prayer if the sun has risen, then the prayer is not in order and should be repeated as postponed prayer or delayed prayer after the sun has risen and brightened. But if while offering *Asr* prayer the sun has set, then the prayer is in order and repetition is not required.

11—Sleeping before *Isha* prayer is execrable. One should sleep after offering *Isha* prayer. But if one is sick or tired on account of journey and asks some one to wake him up at prayer time, then sleeping is allowed.

12—It is appreciable for men to begin *Fajr* prayer at such time when light has spread and there is so much time in which forty verses of the Holy Quran may be recited in the prayer ; or if any prayer is to be repeated after that prayer with recitation of forty verses, then there should be time for it also. Women should always offer *Fajr* prayer while it is yet dark. It is appreciable for men to offer *Fajr* prayer in dark during *Haj* at Muzdalefa.

13—The time of the *Juma* prayer is the same as that of *Zuhr* prayer but *Juma* prayer is offered in its early time as it is *Sunna* according to the Traditions and is also general consensus.

14—The time of the *Eid* prayers begin when the sun has risen fully and remains till a little before mid-day. The full rising of the sun means that its paleness is gone and its glare becomes so strong that eyes cannot bear it—that is the sun should be as high as the length of a spear.

15—It is appreciable to offer prayers of both the *Eids* in early time. But the prayer of *Eid-ul-Fitr* should be offered a bit late.

## INSTRUCTIONS FOR PRAYER 87

16 – When the *Imam* has stood up for Sermon—whether of Friday or *Eids* or *Haj*-offering of prayer at these times is execrable. In the same way at the time of *Nikah* or *Khatm-e-Quran* it is execrable to offer prayer when the Sermon has begun.

17—When *Takbirs* of *Fard* prayer are being called, and *Sunnah* prayer has not been offered and one is certain or has strong hope that he would join the congregation in at least one *Raka'at*, then offering of *Sunna* prayer is not execrable. Or if the offering of essential *Sunna* has been begun, then it should be completed.

18 —Offering of *Nafl* prayer before both *Eid* prayers whether at home or in *Eidgah* is execrable and after *Eid* prayer in *Eidgah* only.

# CONDITIONS OF PRAYERS

1—Some acts are essential before beginning of prayer i.e.:—
   (a) Ablution should be performed if not already done. If one is in need of bath, then one should bathe.
   (b) If there is any filth or pollution on clothes or body, it should be removed.
   (c) The place of offering prayer should also be clean.
   (d) Women should cover their whole body from head to feet with the exception of face, palms and feet. Men should not be naked from below the navel upto and including the knees.
   (e) Face should be towards Ka'aba and one should think of the prayer which is to be offered.
   (f) Intent for the prayer—it may just be said within oneself.
   (g) To offer prayer at its appointed time.

All of the above are requisites of prayer and if anyone of these is omitted, the *Namaz* will not be in order.

2—It is not proper for women to put on a very thin scarf while offering prayers.

3—If one-fourth of the calf or thigh of a woman opens in prayer and remains exposed for such a period in which *Subhan-Allah* can be recited thrice, then the prayer will be disrupted and it should be repeated. But if it was not exposed for such period and was covered immediately, then the prayer will remain in order.

Thus if one-fourth part of the body which is essential to be covered by men and women both, is exposed for more than the above mentioned period during a prayer, then the prayer shall be disrupted.

4—If the scarf of a girl, who has not attained maturity, falls during the prayer, then the prayer will not be disrupted.

5—If there is some filth on body or clothes and water is not available any where, then prayer may be offered in the same condition.

6—If the whole clothe is filthy or less than one-fourth of it is clean and the rest is unclean and there is no other clothe to wear, then it is in order to offer prayer with that clothe. It is also proper to remove that clothe and offer prayer in nakedness. But it is better to offer prayer with unclean clothe than in nakedness.

7—If one has no clothes to wear, then prayer should be offered in nakedness. But should be offered in seclusion where no one can see him or her. In such condition one should not stand and the prayer be offered in sitting position and for bowing (*Ruku*) and prostrations only motion be made.

8—While in a journey if one has a very small quantity of water with him and has to make ablution and wash filth also, that is, if the water is used to wash the filth then nothing is left for ablution. In such condition filth should be washed with the water and *Tayammum* be made for ablution.

9—If one has offered *Zuhr* prayer and later realised that the *Zuhr* time had passed and it was *Asr* time, then he should not repeat the prayer and the offered prayer will be counted as postponed or delayed prayer.

10—If any prayer has been offered before its time then it would not be in order and should be repeated in its time.

11—If a sheet of cloth is large enough that its filthy part does not move with the movements of one offering prayer with it, then there is no harm. All the things carried on person of one offering prayer should be clean. For example one has pollution or filth on the body which is in its place of birth and has no outward sign of it, then it is not objectionable i.e. anyone has a stale egg in his pocket. Its yellow substance has changed to blood but it has no outward expression or effect of its rottenness, then it is not objectionable to carry it in pocket while offering prayer.

12—The place where prayers are offered should be clean and free from all real pollutions and filth i.e. urine, excretion and semen etc. But if it is within permissible limit then there is no objection. The place of prayer means where a person puts feet, knees, hands, fore-head and nose while offering *Namaz* (prayer).

13—If the spot under one foot is clean and the other foot is kept raised during prayer, then it is permissible.

14—If prayer is offered on a cloth then its cleanliness to the extent explained above is essential. Cleanliness of the whole cloth is not necessary whether it is small or large in size.

15—If prayer is offered on a clean cloth spread over unclean ground, then the cloth should not be so thin that the ground under it is visible.

16—There is no harm if one's cloth falls over dry polluted ground while offering prayer.

17—If a person having no clothes offers prayer without them, then there is no objection and repetition of prayer is not necessary. But if the inability to wear clothes is due to other person's act, then prayers should be repeated after the removal of the inability. For instance one is in jail and wardens have removed his clothes, then in such case repetition of prayer is essential.

18—If anyone possesses only one cloth with which he can either cover his body or spread it for prayer, then he should cover his body with it and offer prayer on bare ground even if it be polluted and no other place is available. If clean spot is available then the prayer should be offered on it.

### Intent for Prayer

1—It is not essential to express the intent for prayer in words, it is enough just to think in one's mind that he is offering that day's certain prayer i.e. *Zuhr* and if it is *Sunna* prayer of *Zuhr*, then just think that he is offering *Sunna* prayer of *Zuhr* and saying *Allah-o-Akbar* cross his hands below the navel and the prayer would be in order. The recitation of the long customary intent is not necessary.

2—If the intent is expressed in words then it is sufficient to say that he intends to offer that day's *Fard* or *Sunna* prayer and cross his hands in front after saying *Allah-o-Akbar*. It is not necessary to say, "Four *Raka'at* of *Zuhr* etc. and facing the Ka'aba".

3—If one intends in mind to offer *Zuhr* prayer and the word *Asr* slips out even then the prayer would be in order.

4—If unintentionally instead of saying "four *Raka'at*" six or three is uttered, even then the prayer would be in order.

5—If lot of prayers have been missed and one intends to offer them, then the person should intend for the particular time of prayer which he wants to offer. He should intend thus : "I intend to offer the missed prayer of *Fajr* or *Zuhr*". Only saying that he was offering a missed prayer would not be in order and the prayer should be repeated.

6—If prayers of several days have been missed, then while intending the date and day should also be specified i.e. if anyone has missed the prayers of four days — Saturday, Sunday, Monday, Tuesday. Then it is necessary to specify the day and should intend such that he is offering the missed prayer of *Fajr* of Saturday or Monday. After completing all the missed prayers of one day, he should offer prayers of next day and so on.

7—If prayers of several months or years have been missed, the year and month should also be specified while intending to offer them and should say that he is offering the missed prayer of such time and of such and such month and year. Without intending in this way the missed prayers would not be said.

8—If one does not remember the day, date, month or year of the missed prayer he should intend thus : "Of all the missed prayers of *Fajr*, *Zuhr* etc. due towards him he is offering that which is the first of them". When he is satisfied in his mind that all of his missed prayers have been offered, then he should stop offering missed prayers.

9—While offering *Sunna* or *Nafl* prayers if only praying has been intended without specifying *Sunna* or *Nafl*, then it would be in order. But while offering *Sunna Tarawih* care should be taken to specify it as such.

10—The follower should also intend to follow the Imam,

11—While the Imam should intend for his prayer only. It is not necessary for him to intend to lead the prayer. But if a woman wants to follow him in prayer and she stands along with men and it is not funeral, Friday or *Eid* prayer, then to justify his leading the prayer he (Imam) may intend so. But if the woman does not stand with men or it is a funeral, or Friday prayer, then it is not necessary.

12—It is not necessary for the follower to specify the Imam in his intent. It is just enough to intend that he is following the Imam. If anyone specifies the Imam and he (Imam) happens to be someone else, then the prayer of that person shall be lost.

13—In the prayer of a funeral one should intend that he is offering the prayer for the pleasure of Allah and pray (*Dua*) for the deceased. If the follower does not know the gender of the dead person then he should intend that whose prayer is being led by the Imam he also intends for the same.

**To Face Ka'aba While Praying**

1—If one is at such a place where he cannot be sure or ascertain the direction of Ka'aba, nor is there anyone else from whom he can enquire, then he should judge within himself and offer prayer in the direction towards which his heart testifies. If he offers prayer without thinking then the prayer would not be in order but if later on it is discovered that the direction was correct, then the prayer would be in order.

2—If there was some one and a woman did not ask him about the direction of Ka'aba due to shyness or purdah and offered prayer, then it would not be in order. She should not feel shy on such occasions.

3—If there was no one to tell the direction of Ka'aba and prayer was offered towards the direction indicated by heart and later on it was found that the direction was wrong even then the prayer would be in order.

4—If anyone was offering prayer facing the wrong direction and during prayer it was discovered that Ka'aba was not in that direction, then he should turn towards the correct direction. If after knowledge of the correct direction, one still continues to offer prayer in the wrong direction, the prayer would not be in order.

5—Offering of prayer inside the *Ka'aba* is proper and there the prayer can be offered in any direction.

6—In the premises of *Ka'aba* all kinds of prayer i.e. *Fard, Sunna* or *Nafl* are proper and in order.

7—In congregational prayer without the knowledge of the correct direction of *Ka'aba*, the Imam and the followers should act according to their strong presumption or consensus.

## Method of Offering Fard Prayer

1—(a) After making intent in mind, say *Allah-o-Akbar* and raise both the hands upto the ears with palms facing *Ka'aba* and then cross both hands below the navel holding the left wrist with the thumb and small finger of right hand and the remaining three fingers of the right hand stretched on the left wrist. The fingers of the left hand should also remain stretched.

Women while saying *Allah-o-Akbar* should raise their hands upto their shoulders only keeping their hands in the covering (*dupatta*). Then they should put their hands on the chest instead of below the navel keeping the palm of right hand on the back of the left hand.

(b) Then they, men and women, should recite this prayer :

$$سُبْحَانَكَ اللّٰهُمَّ وَبِحَمْدِكَ وَتَبَارَكَ اسْمُكَ وَتَعَالٰى جَدُّكَ$$
$$وَلَا اِلٰهَ غَيْرُكَ$$

(c) Then after reciting *Aa'oo-dho-Billah* and *Bismillah* recite *Sura Fateha (Alhamd)* and say *Aameen* after

$$وَلَا الضَّآلِّيْنَ$$

*Walad-Duallin* i. e. at the end of *Sura*. Then reciting *Bismillah* again recite some *Sura* of the Holy Quran.

(d) Then go in *Ruku* (bowing) saying *Allah-o-Akbar* once. In *Ruku* (bowing) recite

$$سُبْحَانَ رَبِّيَ الْعَظِيْمِ$$

*Subhana-Rabbi-Yal-Azeem* for three, five or seven times.

In *Ruku* men should hold their knees with fingers spread apart, arms spread and a little distance between the feet. They should bow so well that their head, back and haunches are in one line.

In *Ruku* women should bow to the extent that their hands reach the knees. They should keep their fingers joined while holding knees and their arms passed to their sides and keeping their ankles joined.

(e) Then from *Ruku* the head should be raised saying

سَمِعَ اللهُ لِمَنْ حَمِدَه

*Same-Allah-Holeman-Hameda* and

رَبَّنَا لَكَ الْحَمْدُ ط

*Rabbana-Lakal-Hamd* and should stand erect for a while.

(f) Then go for prostration (*Sajda*) saying *Allah-o-Akbar* placing the knees on the ground first and keeping hands in line with the ears put the fore-head on the ground between the hands. In this posture the fore-head and nose should touch the ground and the fingers of the hands and feet should be towards *Ka'aba*. In prostration recite *Subhana-Rabbi-Yal-Aa'la* at least three times. Then raise head saying *Allah-o-Akbar*, sit properly for a while and then saying *Allah-o-Akbar* perform the second *Sajda* in the manner described above and stand up saying *Allah-o-Akbar*. Thus one *Raka'at* is completed.

In *Sajda* women should keep their belly and arm-pits joined together and pressed against the thighs. They should not keep their feet standing on toes. They should place their elbows flat on ground while men keep them raised from the ground.

(g) To begin the second *Raka'at* one should stand up from the *Sajda* without putting hands on the ground. The second should be completed like the first *Raka'at*

## CONDITIONS OF PRAYERS

and after performing the second *Sajda* of this *Raka'at*, put the left foot on the ground and sit over it keeping right foot standing with its fingers facing the *Ka'aba* and recite *Attahiyaat* as under :

اَلتَّحِيَّاتُ لِلهِ وَالصَّلَوَاتُ وَالطَّيِّبَاتُ اَلسَّلَامُ عَلَيْكَ اَيُّهَا النَّبِيُّ وَرَحْمَةُ اللهِ وَبَرَكَاتُهُ اَلسَّلَامُ عَلَيْنَا وَعَلٰى عِبَادِ اللهِ الصَّالِحِيْنَ ط

While reciting *Attahiyaat* when one reaches the *Kalima* he should make a circle with the thumb and middle finger of the right hand and raise the first finger while reciting *Ashhado-An-La-Ilaha-Illal-lah* and drop the finger at *Illallah*; but the circle should be kept till the end of the prayer or rising for the third *Raka'at*. If four *Raka'ats* are to be offered then nothing should be recited after *Attahiyaat* but stand up saying *Allah-o-Akbar* and offer two more *Raka'ats* in the manner described above. In the last two *Raka'at* of *Fard* prayer no other *Sura* should be added with *Sura Fateha* and in the sitting after the second *Sajda* of the fourth *Raka'at* should recite *Darood Sharif* after *Attahiyaat* as under :

اَللّٰهُمَّ صَلِّ عَلٰى مُحَمَّدٍ وَّعَلٰى اٰلِ مُحَمَّدٍ كَمَا صَلَّيْتَ عَلٰى اِبْرَاهِيْمَ وَعَلٰى اٰلِ اِبْرَاهِيْمَ اِنَّكَ حَمِيْدٌ مَّجِيْدٌ ط اَللّٰهُمَّ بَارِكْ عَلٰى مُحَمَّدٍ وَّعَلٰى اٰلِ مُحَمَّدٍ كَمَا بَارَكْتَ عَلٰى اِبْرَاهِيْمَ وَعَلٰى اٰلِ اِبْرَاهِيْمَ اِنَّكَ حَمِيْدٌ مَّجِيْدٌ ط

or say this prayer (*dua*)

رَبَّنَا اٰتِنَا فِى الدُّنْيَا حَسَنَةً وَّفِى الْاٰخِرَةِ حَسَنَةً وَّقِنَا عَذَابَ النَّارِ ط اَللّٰهُمَّ اغْفِرْلِىْ وَلِوَالِدَىَّ وَلِجَمِيْعِ الْمُؤْمِنِيْنَ

$$\text{وَٱلْمُؤْمِنَاتِ وَٱلْمُسْلِمِيْنَ وَٱلْمُسْلِمَاتِ ٱلْاَحْيَاءِ مِنْهُمْ}$$
$$\text{وَٱلْاَمْوَاتِ ط}$$

or recite any other *Dua* (prayer) which is mentioned in Holy Quran or Traditions.

Women while sitting for *Attahiyaat* should sit on the left haunch and spread both the feet towards right side in such a way that the right thigh is over the left and the right calf over the left.

 (h) After reciting the above *Dua* one should turn his or her face first toward right saying *Assalam-o-Alaikum Warah-Matullah*

$$\text{ٱلسَّلَامُ عَلَيْكُمْ وَرَحْمَةُ ٱللهِ}$$

and then turn towards the left repeating the same words. While saying these words one should think of sending salutations to the angels and the other *Namazees* present in the congregation on his left or right. So this is the method of offering prayers.

Some of the above mentioned items are *Fard* (obligatory) and if any of them is missed or omitted whether deliberately or inadvertently the prayer would not be performed.

Some items are essential (*Wajib*). If their omission in deliberate, the prayer becomes worthless and bad and should be offered again. If not offered again, no doubt the *Fard* would be fulfilled but it is a major sin. If omission is inadvertent then *Sajda-e-Shahav* (prostration for omission) will complete the paryer. In the same way some items are *Sunna* and some *Mustahab* (appreciable).

2— In prayer six items are *Fard* (obligatory):
i —To say *Allah-o-Akbar* after intent.    ii—To stand.
iii—To recite some Surah or verse of the Holy Quran.
iv—To bow (perform *Ruku*).
v —To perform both prostrations (*Sajda*).
vi—To sit for the time required for recitation of *Attahiyaat*.

## CONDITIONS OF PRAYERS

3—The essentials (*Wajib*) of prayer are :
  (a) The recitation of *Sura Fateha* and adding some *Sura* with it.
  (b) To perform each *Fard* item properly and in order.
  (c) To recite *Sura Fateha* and some other *Sura* within it standing.
  (d) To bow (*Ruku*) and offer *Sajda*.
  (e) To sit after two *Raka'at* to recite *Attahiyaat* in both sittings.
  (f) To recite *Dua-e-Qunoot* in *Witr* prayer.
  (g) To turn face right and left at the end to offer *Salam* saying *Assalam-o-Alaikum-Warahmatullah*.
  (h) To perform all the items slowly and with patience and not make haste in their performance.

4—With the exception of above items the rest are either *Sunna* or *Mustahab* (appreciable).

5—If anyone does not recite *Sura Fateha* in prayer and recites some other *Sura* or verse or does not add any other *Sura* with it or does not sit after offering two *Raka'at* and stands up for the third without reciting *Aitahiyaat* or sat but did not recite it then in all these cases no doubt *Fard* would be fulfilled but the prayer would be worthless and bad and it is essential to repeat it. It would be major sin not to repeat the prayer. If the omission has been inadvertent, then *Sajda-e-Sahav* would complete it.

6—If one did not turn his or her face to right and left while offering *Salam* at the end of prayer and instead spoke to some one or began to talk or went out or did any thing which disrupts the *Namaz*, then in all such cases repeating of the prayer is essential and not to repeat it would be a major sin.

7—If some one recited any other *Sura* first and then *Sura Fateha*, then the prayer should be repeated. But if it was done inadvertently then *Sajda-e-Sahav* should be performed.

8—After reciting *Alhamd* three other verses should be recited. If only one or two verses are recited and one is so long that it is equal to three verses, then it would be proper.

9—If any one did not say

$$\text{سُبْحَانَ رَبِّیَ الْعَظِیْم}$$

*Subhana-Rabbi-Yal-Azim* in *Ruku* or

$$\text{سَمِعَ اللهُ لِمَنْ حَمِدَهُ}$$

*Sami-Allah Holeman-Hamedah* while rising from *Ruku* or did not recite

$$\text{سُبْحَانَ رَبِّیَ الْاَعْلٰی}$$

*Subhana-Rabbiyal-Aa'la* in *Sajda* or did not recite *Darud Sharif* after *Attahiyaat* in the final sitting, then the prayer would be complete no doubt but it would be against *Sunna*.

10—It is *Sunna* to raise hands at the time of intent. If anyone omits it, the prayer would be complete but it would be against the *Sunna*.

11—*Bismillah* should be recited before *Sura Fateha* in each *Raka'at*. It is also appreciable to recite *Bismillah* before adding a *Sura* with it.

12—While offering *Sajda* if the forehead and nose both are not placed on the ground but only the fore-head and not the nose, then the prayer would be proper. But if only the nose and not the fore-head, is placed on ground, then the prayer would not be in order. Due to some incapacity and inability nose alone is allowed to be placed on the ground.

13—Not to stand erect after bowing (*ruku*) and to go in *Sajda* raising the head slightly, would make the prayer defective and should be repeated.

14—If one did not sit properly between the two *Sajda* and went into the second immediately after raising the head a bit, then if the head has been raised slightly it would not be counted as one *Sajda* and the prayer would not be complete. But if the head was raised to the position of near sitting, the prayer would be offered but it would be defective and bad and should be repeated. It would be a major sin not to repeat it.

15—If a *Sajda* is offered on grass or cotton then the forehead should be so pressed upon it that further pressing is not possible. If the head is merely touched then the *Sajda* shall not be accomplished.

16—In the last two *Raka'ats* of *Fard* Prayer if some *Sura* is recited along with *Sura Fateha*, then there would be no defect in the prayer.

17—If in the last two *Raka'at Sura Fateha* is not recited by some one and said *Subhanallah* three times, then it is also in order. But recitation of *Alhamd* (*Sura Fateha*) is better. But if one does not recite any thing and just remains standing silently till such time in which *Subhan Allah* can be said thrice, even then there is no harm and the prayer is in order.

18—It is essential to add some *Sura* with *Alhamd*. If other *Sura* is not added in the first two *Raka'at*, then it should be recited in the last two *Raka'at*. If the omission was inadvertent *Sajda-e-Sahav* should be performed. But if the omission was intentional, then the prayer should be repeated.

19—While offering a prayer alone, *Sura Fateha* and other *Sura* etc., should be recited very quietly and in a very low tone, but in such a voice that it is audible in one's own ears. If it is not so then the prayer shall not be completed.

20—No particular *Sura* or verses should be reserved or fixed for any prayer. Any *Sura* may be recited. To fix any *Sura* is execrable.

21—A larger *Sura* should not be recited in the second *Raka'at* than the first.

22—All women should offer their prayer individually and not in congregation. They should also not go to the mosque to offer prayer in congregation with the men. If any woman makes a congregation with her husband or some *Mahram*, then she should not stand in line with him but behind him, otherwise the prayer of both shall be spoiled.

23—If ablution is breached while offering a prayer then

the prayer should be repeated after making fresh ablution.

24—While offering prayer it is appreciable that eyes should remain focussed at the point of *Sajda* while standing on feet while bowing (*Ruku*) and on nose while in prostration and while concluding the prayer with *Assalam-o-Alaikum-Warahmatullah* eyes should be towards the shoulders.

If yawning is felt during prayer, the mouth should be pressed hard and if not checked thus the back side of the palm should be used. In case of irritation in the throat, coughing should be checked and prevented.

25—Some ignorant persons when they enter the mosque and find the Imam in *Ruku*, they also hurriedly join him in that posture saying *Allah-o-Akbar*, then their prayer is not offered because *Allah-o-Akbar* (*Takbir Tahrimi*) is necessary for a prayer and for it standing is essential. When one did not stand, it is not correct and consequently the prayer is not offered.

**Some Requisites of Fard Prayers**

1—While reciting *Sura Fateha* in a prayer, the letter "Alif" in *Aameen* should be prolonged in pronunciation and thereafter recite any other *Sura* of the Holy Quran.

2—While in a journey or any urgent need, one may recite any *Sura* after *Sura Fateha*, but when resident or not in any urgent need then *Sura Hujurat* or *Sura Barooj* should be recited in *Fajr* and *Zuhr* prayers or any other *Sura* that come between them in the Holy Quran. A lengthy *Sura* should be recited in the first *Raka'at* of *Fajr* prayer then the second one. In other prayers the *Suras* should be equal. The difference of one or two verses is immaterial.

In the prayer of *Asr* and *Isha Sura Al-Ta'ariq* or *Sura Al-Bayyana* or any other *Sura* between them should be recited, while in *Maghrib* prayer *Sura Zilzal* upto the end should be recited.

3—When rising from *Ruku* (bowing) the Imam will say only :

سَمِعَ اللهُ لِمَنْ حَمِدَه

*Same-Allah-Holeman-Hameda* and the followers will respond with

$$رَبَّنَا لَكَ الْحَمْدُ$$

*Rabbana-Lakal-Hamd* only in congregational prayers. But when praying alone one should say both and then saying *Takbir* and holding both the knees with hands should perform *Sajda* and care should be taken that *Takbir* should end exactly when prostration begins.

4—While performing *Sajda* first knees should be placed on ground, then hands, nose and lastly the fore-head. The face should be between the hands with their fingers joined together and stretched towards *Ka'aba* and both the feet should stand on their fingers pointing towards *Ka'aba*, the abdomen should remain away from the things and the arms from arm pits. There should be so much difference between the abdomen and the ground that a very small kid may pass through it.

5—In the first two *Raka'at* of *Fajr*, *Maghrib* and *Isha* prayers *Sura Fateha*, another *Sura*, *Same Allah-Holeman-Hameda* and all the *Takbirs* should be said in a loud voice by the Imam. But one offering prayer alone may recite as he likes, but *Same Allah Holeman Hameda* and other *Takbir* should be said in a low voice. In the prayers of *Zuhr* and *Asr* the Imam should say only *Same Allah Holeman Hamedah* and the *Takbir* loudly. The followers should respond in a low voice all the times.

6—After concluding the prayer one should raise both hands upto the chest and pray for one's self and if he is Imam he should pray for all the followers also. After the pray (*dua*) both hands should be passed over the face. The followers should either pray for themselves or just say "Ameen" in response to Imam's prayer (*dua*).

7—In prayers which are followed by *Sunna* i.e. *Zuhr*, *Maghrib* and *Isha* the prayer (*dua*) should not be very long, one should pray shortly and begin performing *Sunnas*. But in prayers which have no *Sunna* after *Fard* like *Fajr* and *Asr* the prayer (*dua*) may be as long as one desires. In such prayers the Imam should turn his face towards right or left and pray facing the followers provided no *Masbuq* is offering his missed prayer opposite the Imam.

8—After *Fard* prayer, if there are no *Sunna* after them, or after *Sunna* prayer it is appreciable to recite thrice.

اَسْتَغْفِرُ اللهَ الَّذِىْ لَآ اِلٰهَ اِلَّا هُوَ الْحَىُّ الْقَيُّوْمُ

*Astagh-Ferullah-Ulladhi-La-Ilaha-Illa-Ho-Wal-Hayyul-Qay-yum, Aayatul-Kursi, Sura Ikhlas, Sura Falaq* and *Sura Naas* once each and

سُبْحَانَ اللهِ

*Subhan-Allah,*

اَلْحَمْدُ لِلّٰهِ

*Alhamdolillah* 33 times each and

اللهُ اَكْبَرُ

*Allah-o-Akbar* 34 times.

### Difference in Postures for Men and Women in Prayers

Women should also pray like men with the following differences :—

1—At the time of *Takbir Tahrima* (saying *Allah-o-Akbar* in the beginning) men should raise their hands upto the ears by taking them out of covering, if any, while the women should raise their hands upto their shoulders without taking them out of their covering (*duppatta*).

2—After *Takbir Tahrima* men should cross their hands below the navel, but women should put them on their chests.

3—Men should make a circle with the little finger and thumb of the right hand to catch the left wrist and spread the remaining three fingers over the left wrist, while women should put the right palm over the back of the left palm and should not make a circle or catch the left wrist.

## CONDITIONS OF PRAYERS

4—In *Ruku* men should bow so much that their head, back and haunches be in one line, but women should bend only so much that their hands reach their knees.

5— In *Ruku* men should keep their fingers of hands spread over the knees, while women should keep their fingers joined together on the knees.

6—In *Ruku* men should keep their elbows apart from their sides, while women should keep them pressed to their sides.

7—In *Sajda* men should keep their bellies apart from the thighs and arms from arm-pits but women should keep them joined.

8—In *Sajda* men should keep their elbows away from the ground, but women should keep them spread on the ground.

9—In *Sajda* men should keep both of their feet standing on the toes but women should not, but should spread both feet towards right side.

10—In sitting men should sit on left foot and keep the right foot standing on its toe, while women should sit on the left haunch and spread both the feet towards right side in such a way that the right thigh is over the left thigh and the right calf on the left calf.

11—Women are not allowed to recite the Holy Quran loudly at any time, but should always recite in a low voice.

## THINGS OR ACTS WHICH DISRUPT NAMAZ

1—If anyone speaks deliberately or otherwise, the prayer is disrupted.

2—Prayer will also be disrupted if anyone utters "Oh", "Ah", or "O", or cries loudly during the prayer. But the prayer will not be disrupted if someone's heart is moved on remembering Hell or Heaven and some sound or words or exclamation or sorrow are uttered involuntarily.

3—Coughing or to clear the throat unnecessarily in such a way that some letter is also uttered disrupts the prayer. But mere coughing is permissible when it is inevitable.

4—If one sneezes during a prayer and responds it with *Alhamdolillah*, then it will not disrupt the prayer, but it is better not to say so. If some one else sneezes and one in prayer says *Yarhamak-Allah*, in response, then the prayer will be disrupted.

5—Prayer will be disrupted if verses are recited during it by seeing in the Holy Quran.

6—While in prayer if one turns to the extent that his or her chest also turns from the direction of Ka'aba, then the prayer will be disrupted.

7—In response to someone's greetings if one says *Waalaikumussalam* in the prayer, then it would be disrupted.

8—If a woman collects and ties the knot of her hair during a prayer, then the prayer will be disrupted.

9—Prayer is disrupted if anything is eaten or drunk during it—even if a very small quantity like the sesame seed or a bit of betel nut is picked up and placed in mouth, it would disrupt the prayer. But if a bit of betel nut etc. is stuck between the teeth and it is less than the size of a gram and is swallowed, it will not disrupt the prayer. But if it is equal to or larger than a gram then the prayer is disrupted.

10—If while offering prayer a person has a betel leaf in his mouth and its juice enters his throat, then the prayer is disrupted.

11—If anything sweet was eaten by someone and after cleaning the mouth starts offering prayer but its taste is still in the mouth and goes down the throat with saliva, then the prayer will not be disrupted.

12—If during a prayer hearing good news one says *Alhamdolillah* or hearing some death news says *Innalillah-e-wa-Innailaihe-Raj-e-oon*, then the prayer will be disrupted.

13—If during a prayer suckling baby sucks the milk of mother, then the prayer of the mother is disrupted. But if the milk did not come out then the prayer is not lost.

14—If *Bismillah* is uttered by one in prayer on the falling of someone, then the prayer is disrupted.

15—Prayer is also lost if any letter of verse is prolonged in recitation or pronounced wrongly.

16—Prayer will not be disrupted if during it anyone on seeing a letter or book, reads or understands it within himself without reading aloud.

17—Prayer will not be disrupted by passing of a person or an animal in front of a person offering prayer. But it is advisable to offer one's prayer at such a place where no one may pass in front of him and others also may not be inconvenienced. If no such place is available, then a *Satra* be fixed in the ground in front. But it should not be exactly in the centre but towards the right or left eye. If a stick is not available then something of the height of a chair or stool be kept in front. Now it would be permissible to pass in front of such a person.

18—If on account of some reason a step is advanced towards Ka'aba or receded, it will not disrupt the prayer provided that the chest remains in the direction of Ka'aba. But if one advances beyond the spot of *Sajda*, then the prayer will be disrupted.

## EXECRABLES OF PRAYERS

1—*Makrooh* (execrable) is an act which, though does not disrupt *Namaz*, but spoils it and reduces its credit. It is a sin also.

2—It is execrable to toy or play with one's clothes or ornaments or remove pebbles etc. during a prayer. But if due to the pebbles or gravels *Sajda* is hindered, then one can remove them or level the ground once or twice with hands.

3—To crack fingers or put hand on haunch or to turn face and look left and right while offering prayer is execrable.

4—While praying it is execrable to sit with both knees up or squat or sit like a dog. But in case of illness one may sit in any posture.

5—To raise hand in reply of greeting is execrable while praying and if the reply is uttered then the prayer will be disrupted.

6—To collect clothes in order to prevent their being soiled is execrable in prayer.

7—It is execrable to offer prayer at such a place where there is an apprehension that someone may make him laugh or his mind will be distracted or there is any likelihood of some omission.

8—If anyone is sitting in front and is engaged in talking someone, then it is not execrable to offer prayer facing the back of such a person. But if that person feels inconvenienced by being checked to move, then prayer should not be offered behind his back.

In the same way if people are talking so loudly that a prayer may be disturbed, then it is execrable to offer prayer at such place. It is also execrable to offer prayer face to face with another person.

## EXECRABLES OF PRAYERS

9—There would be no harm in prayer if the Holy Quran or a sword is hung in front of a person praying.

10—Praying on a floor painted with pictures is in order but *Sajda* should not be offered on pictures. To keep pictured prayer-mat is execrable and it is a sin to keep pictures in house.

11—At a place where a picture is over the head or in the ceiling or canopy or it is in front or on right or left, then it is execrable to offer prayer there. But it is not execrable if the picture is under the feet. If the picture is so small that one can not see it while standing if placed on ground, then there is no harm. If it is not a complete picture or its head is cut off or defaced, then such picture does not disrupt and execrate the prayer in whatever position it may be.

12—It is execrable to offer prayer wearing a picture printed cloth.

13—It is not execrable if the picture is of a house, tree or an inanimate object.

14—To count on fingers the verses of the Holy Quran or any other thing in prayer is execrable. But there is no harm in counting by pressing the fingers.

15—It is execrable to make the second *Raka'at* longer than the first one.

16—It is also execrable to fix any particular *Sura* for a prayer and to recite it always and no other *Sura*.

17—It is execrable to offer prayer with a shawl or sheet hanging over the shoulders.

18—It is execrable to offer prayer wearing very bad and dirty clothes, but it is allowed if one has no other clothes.

19—It is not proper and is execrable to offer prayer with some coin etc. in the mouth. If it is such a thing which obstructs the recitation of the Holy Quran, then prayer is disrupted and lost.

20—It is execrable to offer prayer when there is an urgent need of passing urine or easing one's self.

21—If a person is hungry and food is also ready, then he should eat first and offer prayer afterwards. In such case to offer prayer without taking food is execrable. But if the time of prayer is about to end, then he may offer prayer first and then take the food.

22—It is not proper to pray with eyes closed. But if the closing of eyes enhances concentration in prayer, then there is no harm.

23—To spit or clean the nose in prayer, is execrable; but permissible when obliged to do so. For example if someone coughed and the mouth was filled with phlegm, then in such case he may spit towards his left or rub it by taking in a cloth. But he should not spit towards his right or in the direction of Ka'aba.

24—If a bug bites one while in prayer, it should be caught and thrown and to kill it is not proper. If it has not stung, then it should not be caught either as it is execrable.

25—In *Fard* prayer it is execrable to stand with the help of wall etc.

26—If one has not completed the *Sura* and went into bowing in haste and finished the *Sura* while bowing, then it is execrable and the prayer is lost.

27—If the spot of *Sajda* is higher than the position of feet, i.e. if anyone has to offer *Sajda* on a thresh-hold, then it should be judged as to how much high it is. If it is higher than a span (distance between stretched thumb and small finger of a hand) then the prayer will not be in order. But if it is just equal or less than a span, then it is permissible. But to do it is execrable except in necessity.

28—It is prohibited execrably to wear clothes in a disorderly manner, i.e. against the common usage and as are not put on by civilised men. If one covers himself with a sheet but does not throw its corners over the shoulders, or wears a shirt but does not put arms into the sleeves, then it will make the prayer execrable.

29—It is execrable to offer prayer bare-headed. But if it is done out of humility and devotion then there is no harm.

## EXECRABLES OF PRAYERS

30 —If one's turban or cap falls down while in prayer, then it is preferable to pick it up and put on. But if it requires substantial act to pick it up, then leave it.

31—It is prohibited execrably for men to spread their arms flat on the ground while offering *Sajda*. The elbows should be kept raised.

32—It is milder execrability for the Imam to stand inside the arch, but if stands outside and performs the *Sajda* inside the arch, then it is not execrable.

33—It is milder execrability for the Imam to stand alone on a higher place than the followers without any necessity. If some followers are also with him, then it is not execrable. If there is only one follower, even then it is execrable. According to some jurists it is execrable if the height is equal to one armlength or more and according to some even if it is less than that.

34—It is milder execrability for all the followers to stand at a higher place than the Imam without any necessity. It is not execrable if the congregation is large and the space is not sufficient. Or if some of the followers stand at the level of the Imam and others on a higher level.

35—To perform any act of prayer before the Imam is prohibited execrability for the followers.

36—The followers should not recite any *Sura* of the Holy Quran, even *Sura Fateha* or any prayer (*dua*) while the Imam is engaged in recitation in standing posture. It is prohibited execrability.

**Breaches in Prayers**

If there is some breach of purity, then if it is a stronger breach necessitating a bath, the prayer shall be lost. But if it is a minor breach, either voluntary or involuntary and in its occurrence a person's will or intention may not play a role, the prayer is not lost. If the will or intention was there, then the prayer shall be lost.

For example if one laughs loudly in a prayer or causes some injury to himself leading to bleeding or intentionally passes gases or while walking on a roof causes some stone or brick to fall down injuring a person offering prayer and he bleeds, then in all such cases the prayer shall be lost as in all these actions the human will and intention is present. If it is involuntary, then it may be either rare occurrence i.e. insanity, unconsciousness or death of the Imam ; or of common occurrence such as passing of gases, urination, stool or *Midhi*. Then if it is a rare occurrence, the prayer shall be lost. But the person may remove the impurity and complete the remaining part of the prayer. This is called *Bina*. But it is better to repeat the prayer.

In case of *Bina* the prayer will not be spoiled with the following conditions :

(a) No item of prayer should be offered during breach of purity.

(b) No item of prayer should be offered while walking i.e. when he goes to make a fresh ablution or returns then he should not recite the Holy Quran because recitation is an item of prayer.

(c) Should do no such action which is against the prayer or avoidable.

(d) After breach of purity one should not wait so long in which an item of prayer can be performed, but should immediately go to make fresh ablution. But if delayed due to some unavoidable reason, then there in no harm such as the lines of congregation are many and he was in the first line and it is very difficult to go after disturbing them.

1—If the breach of purity occurred to a person praying singly, then he should immediately make fresh ablution with all its requisites as soon as possible and should not talk in meantime and complete the remaining part of his prayer preferably at the same spot or where he was offering prayer before. But it is better to break the prayer intentionally after the breach by saying *Salam* and repeat it in full after making ablution.

2—If the breach occurs to the Imam, then even if he is in the last sitting of the prayer, he should immediately go to make a fresh ablution and it is better for him to appoint some one from the followers as his substitute whom he thinks qualified to be the Imam. It is better to appoint a *Mudrik*[1] as substitute. It is also permissible if a *Masbuq*[2] is appointed as substitute, but the Imam should tell him by signs as to how many *Raka'at* are due. The number of *Raka'at* should be pointed out by raising fingers, *Ruku* by keeping hands on the knees, *Sajda* by putting hand on fore-head and recitation by putting hand on mouth and so on.

After making ablution the Imam should join the congregation, if still continuing, as follower of his substitute. But if the congregation has ended he may either complete his prayer at the place where he made his ablution or at his original place.

3—If the water is available within the floor of the mosque, then it is not necessary for the Imam to appoint a substitute— may or may not appoint—but should go for making ablution and on return resume the Imam-ship and during this period the followers should wait for him.

4—After appointing a substitute an Imam does not remain an Imam but becomes a follower of his substitute and if the congregation has ended, he should perform his prayer like a *Lahiq*. If the Imam did not appoint a substitute and the followers appoint someone from amongst themselves or a follower himself advances and occupies the place of the Imam and intends to be the Imam, then it is proper provided that in the meantime the Imam has not gone out of the mosque and if the prayer is not in a mosque, then if the Imam has not gone out of the lines or the Satra. If he has crossed these limits, then no one else can be the Imam and the prayer will be spoiled.

5—If a breach occurs to a follower, he should immediately make a fresh ablution and if the congregation is still continuing, he should join it and if not he should complete his prayer.

---

1. One who joined the prayers without losing any *Raka'at*.
2. One who joined the prayers after losing one or more *Raka'at*.

It is better for him to complete his prayer at the place of ablution.

6—If a *Masbuq* has been appointed as substitute by the Imam, then the *Masbuq* after leading the *Raka'at* which were due to the Imam should appoint some *Mudrik* as Imam so that the *Mudrik* may offer the *Salam* and the *Masbuq* should perform his missed *Raka'at*.

7—These problems are very delicate and everyone cannot understand them. Hence the better course in case of breach of purity, is not to resort to *Bina* but one should end his prayer by offering *Salam* and should repeat the whole prayer after ablution.

## Conditions when Break in Prayers is Proper

1—If the train starts when one is engaged in offering prayer and his luggage or family members are in the compartment, then it is allowed to break the prayer to catch the train.

2—If a snake appears while someone is praying, then it is permissible to break the prayer on account of fear of the snake.

3—If anyone has lifted the shoes of one who is engaged in prayer with the intention of stealing them and it is apprehended that the man may disappear with the shoes, then it is allowed to break the prayer to get them.

4—A hen was left from being caged at night and a cat has come near it, then it is permissible to break the prayer to save the hen.

5—If a woman engaged in prayer feels that the pot on the oven is over-boiling or the food-stuff in it is being burnt and its cost is Re. 1/- to Re. 1/50, then it is permissible to break the prayer and look after it.

6—If one feels a strong urge to pass urine or to ease himself, then it is permitted to break the prayer. Ease oneself and then offer the prayer.

7—If a blind person is going and there is a well on the path and there is an apprehension of the blind person falling into the well, then it is compulsory to break the prayer to save the blind man. If one neglects it and the blind falls into the well and dies as a result, then the person offering prayer would commit a sin.

8—If a child or anyone's clothes catch fire, it is permissible to break the prayer to save him.

9—If anyone's parents, grand-parents—paternal or maternal, call him due to some distress or some genuine need, then it is essential (*Wajib*) for him to break the prayer, *Fard* prayer even, to attend them.

For instance if anyone of the parents is ill and while going to or coming back from the latrine slipped and fell down. Then it is compulsory to break the prayer and look after them. But if there is someone else to help them, then prayer should not be broken.

10—Prayer may also be broken if anyone of the parents is about to fall and has called for help. If not called then it is not proper to break *Fard*.

11—If one is offering *Sunna* or *Nafl* prayer and anyone of his parents call him not knowing that he is engaged in prayer, then it is essential for him to break the prayer to attend them. Whether they call for an urgent need or not. If the person does not respond, he will commit a sin. But if the parents are aware that the person is engaged in prayer and even then call, then the prayer should not be broken unless it is in some distress or urgent need.

# THE SUNNA AND NAFL PRAYERS

1—Before offering the *Fard* prayer of *Fajr*, offering of two *Raka'ats* is *Sunna*. Their importance has been greatly stressed in the Traditions and should never be omitted. If one has been delayed and prayer time is short, then two *Raka'ats* of *Fard* may be offered in time and the *Sunna* be offered as postponed prayer after sun-rise.

2—In *Zuhr* prayer first four *Raka'ats* of *Sunna*, then four *Raka'ats* of *Fard* and then two *Raka'ats* of *Sunna* are offered. These six *Raka'ats* of *Sunna* at *Zuhr* time are essential and have been stressed in the Traditions. Their omission is a sin.

3—At *Asr* time first four *Raka'ats* of *Sunna* and then four *Raka'ats* of *Fard* should be offered. But the *Sunna* prayer of *Asr* has not been stressed and if offered one will get much credit or reward for them.

4—In the prayer of *Maghrib* first three *Raka'ats* of *Fard* and then two *Raka'ats* of *Sunna* are offered. These two *Raka'ats* of *Sunna* are also essential and their omission is a sin.

5—At the time of *Isha* prayer it is better and appreciable to offer first four *Raka'ats* of *Sunna*, then four *Raka'ats* of *Fard*, then two *Raka'ats* of *Sunna* and then, if desired, two *Raka'ats* of *Nafl* may be offered. The two *Raka'ats* of *Sunna* prayer after the *Fard* have been stressed much and their omission is a sin. Thus there are six *Sunna Raka'ats* in *Isha* prayer. If one does not want to offer all the six *Raka'ats*, then he may offer only two *Raka'ats* of *Sunna* after the *Isha Fard* prayer and then offer *Witr* prayer.

6—The *Tarawih* prayer in the month of Ramazan is also *Sunna*. It has also been stressed and its omission is a sin. Women often miss these. They should not do so.

## THE SUNNA AND NAFL PRAYERS 115

7—After offering the two *Sunna Raka'ats* after *Isha Fard* prayer, twenty *Sunna Tarawih* should be offered. One may intend in *Tarawih* for two or four *Raka'ats* ; but it is appreciable to intend for two. After completing the twenty *Raka'ats* of *Tarawih Witr* prayer should be offered.

The Sunna whose offering is essential are called *Muakkada* i.e. stressed. They are twelve during the day and night—two before *Fajr* prayer, four before and two after *Zuhr*, two after *Maghrib* and two after *Isha* prayer. *Tarawih* in Ramazan is also *Sunnat-Muakkada*. Some scholars and jurists count *Tahajjud* also as *Sunnat-e-Muakkada*.

All the prayers, other than *Fard* and *Sunna*, are *Nafl* prayers. There is no limit to them and the more *Nafl* one offers the greater will be the credit and reward for them. There have been such servants of Allah who used to offer *Nafl* prayers throughout the night and did not sleep.

8.—Of all the *Nafl* prayers some have a very great credit. Therefore it is better to offer those instead of others because a little amount of extra labour entitles one for greater reward. They are :

(i) *Tahiyatul Wudu*, (ii) *Tahiyatul Masjid*, (iii) *Ishraq*, (iv) *Chasht*, (v) *Awwabin*, (vi) *Tahajjud* and (vii) *Salatut-Tasbih*.

9—*Tahiyatul-Wudu* is of two *Raka'ats* and is offered whenever ablution is performed. Its virtue has been greatly mentioned in the Traditions.

*Tahiyatul-Masjid* is of two *Raka'ats* and may be offered on entering the mosque before sitting.

10—*Ishraq* : After offering *Fajr* prayer one should remain sitting on the prayer-mat till the sun rises and is sufficiently high : but during this period one should remain reciting *Darood Sharif* or *Kalima* or remembering Allah or any other prayer (*dua*) and should not indulge in useless worldly talks or business. When the sun is high, offer two or four *Raka'ats*,. Its reward is equal to the reward of a *Haj* or *Umra*.

But if one got engaged in worldly affairs after *Fajr* prayer and then offered *Ishraq* prayer; then it be proper, but its reward will be decreased.

11—*Chasht* : When the sun is sufficiently high and hot, two or four *Raka'ats* are offered as *Chasht* prayer. Its reward is also very great.

12—*Awwabin* : After the *Fard* and *Sunna* prayers of *Maghrib*, six to twenty *Raka'ats* are offered as *Awwabin* prayer.

13—*Tahajjud* : Offering of prayer on rising after mid-night, is of great merit and virtue. This is called *Tahajjud* prayer. This is most acceptable to Allah and its credit and reward is the greatest. At least four and twelve at the most are its *Raka'ats*. If not four, only two may also be offered. If one cannot be sure to get up after mid-night, then he may offer it after *Isha* prayer; but its reward will not be to that extent. In addition to these as many *Nafl* prayer may be offered as one wishes.

14—*Salatut-Tasbih* : Great merit and reward has been attributed to this prayer in the Traditions. This was taught by the Holy Prophet (SAW) to his uncle Hadrat Abbas and told that on account of offering this prayer all of his past and future, old and new, great and small sins will be forgiven by Allah and said that if possible this should be offered daily, once a week, or once a month, or once a year and even if this is not possible, then once in the whole life.

### Method of its Performance

One should intend for four *Raka'ats* and after reciting *Subhana Kalla Humma*, *Alhamd* (*Sura Fateha*) and any other *Sura*, recite the following prayer (*dua*) fifteen times before bowing (*Ruku*) :

سُبْحَانَ اللهُ وَالْحَمْدُ لِلَّهِ وَلَا اِلَهَ اِلَّا اللهُ وَ اللهُ اَكْبَرُ

Then bow and after reciting *Subhana-Rabbial Azeem* recite the above prayer ten times. Then rise from bowing saying *Same-Allah-o Leman-Hamedah* stand and recite the same prayer ten times. Then go into the first *Sajda* after reciting *Subhana-Rabbial-a'ala* recite the very prayer ten times and on rising from *Sajda* again recite it ten times. Then perform the second

## THE SUNNA AND NAFL PRAYERS

*Sajda* and in it also recite the prayer ten times. Then on rising from the *Sajda* and before standing up for the second *Raka'at* again recite the prayer ten times. Then complete the second *Raka'at* in the same way as described above and while sitting for *Attahiyat* recite this prayer ten times before *Attahiyat*. In this manner the four *Raka'ats* should be completed. In each *Raka'at* this prayer shall be recited seventyfive times.

15—No particular *Suras* are prescribed for these four *Raka'at* any *Sura* may be recited after *Sura Fateha*.

16—When *Nafl* prayers are offered during the day, then each should be of two or four *Raka'ats* only. To intend for more than four *Raka'ats* in one prayer during the day is execrable. But at night six or even eight *Raka'ats* at a time may be intended. But to intend for more than eight *Raka'ats* in one prayer is execrable even at night.

17—If the intent is for four *Rak'ats* of *Nafl*, then while sitting after two *Raka'ats* he may either recite *Attahiyat* only and stand up for the third *Raka'at* or he may recite with it *Darood Sharif* and *dua* also and then stand up for the third *Raka'at* without *Salam* and begin it by reciting *Subhana Kalla*, *Aoudho Billah*, *Bismillah* and *Alhamd* and at the end of the fourth *Raka'at* after reciting *Attahiyat*, *Darood Sharif* and *dua* etc. conclude it with *Salam*. If the intent is for eight *Raka'ats* in one prayer, then he should not conclude at the fourth *Raka'at* but after the eight in the same manner as described above.

18—It is essential in all *Raka'ats* of *Sunna* or *Nafl* prayers to add some *Sura* with *Sura Fateha*. It would be sinful if the *Sura* is omitted deliberately. If the omission is due to forgetfulness, then *Sajda-e-Sahav* (prostration for forgetfulness) should be offered.

19—It is essential to complete a *Nafl* prayer after intending. It is sinful to break it and such prayer should necessarily be offered as postponed (*Qada*) prayer. But in *Nafl* every two *Raka'ats* are separate unit. If the intent of the broken prayer was for four or six *Raka'ats*, then offering of the same number is not essential—only two *Raka'ats* will be due. In the same way there is no harm if anyone intended for four *Raka'ats* but concluded after two *Raka'ats* only.

20—If one had intended for four *Raka'ats* but broke it before even two were completed, then postponed prayer of only two *Raka'ats* shall be due.

21—If one had intended for four *Raka'ats*, but after two broke up the intent or in the third or fourth, then if he had recited *Attahiyat* etc. after second *Raka'at*, then only two *Raka'ats* of postponed prayer will be due. But if he did not sit after the second *Raka'at* and stood up deliberately or unintentionally without reciting *Attahiyat* etc. then postponed prayer for all the four *Raka'ats* has become due and should be offered.

22—If the intent for four *Sunna Raka'ats* of *Zuhr* is broken, then all the four *Raka'ats* have to be repeated whether *Attahiyat* was recited or not in the first sitting.

23—It is allowed to offer *Nafl* prayer in sitting posture, but in such case the reward or credit is reduced to half. So it is better to offer *Nafl* prayer in standing position. *Nafl* prayer after *Witr* also comes under the same category. But if it is not passible to stand due to some illness, then *Nafl* prayers may be performed in sitting and in this case its credit would be full. *Fard* and *Sunna* prayers are not permissible to be offered in sitting postiion unless there is some legitimate cause for it.

24—If *Nafl* prayer was begun while sitting and then after performing some part of it one stood up, then the prayer is in order.

25—In the same way it is also in order if the *Nafl* prayer is begun in standing position and then sat down after performing some part of it.

26—If one started *Nafl* prayer in standing and being tired due to weakness took the support of a stick or wall, then it is permissible.

**Witr Prayer**

Three essential *Raka'ats* are offered after *Isha* prayers. It is called *Witr*.

1—*Witr* prayer is *Wajib* (essential). *Wajib* is nearly equal to *Fard* and its omission is a major sin. If ever missed, it should be performed whenever there is an opportunity.

2—There are three *Raka'ats* prescribed for *Witr* prayer. After the second *Raka'at* one should sit for *Attahiyat* but should not recite *Darood Sharif* and should get up immediately after *Attahiyat* for the third *Raka'at*. In the third *Raka'at* after reciting *Sura Fateha* and some other *Sura*, hands should be raised upto the ears by men and up to shoulders by women saying *Allah-o-Akbar* and cross hands again in front and recite *Dua-e-Qunnut* and then complete the *Raka'at* performing *Ruku* and *Sajda* and sit for reciting *Attahiyat*, *Darood Sharif* and the prayer with *Salam*.

3—*Dua-e-Qunnut* is as under :

اَللّٰهُمَّ اِنَّا نَسْتَعِيْنُكَ وَ نَسْتَغْفِرُكَ وَنُوْمِنُ بِكَ
وَنَتَوَكَّلُ عَلَيْكَ وَنُثْنِيْ عَلَيْكَ الْخَيْرَ وَ نَشْكُرُكَ
وَلَا نَكْفُرُكَ وَ نَخْلَعُ وَ نَتْرُكُ مَنْ يَفْجُرُكَ ط اَللّٰهُمَّ
اِيَّاكَ نَعْبُدُ وَلَكَ نُصَلِّيْ وَ نَسْجُدُ وَ اِلَيْكَ نَسْعٰى
وَ نَحْفِدُ وَ نَرْجُوْا رَحْمَتَكَ وَ نَخْشٰى عَذَابَكَ اِنَّ
عَذَابَكَ بِالْكُفَّارِ مُلْحِقٌ ط

4—Some *Sura* of the Holy Quran must be added with *Sura Fateha* in all the three *Raka'at* of *Witr* prayer.

5—If one forgets to recite *Dua-e-Qunnut* in the third *Raka'at* and goes for *Ruku* and remembers it there, then he may not recite it but should offer *Sajda-e-Sahav* in the end. But if he got up from *Ruku* and recited it, no doubt the prayer would be offered but it should not be done and *Sajda-e-Sahav* is essential in such case also.

6—Due to forgetfulness *Dua-e-Qunnut* was recited in the first or the second *Raka'at*, then it would not be counted. It should be recited again in the third *Raka'at* and a *Sajda-e-Sahav* is also essential.

7—If anyone has not learnt by heart *Dua-e-Qunnut*, he may recite this prayer :

رَبَّنَا اٰتِنَا فِى الدُّنْيَا حَسَنَةً وَّ فِى الْاٰخِرَةِ حَسَنَةً وَّقِنَا عَذَابَ النَّارِ

Or say three times, *Ya Rabbi, Ya Rabbi, Ya Rabbi* and the *Witr* prayer will be performed in order.

# PRAYER FOR GUIDANCE
## (NAMAZ-E-ISTAKHARA)

1—When one intends to do certain thing of which he is not sure whether it is beneficial for him or not, he should seek guidance and help from Allah by prayer. This is called *Istakhara*. Great merit and inducement have been described for this prayer in the Holy Traditions. The Holy Prophet (S.A.W.) is reported to have said that it was a great misfortune if one does not seek Divine Guidance and Help in his affairs. If Divine Help is sought by some one in matters of marriage, journey or any other business, then such a person shall never be disappointed.

2—The method of offering *Istakhara* prayer to seek Divine Guidance is to offer two *Raka'ats* of *Nafl* prayer with full devotion and then recite :

اَللّٰهُمَّ اِنِّىْ اَسْتَخِيْرُكَ بِعِلْمِكَ وَاَسْتَقْدِرُكَ بِقُدْرَتِكَ

وَاَسْئَلُكَ مِنْ فَضْلِكَ الْعَظِيْمِ فَاِنَّكَ تَقْدِرُ وَلَا اَقْدِرُ

وَتَعْلَمُ وَلَا اَعْلَمُ وَ اَنْتَ عَلَّامُ الْغُيُوْبِ اَللّٰهُمَّ اِنْ

كُنْتَ تَعْلَمُ اَنَّ هٰذَا الْاَمْرَ خَيْرٌ لِىْ فِىْ دِيْنِىْ وَ

مَعَاشِىْ وَعَاقِبَةِ اَمْرِىْ فَاقْدِرْهُ لِىْ وَيَسِّرْ لِىْ ثُمَّ

بَارِكْ لِىْ فِيْهِ وَ اِنْ كُنْتَ تَعْلَمُ اَنَّ هٰذَاالْاَمْرَ شَرٌّ

$$\text{لِّى فِىْ دِيْنِىْ وَ مَعَاشِىْ وَعَافِيَةِ اَمْرِىْ فَاصْرِفْهُ عَنِّىْ}$$

$$\text{وَ اصْرِفْنِىْ عَنْهُ وَ اقْدُرْلِىَ الْخَيْرَ حَيْثُ كَانَ ثُمَّ}$$

$$\text{اَرْضِنِىْ بِهٖ}$$

On reaching the words *Hadhal Amra*, one should think of the business for which *Istakhara* is being done and sleep on a clean bed facing *Ka'aba* with ablution in tact and on waking up whatever is prominent in his mind is better and should act accordingly.

3—If nothing definite comes to the mind on the first day and the mental hesitation and disturbance is not removed, he should repeat it on the second day. If still undecided, then he should repeat for seven days, continuously during which period he is sure to realise the suitability or otherwise of the business.

4—This prayer should not be offered while going for Haj pilgrimage seeking whether he should go or not. But should seek as to which day shall be most suitable to go on the journey for Haj.

**Prayer for repentance (Namaz-e-Tauba)**

If anyone commits an anti-*Shariat* (Religion) act he should offer two *Raka'ats* of *Nafl* prayer and very humbly and beseechingly seek Allah's forgiveness expressing sincere repentance on his act and should resolve not to commit such act again and by the Grace of Allah his sin will be forgiven.

# OFFERING OF MISSED PRAYERS
## (QADA NAMAZ)

1—Anyone who has missed any prayer, should offer it immediately when he recollects it. Delay in offering missed prayers without any legitimate cause, is a sin. If anyone who has missed a prayer did not offer it at the first opportunity and continued to postpone it from day to day and died before that time, then he would commit a double sin—one for missing the prayer and the second for not offering the missed prayer.

2—If anyone has missed several prayers, then he should offer all the missed prayers as soon as possible and if possible he should take courage to offer all of them at one time. If the missed prayers are of several months or years, then these should be offered as soon as possible and two or more of them can be offered at one time. If there is any difficulty then only one missed prayer may be offered at a time. But this is the least.

3—There is no fixed or specific time for offering the missed prayers. Whenever one has time, make ablution and offer the prayer ; but care should be taken that the time should not be the prohibited one or execrable.

4—If anyone has missed one prayer only or he has offered all the previously missed prayers and only this one is due, then he should offer this prayer first and then another prayer. If he performs the prayer of that day or time without offering the missed prayer, then the prayer of the day or time will not be in order and should be repeated after performing the missed prayer. If he forgot the missed prayer, then the prayer of the time would be in order and whenever he remembers the missed prayer, he should offer it and not repeat the prayer of time.

5—If the time is so that if one offers the missed prayer,

then there would be no time left for the prescribed prayer of the time, then the prayer of the time should be offered first and the missed one thereafter.

6—If someone has missed two to five prayers and no other prayer is due to him or that since he attained maturity or puberty no prayer other than these have been missed by him or he has offered all the other missed prayers, then it is not permissible for him to offer any prayer of the time unless he has offered all these missed prayers. While offering these missed prayers consideration should be kept that the prayer missed first should be offered first then the next and so on till all the missed prayers have offered, otherwise the prayer of the time will not be offered and will remain due. For instance one has not offered one full day's prayers, then he should first offer *Fajr*, then *Zuhr*, then *Asr*, then *Maghrib* and at last *Isha* missed prayer.

7—If a person has missed six prayers, then it is allowed for him to offer the prescribed prayer of the time first and then offer these six missed prayers and it would not be essential to offer the first missed prayer first. He may offer these missed prayers in any order.

8—Several months or years ago someone had missed six prayers and has not offered them yet, but after that he has offered all prescribed daily prayers regularly and after such a long time he missed one more prayer. Then in such case also it is proper to offer the prescribed prayer without first offering the missed prayers and the order is not maintainable.

9—If six or more prayers were due to someone and as such it was not essential for him to offer these prayers in order and he has offered them in twos and fours and no missed prayer was left and now again he missed one or upto five prayers, then it is essential for him to maintain the order and offering of prescribed prayer is not permissible for him to offer without offering the missed prayers.

10—If anyone has missed many prayers and has offered most of them and now only four or five remain, then it is not essential to offer these in order. He can offer these as he wishes and offering of the prescribed time prayer is proper without offering remaining missed prayers.

11—If one has missed *Witr* prayer only and no other missed prayer is due to him, then to offer *Fajr* prayer without offering the missed *Witr* prayer, is not permissible. If one remembers the missing of *Witr* prayer and still offers the *Fajr* prayer, then it would not be in order and accomplished and must be repeated after offering the missed *Witr* prayer.

12—If one went to sleep after offering the *Isha* prayer only and then rose at *Tahajjud* and *Witr* prayers. He remembered in the morning that he had offered *Isha* prayer without ablution in omission, then he should offer *Isha* prayer only as missed prayer and not the *Witr* prayer.

13—Only the missed prayers of *Fard* and *Witr* are essential to be offered and not the *Sunna* prayers. But if the *Fajr* is missed, then both *Fard* and *Sunna* should be offered if offered before the mid-day and if offered after mid-day then only two *Raka'ats* of *Fard* are to be offered as missed prayer.

14—If due to narrowness of time only *Fard* prayer of *Fajr* was offered, then it is appreciable to offer the *Sunna Raka'ats* after sun-rise but before mid-day.

15—If one who has not offered prayers in his whole life but repented and sought forgiveness, then it is essential for him to offer all the missed prayers. He is not excused of offering the missed prayers by repentance and only sin of omitted prayers may be forgiven by Allah. It would be a sin if the missed prayers are not offered and duly made up.

16—If prayers are missed by someone and did not have the opportunity of offering them, then before his death it is essential for him to leave a will that compensation (*Fidya*) be given for his missed prayers otherwise it would be a sin.

Compensation (*Fidya*) will be discussed in a separate Chapter.

17—If a number of persons have missed their prayer of any time, they should offer it in congregation with all its requisites—with loud or low recitation as is necessary for the prayers of that time.

18—If a minor boy sleeps after *Isha* prayer and on waking up in the morning finds stains of semen on clothes which prove that he had a wet dream then according to predominant view he should offer *Isha* prayer again. If the stain is found on waking up before dawn then according to unanimous opinion he should offer *Isha* prayer again.

# PROSTRATION FOR CORRECTION
## (SAJDA-E-SAHAV)

1—If any of the items which are essential (*Wajib*) in prayer, are omitted inadvertently, then a prostration for the omission is offered to rectify it. This is called *Sajda-e-Sahav*. This prostration, if not offered, then the prayer should be repeated.

2—If an obligatory item of prayer is missed, then *Sajda-e-Sahav* would not rectify it. The prayer shall have to be repeated.

3—The method of offering *Sajda-e-Sahav* is that in the final sitting of a prayer recite *Attahiyat* only and then turn towards right only for *Salam* and offer two *Sajdas* and thereafter yit again to recite *Attahiyat*, *Darood Sharif* and *Dua* and conclude the prayer with *Salam*. The two *Sajdas* offered thus are *Sajda-e-Sahav*.

4—If anyone performed *Sajda-e-Sahav* before offering one *Salam*, then it is accomplished and the prayer is rectified.

5—*Sajda-e-Sahav* becomes essential if anyone inadvertently has offered two *Rukus* (bowing) or three *Sajdas* in one *Raka'at*.

6—*Sajda-e-Sahav* is essential for one if he forgot to recite *Sura Fateha* (*Alhamd*) and only recited some *Sura* or recited *Alhamd* after the *Sura*.

7—If someone forgot to add some *Sura* with *Sura Fateha* in the first two *Raka'ats* of a *Fard* praper, then he may add it in the last two *Raka'ats* and offer *Sajda-e-Sahav* also. If the *Sura* was not added in anyone of the first two *Raka'ats* then it should be added with anyone of the last two *Raka'ats* and offer *Sajda-e-Sahav* also.

If the adding of *Sura* was forgotten in all the four *Raka'ats* and the omission was recollected while reciting *Attahiyat*, then

*Sajda-e-Sahav* should be offered after *Attahiyat* and prayer would be rectified.

8—It is essential to add some *Sura* in all the *Raka'ats* of *Sunna* and *Nafl* prayers and if forgotten in any one *Raka'at*, *Sajda-e-Sahav* is essential.

9—If after reciting *Sura Fateha* if one begins to think as to which *Surah* be added and in this thinking so much time is spent during which *Subhanallah* can be recited three times, then *Sajda-e-Sahav* becomes due and essential.

10—If in the first sitting after reciting *Attahiyat* and *Darood Sharif* a doubt cropped up in mind whether he has offered three or four *Raka'ats* and in this fix he remained silent so long in which *Subhanallah* may be recited three times and then remembered that he has offered all the four *Raka ats*, then *Sajda-e-Sahav* is due.

11—After reciting *Alhamd* and a *Sura* if one began to think something in forgetfulness and delayed bowing (*Ruku*) to the extent of the abovementioned time, then *Sajda-e-Sahav* is essential.

12—In the same way someone stopped while reciting and began to think something else and it took so much time as mentioned above, or in the first or final sitting instead of reciting *Attahiyat* immediately began to think for so much time, or when rose from *Ruku* or when sat between the two *Sajdas* and began to think something else and took so much time as described above, then in all these cases *Sajda-e-Sahav* is due and should be offered. In short if in forgetfulness one delayed so much or spent as much time, then, *Sajda-e-Sahav* is due and essential.

13—In *Fard* prayer of three or four *Raka'ats* in the first or second sitting *Attahiyat* was recited twice, then *Sajda-e-Sahav* becomes essential. If after *Attahiyat* he began to recite *Darood Sharif* also and has said *Allahumma Salle Ala Muhammad* or more and then realised the omission and stood up, even then *Sajda-e-Sahav* is essential. But if recited less than that then it would not be due,

## PROSTRATION FOR CORRECTION

13—In *Nafl* prayer it is permissible to recite *Darood Sharif* with *Attahiyat* after two *Raka'ats*. So *Sajda e-Sahav* is not due in *Nafl* prayer for reciting *Darood Sharif* with *Attahiyat* in the first sitting. But if *Attahiyat* is recited twice, then *Sajda-e-Sahav* becomes due and should be offered.

15—If one sat for *Attahiyat* and instead of it began to recite *Alhamd* or anything else, then *Sajda-e-Sahav* becomes essential.

16—*Sajda-e-Sahav* is not essential if after making intent one began reciting *Dua-e-Qunut* instead of *Subhana-Kalla-Humma*. It is also not essential if in the third or fourth *Raka'at* of a *Fard* prayer one recited *Attahiyat* or something else in place of *Sura Fateha*.

17—In a prayer of three or four *Raka'ats* if one forgets to sit in the middle for *Attahiyat* and stands up for the third *Raka'at*, so if half of the lower part of the body is still bent and not straightened, then he should sit down and recite *Attahiyat* and no *Sajda-e-Sahav* would be due. But if the lower part of the body has straightened, then he should not sit down and should complete the three or four *Raka'ats* and sit down in the last and conclude the prayer with *Sajda-e-Sahav* which has become due. If the body had straightened and then he sat down and recited *Attahiyat*, then it is an act of sin and *Sajda-e-Sahav* is also due.

18—If anyone forgets to sit after the fourth *Raka'at* and is in the posture of standing then if the lower portion of the body is still bent, he should sit down and complete the prayer and no *Sajda-e-Sahav* is due. But if stood erect and even recited *Alhamd* and a *Sura* also; or has bowed even and then remembered, even then he should sit down and after reciting *Attahiyat* conclude the prayer with *Sajda e-Sahav* which has become due. But if he did not remember even after bowing and also performed the *Sajdas* of the fifth *Raka'at*, then if it is a *Fard* prayer, it should be repeated. It becomes a *Nafl* prayer and sixth *Raka'at* should be added and conclude with *Sajda-e-Sahav* which has become essential. But if the sixth *Raka'at* was not added and concluded after the fifth, then four of these five *Raka'ats* will be counted as *Nafl* prayer and the fifth would go waste.

19—After reciting *Attahiyat* in the second sitting of a *Fard* prayer one stood up for the fifth *Raka'at* and remembers the omission before going into *Sajda*, then one should sit down and immediately turn for *Salam* without reciting *Attahiyat* again and conclude with *Sajda-e-Sahav*. But if remembered after having performed the *Sajda* of the fifth *Raka'at*, he should then add the sixth *Raka'at* to it—of these four will be counted as *Fard Raka'ats* and the remaining two as *Nafl* prayer—and offer *Sajda-e-Sahav* at the end of sixth *Raka'at*. But if the prayer was concluded after the fifth *Raka'at* and *Sajda-e-Sahav* was also offered, he did wrong as now four of these *Raka'ats* will be counted as *Fard* and the fifth would go waste.

20—If four *Raka'ats* of *Nafl* prayer were offered but one forgot to sit after the second *Raka'at*, then if it is remembered before going for *Sajda* of the third *Raka'at* one should sit down or even if he has performed the *Sajdas*, the prayer would be accomplished, but *Sajda-e-Sahav* is essential in both the cases.

21—If anyone is in doubt whether he has offered three or four *Raka'ats*, then if the doubt is by chance and it is not usual with him, he should repeat the prayer. But if he usually has his doubt, he should weigh in his mind both the sides and if it is in favour of three, he may offer one more *Raka'at* and no *Sajda-e-Sahav* is essential. But if the indication is more towards four *Raka'ats*, then he may conclude the prayer without *Sajda-e-Sahav*.

If even after weighing in mind one is in suspense and his mental indication is neither towards three nor four *Raka'ats*, then he should take it as three and offer one more *Raka'at*; but in such case he should recite *Attahiyat* in that *Raka'at* also and then stand up for the fourth and complete the prayer with *Sajda-e-Sahav*.

22—If one is in doubt whether it is the first or the second *Raka'at*, then it should also be performed as described above; but in such case *Attahiyat* has to be recited in all the *Raka'ats* and should be concluded with *Sajda-e-Sahav*.

## PROSTRATION FOR CORRECTION

**23**—In the same way if there is doubt whether it is the second or third *Raka'at*, then it is also governed by the above rule and if the mental inclination is towards none, then after the second sitting he should perform the third *Raka'at* and sit for *Attahiyat* and then perform the fourth and conclude with *Sajda-e-Sahav*.

**24**—If some doubt crept up at the end of a prayer whether three or four *Raka'ats* have been offered, then it is not reliable. The prayer has been accomplished. But if it is definitely remembered that only three *Raka'ats* have been offered, then he should stand up and offer one more *Raka'at* and conclude with *Sajda-e-Sahav*. But if he spoke or did something which disrupts the *Namaz*, then he should repeat the prayer. The same is true if the doubt occurs after recitation of *Attahiyat*, then, unless anything is definitely remembered, the doubt should not be taken into account. But it would be better if the prayer is offered again to remove the doubt and clear the mind.

**25**—If several such things have occurred in a prayer which necessitate *Sajda-e-Sahav*, offering of *Sajda-e-Sahav* once would be sufficient for all. The *Sajda-e-Sahav* is not offered twice in one prayer.

**26**—If after performing *Sajda-e-Sahav* any such thing happens which necessitates *Sajda-e-Sahav*, the first *Sajda-e-Sahav* will do and there is no need for another one.

**27**—If there has been an omission in the prayer for which *Sajda-e-Sahav* is essential and performing the same was also forgotten and the prayer was concluded; but he is still sitting at the same place and has not turned his chest from the direction of Ka'aba nor has spoken to anyone or did anything which disrupts *Namaz*, then he may offer *Sajda-e-Sahav*.

Even if he has recited *Kalima* or *Darood Sharif* or any other prayer (*Dua*) while sitting, then there is no harm if he performs *Sajda-e-Sahav*. The prayer will be complete and performed in order.

**28**—If *Sajda-e-Sahav* had become due but one deliberately concluded the prayer and resolved not to offer the same, so if no such thing has happened which disrupts the *Namaz*, then he still has the discretion to offer *Sajda-e-Sahav*.

29—If in a prayer of three or four *Raka'ats*, one concluded it after the second *Raka'at* and then remembered, he should get up immediately and complete the prayer and conclude with *Sajda-e-Sahav*. If after ending the prayer after two *Raka'ats* he did any such thing which disrupts the *Namaz*, then it should be repeated.

30—If in forgetfulness one recited *Dua-e-Qunut* in the first or second *Raka'at* of *Witr* then it is immaterial. He should recite it again in the third *Raka'at* and conclude with *Sajda-e-Sahav*.

31—In *Witr* prayer a doubt cropped up whether it was the second or third *Raka'at* and the mind is not inclined towards any side, then he may recite *Dua-e Qunnut* in the same *Raka'at* and then sit and recite *Attahiyat* and stand to offer one more *Raka'at* and again recite *Dua-e-Qunnut* in that and conclude with *Sajda-Sahav*.

32—In *Witr* prayer one recited *Subhana-Kalla-Humma* instead of *Dua-e-Qunut* and upon remembering also recited *Dua-e-Qunut*, then *Sajda-e-Sahav* is not due.

33—One forgot to recite *Dua-e-Qunut* in *Witr* prayer and went into bowing (*Ruku*) after reciting the *Sura* then *Sajda-e-Sahav* is essential.

34—If after reciting *Sura Fateha* two and three *Suras* were recited, then there is no harm and *Sajda-e-Sahav* is not essential.

35—In a *Fard* prayer if *Sura* was also recited in the last one or two *Raka'ats*, then *Sajda-e-Sahav* will not be due.

36—If one forgot to recite *Subhana-Kalla-Humma* in the beginning of the prayer or did not say *Subhana-Rabbial-Azeem* in *Ruku* or *Subhana-Rabbial-Aala* in *Sajda* or to say *Sami-Allaholeman-Hamedah* while rising from *Ruku* or did not raise hands upto ears (upto shoulders by women) while making intent or did not recite *Darood Sharif* and *Dua* in the last sitting and concluded the prayer, then in all these cases *Sajda-e-Sahav* is not essential.

37—In the last two *Raka'ats* of a *Fard* prayer or in anyone of them, one forgot to recite *Alhamd* and simply stood silent and performed *Ruku* etc. then *Sajda-e-Sahav* is not due.

38—Things on which *Sajda-e-Sahav* is essential if done in forgetfulness, if they are done intentionally, then the prayer should be repeated as *Sajda-e-Sahav* will not rectify the prayer. Even if the *Sajda-e-Sahav* is offered the prayer will not be in order. Things which are neither *Fard* (obligatory) nor *Wajib* (essential) in a prayer, their omission in fotgetfulness does not make *Sajda-e-Sahav* essential.

39—If any individual or Imam recites loudly in a prayer to be offered with lower tone recitation or the Imam recites in lower tone in prayer of loud recitation, then *Sajda-e-Sahav* should be offered.

40—If in a prayer of lower tone recitation just two or three words are recited loudly or in a prayer with loud recitation a few words only are recited in a low tone which are not sufficient for a prayer to be in order, then in both cases *Sajda-e-Sahav* is not essential and the prayer would be in order.

# PROSTRATION OF RECITATION
## (SAJDA-E-TALAWAT)

1—There are fourteen prostrations of recitation in the Holy Quran and they are to be offered after reading or reciting the verse wherever the word *Sajda* is written on the margin of the Holy Quran. *Sajda-e-Talawat* is essential on reciting or hearing the verses.

2—The method of performing this *Sajda* is to prostrate saying *Allah-o-Akbar* without raising hands and recite in *Sajda Subhana-Rabbial-Aala* at least three times and raise the head saying *Allah-o-Akbar*. This is called *Sajda-e-Talawat*.

3—It is better first to stand up and then go to *Sajda* saying *Allah-o-Akbar* and recite *Subbana-Rabbial-Aala*. It is also permissible to perform it sitting.

4—*Sajda-e-Talawat* is essential for both — one who recites and the one who hears the verse whether he is sitting with the intent to listen the Holy Quran or is engaged in some work and hears the *Sajda* verse unintentionally. It is, therefore, advisable to recite the *Sajda* verse in a low tone so that the *Sajda* may not be imposed upon other listeners.

5—The things which are essential for prayer are also essential for *Sajda-e-Talawat* i.e. ablution, cleanliness of clothes and place and direction of Ka'aba.

6—*Sajda-e-Talawat* should be offered in the same manner as *Sajda* of a prayer. *Sajda* on the Holy Quran is not proper and if done, it remains due.

7—If one is not with ablution when he hears the *Sajda* verse, then he should perform it at some other time after making ablution. But it is preferable if it is performed immediately as one may forget it later on.

8—If several or many *Sajda-e-Talawat* are due towards anyone and he has not offered them, then he should perform them now. These should be performed during life-time. If not performed, it would be a sin.

9—If a woman heard the *Sajda* verse while in her menses or after-birth discharge, then *Sajda-e-Talawat* is not essential for her. But if she heard it when she was in need of bath, then she should offer it after taking a bath.

10—If someone hears the *Sajda* verse in his illness when he is too weak to rise and offer *Sajda*, then he should accomplish the *Sajda* with gesture.

11—If one recites *Sajda* verse in prayer, he should go in *Sajda* immediately then rise and complete the *Sura* and perform *Ruku*. It is also permissible to recite two or three verses after the *Sajda* verse and then perform the *Sajda-e-Talawat*. But if one recites more verses and then goes in *Sajda*, then *Sajda* will be offered but it would be sinful to do so.

12—If one recited *Sajda* verse in a prayer and did not offer *Sajda-e-Talawat* in the prayer then it will not be accomplished if offered after the prayer and it would be a perpetual sin. It can be pardoned only through repentance and beseechingly seeking forgiveness of *Allah*.

13—If one goes to *Ruku* immediately after reciting the *Sajda* verse and intends in *Ruku* that the *Ruku* is also for *Sajda-e-Talawat*, then the *Sajda-e-Talawat* will be accomplished. But if no such intent was resolved while bowing and when he goes into *Sajda* it will also be fulfilled whether it was intended or not.

14—While offering prayer if one hears *Sajda* verse from someone else, then he should not offer *Sajda-e-Talawat* while in prayer but should offer it after the prayer. If it is offered during the prayer, it would not be accomplished and would be a sin.

15—If the *Sajda* verse is repeated several times while sitting at the same place, then only one *Sajda-e-Talawat* is due whether performed after the first recitation of the verse or after the last recitation. If the place is changed and the same *Sajda* verse is repeated and then again changed the place, then for every repetition *Sajda-e-Talawat* should be offered.

16—If several *Sajda* verses are recited while sitting at one place, then *Sajda-e-Talawat* should be offered for each verse.

17—If someone recited *Sajda* verse while sitting and then stood up but did not walk and repeated the verse standing just on the spot where he was sitting, then only one *Sajda-e-Talawat* is essential.

18—After reciting *Sajda* verse sitting at a place one goes out for some business and on coming back to the same spot repeated the same *Sajda* verse, then in this case two *Sajda-e-Talawat* are essential.

19—If one recited a *Sajda* verse sitting at a place and after recitation of the Holy Quran he engaged himself in some other business on the same place i.e. started taking food, writing or stitching etc. and then again repeated the same verse, then two *Sajada-e-Talawat* will be due. The engagement in some other business amounts to change of place.

20—If a *Sajda* verse is recited in one corner of a room or cell and then repeated in the other corner, then only one *Sajda-e-Talawat* will be sufficient and it does not matter as to how many times the verse was repeated. But if one is engaged in some other work after reciting the verse and again recites the same verse after work, then two *Sajdas* would be essential and so on.

21—However, if the house is large, then reciting and repeating the same *Sajda* verse at its every corner will make *Sajda-e-Talawat* essential for each repetition.

22—The same is the case of a mosque as that of a small room. If a *Sajda* verse is repeated several times at one place or places in a mosque or while walking in it, then only one *Sajda-e-Talawat* is essential.

23—If the same *Sajda* verse is repeated several times in a prayer, then also only one *Sajda-e-Talawat* is essential. It may be offered after the first recitation or at the end of all repetitions whether in the same *Rak'at* or any subsequent *Raka'at*.

24—If someone recited *Sajda* verse but did not offer *Sajda-e-Talawat* and began to pray at the same place after making intent and in the prayer he again recited the same *Sajda* verse and offered *Sajda-e-Talawat*, then it would suffice for both. But if he changed the place to offer the prayer then two *Sajda-e-Talawat* are essential.

25—If *Sajda* verse was recited and *Sajda-e-Talawat* was also offered and then he began to offer prayer on the same place in which the same *Sajda* verse was again recited then another *Sajda-e-Talawat* should be performed in the prayer.

26—If anyone is repeating a *Sajda* verse again and again sitting at one place and someone else heard it and changed his place and then heard it for the third time and so on ; then in this case only one *Sajd-a-Talawat* for one who was reciting it but three or as many *Sajda-e-Talawat* are essential for the hearer as many times he heard it at different places.

27—In the above case if the place of the hearer is not changed but that of the reciter has changed, then the hearer has to offer only one *Sajda-e-Talawat* but the reciter should perform as many *Sajda-e-Talawat* as he has changed places.

28—It is prohibited and execrable to recite whole *Sura* and leave out only the *Sajda* verse. Only to avoid *Sajda-e-Talawat* that verse should not be left as it will mean the rejection of the *Sajda*.

29—There is no harm if only *Sajda* verse is recited out of a *Sura* and no other verse is recited. If it is done in prayer then the verse should be so long as to be equal to two three small verses But it is better to recite *Sajda* verse with one or two verses in prayer.

30—If anyone hears the *Sajda* verse from the Imam and joins the congregation, then he should offer the *Sajda* with the Imam. If the Imam has already offered the *Sajda-e-Talawat* then there are two coures—if he got the *Raka'at* in which the *Sajda* verse was recited by the Imam, then this man may not offer the *Sajda* as the same has been fulfilled by joining the same *Raka'at*. But if he did not join the same *Raka'at*, then he should offer it after ending the prayer.

31—If the *Sajda* verse is heard from a follower in congregation, then *Sajda-e-Talawat* will not be essential for him or for his Imam or for anyone else in the congregation. But for those who are not in the congregation and whether they are offering some other prayer or not, *Sajda-e-Talawat* would be essential.

32—Laughter in *Sajda-e-Talawat* will not break the ablution, but the *Sajda* in itself will be disrupted.

33—Standing of a woman by one's side will not disrupt the *Sajda-e-Talawat*.

34—If *Sajda-e-Talawat* has become due in a prayer, its immediate performance is essential. Delay is not permissible.

35—*Sajda-e-Talawat* which became due out of prayer, if offered in prayer, or which became due in prayer and offered out of prayer or in another prayer, will not be in order. So if anyone recite *Sajda* verse in prayer and does not offer *Sajda-e-Talawat* in prayer, will commit a sin as already described.

36—A *Sajda* verse should not be recited in *Juma* or *Eid* prayers and also in prayers of low tone recitation as the followers may be perturbed by the prostration.

## PATIENT'S PRAYER (NAMAZ)

1—Offering of prayers should not be given up under any circumstance. So long as one is able, he should stand up and offer prayers; but if unable to stand he should offer prayer in sitting position and perform *Ruku* and both *Sajdas*. In *Ruku* he should bend so much that fore-head comes in line with the knees.

2—If one is not able even to offer *Ruku* and *Sajda* in sitting position as described above, he may perform them by gestures but should bend more in *Sajdas* than in *Ruku*.

3—It is not proper to place a pillow or anything else for performing *Sajdas* upon that. If one is unable to perform *Sajda*, he may do so by gestures.

4—If anyone has the strength to stand but it causes pain or there is an apprehension of an increase in his illness, it is permissible for him to offer prayer in sitting position.

5—One can stand but cannot offer *Ruku* and *Sajda*, then he may either offer prayer in standing or sitting position and offer *Ruku* and *Sajda* with gestures. But it is better to offer prayer in sitting position in this condition.

6—If one is unable even to sit, then he may place big pillow behind his back and lie down in such a position that his head remains sufficiently raised nearing about sitting position and stretch his leg in the direction of Ka'aba and offer prayer with gestures. It is better, if one has the strength, to keep his knees standing instead of stretching. The *Ruku* and *Sajdas* should be offered with gestures of head but the gestures for *Sajda* should be lower than *Ruku*. If he is unable even to lie with the help of a big pillow with head and chest raised high, then he may lie flat and stretch his legs towards Ka'aba but a pillow should be placed under his head so that the face may be

139

in the direction of *Ka'aba* and not towards the sky and in this position he should offer *Ruku* and *Sajda* with gestures of head bending a little more for *Sajdas* than *Ruku*.

7—If any such person instead of lying flat on his back, lies on his right or left side with his face towards *Ka'aba* and offers *Ruku* and *Sajdas* with gestures of head, then it is also permissible ; but it is better to lie flat on his back.

8—If one is so weak that he is unable to pray even with gestures of head then he may not offer prayer at all and if this condition remains for one day and night, the prayer is remitted completely. But if the condition of weakness remains for less than one day and night and he gets back the strength to offer prayer with gestures, then he should offer the missed prayers with signs and should not postpone the same to be offered after complete recovery because he may die and as such he would be a sinner.

9—In the same way if a healthy person falls unconscious and this condition does not remain for more than one day and night, offering of missed prayers is essential. But if the unconsciousness continued for more than one day and night, then offering of missed prayers is not essential.

10—While beginning a prayer one was quite healthy but during it some of his nerve was disturbed and it became so painful that he cannot stand, then he may offer the remaining part of prayer in sitting position and perform *Ruku* and *Sajdas* if possible, otherwise with gestures of head. But if his condition grew so worse that he cannot even sit, then he should complete the prayer by lying flat on his back with legs stretched towards the Ka'aba.

11—If anyone offered some part of his prayer in sitting position on account of his illness and recovered strength while still in prayer, then he should complete the remaining prayer in standing position.

12—If anyone was unable to perform *Ruku* and *Sajda* due to some illness and performed them with gestures and during the prayer he regained strength to perform them, then the prayer is lost and instead of completing the remaining prayer, he should offer the whole prayer again.

13—If anyone is attacked with paralysis and is so ill that he cannot perform an *Istanja* with water, then he should clean with a clean cloth or a clod of earth and offer prayer. If he is unable to make *Tayammum* himself, then someone else should help him. But if he is so incapacitated that he cannot clean even with a clean cloth or clod of earth, then he should offer prayer as he is and the prayer should not be missed. It is not proper for anyone else to see his or her private parts—even the father, mother, son or daughter are not allowed. However, it is permissible for husband and wife to see the private parts of each other in such circumstances and for no one else.

14—If anyone missed some prayers while he was healthy and then fell ill, then he should offer these missed prayers in illness in whatever manner it is possible for him and should not wait for recovery or for gaining strength to offer *Ruku* and *Sajdas*. All such thoughts are satanic. Religion demands that these should be offered immediately and without delay.

15—If the bed of a patient is filthy and cleaning it would be painful to the patient then he may offer prayer on the same.

16—If anyone's eye has been operated upon and it is prohibited for him to move, then he should offer his prayers in lying position.

17—If anyone is tired on account of lengthy recitation in a prayer, then it is not execrable for him to take the support of a wall or a stick or a tree. Old and infirm people are sometimes in need of such support in the *Tarawih* prayers.

## PRAYER (NAMAZ) OF A TRAVELLER

1—If anyone goes on a journey of one or two *Manzils*[1] only, then religious injunctions are not modified in his case and according to *Shariat* he will not be treated as a traveller. He is required to observe everything as if he is at home and resident. He should offer four *Raka'ats* of prayer in which there are four. If he is wearing a hose, then he can perform *Masah* over them for one night and day only and after it not permissible.

2—One who goes on a journey with an intent of travelling three stages (*Manzils*), then according to religious code he will be treated as a traveller and becomes so when he goes out of the population of his town. So long as he walks and remains within the population of his town, he is not a traveller. If the railway station happens to be within the population, then it is also treated as part of the population, and if it is without the population, then one will become a traveller on reaching it.

3—Three *Manzils* or stages is the distance which is covered by a pedestrian in three days. In countries where journey is not by sea or through mountains, its estimate is forty eight miles or about seventy two Km.

4—If the distance is three stages if covered on foot i.e. coverable in three days, but while travelling by fast conveyance or by railway train it may be covered in a very short time, then according to religious code (*Shariat*) anyone travelling such a distance is a traveller whatever may be the means of his journey.

5—One who is a traveller according to *Shariat*, should offer only two *Raka'ats* in each of *Zuhr*, *Asr* and *Isha* ; and *Sunna*

---

1. *Manzil* (stage) is the distance covered by a traveller on foot and is equal to sixteen British miles or about 24 K.M.

prayers with the exception of *Fajr Sunna*, may be omitted if in a hurry there would be no sin. But if he is not in a hurry and there is no risk also of being separated from other fellow travellers, then he must offer. There is no reduction in them.

6—There is no reduction in the prayers of *Fajr*, *Maghrib* and *Witr*. These should be offered in full as usual.

7—In the prayers of *Zuhr*, *Asr* and *Isha* more than two *Raka'ats* in each prayer should not be offered. The offering of all the four *Rak'ats* is a sin.

8—If anyone in forgetfulness has offered all the four *Raka'ats*, then if he has recited *Attahiyat* after the second *Raka'at*, two will be counted as *Fard* prayer and two as *Nafl* prayer. But he should offer *Sajda-e-Sahav*. If he did not sit in the second *Raka'at* then all the four *Raka'ats* will be counted as *Nafl* prayer. He should offer *Fard* prayer again.

9—If anyone breaks his journey on the way with an intent of staying there for less than fifteen days, then he will continue to be a traveller and should offer prayers as a traveller. But if the intent is to stay for more than fifteen days, then he no longer remains a traveller and should offer prayers in full. But if he again changes his intent and starts on the journey before fifteen days, even then he will not be a traveller and should offer prayers in full. When he restarts from that place and his next destination is a distance of more than three stages, he will again become a traveller and if the distance is less than that, he will not be a traveller.

10—One goes on journey with an intent of going three stages and also intended to stay at a certain place for fifteen days (provided the place is at a distance of less than three stages from his town) then he will not be treated as a traveller. He should offer all the prayers in full on his way.

11—One has intended to go three stages but at the first or second stage his home happens to be ; then he will not be a traveller.

12—A woman started on journey with the intent of going four stages but during the first two stages she was in her monthly course, then she will not be treated as a traveller.

After bathing and cleaning herself she should offer full prayers. But after purification from the monthly course, if her destination is still three stages or that she was clean when she started and the menses came on her way, then she will remain a traveller and after being clean she can offer prayers as a traveller.

13—A traveller while offering prayer intends to stay for more than fifteen days, then he no longer remains a traveller and he should offer even that prayer in full.

14—If one broke his journey for two or three days but due to some reasons he cannot resume his journey and every day he thinks of starting next day or the day after but cannot proceed and in this way his stay continues for fifteen or twenty days or a month or more but there was no intent to stay for fifteen days, then he will continue to be treated as a traveller howsoever long a period may pass in this way.

15—One started on a journey to go to three stages but after going some distance he changed his mind and came back home, then from the time he changed his mind he is no longer remains a traveller.

16—If husband and wife are travelling together and on the way wife will stay for as many days as her husband will stay, then in this case the intent of the husband shall be counted. If the husband intends to stay for fifteen days then the wife would also become a non-traveller with her husband whether intended to stay so long or not. If the husband intends to stay for less than fifteen days, then the wife will also remain a traveller.

17—If after travelling three stages a person reaches such a place where he has his house, then he will not remain a traveller whether he stays there for a long or short period and should offer prayers in full. If he has no house and intends to stay for fifteen days then also he will not remain a traveller.

18—If someone intends to stay at several places during a journey for ten days here and for five days there but no where for full fifteen days, then such a person shall continue to be a traveller.

## PRAYER (NAMAZ) OF A TRAVELLER

**19**—If anyone has left his home town permanently and built a house in another town and began to live there ceasing all connection with his old house, then that town or any other out side place is equal and if in a journey such a person happens to stay in his old home town for a few day (less than fifteen days) then he will remain a traveller.

**20**—If someone missed his prayers while travelling then on returning home he should offer only two *Raka'ats* of *Zuhr*, *Asr* and *Isha* missed prayer. But if some prayers were missed before going on journey, then he should offer those missed prayers in full while travelling.

**21**—If after marriage a woman lives with her husband permanently then her husband's home becomes her real home. If now she goes to her parent's house at a distance of three stages and does not intend to stay for fifteen days there, then she will remain a traveller and should observe prayers, fast etc. as a traveller. But if she did not intend to live permanently with her husband, then her parent's house shall continue to be real home.

**22**—If prayer time comes while travelling in a boat, then one should offer prayer in it.

If one feels giddy in offering prayer in standing, he may offer the prayer in sitting position.

**23**—The above rule is also applicable to a journey by railway train.

**24**—If during a prayer the train takes a turn and the direction of Ka'aba is changed, then one should turn his face towards Ka'aba in prayer.

**25**—If a woman has to go on a journey for three stages, she should not go unless accompanied by some Mahram (permitted person) or her husband. It is a major sin to travel without a Mahram. Even if she has to go one or two stages, it is not proper to go without a Mahram. It has been forbidden in Traditions.

**26**—It is also not proper for a woman to travel in company of such a Mahram who has no fear of Allah and the Holy Prophet (SAW) and also does not observe the laws of religion.

27—If one is travelling by an animal drawn conveyance and the time of prayer comes, then one should come down from the conveyance and should offer prayer. In the case of a woman, she should make ablution and offer prayer in cover of something i.e. with purdah.

28—If one is so ill that prayer in sitting is permissible for him, even then he should not offer prayer in a running carriage. Prayer on carriage may be offered after disengaging the animals from it.

29—The same is true for women travelling in palanquins. While it is on the shoulders of the carriers, no prayer should be offered in it.

30—If there is risk in getting down from an animal or a cart, then it is permissible to offer prayer sitting on them.

31—Before starting on a journey it is appreciable (*Mustahab*) for a person to offer two *Raka'ats* of *Nafl* prayer at his house and on returning from a journey it is appreciable for men to go to a mosque first and offer two *Raka'ats*. Great credit has been assigned to it in traditions.

32—It is also appreciable for a traveller that during the journey when he reaches a *Manzil* and intends to stay there, he should offer two *Raka'ats* of *Nafl* prayer before sitting.

33—If a person intends to stay for fifteen days at two places and the distance between them is so much that voice of one place cannot reach the other, then in this case he will be treated as a traveller.

34—If in the above problem he intends to stay all the nights at one place and days at the other, then the place where he has intended at night will become his residence town and there he is not allowed to offer *Qasr* prayer i.e. two *Raka'ats* in prayers of four *Raka'ats*. Now if the other place where he stays for the day is at the prescribed distance then he will become a traveller, otherwise not.

35—In the same problem if the two places are so near that voice of *Adhan* of one place reaches the other, then he will be treated as resident if he intends to stay for fifteen days at both places.

## PRAYER (NAMAZ) OF A TRAVELLER

36—A resident's prayer if led by a traveller, is proper in all cases whether it is a prayer of the fixed time or a postponed prayer. In such case when the traveller Imam concludes his prayer after two *Raka'ats* the resident follower should stand-up and complete the prayer, but he should not recite in these *Raka'ats* and only should stand silently as he is a *Lahiq*. The first sitting of the prayer will be *Fard* on the follower alongwith the Imam. It is appreciable for the traveller Imam to inform the followers that he is a traveller.

37—A traveller can also follow a resident Imam but within the time of the prayer and he will offer full prayer with the resident Imam. If the time of prayer has passed then he can follow the Imam in *Fajr* and *Maghrib* prayers only but not in *Zuhr*, *Asr* and *Isha* prayers.

38—If a traveller decides to stay while offering a prayer, whether in the beginning or in middle or in the end but before *Salam* or *Sajda-e-Sahav*, then he should offer that prayer in full and no *Qasr* (reduction) is permissible.

## RECITATION OF THE HOLY QURAN

1—It is essential to recite the Holy Quran correctly and each word should be pronounced properly bringing out their correct voice. Some of the Arabic letters and signs have similar voice, care should be taken to pronounce them in their correct intonation. One letter should not be pronounced instead of other.

2—If anyone is unable to pronounce any letter correctly or propely, then such a person should try his best to learn the correct pronunciation. It would be a major sin if effort is not made to learn the correct pronunciation and none of his prayers would be in order. If in spite of best efforts the pronunciation could not be corrected, then it is excusable.

3—If the pronunciation of letters of similar voice is correct, but one recites them so carelessly that the voice of one is pronounced in place of the other, then the prayer shall not be accomplished and it is a sin also.

4—If the *Sura* recited in the first *Raka'at* is also recited in the second, then there is no harm. But it is not better to do so.

5—The arrangement of *Suras* as is in the Holy Quran should be maintained in the prayers and it should not be changed. For example if a *Sura* is recited in the first *Raka'at* then in the second *Raka'at* the *Sura* occurring in the Quran after the first one should be recited and not such a *Sura* which is before the one recited in the first *Raka'at*. It is execrable to change their order in recitation. However if done in forgetfulness, then there is no harm.

6—If one has started reciting a verse, it is execrable to give it up in the middle and start another one without proper

## RECITATION OF THE HOLY QURAN 149

cause.

7— If anyone is quite ignorant of the method of offering a prayer or is a new convert to Islam, then such a person may recite *Subhan Allah* in every posture and the *Fard* prayer shall be accomplished. But such a person should continue to learn the correct method and would commit a sin if not done so.

8— Women should not recite the Holy Quran in a loud voice in any case. They should recite it in a low tone.

## CALLING FOR PRAYER
### (ADHAN AND IQAMAT)

1—If *Adhan* is called for a prayer, then it is essential that it should be called at its proper time. It would not be correct if the *Adhan* is called before time and it will have to be repeated at its proper time whether it is of *Fajr* or some other.

2—It is necessary to call *Adhan* and *Iqamat* in the same Arabic words which have been narrated by the Holy Prophet (SAW). If these are called in any other language or different Arabic words then it would not be correct, though hearing it people may take it for *Adhan*.

3—The caller of *Adhan* should be a male. It is not proper for a woman to call it. If a woman has called it, it should be repeated and if not repeated the prayer will be regarded as offered without *Adhan*.

4—The *Adhan* caller must be sane. If a minor boy or insane person or one inebriated calls *Adhan*, then it would not be reliable.

5—The *Masnoon* (Traditional) way of calling *Adhan* is that one who calls it should be clean from all those impurities which breach cleanliness and should stand on a raised place separate from the mosque facing Ka'aba, closing the holes of his ears with the index fingers of his both hands, should recite the following at the full pitch of his voice :

*Allah-o-Akber* four times ; then *Ash-hado-Anla Ilaha-Illallah* two times ; then *Ash-hado-Anna-Muhammadar-Rasulullah* two times ; then *Haiyya-alas-Salah* two times ; then *Haiyya-alal-Falah* two times ; then *Allah-o-Akbar* two times and should be concluded with *La-Ilah-Illallah* calling once only.

While calling *Haiyya-alas-Salah* he should turn his face a

little to the right side and while calling *Haiyya-allal-Falah* should turn to the left in such a way that in both turnings his chest and feet remain towards Ka'aba.

In the *Adhan* of *Fajr* prayer "*Assalato-Khairum-Minan-Naum* should be called twice after *Haiyya-alal-Falah*. Thus there are fifteen phrases of *Adhan* in general and seventeen in *Fajr* prayer. *Adhan* should not be called in a singing way and there should be a pause between each phrase so that the hearer may repeat it.

6—*Iqamat* is similar to *Adhan* with the only difference that *Adhan* is called outside the mosque and *Iqamat* inside the mosque. *Adhan* is called in a loud voice and *Iqamat* in a low voice. *Assalato-Khairum-Minan-Naum* is not called in *Iqamat* but instead of it *Qad-Qamatissala* is said twice in all the five prayers.

7—While saying *Iqamat* the holes of the ears are not closed with fingers and no turning of face towards right or left while saying, *Haiyya-Alas Salah* or *Haiyya-alal-Falah*.

### Injunctions for Adhan and Iqamat

1—It is emphasised *Sunna* (*Moa'kkada*) to call *Adhan* for all compulsory prayers for males whether they are travellers or resident and praying in congregation or alone and in timely or missed prayers. For Friday prayer there are two *Adhans* one of the time and the other just before the beginning of the Sermon (*Khutba*).

2—If a prayer has been missed or postponed for some such reason which cannot be made public, then *Adhan* for such a prayer should also be called secretly so that other people may not learn about missed prayer because missing of a prayer on negilgence and laziness is a sin according to religion. It is not good to expose a sin. If several prayers have been missed and they are being offered at one time then *Adhan* for the first prayer is *Sunna* and *Iqamat* for the rest.

3—For a traveller when all of his fellow travellers are present, *Adhan* is appreciable and compulsory *Sunna*.

4—One who offers prayer at home alone or in congregation,

*Adhan* and *Iqamat* are appreciable for him, provided the same have not been said in the mosque of the area because of the *Adhan* and *Iqamat* of mosque is sufficient for the residents of the area.

5—In a mosque where *Adhan* and *Iqamat* have been said and prayer offered, it is execrable to call another *Adhan* or *Iqamat* for the same prayer. But if there is no permanent *Adhan* caller or Imam in a mosque, then it is not execrable but better.

6—If a person is at such a place where conditions for Friday prayer exist and it is also offered, then if he wants to offer *Zuhr* prayer, calling of *Adhan* and *Iqamat* are execrable for him though he may be offering the *Zuhr* prayer on account of any legitimate cause or not; or is offering it before or after the *Juma* prayer.

7—Calling of *Adhan* and *Iqamat* are execrable for women whether they pray alone or in congregation.

8—Except for obligatory *Fard* prayers *Adhan* and *Iqamat* are not *Sunna* for any other prayer whether it be a *Kifaya* (sufficed) *Fard* prayer of funeral or essential prayer of *Witr*, the prayer of both *Eids* or *Nafl* prayers etc.

9—Any one who hears the *Adhan*, male or female, clean or unclean, it is apprecible for him or her to respond to it by repeating the same words which the caller says. But in response to *Haiyya-alas-Salah* and *Haiyya-alal-Falah*, they should say *La-haula-wala-Quwwata-Illa-Billah* and in response to *Asslato-Khairum-Minan-Naum* one should say *Sadaqta-Wa-Barakta*. After *Adhan* the following *Dua* should be recited:

اَللّٰهُمَّ رَبَّ هٰذِهِ الدَّعْوَةِ التَّامَّةِ وَ الصَّلٰوةِ الْقَائِمَةِ

اٰتِ سَيِّدَنَا مُحَمَّدَنِ الْوَسِيْلَةَ وَ الْفَضِيْلَةَ وَابْعَثْهُ

مَقَامًا مَحْمُوْدَنِ الَّذِيْ وَعَدْتَّهُ اِنَّكَ لَاتُخْلِفُ الْمِيْعَاد

# CALLING FOR PRAYERS

**10**—On hearing the first *Adhan* of *Juma* prayer it is essential to suspend all the business and should go to the mosque for *Juma* prayer. To remain engaged in other work or transact any business after the *Adhan* is forbidden (*Haram*).

**11**—Response to *Iqamat* is appreciable but not essential and in reply to

قَـدْقَامَتِ الصَّلٰوةُ

one should say :

أَقَامَهَا اللهُ وَ أَدَامَهَا

**12**—In eight cases *Adhan* should not be responded viz. (1) While in prayer. (2) When listening to a Sermon whether of Friday or any other. (3) In monthly course. (4) During after birth discharge. (5) While teaching or learning religious lessons. (6) When engaged in sexual course. (7) While passing urine or stool and (8) While taking food.

If sufficient time has not passed after the calling of *Adhan*, then after finishing or being relieved of the above acts, response should be made otherwise not.

## Appreciables of Adhan and Iqamat

There are two kinds of appreciables, some are related to the *Adhan* caller (*Moadhdhin*) and some are about *Adhan* and *Iqamat*.

## About Moadhdhin

**1**—An *Adhan* caller should be a male. *Adhan* and *Iqamat* said by a woman are highly execrable and *Adhan* by a woman should be repeated.

**2**—The *Adhan* caller should be a sane person. *Adhan* and *Iqamat* by an insane or inebriated or a minor boy are execrable and such *Adhan* only should be repeated and not *Iqamat*.

**3**—The *Adhan* caller should be fully conversant with essential injunctions and timings etc. of prayers. If *Adhan* is called by an ignorant person then he will not get as much reward or credit as *Moadhdhin*.

**4**—The *Moadhdhin* should be an abstainer and God fearing person, well informed about the people of the area and be able to exhort those who do not attend the prayers provided there is no fear of being molested.

5—The *Moadhin* should possess a loud voice.

**About Adhan and Iqamat**

1—*Adhan* should be called from a high place outside the mosque i.e. the place where prayer is not offered in the mosque. *Iqamat* should be called inside the mosque. To call *Adhan* inside the mosque is a milder execrability, but the second *Adhan* of Juma prayer is called inside the mosque and in front of the pulpit and it is not execrable.

2—*Adhan* should be called standing and it is execrable to call *Adhan* while sitting and if called it should be repeated.

3—*Adhan* should be called in a loud voice and it may be called in a low voice if it is for one's own prayer. But there is great credit for calling it in a loud voice.

4—It is appreciable to close the holes of both the ears with the index fingers of hands while calling *Adhan*.

5—Each phrase of the *Adhan* should be called with a pause between them so that the same may be repeated by the listeners. But *Iqamat* should be said hurriedly.

6—It is *Sunna* to turn face towards right while saying *Haiyya-alas-Salah* and towards left while saying *Haiyya-alal-Falah* in *Adhan* only but the chest and feet of the caller should remain towards Ka'aba while turning.

7—While saying *Adhan* or *Iqamat* one should face Ka'aba, otherwise it would be a minor execrability.

8—While calling *Adhan* it is *Sunna* to be free from strong impurity and to be free from all impurities and uncleanliness is appreciable. While saying *Iqamat* it is appreciable to be quite clean and free from stronger and milder impurities. If anyone calls *Adhan* while in stronger impurity, then it is highly execrable and its repetition is appreciable. So if one says *Iqamat* while in any type of impurity, it is also highly execrable but its repetition is not appreciable.

9—It is *Sunna* to pronounce the words of *Adhan* or *Iqamat* in their order.

## CALLING FOR PRAYERS

10—One should not talk in *Adhan* and *Iqamat* even for *Salam* or response to *Salam*. The injunction is for both – calling or listening the *Adhan* or *Iqamat*.

### Injunctions

1—If anyone forgot to respond the *Adhan* and recollects it later, then if much time has not passed, he may repeat the phrases of *Adhan*, otherwise not.

2—If *Iqamat* has been said and long time has passed and the congregation was not started, then *Iqamat* should be repeated. If much time did not pass, it should not be repeated.

3—If *Iqamat* has been said and the Imam who had not offered the *Sunna* prayer of *Fajr* begins to offer it now, then this would not be treated as much delay and *Iqamat* may not be repeated.

4—If the caller of *Adhan* dies in the middle of *Adhan* or becomes unconscious or his voice fails or he forgets some phrase and there is no one to correct him or any breach of cleanliness happens and he goes to rectify it, the repetition of the *Adhan* is imperative.

5—If any milder breach of cleanliness happens to the caller of *Adhan* or *Iqamat* during its calling, then it is better to complete the same and then go to clean himself and should not break it.

6—Calling of *Adhan* of the same time in two mosques by the same man is execrable. He should call *Adhan* in that mosque only where he offers his *Fard* prayer.

7—Saying of *Iqamat* is the right of the person who called the *Adhan*, but if he goes away or permits anyone else to call *Iqamat*, then it is permissible.

8—Calling of *Adhan* by several persons together is also permissible.

9—The *Moadhin* should conclude *Iqamat* at the same spot where he began it. That is, he should not move while saying the *Iqamat*.

10—The intent for *Adhan* or *Iqamat* is not necessary but there is no credit without it. The intent for *Adhan* is just to resolve in mind that he is calling *Adhan* for the pleasure of Allah to gain credit and for no other purpose.

# PRAYER ON ENTERING THE MOSQUE
## (TAHIYATUL MASJID)

1—This prayer is for one who enters a mosque.

2—This prayer is in fact in honour of the mosque which in other words is Glory of Allah because a house is honoured on account of its owner and not for itself. The mosque is the house of Allah.

3—Two *Raka'ats* of *Tahiyatul Masjid* prayer be offered on entering the mosque before sitting. If the time when one enters the mosque is execrable for prayer, then the following phrases be recited four times :

سُبْحَانَ اللهِ وَ الْحَمْدُ لِلهِ وَلَا اِلٰهَ اِلَّا اللهُ وَ اللهُ اَكْبَرُ

and recite *Darood Sharif* thereafter.

4—The intent for this prayer is :

نَوَيْتُ اَنْ اُصَلِّىَ رَكْعَتَىْ تَحِيَّةِ الْمَسْجِدِ

*Navaito-an-Osalli-Raka'atai-Tahiyatul-Masjid* or in one's own language such as, "I intend to offer two *Raka'ats* of *Tahiyatul Masjid*."

5—There is no restriction of two *Raka'ats*. If four *Raka'ats* are offered, there is no harm. If immediately on entering the mosque some *Sunna* or *Fard* prayer is offered, then it would fulfil the *Tahiyatul Masjid* and will get reward for it also even if it was not intended.

6—If one sits down after entering the mosque and then offers *Tahiyatul Masjid*, then there is no harm ; but it is better to offer it before sitting.

7—If anyone has occasions to go to mosque several times, then it is enough to offer *Tahiyatul Masjid* once only either in the beginning or in last.

# TARAWIH PRAYERS OF RAMADAN

1—Offering of *Tarawih* prayer in the month of *Ramadan* is *Sunna*. It has been greatly stressed and its omission is a sin. Twenty *Raka'ats* of *Tarawih* are to be offered after the *Fard* and *Sunna* prayers of *Isha* with an intent of two or four *Raka'ats* at a time. But it is preferable to offer *Tarawih* in two *Raka'ats* and in congregation. It is better to offer *Witr* prayer after *Tarawih*, but if offered before, even then there is no harm.

2—While offering *Tarawih* it is appreciable to sit after every two *Raka'ats* for as much time as is spent in offering four *Raka'ats*. It is also permissible to sit for lesser time if men feel inconvenience or there is fear of congregation being reduced. During this sitting it is permissible to offer *Nafl* prayer or recite some *Dua* or simply remain sitting silent.

3—If anyone has offered *Tarawih* prayer after *Isha* and later on found that there was some lacuna in the *Isha* prayer due to which the same stands disrupted, then offering of *Tarawih* also becomes essential after repeating the *Isha* prayer.

4—If *Isha* prayer has not been offered by someone in congregation, then *Tarawih* also should not be offered in congregation as *Tarawih* is subject to *Isha* prayer. But if other people after performing *Isha* prayer in congregation are engaged in congregational *Tarawih* prayer, then it would be in order for such a person, who did not offer *Isha* prayer in congregation, to join the *Tarawih* congregation.

5—If anyone reached the mosque when *Isha* prayer has been offered, then he should first offer *Isha* prayer and then join the *Tarawih* congregation. If due to this delay some *Tarawih* have been missed, then he should offer missed *Tarawih* before *Witr* and the *Witr* should be offered in congregation.

6—It is *Sunna Moakkeda* (Emphasised *Sunna*) to hear one complete recitation of the Holy Quran in its order during the month of Ramadan. It should not be missed on account of laziness or lassitude. But if it is feared that if one complete Quran is recited, it will prevent people from coming to *Tarawih* or will disrupt the congregation, then only so much be recited as is agreeable to the people.

7—Only ten *Suras* of the Holy Quran from *Sura Fateha* to *Sura Nas* may also be recited in *Tarawih*—one *Sura* in each *Raka'at* and the same *Sura* be repeated in the remaining ten *Raka ats*. Recitation of other *Sura* is also permitted.

8—Not more than one complete Holy Quran should be recited in the whole of Ramadan unless it is found that people are interested in more than one.

9—Reciting of one complete Holy Quran in one night is permissible provided people are interested and it would not be disagreeable to them. If people are inconvenienced by it, then it is execrable.

10—In *Tarawih* prayer once in the beginning of any *Sura Bismillah* should be recited loudly as it is a verse of the Holy Quran, though not the part of any *Sura*. So if *Bismillah* is not recited even once, then the Holy Quran would not be complete being short of one verse and if it is recited in a very low voice, then the hearing of Holy Quran by the followers will not be complete.

11.—It is *Sunna* to offer *Tarawih* prayer in the whole month of *Ramadan*, even if the recitation of Holy Quran has been completed before the end of the month. For instance if the Holy Quran has been completed in ten or fifteen days, then during the remaining days, the offering of *Tarawih* is *Sunna Moakkeda* (Emphasised *Sunna*).

12—It is correct that reciting of *Sura Ikhlas* thrice in *Tarawih* is execrable.

# PRAYER FOR RAIN
## (NAMAZ-E-ISTASQA)

When rains have failed and it does not rain, then in such time it is *Sunna* to pray to Allah for rains. The appreciable method of this prayer according to *Sunna* is that all Muslims along with their sons, the aged men and their animals should go on feet to the jungle, dressed ordinarily and in a very humble way.

There they should repent and should discharge their rights and dues of those which may be due. They should not take any non-believer or rejector with them. They should then offer two *Raka'ats* of prayer without *Adhan* and *Iqamat* in congregation and the Imam should recite loudly. Then the two sermons like *Eid* should be read and then the Imam should stand up facing the Ka'aba and raising both hands should pray to Allah for rain and all the followers should also pray. This should be done successively for three days and not more. But if it rains before going to the jungle or just after one day of the prayer even then three days should be completed. It is appreciable to fast during the three days and give alms before going for the prayer.

# PRAYERS DURING ECLIPSES
## (NAMAZ-E-KASUF-WA-KHASUF)

*Kasuf* means Solar eclipse, and *Khasuf* means Lunar eclipse.

1.—To offer two *Raka'ats* of prayer at the time of solar or lunar eclipse is *Sunna*.

2.—The solar eclipse prayer should be offered in congregation provided the Imam of such congregation is the Imam of *Juma* prayer or the ruler of the time or his representative. It has been stated in one report that the Imam of every mosque can lead such prayer in his mosque.

3.—*Adhan* and *Takbir* are not necessary for such prayer, but to call the people together for such prayer, it may be called ;

الصَّلوةُ جَامِعَةٌ

(Assalato-Jamiyatun)
i.e. gather for prayer.

4.—It is *Sunna* to recite lengthy *Suras* like *Suras Baqarah* and stay longer in *Ruku* and *Sajda*. Recitation of the Holy Quran should be done loudly.

5.—Immediately after ending the prayer the Imam should devote himself to *Dua* (Pray) and the followers should say, *Ameen* and in this way praying (*Dua*) should continue upto the end of eclipse. But if in this condition the sun sets or the time of some prescribed prayer comes, the praying should be stopped and the prayer of the time should be offered.

6.—At the time of lunar eclipse also two *Raka'ats* of prayer are *Sunna*, but congregation is not essential. These should be offered individually in homes only.

7.—When there is some fear or trouble, offering of prayer is

# PRAYERS DURING ECLIPSES

*Sunna* i.e. in a storm or earth-quake or lightning or shooting of stars in large number or hail storm or heavy rains or spreading of some epidemic or there be fear of enemy etc. In prayers of all such occasions there should be no congregation. These should be offered individually in homes. Whenever the Holy Prophet was in trouble he used to offer *Namaz*.

# SOME OBLIGATORY AND ESSENTIAL
## (PROBLEMS OF NAMAZ)

1—Recitation is not for Mudrik follower. The recitation of Imam is sufficient for all the followers. According to Imam Abu Hanifa recitation by the followers behind the Imam is execrable.

2—For Masbuq it is essential to recite in one or two *Raka'ats* of his missed prayer in which recitation is essential.

3—In short, in the presence of Imam the followers should not recite Holy Quran except the Masbuq who has to recite as there will be no Imam in the missed part (*Raka'ats*) of his prayer.

4—The place should not be higher than 18 cm. from the feet. If *Sajda* is offered on a higher place than this, it would not be in order. But in case of urgency and there being no other way, then it is permissible.

5—In the prayers of both the *Eids* in addition to the usual *Takbirs*, six more *Takbirs* are essential.

6—It is essential for the Imam to recite loudly in both the *Raka'ats* of *Fajr* ; in the first two *Raka'ats* of *Maghrib* and *Isha* ; the two *Raka'ats* of Friday prayer ; in both the *Eid* prayers. *Tarawih* and *Witr* of the month of Ramadan.

7—It is permissible for one praying individually to recite loudly or in a low voice in the *Raka'ats* of *Fajr* or in the first two *Raka ats* of *Maghrib* and *Isha* prayers. Jurists have defined the limit of louder voice as one which can be heard by another person and the low tone which only be heard by one reciting but no one else.

8—For the Imam and one who is offering prayer individually, it is essential to recite in low voice in all the *Raka'ats* of *Zuhr*

## SOME OBLIGATORY AND ESSENTIAL PROBLEMS OF NAMAZ

and *Asr* and in the last *Raka'ats* of *Maghrib* and *Isha prayers*.

9—Recitation in *Nafl* prayers offered during the day, should be in a low tone ; but in *Nafl* prayers offered at night the recitation may be in a low or loud voice.

10—If anyone offers missed prayer of *Fajr*, *Maghrib* or *Isha* individually. It is essential for him to recite in a low voice when offered during day time ; but if offered at night, the voice may be low or loud as he likes.

11—If anyone forgets to add some *Sura* after *Sura Fateha* in the first and second *Raka'ats* of *Maghrib* or *Isha* then he should add a *Sura* in the third or fourth *Raka'ats* and in these recitations louder tone is essential and a *Sajda-e-Sahav* in the end is also essential.

# OFFERING OF PRAYERS IN CONGREGATION
## (NAMAZ-E-JAMA'AT)

To offer prayer in congregation is emphasised (*Sunna Moakkeda*). At least two persons offering prayer together make up the congregation that is, one of them is Imam and the other follower (*Muqtadi*).

Participation of only one person besides the Imam will make up the congregation, whether the person is a man or woman, slave or free or even a minor. But in the prayers of Friday and both the *Eids* at least three persons besides the Imam are essential to constitute a congregation.

It is not necessary for a congregation that it should be for *Fajr* prayer only—even *Nafl* prayer may be offered in congregation. But it is not proper to be habitual of *Nafl* congregation.

**Value of Congregation**

In many Traditions the importance and excellence of congregation has been reported with the definite conclusion that congregation is pre-eminent requisite or condition for perfection of Namaz. The Holy Prophet (SAW) never missed it, even in his illness he went to the mosque with the help of others to offer prayer in congregation. He used to be very angry with those who missed or neglected congregation and wished to award severest punishment to such persons.

**Hadith**

1—The Holy Prophet (SAW) is reported by Ibne Umar to have said that congregational prayer has twenty-seven times more credit than a prayer offered individually.

2—The Holy Prophet (SAW) has said that offering prayer with a person is much better than offering it alone and it is still better to offer it with two others. The larger the congregation the more it is liked by Allah.

3—Once at the time of *Isha* prayer the Holy Prophet (SAW) said to his companions who were present in the congregation that some men have gone to sleep after offering prayer alone, but the time they (who were present) spent in waiting for the congregation is also counted as spent in the prayer.

4—It has been reported by Hadrat Buraida Aslami that the Holy Prophet has (SAW) said that glad tidings be given to those who go to the mosque in dark nights for congregation, that on the Day of Judgement there will be brightest light for them.

5—It has been reported by Hadrat Uthman Ghani that the Holy Prophet (SAW) has said that one who offers his *Isha* prayer in congregation, he will be rewarded credit for that equal to half night's prayer and one who will offer his *Isha* and *Fajr* prayers in congregation will be rewarded by credit equal to whole night's prayer.

6—Hadrat Abu Huraira has reported that one day the Holy Prophet (SAW) said that he wished to order someone to collect fire wood and then order for *Adhan* to be called and deputing someone to lead the prayer he (Prophet (SAW) go to the houses of those who did not come to the congregation and burn their houses.

7—It has been reported by Hadrat Abu Abbas that the Holy Prophet (SAW) has said that one who does not join the congregation after hearing the *Adhan* and has no legitimate excuse also, then the prayer which he offers alone in his house will not be accepted. The companions asked the Holy Prophet (SAW) as to what could be the legitimate excuse, the Prophet (SAW) replied, 'Fear or illness.'

There are lot of Traditions emphasising the importance of congregation. Only a few of them have been described.

**Conditions of Proper Congregation**

1—Persons joining congregation should be male. For women it is not essential.

2—To be major and matured in age. For minor children congregation is not essential.

3—To be a free man. Congregation is not necessary for

a slave.

4—To be free from legitimate excuse.

5—To be a Muslim. The participation of a non-believer is not proper.

6—To be sane. The participation of an insane, unconscious or inebriated in congregation is not proper.

7—While intending for the prayer the follower should also intend to follow the Imam i.e. to say in mind that he intends to offer such and such prayer following that Imam.

8—The place of the Imam and the follower should be the same i.e. both should be in the same mosque or house.

**Injunctions**

(a) If the follower stands on the roof of the mosque and the Imam inside the mosque, then it would be in order as the roof is a part of the mosque. In the same way if anyone's roof adjoins the mosque and there is nothing between them, then that roof will also be treated as part of the mosque for the purpose of following the Imam.

(b) If the mosque is very large or it is house or jungle and the distance between the Imam and the follower is so much in which the rows (Saf) can be formed then both the spots shall be considered apart from each other and in such case following will not be correct.

(c) If there is a canal or some clean tank intervening between the Imam and the followers or there is a common passage and there are no rows in between, then both the places would not be treated as one and it will not be in order for those in one row to follow the row on the other side.

(d) To follow one on horse-back by a pedestrian or of a rider to follow another rider is not in order as the places of both are different. If the persons are riding the same mount then it is permissible for them.

9—The prayer of the Imam and the follower should not be different. If they are different following would not be in order. For example the Imam is offering *Zuhr* prayer and the follower intends for *Asr* prayer. Or the Imam is offering the previous day's *Zuhr* and the follower intends for that day's *Zuhr* prayer, then the following will not be correct. But if the Imam is offering *Fard* prayer and the follower intends for *Nafl* prayer, then the following would be in order.

If the Imam is offering *Nafl* prayers in *Ramadan* and the follower intends for *Tarawih* of *Ramadan*, then also the following will not be correct as the prayer of the Imam is weak while in the above (No. 9) the prayer of the Imam is pre-eminent or strong.

10—The prayer of the Imam should be correct. If Imam's prayer is disrupted then the follower's prayer will also be disrupted automatically whether known during or after the prayer:

(a) If the Imam was without ablution and recollected the same during or after the prayer, then the prayer would be disrupted.

(b) If the Imam had strong pollution stuck to his clothes more than the prescribed limit and it was discovered during or after the prayer, then the prayer would be disrupted.

(c) If the prayer of the Imam has been disrupted and the followers are unaware of it, then it is the duty of the Imam to inform the followers as soon as possible so that they may repeat their prayer. The information may be conveyed through announcement, messenger or even letters.

11—The follower should not stand ahead of the Imam but should be on his side or behind. If he stands ahead of him, following would not be in order.

12—If the heel of the follower is ahead of the Imam, then it will be treated as the follower is standing ahead of the Imam. If the heel of the follower is not ahead of the Imam but the fingers are, following would be in order.

13—The follower should know the changes in Imam's postures like *Ruku, Sajda,* sitting etc. whether by directly seeing him or through the *Takbirs* called by him or someone else or by seeing other followers. If the follower is not aware of the changes in Imam's postures, then the following will not be in order. If they are known somehow in spite of some intervention, then the following would be in order.

14—If it is not known whether the Imam is *Muqeem* (resident) or a traveller but it is guessed that he is resident (provided he is not in a city or village) and leads the prayer like a traveller i.e. observes *Qasr* and ends after two *Raka'ats* and the follower thinks that the Imam has done so in forgetfulness, then the follower should complete his four *Raka'ats*. But the follower should ascertain afterwards about the position of the Imam. If after enquiry it was found that the Imam was actually a traveller, then the prayer of the follower was in order. But if it is found that the Imam did so in forgetfulness, then the follower should repeat his prayer. But if it was not ascertained and the follower remained in doubt even then he should repeat his prayer :

(a) If the Imam is presumed to be a resident but he is leading the prayer outside the city or village and observed *Qasr* in prayer of four *Raka'ats* and the follower thought that it was done in forgetfulness, even then the follower should complete his four *Raka'ats*. It would be better if the correct position of the Imam is ascertained later.

(b) In short the ascertaining of the state of the Imam is necessary when Imam, while in a city or village, leads only two *Raka'ats* in prayer of four *Raka'ats* and the follower has some doubt.

15—Except recitation the follower should remain with the Imam in all other items of *Namaz* whether performed alongwith the Imam or before or after provided that the Imam joins before the completion of the item.

**Example**

(a) The follower bows, prostrates etc. with the Imam.

(b) If the follower bows when the Imam has risen from it.

(c) When the follower bows, prostrates etc. before the Imam performs them, but in this position the action should be

## OFFERING OF PRAYERS IN CONGREGATION 169

so prolonged that the Imam joins him and if the Imam does not join him, then the following would not be in order.

16—The state of the follower should be inferior or equal to the Imam :

(a) It is permissible for one who can stand to follow one who is incapable of standing as according to religious code the sitting of an incapacitated person is like standing.

(b) It is permissible for one who is with ablution and bath to follow who has performed *Tayammum* as in matter of purity bath and *Tayammum* are in the same order—none is more or less than the other.

(c) It is permissible for one who has washed to follow one who has performed *Masah*, because *Masah* and washing are equal in purity.

(d) The following of an incapacitated by another incapacitated is permissible provided both of them are suffering from the same disease as gases or diabetes.

(e) It is permissible for an illiterate person to follow another illiterate person provided there is no *Qari* (literate) among the followers.

(f) The following by a woman or a minor of a male.

(g) It is permissible for a woman to follow a woman.

(h) It is permissible for a minor girl or a boy to follow a minor male.

(i) It is permissible for one offering *Nafl* prayer to follow one who is offering *Wajib* (essential) prayer.

(j) One offering *Nafl* prayer can follow one who is also offering *Nafl*.

(k) It is permissible for one offering a vowed prayer to follow one offering *Nafl* prayer because prayer of an oath is in fact a *Nafl*.

(l) It is also permissible to offer *Nadhar* prayer (vow) following one who is also offering a *Nadhar* prayer.

In the above example from (a) to (l) condition for conregation being in order have been explained. If the Imam is superior or equal to the follower, then the following and the prayer will be correct and in order.

17—Following are cases in which the Imam's state is inferior to that of the follower whether definitely or doubtfully and as such the following would not be in order :

(a) It is not permissible for a major male or female to follow a minor.

(b) It is not permissible for a male, whether major or minor to follow a woman.

(c) The following of an eunuch by another eunuch will not be correct. This type of being is rare and about such persons it cannot be said with certain whether they are men or women.

(d) It is not permissible for a woman who does not remember her period of menses to follow another woman in the same condition because there is an apprehension that this may be the period of the Imam woman and the follower may be clean and the Imam should be stronger and superior in position.

(e) The following of a woman by an eunuch will not be correct as it is just possible that the eunuch may be a male.

(f) It is not permissible for a sane person to follow an insane, inebriated, unconscious and a fool.

(g) It is not permissible for one in cleanliness and purity to follow an incapacitated person.

(h) It is not permissible for one having one excuse to follow one having two excuses, that is, it is not permissible for one suffering from gases to follow one suffering from gases and diabetes.

(i) It is not permissible for one having one kind of incapacity, that is, one suffering from diabetes should not follow one suffering from gases.

(j) It is not permissible for *Qari* (literate) to follow an ignorant. *Qari* (recitor of Quran literally) is one who remembers so much of Holy Quran correctly as is required in the prayers and ignorant (*Ummi*) is one who does not remember even so much.

## OFFERING OF PRAYERS IN CONGREGATION

(k) The following of an ignorant person by another ignorant is not permissible if any one remembering the necessary part of Holy Quran is present in the congregation. In such case not only prayer of the Imam shall be disrupted but that of the followers also consequently.

(l) It is not permissible for an ignorant to follow a dumb person because no doubt the ignorant cannot at present recite the Holy Quran, but he is capable of learning it; but the dumb is not even able to learn it.

(m) One whose neccessary parts of the body are covered, cannot follow a naked or scantly clothed.

(n) It is not permissible for one who can perform *Ruku* and *Sajda* to follow one who is incapable of doing these.

(o) It is not permissible for one offering *Fard* prayer to follow one offering *Nafl* prayer.

(p) It is not permissible for one offering *Nadhar* prayer to follow on offering *Nafl* prayer as *Nadhar* is an essential prayer.

(q) It is not permissible for one having correct pronunciation of words to follow one who cannot pronounce the words correctly or changes the words. But if a letter or two happen to be mis-pronounced, then the following would be correct.

(r) The Imam should not be one who has to remain single at the time of prayer i.e. one who missed some *Raka'ats* of the prayer and has to complete them singly. The following of such a person by anyone would not be in order.

## Excuses for Congregation

There are fourteen excuses when congregation may be given up:

1—When clothes for covering the essential parts of the body are not available.

2—If there is much slush or mud on the road or way to the mosque and it is difficult to walk. But it is appreciable to go.

3—When there is heavy rain ; but it is preferable to go even then.

4.—When it is very cold and there is fear of catching some illness or aggravation of the present illness by going out to the mosque.

5—If there is risk of property and wealth being stolen in absence.

6—When there is fear of confrontation with an enemy on the way.

7—If there is fear of meeting a creditor and being embarrassed by him provided that he is not in a position to repay the debt. If he is capable of repaying the debt then it would not be permissible for him to give up the congregation on this account.

8—If it is pitch dark at night and the path is not visible and one has no other means of light also.

9—It is night and a severe storm is raging.

10—One is attending a patient and it is feared that if he goes to the mosque the patient may feel inconvenience or be worried and there is no one else to look after the patient.

11.—If the meal has been cooked or is nearly cooked and one is so hungry that he may not be able to devote fully to the prayer.

12—When there is immense urge for urination or for easing oneself.

13—When one intends to go on a journey and there is an apprehension that by offering prayer in congregation he may be delayed or miss caravan or the train.

14.—If one is ill and cannot walk due to it or is blind or decrepit or has lost his legs. But if a blind can conveniently walk upto the mosque, he should not neglect or miss the congregation.

### Injunctions for Congregation

1. Congregation in prayers of Friday and both the *Eids*— that is, *Eid-ul-Fitr* and *Eid-ul-Adha*, Individual performance of

## OFFERING OF PRAYERS IN CONGREGATION

these prayers is not in order.

2—In the daily five times' prayers congregation is *Wajib* (essential) provided there is no legitimate excuse.

3—In *Tarawih* congregation is a stressed *Sunna*, even if one has completed the hearing of one whole Holy Quran with congregation before the end of *Ramadan*. It is to be continued till the visibility of *Eid* moon.

4—Performance of *Witr* prayer in congregation during the month of *Ramadan* is appreciable, but on other days besides *Ramadan*, it is mildly execrable if perpetuated. There is no harm if occasionally two or three men offer *Witr* in congregation.

5—In solar eclipse prayer congregation is prohibited execrability and also if *Nafl* prayers are offered with all preparations of a *Fard* prayer i.e. with *Adhan* and *Iqamat*.

6—If two or three persons collect incidentally without calling and offer *Nafl* prayer in congregation, then there is no harm ; but it should not be made a practice or rule.

7—The second congregation of every *Fard* prayer is prohibited execrability under the following conditions :

(a) The mosque is in a mohalla or locality and is not situated on a public highway. The definition of a mohalla mosque is that it has an appointed Imam and men of the locality generally offer their prayers there.

(b) The first congregation has been held with loudly called *Adhan* and *Iqamat*.

(c) Prayer in the first congregation has been offered by the residents of the area and who also have the right of management of the mosque.

(d) The second congregation is also held with all the same preparation and conditions which were observed in the first. This condition has been prescribed by Imam Abu Yusuf alone while according to Imam Abu Hanifa it is execrable even if the conditions have been changed.

So if the second congregational prayer is offered at home

and not in the mosque, then it is not execrable. So if none of the above mentioned four conditions exists, i.e. the mosque is on a public highway and not of the locality and a second or even third or fourth congregation of a prayer is held, it is not execrable. Or if the first congregation was held without the *Adhan* and *Iqamat* being called loudly and the second congregational prayer was offered by such persons who were not residents of that area and have no say in the management of the mosque; or as according to Imam Abu Hanifa the second congregation is not of the same type as the first, then in all such cases it is not execrable.

If the Imam of the second congregation stands at a different place than that of the Imam of the first congregation, then the situation and condition of the second congregation will be changed and it will not be execrable as such.

**Warning**

Though some people follow the opinion of Imam Abu Yusuf but the opinion of Imam Abu Hanifa is logically stronger and sound. Now-a-days when in matters of religion and particularly in congregational prayers there is a general slackness and reluctance in practice, then the proper course would be prescribed execrability even in case of change in conditions and situations because men may be encouraged to deliberately miss the first congregation and may make it a practice to arrange second congregation only.

**About the Imam and the followers**

1—The followers should select as their Imam the person who is most suitable and possess a virtuous conduct from amongst those present for the congregation. If there are several such persons, then the one who is favoured by the majority should be the Imam. If in the presence of a more suitable person some other person is made Imam, then it will be an act against the *Sunna* and would amount to giving up *Sunna*.

2—The person most suited to be the Imam should be one in order of his merits and qualifications :

(*a*) is well versed with the requisites of prayer provided

## OFFERING OF PRAYERS IN CONGREGATION

that there is no apparent impiety in him and he fully remembers the minimum portion of Holy Quran the recitation of which is *Sunna* and recites the Holy Quran correctly.

(b) Then the person who recites the Holy Quran properly according to the rules of intonation.

(c) Then the oldest amongst those present for the congregation.

(d) Then the person who is the most handsome.

(e) Then the most respectable person.

(f) Then the person possessing a sweet voice.

(g) Then the man who is most well dressed.

(h) Then a resident in preference to a traveller.

(i) The person possessing two qualities should be preferred to one who has only one, that is, the person who knows the requisites of prayer and also recites the Holy Quran properly, should be preferred to one who only knows the requisites of *Namaz* but cannot recite the Holy Quran so well.

3—If the congregation of a prayer is held in someone's house, then the owner of the house has the stronger right to be the Imam or anyone else nominated by him. But if the owner is quite ignorant or illiterate and others are fully acquainted with the requisites, then it would be the right of one of them to lead the prayer.

4—If there is permanent Imam of a mosque, then no one else has the right to lead the prayer unless the Imam asks someone else to lead.

5—In the presence of the *Qadi* or a Muslim king no other person has the right to lead the prayer.

6—To lead the prayer without the consent of the community is a prohibited execrability, but if the person is most suited and deserving to lead the prayer and there is no other person so qualified as he, then his leading the prayer is not execrable. People opposing him are wrong.

7—To make an impious and innovator person the Imam is a prohibited execration. But if, may it not be, no other except him, is present then it is not execrable. Similarly if transgressors and innovators are so powerful that they cannot be set aside or there is danger of great disturbance in doing so, then it is not execrable for the followers to follow such a person.

8—To appoint one, who is a slave according to religious code (even though he is liberated) as Imam or a rustic or a blind who does not mind his cleanliness or a person with weak eye-sight at night or a bastard is a milder execrability. But if such people are highly educated and others have no objection to their being Imam then it is not execrable. In the same way it is a milder execrability to make Imam a beautiful youngman whose beard has not yet come up or a foolish man.

9—In all the obligatory and essential requisites of *Namaz* the followers should follow the Imam but it is not necessary in the *Sunna* and *Nafl* prayers.

10—It is prohibited execrability for the Imam to recite longer *Suras* in prayers than allowed by *Sunna* or to perform *Ruku* or *Sajdas* of a longer duration. On the other hand the Imam should have regard for the needs and weaknesses of the followers. It is better, if needed, the Imam should recite a bit little than prescribed by *Sunna* so that people may not suffer and consequently the congregation may not be thinned.

11—If there is only one follower in a prayer, whether major or minor, he should stand on the right side of the Imam with him or a little backward. It is execrable for him to stand on the left side of the Imam or behind him.

12—If the followers are more than one, they should stand in a row behind the Imam. If there are only two followers and they stand on the right and left of the Imam, it is milder execrability. It would be strong execrability to do so if the followers are more than two because it is essential for the Imam to stand ahead of the followers when they are more than two.

13—If at the beginning of prayer there was only one follower and he stood on the right side of the Imam ; but after some time more followers came, then the first follower should move backward so that a row may be formed by all the followers behind the Imam. If the first follower does not move back, the new followers should pull him back. But if the new followers unintentionally stand on both the sides of the Imam, then he (Imam) should step forward so that all the followers may come in one row behind him. In the same way if there is no space for the followers to step backward, the Imam should himself move forward. If the followers are ignorant of the rules of congregational prayer, as is generally the case now-a-days, then the first follower should not be pulled back lest he may do something which may disrupt the prayer itself.

14—If the follower is a woman or a minor girl, then she should stand behind the Imam. It is immaterial whether she is alone or more than one.

15—If there are different types of persons amongst the followers—men, women, minors—the Imam should arrange them in such a way that men are in the first row, the minor male children in the next, then women and in the last row minor girls.

16—The Imam should arrange the rows properly and should allow the followers to stand in disorder. He should direct all to stand in a straight line. The followers should stand so closely in the rows that no vacant space is left between them.

17—It is execrable for one man to stand alone behind the row. In such case he should pull back someone from the front row to stand with him. But if there is the apprehension that the man pulled back may disrupt his prayer or would mind, then he should not be pulled back.

18—If there is space in the first row, then it is execrable to stand in the second row.

19—It is prohibited execrability for a man to be the Imam of a woman only when there is no male or *Mahram* woman (co-related) such as his wife, mother or sister. If a man or a *Mahram* woman is present, then it is not execrable.

20—If a person is offering *Fajr*, *Maghrib* or *Isha* prayer all alone and is reciting in a low tone and someone else comes and begins to follow him in prayer, then there are two options for the first man—one that he may intend in his mind to take up the role of Imam so that the prayer may become a congregational one and the second is that in spite of the knowledge that the other man is following him, he may continue to pray alone. In the first case he should immediately start reciting in a loud voice and if he has already recited *Sura Fateha* or some part of another *Sura*, then he should recite the remaining part loudly, because in the prayers of *Fajr*, *Magrib* and *Isha* it is essential for the Imam to recite loudly. In the second case the prayer of the follower would be correct as for the follower's prayer to be correct the intent of the Imam to lead is not necessary.

21—*Lahiq* is the follower whose all or some of the *Raka'ats* have been disrupted after joining the congregation either due to some such execuse that he fell asleep during the prayer and thereby missed some *Raka'ats* or due to crowded congregation was unable to perform *Ruku* and *Sajda* properly; or his ablution was breached and went for fresh ablution and thus missed some *Raka'ats*.

If a resident follows a traveller in prayer and the traveller shortens his prayer (i.e. offers *Qasr*), then the resident becomes a *Lahiq* just as the traveller concludes his prayer.

Or the *Raka'ats* are missed without any excuse i.e. if one goes in *Sajda* or *Ruku* before the Imam in a *Raka'at*, then that *Raka'at* will become null and void and the man will become a *Lahiq*. So it is essential for the *Lahiq* in such case to first perform his missed *Raka'ats* and then join the congregation if it is still continuing, otherwise should complete his remaining prayer individually.

22—The *Lahiq* will be regarded as a follower for his missed *Raka'ats* and just as the follower is not required to recite but to stand silently and in the same way *Sajda-e-Sahav* is not necessary for the *Lahiq* just as it is not necessary for the follower.

23—If the Imam or a single person is offering prayer at

home or in an open place, it is appreciable for him to fix a stick of one arm-length and about two fingers in thickness in front of his brow on left or right side. This is called *Satra*. But if he is praying in the mosque or at such a place where people do not pass in front of prayer then it is not necessary. The *Satra* of Imam is sufficient for all the followers. Passing before the *Satra* is not objectionable, but it would be a sin for a person if he passes from the inner side of the *Satra*.

24 – *Masbuq* is the person who has already missed some of his *Raka'ats* when he joins the congregation. Such a person should follow the Imam for the rest of the prayer and when the Imam concludes his prayer, he should stand up and perform the missed *Raka'ats*.

25—*Masbuq* should perform his missed *Raka'ats* with recitation like one who prays alone and if he forgets something in these *Raka'ats*, it is essential for him to offer *Sajda-e-Sahav*.

26 – *Masbuq* should offer his missed *Raka'ats* in this order :—

First those in which recitation is essential and then those in which it is not essential. He should offer sittings (*attahiyat*) according to the *Raka'ats* offered with the Imam i.e. in the *Raka'at* which happens to be the second *Raka'at* he should observe the first sitting and in the third *Raka'at* of the prayer having three *Raka'ats* only, he should observe the final sitting and so on.

**Example**

If in the prayer of *Zuhr* one joined the congregation after the third *Raka'at*, then after the Imam has completed the prayer, the follower should stand up and offer the missed *Raka'ats* in this way that in the first *Raka'at* after recitation of *Sura Fateha* and some other *Sura* and performing *Ruku* and *Sajdas*, he should observe the first sitting as according to the *Raka'at* which he had joined it is his second *Raka'at*. Then in the next *Raka'at* after sitting he should recite as prescribed and after *Ruku* and *Sajdas* he should not sit for *Attahiyat* as it is his third *Raka'at*. Then in the third *Raka'at* he should not add any *Sura* to *Sura Fateha* as it would be his last *Raka'at* and should observe final sitting after it and so on.

27—If a person happens to be *Lahiq* and *Musbuq* as well i.e. he joined the congregation after some *Raka'ats* and again missed some *Raka'at*, then he should first offer the missed *Raka'ats* for which he is a *Lahiq*, but in these he should act like a follower that is he should not recite and should observe the Imam's order of *Raka'ats* and then join congregation if it still continues, otherwise offer the prayer alone and thereafter offer those *Raka'ats* for which he is *Masbuq*.

**Example**

If anyone joined the congregation after one *Raka'at* of *Asr* prayer and thereafter his ablution was breached and he went for a fresh ablution and in the meantime the congregation ended, then he should first offer the three *Raka'ats* which were offered in congregation in his absence and then the one which was also offered in congregation before he joined it. In the first three *Raka'ats* he should act as a follower i.e. he should not recite and sit after the first *Raka'at* of these three as it would be Imam's second one and in it the Imam had observed first sitting; but the person should not sit in his second *Raka'at* as it would be the third of Imam. He should sit in his third *Raka'at* as it would be fourth of Imam in which he observed the final sitting. Then he should offer that *Raka'at* which was offered before he joined the congregation and in this he should recite as he is *Masbuq* for it and he should sit after it as it would be his fourth *Raka'at*. *Masbuq* in his missed part of the prayer is like the person who offers his prayer individually.

28—It is *Sunna* for all the followers to perform all the actions of prayer with the Imam without delay. From *Takbir Tahrima* to standing, *Ruku*, *Sajda* and sitting, every action and item should be performed with the Imam. But if in the first sitting the Imam stands up before the follower has completed the recitation of *Attahiyat*, then the follower should complete it and then rise. In the same way in the last sitting if the Imam concludes the prayer before the follower has completed the recitation of *Attahiyat*, then the follower should complete it before concluding the prayer. But in bowing (*Ruku*) and *Sajda* the follower should rise with the Imam even if he had not recited the words of *Ruku* and *Sajda*.

## On Missing of Congregation

1—If anyone reached the mosque of his area when congregation has come to an end, then it is permissible for him to go in search of congregation in some other Mosque. It is also permissible for him to collect his family members in his house and arrange congregation for the prayer.

2—If anyone has offered *Fard* prayer individually at home and then finds the same prayer being offered in congregation, then he should join the congregation provided that it is *Zuhr* or *Isha* prayer. If it is *Fajr*, *Asr* or *Maghrib* prayer, he should not join it because *Nafl* prayer is execrable after *Fajr* and *Asr* prayers while in *Maghrib*, as it is of three *Raka'ats*, and *Nafl* prayer of three *Raka'ats* has nowhere been mentioned.

3—If anyone has begun to offer his *Fard* prayer alone and congregation of the same *Fard* also began just after, then if it is the *Fard* of two *Raka'ats* (*Fajr*) and he has not performed the *Sajdas* of his first *Raka'at*, then he should break his prayer and join the congregation. If he has offered the *Sajdas* of the first *Raka'at* and not of the second, even then he should break his prayer and join the congregation. But if he has offered the *Sajdas* of the second *Raka'ats* also, then he should not break it to join the congregation and should complete his prayer.

If the prayer is of *Maghrib*, then if the *Sajdas* of the second *Raka'at* have not been offered, he should break his prayer to join the congregation. If the *Sajdas* of the second *Raka'at* have been offered, then he should complete his prayer and should not break it.

If the prayer is of four *Raka'ats* i.e. *Zuhr*, *Asr* or *Isha* and one has not as yet offered the *Sajdas* of the first *Raka'at*, then he should break his prayer to join the congregation. If he has offered the *Sajdas* of his first *Raka'at*, then he should conclude his prayer after the first sitting and join the congregation. If he has begun the third *Raka'at* of his prayer but has not offered the *Sajdas* of this *Raka'at*, then he should break his prayer to join the congregation. But if he has offered the *Sajdas* of the third *Raka'at* then he should complete his prayer and not break to join the congregation.

In cases of *Fajr*, *Asr* and *Maghrib* prayers one need not join the congregation if he has offered his prayer alone, but in case of *Zuhr* and *Isha* he should join the congregation.

When a person has to break his prayer to join congregation, he should turn his face once in standing and say *Assalam-o-Alaikum-wa-Rahma-Tullah*.

4—If one has begun offering *Nafl* prayer and during it the congregation of *Fard* prayer begins, then he should not break the *Nafl* prayer immediately but should conclude it after two *Raka'ats* even if he had intended for four *Raka'ats*.

5—If one is offering the stressed *Sunna* of *Zuhr* or Friday prayer and in the meantime the congregation of *Fard* prayer begins, then the apparent view is that he should conclude it after two *Raka'ats* and join the congregation. But according to some jurists it is preferable that he should complete his four *Raka'ats* and then join the congregation. But if he has begun his third *Raka'at*, then it is necessary for him to complete his four *Raka'ats*.

6 – If congregation of *Fard* prayer has begun, then one should not begin offering of *Sunna* etc. as there may be the risk of missing any *Raka'at* of congregation. But if one is sure or has strong hope that no *Raka'at* would be missed, then he may offer *Sunna* etc.

For instance, if congregation of *Zuhr* has begun and there is likelihood of missing some *Raka'at*, then stressed *Sunna* to be offered before *Fard* should be left. In such case after *Fard* of *Zuhr* and Friday prayer, it is better to offer first the two stressed *Sunna* which is offered after *Fard* and then the missed ones.

Since the *Sunna* of *Fajr* prayer are more stressed, the injunction in their case is that even if the *Fard* congregation has started, one should offer these *Sunna* first provided that there is hope of getting at least one *Raka'at* with congregation. But if there is no such hope then these may be left and may be offered after sun-rise.

7—In *Fajr* prayer if it is feared that if *Sunna* is offered with all its requisites, then congregation may be missed, then only *Fard* be offered, *Sunna* be omitted.

8—When congregation prayer has started then *Sunna* prayer, whether of *Fajr* or of any other time, should be offered at a place which is separate from it, because the place where *Fard* prayer is being offered the offering of other prayer at that place is prohibited execrability.

9—If anyone joins the congregation in the last sitting having missed all the *Raka'ats* even then he will get full credit of congregation.

10—If one joins a congregational prayer in bowing (*ruku*) then it will be taken as if that *Raka'at* has been offered by him. If joined after *Ruku* then that *Raka'at* will not be counted to have been performed.

**Things or acts which spoil the Prayer (Namaz)**

1—It will disrupt the prayer if the recitation of Holy Quran by someone other than the Imam, is corrected by anyone in prayer.

2—If the follower corrects the recitation of his Imam, it is correct and the prayer will not be spoiled whether the Imam has recited the necessary verses of the Holy Quran and was corrected then.

3—If the Imam has recited the necessary verses, he should immediately go for *Ruku* and should not force the followers to correct him as it is execrable. The follower should not correct the Imam unless it is absolutely necessary as it is also execrable.

*Absolute Necessity* means that the Imam after wrong recitation wants to proceed further or does not bow (perform *Ruku*) or stands silent. If he was corrected even without absolute necessity, the prayer will not be spoiled.

4—If anyone corrects someone else who is offering prayer and the man correcting is not his follower (whether he is in prayer or not) if the man offering prayer accepts the correction, then his prayer will be spoiled. But if he himself recollects whether before or after the correction and it is not on account of the correction, then there will be no harm in the prayer.

5—If a follower corrects anyone who is not his Imam (whether he is in prayer or not) in every case the prayer of the follower will be spoiled.

6—If the follower on hearing someone else reciting the Holy Quran or by consulting the Holy Quran corrects the Imam, then his prayer will be spoiled and if the Imam accepts such correction he will also spoil his prayer. But if the follower himself remembers on consulting the Holy Quran or by hearing someone's correct recitation and then corrects the Imam, then the prayer will not be spoiled.

7—Similarly while in prayer if one verse is recited after consulting the Holy Quran, then the prayer will be spoiled. But if the verse which was recited after consulting was already in his memory, then the prayer will not be spoiled.

8—The standing of a woman alongside of a man in such a way that any part of the body of one confronts a part of the other, will spoil the prayer with the following provisions :

 (*a*) That the woman has attained maturity or is a minor but competent for sexual intercourse. Thus if a little and minor girl stands alongside of a man in prayer, then his prayer will not be spoiled.

 (*b*) That both are in prayer. If only one is in prayer and the other not, then the prayer will not be spoiled.

 (*c*) That no partition or *Satra* intervenes between them. So if there is some such thing intervening or the distance between both is so much that one man can easily stand between them, then the prayer will not be spoiled.

 (*d*) That the woman is normal and possesses all the requisites of correct *Namaz*. So if a woman is insane or is in her menses or after-birth bleeding, then the prayer will not be spoiled if she confronts anyone in such conditions as she will no be considered in prayer.

(e) That it is not a funeral prayer, because in funeral prayer standing of women alongside of men does not spoil the prayer.

(f) That the confrontation continues for such time in which one item of prayer is completed. So if the confrontation is for a short time only in which a *Ruku* or *Sajda* cannot be performed, then it will not spoil the prayer.

(g) That *Takbir Tahrima* of both is the same i.e. the woman is the follower of this man or both are followers of a third man.

(h) That if the Imam had intended either in the beginning or when she joins, to lead her prayer. If the Imam had not intended for her, then the prayer will not be spoiled by her confrontation but the woman's own prayer will be spoiled.

9 – If the Imam due to breach of his ablution went out of the mosque without appointing any substitute, the prayer of all the followers will be spoiled.

10 – If the Imam in case of breach of his ablution appoints as his substitute such a person who is not competent to be Imam i.e. an insane, a minor child or a woman then the prayer of all including that of the substitute will be spoiled.

11 – If a woman kisses a man while he is praying, then his prayer will not be spoiled. But if the man is excited by her kissing, his prayer will be spoiled. But if a man kisses a woman while she is in prayer her prayer will be spoiled whether he kissed her in excitement or not and also whether she got excited or not.

12 – If anyone intends to pass in front of one engaged in prayer, then to prevent and resist him is permissible provided that it does not amount to substantial acts. If it amounts to substantial act, then the prayer will be spoiled.

# ABOUT DEATH, FUNERAL AND SHROUD
## DEATH

1—When a person is about to die, lay him flat on back with feet towards Ka'aba with head raised high so that the face is towards Ka'aba. His relatives etc. should sit by his side and recite the *Kalima* aloud so that he may also recite the same on hearing it.

The dying person should not be directed to recite *Kalima* as the time of death is very critical and it is possible that he may say anything else which may be objectionable.

2—If the dying person recites the *Kalima* once, then others should now keep silence and should not try to make him repeat it continuously with a view that he may breathe his last with *Kalima* on his lips. The real aim is that the last word that he speaks should be *Kalima* and it is not necessary that he keep it repeating till death. But if he speaks something else after reciting *Kalima*, then others should start reciting *Kalima* again till he repeats it once more.

3—When someone's breath becomes irregular and quick, nose is twisted, legs become relaxed so that he cannot keep them standing and temples are depressed, then it should be understood that his end has come and at such time all present should begin to recite *Kalima* loudly.

4—Recitation of *Sura Yasin* reduces the severity and pangs of death. It should be recited sitting towards his head or somewhere near the dying person.

5—At the time of one's death no such thing should be said which may turn his mind towards worldly affairs because this is time for him to present himself before Almighty Allah. Those present at that time should act and talk in such manner that his mind and heart may turn away from the world and be directed towards Allah. It is in the interest of the dying person that at such time his children or any other thing with which he had attachment should not be brought before him or to talk about them as this may turn his attention towards them and their love may be revived in his heart. It is very bad and most unfortunate that one should leave this world with its love in his heart and, Allah Forbid, it would be a very bad death.

6—If at the time of death one utters something blasphemous, it should not be considered or communicated to others. But it should be taken to be on account of senselessness and should pray for his deliverance and forgiveness by Allah.

7—When a person is dead his limbs should be put properly and a strip of cloth from under his chin over the head be tied so that his mouth may not remain open and his eyes should also be closed. His both the toes should be tied so that his legs may not spread. Cover his body with a clean sheet and expedite his bathing and shrouding.

8—While closing the mouth of the dead recite :

بِسْمِ اللهِ وَعَلٰى مِلَّةِ رَسُولِ اللهِ

(*Bismillah-wa-ala-millat-e-Rasulillah*)

9—After death burn some incense etc. near him. Women in their menses or after-birth bleeding should not come near the dead.

10—It is not proper to recite the Holy Quran near the dead body till it is given bath.

### Bath of the Dead

1—When all the preparations of grave and shroud (*kafan*) are complete, the dead should be given a bath. Wooden platform or plank used for bath should first be perfumed three, five or seven times on all sides. Then the dead body should be placed upon it covered with a cloth from navel to the knees.

2—If the place of bathing of the dead is such that the water will flow out then it is better, otherwise dig a pit nearby for the water to be collected in it. But if the water is spread even

then there is no harm or sin.
## Method of Bath
3—First wash the private parts of the dead without looking at them. To clean these parts, the hand of the person giving the bath should be covered with a cloth and the parts should be cleaned thoroughly under the cloth spreading from the navel to the knees of the dead.

Then perform ablution of the dead without gargling or passing water into the nose or washing his hands upto wrists. It should be done thus : First wash the face, then hands upto and including the elbows, then perform Masah over his head and then wash both feet.

It is also permissible to rub a wet cloth or cotton over the teeth, gums and nostrils. If the person died in need of a bath or a woman died during monthly course or after-birth discharge, then it is essential to wash inner mouth and nose also in this way.

Plug the nose, mouth and ears with cotton so that water may not enter into them at the time of ablution or bath.

After ablution the head of the dead should be washed with some soap etc. Then the body should be turned on its left side and warm water boiled with berry leaves should be flowed thrice over the entire body from head to feet till it reaches under the left side.

Then the body should be turned over his right side and washed in the same manner.

Then raise the body to a little sitting position and rub and press his stomach gently and if some excretion etc. comes out, it should be cleaned and washed well. The ablution or bath should not be repeated in such case.

Then turn the body to its left side again and pour water mixed with camphor all over the body thrice. After wiping the body with some clean cloth it should be shrouded.

4—If water, boiled with berry leaves, is not available, then the body may be bathed with ordinary warm water. This method of bathing a dead is according to *Sunna*. If not given a bath thrice but once only even then the obligation is discharged.

5.—When the body is placed on the shroud its head should be perfumed. If a male, his beard should also be perfumed. Then rub camphor on its fore-head, nose, knees and feet. Some people perfume the shroud or put scented cotton in the ears of the dead, it is not proper. Nothing more should be done than allowed by *Sunna*.

6—Do not comb the hair or clip the nails or cut hair from any part of the body. Let every thing be as it is.

7—If a male dies and there is no other male to give the bath, then no woman other than the wife is allowed to bathe the dead body. Touching the body by a non-permissible woman is not allowed. There is no wife even, then *Tayammum* of the dead be performed with head covered with a cloth or glove.

8—If a husband dies, then it is permissible for his wife to bathe and shroud him. But if the wife dies then it is not permissible for the husband to touch her body. However he can see her and touch her with a covered hand.

9—If woman is in her monthly course or after birth discharge, she should not give bath to a dead body. It is prohibited and execrable.

10—In the case of a female, the woman who is very closely related to the dead should bathe her. If she is unable to do it, then some other pious and religious woman should do it.

11—If anything abnormal or improper is seen while giving bath to dead, it should not be mentioned to anyone else such as if a dead person's face is defaced or turned black. But if he was a drunkard or she was a professional dancer and singer or a prostitute then it may be mentioned so that others may refrain from such things and be penitent.

12—If one died of drowning, then when his body is taken out it is essential to give it a bath as being drowned in water would not be sufficient for bath. But while taking out his body was moved in the water with intent of giving him a bath, then it would amount to a bath.

13—If anyone's head only is found, then it may not be given a bath, but should be buried as it is. If anyone's more than half body is found, whether with or without head, then it is necessary to give it a bath. But if it is not more than half or just half then if it is with head it should be given bath otherwise not. If body is less than half, whether with or without head, it may not be given bath.

14—If a dead body is found and it cannot be ascertained in any way whether he was a Muslim or not, then if it was found within Muslim population, it should be given a bath and funeral prayer should also be offered

15—If anyone's non-believing relative expires, his body should be handed over to his co-religionists. If there is no such man or they refuse to accept his body, then the Muslims should give bath to the body but not according to *Sunna*. No ablution be given to him nor his head cleaned and no camphor be rubbed. But it should be done in the same way as an unclean thing is washed because a non-believer is not purified by washing only. If anyone offers its funeral prayer, it will not be in order.

16—If rebels and robbers are killed in actual fighting, their bodies should not be given bath.

17—If an apostate dies, he should not be given a bath and if his co-religionists claim his body should not be given to them.

18—If due to non availability of water, a dead body was given a *Tayammum* and afterwards water becomes available, then the body may be given a bath.

**Shrouding**

1—According to *Sunna* a man's shroud (*kafan*) consists of three clothes, that is, a loin cloth, a shirt and a sheet. Shrouding him with two clothes *i e.* a loin cloth and covering sheet is also permissible.

2—A woman's shroud consists of five clothes as per *Sunna* i.e one shirt, a loin cloth, a chest band, a head band and a covering sheet. The loin cloth should be from head to feet in length and the covering sheet longer than it by one hand's length. The shirt should be from neck to feet but without sleeves and side pieces. The head piece should be three hands in length. The chest band should be from breast to thighs in length and should be enough in length and breadth so that it may be wrapped round the body.

A woman may be shrouded in three clothes only i.e. loin cloth, a head band, a covering sheet due to lack of cloth or means. But using less than three clothes is execrable and not proper. But in case of exigency or unavoidable circumstances using less than three clothes is also permissible.

3—The chest band may be from the breast to navel, but it is better than it should be upto thighs.

4—The shroud should be perfumed thrice, five or seven times before shrouding.

**Method of Shrouding**

5—First spread the covering sheet, then chest band, then loin cloth and shirt over it. After placing the body over it the shirt should be put on first and spread her hair on her chest by dividing them in two equal parts on right and left side. Spread the head band over head and the hair. It should not be tied or wrapped. Then loin cloth should be wrapped first on the left side and then on right side. Then the chest band should be wrapped and finally the covering sheet should be wrapped first on left side and then on right side. Then tie the whole shroud with strips of cloth on the side of head, chest and feet so that body may not slip out of the shroud on way to the grave-yard.

6—If the chest band is wrapped after head band and before wrapping the loin cloth, then it is also permissible and if it is tied over the whole shroud, then it is also permissible.

7—When a dead has been shrouded, women should part away so that men may offer funeral prayer and take it to the grave-yard to bury it.

8—It is permissible for women to offer funeral prayer.

9—It is not proper to put any pledge or genealogy of his

preceptor or any other prayer (*dua*) in the shroud or grave. It is also not proper to write with camphor or ink some *Kalima* etc. on the chest or shroud. But putting a piece of the cover of Ka'aba or a handkerchief of his preceptor as a blessing is allowed and justifiable.

10—If a baby is born alive and dies immediately or shortly after birth, it should also be given a bath, shrouded as usual and buried after funeral prayer. The baby should also be given a name.

11—If a baby was born dead and no sign of life was in him at birth it should also be given a bath as described above, but instead of proper shroud, it should be wrapped in a clean cloth and buried. Such baby should also be given a name.

12—In case of abortion, if limbs of the child have not been formed, then such a child should be buried without bath and a proper shroud in a piece of cloth. But if the limbs have been formed, it should be buried according to the instructions as for a child. It should also be given a name.

13—At the time of birth of a child only its head has come out when it died, then it should be disposed of as described in No. 11. But if more than the head had come out when it died, then it will be treated as a child born alive and should be disposed of as described in No. 10.

14—If a minor girl, who has not attained puberty dies, she should also be given a shroud of five clothes; but if five clothes are not within the means, then three would also suffice. The instructions about an adult woman also apply to virgin and near maturity girls. But in case of women they are stresses and preferable in case of minor girls.

15—If a very minor girl dies who was not yet near maturity even, she should also be given a shroud of five clothes. But to bury her with two clothes—loin cloth and covering sheet— is also allowed.

16—The same instructions apply to boys but in their case a shroud of three clothes is required.

17—In case of a man a shroud consisting of a loin cloth and

## ABOUT DEATH, FUNERAL AND SHROUD

covering sheet is also permissible. But less than two is execrable. In case of inability to provide two clothes even only one cloth is permissible and it is not execrable in that case.

18—The sheet which is spread over the funeral is not included in the shroud.

19—One should be buried in the grave-yard of the locality when he dies. It is not appreciable to take the body somewhere else at a distance of more than three or four kilometers.

20—If anyone's grave opens and somehow the body also comes out and happens to be without shroud, then it should be shrouded again as described above provided that it has not decomposed and cracked. But if it is cracked then mere wrapping it in a clean cloth will be sufficient and should be buried again.

## THE FUNERAL PRAYER
### (NAMAZ-E-JANAZA)

Funeral prayer as a matter of fact is a prayer (*dua*) for the dead before the Most Merciful Allah.

1—The funeral prayer is essential and therefore its requisites are the same as for other prayers already described above. But there is one condition more in it—one should have the knowledge of the death If one is not aware of the death then the funeral prayer will not be necessary for him to offer.

2—There are two kinds of conditions to make the funeral prayer in order. First are those which concern people who are offering the funeral prayer and are the same as for other prayers, that is, cleanliness, covering of the private parts of body, facing Ka'aba and the intent ; but there is no restriction about some specific time for this prayer as in other timely prayers. *Tayammum* for this prayer is also permissible if there is apprehension of missing the prayer. If the prayer has begun and in making ablution there is risk of missing it, then one may perform *Tayammum* as against other prayers in which *Tayammum* is not permissible even if there is fear of missing the prayer.

Now-a-days some people offer funeral prayer wearing the shoes It is necessary that their shoes and the place where they stand both should be clean If the shoes are removed and he stands on them, then shoes should be clean.

3—The other kind of conditions are those which concern the dead and they are six : (*i*). The deceased must be Muslim. Hence the funeral prayer for a non-believer and an apostate is not proper. A Muslim, even if he is a transgressor or innovator, his funeral prayer is in order. For one who has committed a suicide the correct view is that funeral prayer for him is also in order. The rebels and robbers who are killed in actual fighting or one who has murdered his father or mother and is killed as its punishment, then the funeral prayer for them is not in order. But if they die their natural deaths then for them funeral prayer is in order.

The child, whose father or mother is a Muslim, will be considered a Muslim and funeral prayer for him would be in order.

By a deceased is meant one who was born alive and died. For a still born baby funeral prayer is not in order.

(*ii*) The body of the dead should be clean from all real and prescribed pollutions. But if the real pollution has come out of the body then there is no harm and the funeral prayer will be in order.

(*iii*) The necessary private parts of the dead should be covered. If the dead body is naked, then funeral prayer for it will not be in order.

(*iv*) The dead body should be in front of those offering the funeral prayer. If it is behind then the prayer will not be in order.

(*v*) The dead body or the cot upon which it is put, should be on the ground. If the people are holding the body in their hands or it is placed on a carriage or animal, funeral prayer, if offered in such conditions will not be proper.

(*vi*) The dead body should be present there before those offering the prayer. If it is not there, the funeral prayer will not be in order.

4—If a dead body is not clean according to the prescribed ways i.e. it has not been given bath or *Tayammum* in case of exigency, then funeral prayer for it is not proper. But if it was not possible due to some unavoidable circumstances to give it a bath or *Tayammum* and has been buried without a funeral prayer, then it should be offered at his grave.

5—If funeral prayer was offered for a dead without bath or *Tayammum* and was buried and it was remembered after burial that the body was not given a bath, then the funeral prayer should be offered again at his grave.

6—If a Muslim has been buried without funeral prayer, then it should be offered at his grave provided the body has not decomposed and cracked. If the body has been decomposed, then funeral prayer should not be offered. The time of decomposition of the body is not fixed and it is different for different place. Some have fixed three days while others ten days and even one month.

7—It is not essential that the spot where the dead body is placed for funeral prayer should be clean, provided the body is on a clean cot. If the cot is polluted or body is placed on an unclean ground, then there is difference of opinion about it. According to some, it is necessary that the body should be placed upon a clean ground. If it is placed upon unclean ground, the prayer will not be in order. While according to others the cleanliness of the ground is not at all necessary and the funeral prayer will be in order if the body is put on a clean cot.

8—There are two obligatory items in the funeral prayer:—

(a) To call *Takbir* (*Allah-o-Akbar*) four times. Each *Takbir* shall be equivalent to one *Raka'at*.

(b) The funeral prayer should be offered in standing just as in *Fard* and essential prayers. Standing is *Fard* (obligatory) and it is not permissible to omit it without legitimate excuse.

9—There are no *Ruku* (bowing), *Sajda* or sittings in this prayer.

10—Three things are *Sunna* in funeral prayer:—

(a) To praise Almighty Allah.

(b) To send *Darood Sharif* to the Holy Prophet (SAW).

(c) To pray (*dua*) for the deceased.

Congregation is not a condition for funeral prayer. If only one person, whether male or female, minor or major, offers this prayer alone, then the obligation will be discharged.

11—But congregation in funeral prayer is necessary from

the point of view that it is a prayer (*dua*) for the deceased and gathering of some Muslims for praying to Almighty Allah for anything possess wonderful efficacy as to the descent of Divine Mercy and acceptance of the prayer (*dua*).

12—The *Masnoon* and appreciable method of offering funeral prayer is to place the dead body in front of all praying and the Imam should stand opposite its chest. All should intend :

نَوَيْتُ اَنْ اُصَلِّىَ صَلٰوةِ الْجَنَازَةِ لِلّٰهِ تَعَالٰى وَ دُعَاءً لِلْمَيِّتِ

(*Navaito-an-osalli Salatil Janazati lillāh-e-Taāla wa dua-an lilmayyit*).

I intend to offer funeral prayer which is devotion to Allah and prayer for the deceased and raise both the hands upto the ears as in *Takbir Tahrima* and saying *Allah-o-Akbar* once, join the hands in front as in usual prayers. Then recite *Subhana Kalla Humma* till end. Then say *Allah-o-Akbar* without raising hands and recite *Darood Sharif*, the same which is recited in prayers. Then say *Allah-o-Akbar* once more without raising the hands and pray for the deceased. If the dead was a major—whether male or female—the following *Dua* should be recited :

اَللّٰهُمَّ اغْفِرْ لِحَيِّنَا وَ مَيِّتِنَا وَ شَاهِدِنَا وَ غَآئِبِنَا وَ
صَغِيْرِنَا وَ كَبِيْرِنَا وَ ذَكَرِنَا وَ اُنْثَانَا ط اَللّٰهُمَّ مَنْ
اَحْيَيْتَهٗ مِنَّافَاَحْيِهٖ عَلَى الْاِسْلَامِ وَ مَنْ تَوَفَّيْتَهٗ مِنَّا
فَتَوَفَّهٗ عَلَى الْاِيْمَانِ ط

(*Allahummaghfir lehayyyena wa mayyatena wa shahidina wa ghaibina wa saghirina wa kabirina wa dhakarina wa unthana Allahumma man ahyaytahoo minna fa-ahye-hi alal-Islame waman tawaffaitahoo minna fatawaffa hoo alal Iman*).

"O Allah, pardon our living beings, our males, our present as well as absentees, our minors and our elders, our males and our females. O' Allah whomsoever Thou likest to keep alive amongst us keep him alive on the path of Islam and whomsoever Thou likest to die amongst us, end him on faith."

If the dead was a minor male child, then this prayer should be recited :

اَللّٰهُمَّ اجْعَلْهُ لَنَا فَرَطًا وَّاجْعَلْهُ لَنَا اَجْرًا وَّذُخْرًا وَّاجْعَلْهُ لَنَا شَافِعًا وَّمُشَفَّعًا ۔

(Allahummaj'alho forotan waj'alho lana ajranw wa zukhranw waj'alho lana shāfe-anw wa mushaffa-an).

"O' Allah, make this pleasurable for us. Make it better reward and stock for us. Make this forgiver for us and the one granted forgiveness."

The same prayer should be recited for a minor girl with the difference that at three places *Wajalho-lana* should be substituted by *Wja'lha* and *Shaffe-an wa Mushaffe-an* by *Shafiatan wa Mushaffi-atan*.

After reciting *Dua* say *Allah-o-Akbar* without raising the hands and conclude the prayer with *Salam* as is done in usual prayers. There is no sitting or recitation of *Attahiyat* or of any other verse of the Holy Quran in funeral prayer.

13—The funeral prayer is similar for the Imam and the followers with the difference that the Imam will call *Takbirs* and *Salam* aloud and the followers in a lower tone. The recitation of *Thana, Darood Sharif* and the *Dua* will be done in a lower tone by the Imam and the followers.

14—It is appreciable in the funeral prayer that three rows are formed. Even if there are only seven persons, then one of them should be made Imam, three should stand in the first row, two in the second and one in the last row.

15—Funeral prayer is also disrupted by the same things

which disrupt other prayers with the difference that ablution is not breached by laughter in it nor the inclusion of a woman in it disrupts it.

16—It is highly execrable to offer funeral prayer in the mosque which is meant for daily five time's prayers or for Friday and *Eid* prayers, whether the *Janaza* (dead body) is placed inside or outside the mosque and the congregation is held inside the mosque.

17—It is execrable to delay the funeral in waiting for more people to join it.

18—The funeral prayer is not permissible to be offered in sitting or on a conveyance, unless there is some legitimate excuse.

19—If there are more than one funerals at the same time, it is preferable to offer prayer for each of them separately; but it is also permissible to offer one prayer for all of them. But in such case the funerals be placed in rows so that one funeral is in front of the other and the feet of all are on one side and heads on the other side as such that the chests of all the dead shall be opposite Imam as it is *Sunna*.

20—If the funerals are of different types (sexes), then their order should be that men's funerals should be near the Imam, then of male children, then of women and lastly of minor girls.

21—If anyone joins the funeral prayer when some *Takbirs* have been said before his joining, then he will be *Masbuq* in respect of these *Takbirs*, then he should not immediately join the congregation saying *Allah-o-Akbar* but he should rather wait for the Imam's *Takbir* and join with it which will be his first *Takbir* and just as the Imam concludes the prayer he should say his missed *Takbirs* in which nothing should be recited. But if he joins the congregation when the Imam has said his fourth *Takbir*, then he will not be counted a *Masbuq*. He should immediately say the *Takbir* and join the prayer before the Imam says *Salam* and after its end, he should repeat his missed *Takbirs*.

22—If anyone was present at the time of *Takbir Tahrima* and was ready to join it but due to his laziness or some other reason could not join, then he should immediately say *Takbir* and join without waiting for the second *Takbir* of the Imam and should repeat the first *Takbir* before the Imam says his next *Takbir*.

23—The *Masbuq* of funeral prayer should say his missed *Takbir* and if it is feared that the funeral will be lifted before he says *Dua*, then he should not recite *dua*.

24—If anyone becomes a *Lahiq* during a funeral prayer, then injunctions for him are the same as for usual prayers.

25—The utmost right of leading the prayer of a funeral is that of the ruler even though more pious and abstaining people are present. In the absence of the ruler his representative i.e the head of the city is entitled and if he is also not present, then the *Qadi* of the city and in his absence his deputy. In the presence of these persons, it is not permissible to make anyone else the Imam ; but if none of these is present, then the Imam of the mosque of the area is entitled, provided that there is no one superior to him in the relatives of the deceased, otherwise those of his relatives who have the right to succeed him are entitled to become Imam or the person whom they permit to lead prayer. If without the permission of the relatives, anyone led the prayer who is not entitled to lead then the relatives have the right to offer it again and if buried, may offer it at his grave, provided the body has not been decomposed.

## BURIAL (DAFN) OF THE DEAD

1—The burial of a dead body is a sufficed obligation like its bath and funeral prayer.

2—After the end of funeral prayer the dead body should immediately be taken to its place of burial—grave.

3—If the deceased is a suckling baby or a bit older, then its body should be taken on the hands i.e. the body should be placed on two hands by one man, then on the way another man should take it and in this way it should be carried to the grave-yard changing hands. But if it is the funeral of an adult, then it should be carried on a cot or something like it and each of its legs should be held by one man each and the cot be lifted and put on the shoulders But it is execrable to carry it on shoulders like luggage or some other goods. It is also execrable to carry the funeral on a carriage, but for some legitimate excuse it is permissible, such as the grave-yard is at a long distance.

4—The *Mustahab* (appreciable) way of carrying a funeral is first to lift right leg of the front side of the cot on the right shoulder and walk at least ten steps with it, then lift the right leg of the back on right shoulder and walk at least ten steps. Then the front left leg should be lifted on left shoulder and walk ten steps at least and in the same manner the left leg of back should be lifted and walk ten steps. In this way forty steps will be made up.

5—It is *Sunna* to carry the funeral with fast steps but it should not be so fast that the body be shaken and disturbed.

6—Those who accompany the funeral to the grave-yard should not sit before the funeral is taken down from the shoulders as it is execrable, unless there is some necessity.

7—Those who are not accompanying the funeral but are sitting, they should stand up on seeing the funeral.

8—Those accompanying the funeral should remain behind it, although it is permissible to be ahead of the funeral. But it is execrable if all go ahead of the funeral. It is also execrable to go ahead of the funeral on a conveyance.

9—It is appreciable to accompany the funeral on foot and one who is in a carriage, should remain behind the funeral.

10—It is execrable for those accompanying the funeral to recite some prayer or *Dua* etc. loudly.

11—The grave of the dead should be at least as half of the height of the dead person and its length equal to the length of the body and not more than that. Side-grave is better than the box type grave, but if the earth is so soft that the side-grave may collapse, then such grave should not be made.

12—It is also permissible when a side-grave cannot be made due to softness of the earth, that the body may be buried keeping it in a box whether made of wood, stone or iron and it is better to spread some earth at its bottom.

13—When the grave is ready the dead body should be lowered into it from the side of Ka'aba. Its method is that the funeral be placed near the grave towards Ka'aba and those who have to lower it, should lift the body facing the Ka'aba and place in the grave.

14—The number of those who lower the dead into the grave has not been specified any where by *Sunna*. The Holy Prophet (SAW) was lowered in his sacred grave by four persons.

15—It is appreciable to recite :

بِسْمِ اللهِ وَعَلَى مِلَّةِ رَسُولِ اللهِ

(*Bismillah-wa-ala-millate-Rasulillah*)

while putting the dead body in the grave :

16—After laying the dead in the grave the knot of the shroud, which was tied so that the shroud may not slip, should be loosened.

17—Then the grave should be closed with mud bricks or straw. It is execrable to close it with burnt bricks or stones. But if the earth is very loose and there is apprehension of collapse of the grave, then it is permissible to close it with burnt bricks or planks or even by putting the dead body in a box.

18—It is appreciable, while lowering the body of a woman in the grave, to draw curtains around the grave. If it is feared that the body may be exposed, then the drawing of curtains is essential.

19—No curtain be drawn while burying a man in a grave, but if there is unavoidable excuse, such as it is raining or snow is falling or it is too hot, purdah or covering of the grave is permissible

20—After putting the dead body in the grave all the earth which came out of the grave while digging it, should be thrown over it. To add other earth with it is execrable.

21—While throwing earth over the grave it is appreciable to begin from the side of the head of the dead and each man taking the earth in both hands should throw it over the grave reciting :

مِنْهَا خَلَقْنَاكُمْ وَ فِيهَا نُعِيدُكُمْ وَ مِنْهَا نُخْرِجُكُمْ تَارَةً أُخْرَى ۔

*Minha Khalaqnakum* meaning "We created you from the earth"—with the second handful of earth recite :

*Wa Feeha Nueedokum* meaning "and will turn you in the earth"—with the third throwing recite :

*Wa Minha Nukhrijokum Tara'an ukhra* meaning "and will raise you again from the same."

22—It is appreciable to stay for a while at the grave after burial and to pray for forgiveness of the sins of the dead or to recite Holy Quran for the benefit of the deceased.

23—When the grave is covered with earth, it is appreciable

to sprinkle some water over it.

24—No dead body, whether of an adult or child, should be buried in the house as this is specially meant for the Prophets.

25—It is execrable to prepare a grave in square shape. The appreciable way is to build it in a mound like a camel's hunch. Its height should be one span or more.

26—To raise the grave more than one span in height, is highly execrable. It is also execrable to cement the grave.

27—It is forbidden and execrable to build any superstructure like a dome etc. over the grave for decoration or even for strengthening it. It is permissible, if necessary, to write something on the grave for remembrance; but since these days people have spoiled their actions and beliefs and on account of these even permissibles become prohibited. Hence such acts will not be permissible.

### Instructions for Proper Funeral

1—If it is forgotten to turn the face of the dead towards Ka'aba and it is remembered after burial and covering earth, then it is not permissible to reopen the grave for this purpose only. But if only planks have been put and earth has not been filled, then the planks may be removed and the face of the body be turned towards Ka'aba.

2—It is prohibited execrability for women to accompany the funeral. Their weeping and stating is also prohibited.

3—At the time of lowering the dead body in the grave to call *Adhan* is an innovation.

4—If in a funeral prayer the Imam says more than four *Takbirs* then the followers of *Hanfi* school should not follow the Imam in those extra *Takbirs* but should remain silent and end the prayer when the Imam concludes it.

5—If anyone dies while travelling by a boat or ship and the land from that place is so distant that the body may be decomposed till reaching the land, then in such case the dead should be given bath, shrouded and after offering funeral prayer for the same, the body should be lowered into the water

## BURIAL (DAFN) OF THE DEAD

But if the land is not so far off and it is expected to reach there soon, then the body should be preserved till then and buried in the ground.

6—If anyone does not remember the prescribed prayer (*dua*) of funeral, it is enough for such a person to say:

اَللّٰهُمَّ اغْفِرْ لِلْمُؤْمِنِينَ وَ الْمُؤْمِنَاتِ

*Allahummagfir lil momeneena wal momenat*
"O' Allah forgive Muslim men and women."

If one cannot say even so much, then he should say the four *Takbirs* only and it would be sufficient for him.

7—It is not proper and permissible to reopen the grave after it has been covered with earth, provided :

(a) The ground where the body has been buried belongs to someone who does not permit burial there.
(b) If someone's property has fallen in the grave while burying the dead.

Then in such cases the reopening of the grave is permissible.

8— If a woman dies with a live child in her womb, then the child should be taken out by operating the womb. In the same way if one died by swallowing someone's property and the owner claims it, then the property should be taken out by opening stomach. But if the dead has left some property, then the claimant may be paid from that property and the stomach should not be slashed.

9—It is not proper to carry the body of a dead person from one place to another for burial provided the other place is not more than one or two miles away from the first. To dig out a buried body after its burial is not permissible in any condition.

10—It is permissible to praise the deceased whether in prose or poetry, provided there is no exaggeration in it and such qualities are not attributed to him which were not in him.

11—To console the bereaved members of the family of the deceased by advising them to keep patience and for the excellence and reward of patience and also to pray for the deceased, is permissible and it is called condlence. To express condolence after three days of death is a minor execrability. But if the relatives of the deceassed who were out at the time of the death and return after three days, then expressing condolence to them or by them after three days is not execrable. One who has expressed condolence once, it is execrable for him to express it again.

12—To keep prepared one's own shroud is not execrable, but to get his own grave prepared is execrable.

13—It is permissible to write with the movement of fingers and without ink *Bismillah-hir-rehman-ir-rahim* on the chest of the dead or some prayer on his shroud or *Kalima* on his forehead; but this is not mentioned in any Tradition and hence it should not be regarded as *Sunna* or appreciable.

14—It is appreciable to place a green twig on the grave; but it is execrable to cut down a tree etc. if growing near the grave.

15—Not more than one person should be buried in one grave, but in case of necessity or exigency it is permissible. In case of several bodies of males the best of them should be put ahead and the rest according to their position should be put behind him. But if the bodies are mixed—males and females, then the males should be put first and ahead and the women behind them.

16—It is appreciable for men to visit the graves and it is better to visit the graveyard on Friday. It is permissible to visit the graves of the pious (saints) even by travelling some distance, provided that no deed or action against the *Sunna* is done or some creed against *Sunna* is practised.

### About Shaheed (Martyr)

Apparently martyrs are dead bodies but all the injunctions about ordinary dead bodies are not applicable to them. The excellence of martyrdom is also very high. Hence its injunctions are different and described here.

A *Shaheed* is one in whom the following requisites are

found :

(a) To be a Muslim. So a non-Muslim cannot be categorsied as martyr.

(b) To be responsible, mature and sensible. If one is killed in a state of insanity or when not yet matured, the injunctions of martyrdom will not apply to him.

(c) To be free from major pollution. If anyone is killed in need of a bath or a woman in her menses or afterbirth bleeding, will not be covered by the injunctions of martyrdom.

(d) To be killed innocent and without fault. If anyone was not killed innocent or was executed as punishment for violence of religious code, then injunctions of martyrdom will not apply to him.

(e) If killed by a Muslim or Dhimmi by an aggressive weapon. If one is killed by a Maslim or a Dhimmi with a non-aggressive weapon like stone, then he will not be covered by the injunctions. Iron is decidedly an aggressive weapon whether it has a sharp edge or not.

If anyone is killed by aggressive non-believers, rebels or robbers or was found dead in the battle-field, then the condition of an aggressive weapon is not necessary. Even if he was killed by stones etc., he will be counted as a martyr.

For instance an aggressor crushed a Muslim under the feet of his animal which he was riding

(f) No monetary compensation has been fixed in the 'beginning' as a punishment for one's being killed but *Qasas* (retaliation) has been ordered. If monetary compensation has been allowed, then the injunctions of martyrdom will not apply even if he has been killed very cruelly.

For example if a Muslim kills another Muslim intentionally with an aggressive weapon or Muslim is killed by another Muslim accidentally or a person was dead somewhere and not in a battlefield and it is also not known as to who killed him, then in all such cases monetary compensation is allowed and not retaliation, hence injunctions of martyrdom will not apply.

In case of monetary compensation the condition of "in the beginning" means that while deciding such a case if punishment by retaliation has been awarded but later on due to some valid reasons it was changed to monetary compensation, then injunctions of martyrdom will apply. If monetary compensation was allowed in the beginning, then the injunctions of martyrdom will not apply.

(g) To be a martyr no act of comfort such as eating, drinking, sleeping, taking medicine or any worldly transaction should have been committed by one after being wounded. He has not been in his senses for in which a period one prayer can be offered nor was brought from the battlefield in his senses provided with the fear that he may not be trampled upon by an animal.

So if one talks a lot after being wounded, he will not be counted as a martyr as talk is the sign of life.

If one makes a will on worldly matters then he will not be regarded as a martyr. If anyone is killed in battlefield and has committed any of these things, then he will not be counted as a martyr. But if he committed any of these things in the battlefield while the battle is going on, then he will be counted as a martyr.

### Injunctions About Martyrdom

1—A martyr to which all the abovementioned conditions and requisites are found, will neither be given a bath nor the blood should be removed or washed from his clothes and body ; but will be buried as he is.

2—That the clothes he is wearing should not be removed from his body. But if his clothes are short of the minimum

## BURIAL (DAFN) OF THE DEAD

prescribed by *Sunna*, then more be added. If his clothes are more than the shroud prescribed by *Sunna*, then the extra ones should be removed. If his clothes are such with which shroud cannot be made as parchment, then these should be removed. Cap, shoes and weapons etc. should in all cases be removed.

Other injunctions of ordinarily dead such as funeral prayer etc will apply to him also. If in any person any of these conditions and requisites are not found, then he will be given a bath and shrouded like other dead bodies.

# THE MOSQUE
## (INJUNCTIONS ABOUT MOSQUE)

1—It is highly execrable to keep the doors of a mosque closed provided that it is not the time of prayer and the door has been closed for the safety of the property of the mosque. In such case it is permissible.

2.—The entire building in which there is a mosque does not come under the definition of a mosque. In the same way the places assigned for *Eid* or funeral prayers are not mosques.

3—To decorate a mosque with one's own money is permissible but it is execrable on the arch (*Mehrab*) or the wall of arch. It is not permissible to spend the income of the mosque on such decoration.

4—It is not good to write or inscribe the verses or Suras of the Holy Quran on the walls of the mosque.

5—To pass urine or ease oneself or indulge in sexual intercourse on the roof of the mosque is such as if these have been committed in the mosque.

6—It is very bad and not desirable to spit or clean one's nose in the mosque or on its walls. In case of urgent need it should be taken in a hand-kerchief or lapel of the shirt.

7—It is highly execrable to perform ablution or gargle in the mosque.

8—It is a sin for one in need of a bath or in menses to enter mosque.

9—It is highly execrable to enter into buying or selling in a mosque, but it is permissible for one who is in *Aitikaf* to make necessary purchase or selling, provided that the thing is not in mosque.

10—It is execrable to clean the dust or mud of the feet on

the walls or with the pillars of a mosque.

11 – To plant trees in a mosque is execrable as it is the custom of Christians and Jews.

12— To make a mosque a passage is not permissible. But in case of some urgent need passing through the mosque is permissible.

13— Mosque is intended for prayers, so it is not permissible for anyone to carry his profession in a mosque. Even one who teaches the Holy Quran on remuneration is included in the professionals and he should teach outside the mosque.

**Offering of Prayer Inside Ka'aba**

1— Just as it is correct and proper to face the Ka'aba while praying away and outside of it, it is also permissible to offer prayer inside the Ka'aba and there is no restriction of facing a particluar side. Whichever side one faces it will be correct as there is Ka'aba on every side and in every direction *Fard* and *Nafl* both types of prayers are offered inside the Ka'aba.

2— If prayer is offered on the roof of Ka'aba, even then it would be proper because the spot where Ka'aba is situated, it is Ka'aba from earth to sky. Ka'aba is not confined to its walls only. So if anyone offers prayer standing on a high mountain from where the walls of Ka'aba are not in a straight line, his prayer is justified by consensus. But because it amount to dis-respect of Ka'aba. The Holy Prophet (SAW) has prohibited the offering of prayer on its roof.

3— In Ka'aba it is permissible to offer prayer individually or in congregation and also there is no restriction that the Imam and the followers should face the same direction. It is Ka'aba in all the sides there. While offering prayer in congregation inside Ka'aba the only condition is that the followers should not stand ahead of the Imam. It is also permissible, though execrable, if the faces of the followers are in front of the Imam. It is execrable to face any other person in prayer, but if something is placed in between, then it will not be execrable.

4— If the Imam is inside Ka'aba and the followers are

standing outside in a circle even then the prayer shall be accomplished. But if only the Imam is inside and no follower is with him there, then the prayer will be execrable as in this case the ground inside the Ka'aba being higher than outside, the place of the Imam will be higher than that of followers by the size of a man's height.

5—If the followers are inside the Ka'aba and the Imam is outside even then the prayer will be justified provided that the followers are not ahead of the Imam.

6—As is usual there, it is also permissible if all the followers are outside and the Imam inside the Ka'aba and the followers surround him on all four sides with the condition that on the side on which the Imam is standing no follower should be nearer the Ka'aba than the Imam as in that case he will be treated as ahead of the Imam and it is against the following and is prohibited. But if the followers of the other side are nearer the Ka'aba than the Imam, then there is no harm and the following would be proper. It can easily be understood by the following illustration :

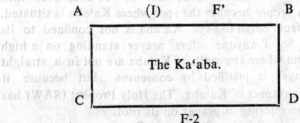

In the above illustration ABCD is the Ka'aba and I is the Imam who stands at a distance of two meters from the Ka'aba and F' is a follower who is standing on the side of the Imam and F-2 another follower on the other side of the Ka'aba. Both the followers are at a distance of one meter only from the Ka'aba. In this case the prayer of F-2 will be in order but not of F' as he will be standing ahead of the Imam.

## *JUMA* (FRIDAY) PRAYER

Nothing is more appreciable and likeable to Allah than offering of prayer by human beings. No other act of devotion is so much emphasised and given so much credit in *Shariah* (religion) as the prayer and that is why Allah has fixed five times prayer daily as an expression of gratitude for Hir unlimited favours and blessings bestowed upon the creatures from birth to death—even since before birth and after death its continuance is not cut off. Allah's blessings and favours are bestowed more on Fridays than other days. Even Hadrat Adam, fore-father of all human beings, was created on Friday. So due to its excellence, a special prayer has been enjoined for Friday. The benefits and consideration of congregation have already been described and it should now be clear to the reader that the larger the congregation will be, the greater will be its reward and credit. This is only possible when residents of all mohallas, localities, villages, and majority of people assemble and offer the prayer in congregation. Had it been enjoined for all the *Fard* daily prayers, then it would have been very inconvenient for all to come from distant places for daily prayers. So in view of this inconvenience *Shariah* has fixed one day in the week for this special prayer in which Muslims of all localities and areas should assemble together to offer this prayer in congregation. Since Friday has been assigned greater excellence than other days, hence this distinction has been given to this day.

Allah had also ordered former *Ummahs* (Communities) to offer prayer on this day; but due to their ill-luck they differed and on account of their negligence and insubordination they have been deprived of this great boon and ultimately the Muslims have been favoured with it. The Jews fixed Saturday of their own thinking that on this (Saturday) day Allah completed the creation of all creatures. The Christians fixed Sunday presuming it to be the day of the beginning of creation of the universe. So upto this day these two communities observe and make great preparation on their respective days and giving up all worldly affairs devote themselves to praying. That is why in all Christian countries weekly holiday is observed on Sundays.

**Virtues of Friday**

1—The Holy Prophet (SAW) has said that Friday is the best of all the days. Hadrat Adam was created on this day. He was admitted to Paradise on this day and was also taken out on this day. The Day of Judgement will also be on Friday.

2—Hadrat Imam Ahmad says that the virtue of Friday night is more than *Lailatul Qadar* (Night of Excellence). Among other grounds its excellence is also great because on this night the Holy Prophet (SAW) came to the womb of his mother and the events of his coming is superior to all the blessings of this world and hereafter and has been the cause of unlimited blessings.

3—The Holy Prophet SAW has said that in Friday there is such a moment that if a Muslim in this moment seeks Allah for some prayer (*dua*) then it is sure to be accepted.

4—The Prophet (SAW) has said that of all the days Friday is the best day. On this day recite *Darood Sharif* abundantly as the same will be presented to him on this day.

5—Allah has sworn by this day thus :

وَالسَّمَاءِ ذَاتِ الْبُرُوجِ ٥ وَالْيَوْمِ الْمَوْعُودِ ٥ وَ شَاهِدٍ وَ مَشْهُودٍ ٥ ط

This is in *Sura Burooj* and the Prophet (SAW) has said that the word "Shahid" means Friday and there is no other day more virtuous than it.

6—The Prophet (SAW) has said that Friday is the chief of all days and most honoured by Allah and its virtue is greater than even *Eid-ul-Fitr* and *Eid-ul-Adha*. (Ibne Maja).

7—The Holy Prophet (SAW) is reported to have said that if any Muslim dies on Friday or its night Allah will protect him from the punishment of grave (Tirmidhi).

8—Hadrat Ibn Abbas once recited the verse :

اَلْيَوْمَ اَكْمَلْتُ لَكُمْ دِيْنَكُمْ

This day I have completed your religion.

A Jew who was sitting with him at that time said that had such a verse been revealed to them, they would have celebrated that day as *Eid*. Hadrat Ibn Abbas replied that "the verse was revealed on two *Eids*— i.e.—it was Friday and Arafa and there was no need of any special celebration as those days were *Eid* in themselves."

9—The Holy Prophet (SAW) has said that Friday night is a refulgent night and its day is bright.

10—After the doomsday when Allah would have sent those to Paradise who deserves Paradise and those who deserve Hell to Hell, then there will be all the days (Fridays to Thursday) though there will be no day and night. But Allah would teach them to count these days. On Friday at that time when in the world Muslims used to go out to assemble for *Juma* prayer, a caller will call all the dwellers of Paradise to assemble in a jungle the length and breadth of which, no one but Allah knows. There will be sky high heaps of *Mushk*. All the Prophets shall be seated on thrones of *Noor* (light) and *Momins* (believers) on chairs of *Yaqut* (precious red stone). There on the request of all, Allah will appear before them.

11—The fire of Hell is stirred up every day at noon but not on Friday because of its virtue.

12—The Holy Prophet (SAW) once said on a Friday, that Allah has given the status of *Eid* to Friday and all Muslims should take a bath on this day and those who possess perfume should apply it to their bodies and cleaning teeth with *Miswak* should be made essential on this day.

## Respect and Reverence of Friday

1—Every Muslim should make preparations for *Juma* (Friday) from Thursday. After the prayer of *Asr* one should pray to seek forgiveness of Allah. He should arrange for clean clothes and perfume them. If there is no perfume in the house, it should also be brought on Thursday for use on Friday and no such preparation be left for Friday. Earlier Muslim saints and learned men have observed that one who had been waiting for Friday and remained preparing for it since Thursday, will get the greatest benefits of Friday. Most unfortunate is the person who does not know when Friday is and asks about it in the morning as to what day it was.

2—One should bathe properly on Friday and clean his body and hair of the head. Use of *Miswak* (tooth-stick) is also of great virtue on Friday.

3—On Friday one should wear the best clothes available to him, use perfume if possible and get his nails clipped.

4—One should go very early to the *Juma Masjid*, because the earlier one goes, the greater will be the reward for him. The Holy Prophet (SAW) has said that on Friday angels stand at the gates of mosque where *Juma* prayer is offered and note down the names of those who enter the mosque in serial order and they also get credit accordingly.

5—If one goes to offer *Juma* prayer on foot, then his every step is rewarded credit equal to one year's fasting.

6—On Friday in *Fajr* prayer the Holy Prophet (SAW) used to recite *Sura Alif Lam Mim Sajda* and *Sura Hal Ata'alal Insan* so occasionally these *Suras* be recited in the morning prayer. It is appreciable, but omit them some time so that people may not begin to treat them as obligatory.

7—In *Juma* prayer the Holy Prophet (SAW) used to recite *Sura Juma* and *Sura Munafiqeen* or *Sabbeh Isme Rabbe kal, A'la* and *Hal Atāka Hadithul Ghāshia*.

8—The recitation of *Sura Kahaf* on Friday either before or after the prayer has great credit. The Holy Prophet (SAW) has said whosoever recited this *Sura* on Friday, a light will appear for him from under the Divine Throne (*Arsh*) as high as the sky and this will serve him in the darkness on the Day of Judgment and all of his sins from the last Friday till this one will be forgiven. Scholars have commented that in this Tradition by sins is meant the minor sins only because major sins cannot be forgiven without repentance.

9—Reciting of *Darood Sharif* on Friday possesses great credit so it has been stressed in the Tradition to offer *Darood Sharif* abundantly on Fridays.

10—It is a pity that Muslims of to-day have greatly decreased the regard of Friday and they do not even know its importance and excellence. The blessed day which, once was a day of *Eid* for the Muslims and of which the Holy Prophet (SAW) was so proud, the day with which the earlier communities were not favoured, is being so much neglected by the Muslims that the great boon conferred by Allah in the shape of Friday is being wasted thanklessly and the consequences of which are before us.

## Importance of Friday Prayer

Friday prayer is totally obligatory as proved by the Holy Quran, a series of traditions and the consensus of the community (*Ummah*). It is one of the great tenets of Islam and its rejector is an apostate and who misses it without any legitimate cause is a transgressor.

**1—The Holy Quran says :**

يَا أَيُّهَا الَّذِينَ آمَنُوا إِذَا نُودِيَ لِلصَّلَاةِ مِنْ يَوْمِ الْجُمُعَةِ فَاسْعَوْا إِلَى ذِكْرِ اللَّهِ وَذَرُوا الْبَيْعَ ذَلِكُمْ خَيْرٌ لَكُمْ إِنْ كُنْتُمْ تَعْلَمُونَ ۞

"When the call for *Juma* prayer is made you should rush

for remembrance of Allah and give up all transactions, this is best for you if you know.

In this verse 'remembrance' of Allah means Friday prayer and its sermon and 'rushing' means to go with eagerness and full preparations.

2—The Holy Prophet (SAW) is reported to have said that one who bathes and cleans as far as possible, oils his hair, applies perfume to his clothes and then goes for Friday prayer on Friday and on entering the mosque does not sit by removing another from his place, offers as many *Nafl* prayers as destined to him and sits silently when the Imam delivers the sermon (*Khutba*), then all of his sins from the last Friday to the present one will be forgiven.

3—The Holy Prophet (SAW) has said that whosoever bathes on Friday and goes to the mosque early on foot and not in conveyance, listens to the *Khutba* does not talk loosely or nonsense, then for his each step he will get reward equal to one year's prayers and fasts.

4—Hadrat Ibn Umar and Abu Huraira have reported the Holy Prophet (SAW) as saying that people should avoid neglecting *Juma* prayers otherwise Allah will put a seal to their hearts and then they will fall into great negligence and indifference.

5—The Holy Prophet (SAW) is reported to have said that whosoever neglects three Friday prayers successively without a legitimate excuse, then Allah puts a seal to his heart and in another report it is said that Allah is disgusted with him.

6—Hadrat bin Shahab has reported the Holy Prophet (SAW) to have said that Friday prayer in congregation is obligatory for every Muslim except four i.e. (1) slave obtained according to *Shariah*, (2) Women, (3) minor child and (4) a patient.

7—Hadrat Ibn Umar reports that the Prophet (SAW) has said about those who neglected Friday prayers that he wished to appoint some one in his place to lead the prayer and himself go out to burn the houses of those who do not come to offer

Friday prayer. There is another report of the same type about neglecting the congregation which has already been mentioned.

8—Hadrat Ibn Abbas has reported the Holy Prophet (SAW) to have said that, whosoever avoids Friday prayer without a legitimate cause, his name is entered as on atheist in a book which is protected against change or alteration and that he will be even regarded as such unless he repents or the Most Mercifull (*Allah*) forgives him out of His Mercy. It does not mean that he actually has become an atheist but he is said to possess the qualities of an atheist and it is a sin to be so.

9—Hadrat Jabir has reported the Holy Prophet (SAW) to have said that whosoever believes in Allah and the Day of Judgement, he must offer Friday prayer except the sick, a traveller, woman, a child and a slave. If anyone at the time of *Juma* prayer engages himself in useless act or business, then Allah also ignores him. Allah is Independent and Praise Worthy—He neither cares for anyone's prayer nor is benefited by it. He is endowed with all the best qualities whether He is praised by any one or not.

10—It is reported by Hadrat Ibn Abbas that whosoever neglected successively several Friday prayers, in fact ignored Islam.

11—Once someone asked Hadrat Ibn Abbas that a man who did not attend the congregation of Friday has died, what would he (Hadrat Ibn Abbas) say about him. Ibn Abbas replied that he was in Hell. Then the same man continued to ask him the same question continuously for one month and every time the reply was the same. Thus traditions have clearly indicated that *Shariah* has greatly stressed the importance of Friday prayer and also very grave warnings have come for those who deliberately neglect it. In view of these, can anyone claiming to be Muslim still dare to neglect this *Fard* of Islam.

### Conditions for Juma Prayer to be Wajib

1—To be a resident. So *Juma* prayer is not essential for a traveller.

2—To be healthy and fit. Friday is not obligatory for a sick, blind and who has become so weak due to old age that he cannot walk to the mosque. The men suffering from these excuses shall be regarded as patients.

3—To be a free man. Friday prayer is not obligatory for a slave.

4—To be male. Hence *Juma* prayer is not obligatory on women.

5—To be free from the excuses on account of which to join congregation is excused as explained above. If any of these exist, *Juma* prayer will not be obligatory i e. (1) If it is raining heavily. (2) If one is attending a patient. (3) Risk of an enemy in going to mosque. (4) The condition for other prayers to be obligatory such as to be sane, mature and a Muslim.

If in the absence of these conditions anyone offers *Juma* prayer, then it will be proper as the obligation of *Zuhr* prayer shall be fulfilled.

### Conditions for Juma Prayer to be Correct

1—It should be a city or town. *Juma* prayer in a village or jungle is not proper. But it is permissible in a village having a population of three or four thousand.

2—The time should be a *Zuhr* prayer. So *Juma* prayer is not proper before or after *Zuhr* prayer time so much so that even if in the middle of *Juma* prayer or last sitting after *Attahiyat* the time of *Zuhr* comes to an end, then the *Juma* prayer will be spoiled and that is why there is no postponed Friday prayer.

3—The *Khutba* (Sermon) that is to praise Allah before the prayer, even if *Subhan Allah* or *Alhamdo Lillah* only is said. But only to say these words would be against *Sunna*.

4—The *Khutba* (Sermon) to be delivered before prayer. If delivered after the prayer, it will be spoiled.

5—*Khutba* to be delivered within the time of *Zuhr*. If it is before the *Zuhr* prayer, then the prayer will not be accomplished.

6—In the congregation there must be at least three persons

besides the Imam from the beginning of *Khutba* to the first *Sajda* of the first *Raka'at* though the three men in prayer are different from the three present at the time of *Khutba*. But the condition is that these three must be such who can lead the prayer. So if there are only women or minor children in the congregation, then the prayer will be spoiled.

7—If people leave the congregation before *Sajda* and less than three or none are left, then the prayer will be spoiled. But if they leave after offering first *Sajda*, then there will be no harm.

8—To offer *Juma* prayer openly and with public announcement. It is not permissible to offer *Juma* prayer secretly or at a hidden place. If *Juma* prayer is offered at such a place where commoners are not allowed to enter, or if the doors of mosque are closed, then the prayer will not be accomplished.

If *Juma* prayer is offered in the absence of the abovementioned conditions, it will not be accomplished and *Zuhr* prayer will be necessary and in the absence of these essentials the offering of *Juma* prayer is a prohibited execrability.

### Khutba (Sermon) of Juma and Juma Prayer

*Method of Prayer* : After the first *Adhan* of *Juma* prayer and before the second, four *Raka'ats* of *Sunna* prayer should be offered which are essential. Immediately after the *second Adhan* two sermons are delivered by the Imam. After the sermon two *Fard Raka'ats* of *Juma* are offered in congregation following the Imam. After *Fard* four *Raka'ats* of essential *Sunna* are offered and then two *Raka'ats* of *Sunna* which are also essential according to some and lastly two *Raka'ats* of *Nafl*.

When people have assembled in congregation in the mosque, the *Imam* should sit on the pulpit and the *Moadhan* (caller of *Adhan*) should call the *Adhan* after which the *Imam* should immediately stand up and deliver the *Khutba*. The following twelve items are *Sunna* in the *Khutba* :—

(a) The person who delivers the *Khutba* (sermon) should **remain standing while delivering the *Khutba*.**

(b) To deliver two *Khutbas*.

(c) To sit between the two *Khutbas* for such time in which *Subhanallah* may be recited three times.

(d) The *Khutba* deliverer should be clean from both the kinds of pollutions.

(e) To face the audience (congregation) while delivering the *Khutbas*.

(f) Before beginning the *Khutba* the deliverer should within himself say *Aoozobillah-e-Minash-Shaitanir-Rajeim*.

(g) The *Khutba* should be delivered in a loud voice so it be heard by the audience distinctly.

(h) The *Khutba* should consist of eight topics :—
(1) Thanks and gratitude to Allah. (2) Praise of Allah. (3) Oneness of Allah. (4) Affirmation of Holy Prophet (SAW) (5) *Darood Sharif* to the Holy Prophet (SAW) (6) Advice and admonition. (7) Recitation of a *Sura* or some verses of the Holy Quran. (8) To repeat all these in the second *Khutba* with the difference that instead of advice and admonition, there should be prayer (*dua*) for the Muslims.

(i) The *Khutba* should not be very long. It should take less time than the prayer.

(j) The *Khutba* should be delivered from the puplit and if there is no pulpit the support of a stick should be taken. Putting one hand over the other, as is usual these days, has not been mentioned in the Traditions.

(k) Both the sermons should be delivered in Arabic. To deliver *Khutba* in any other language or to add verses of any other language is against Traditions and is highly execrable.

(l) The listeners during the *Khutba* should face the Ka'aba. It is appreciable to pray in the second *Khutba* for the Progeny, Companions, the Consorts of the Holy Prophet (SAW) and particularly the four

Caliphs— (Hadrat Abu Bakr Siddique, Hadrat Umar, Hadrat Usman, Hadrat Ali) and Hadrat Hamza and Hadrat Abbas. Praise of the Muslim ruler is also permissible but to praise him with such words or to attribute such qualities to him which are not true, is execrable.

**Injunctions for Juma Sermon**

1—It is highly execrable to offer any prayer or talk when *Khutba* is being delivered. But offering of postponed prayer is allowed and essential.

2—When the *Khutba* has begun it is essential for all present to listen it whether they are sitting near the *Imam* or at some distance. It is highly execrable to do anything which obstructs the hearing of *Khutba*. To eat, drink, talk, walk, greet, respond to greeting, to recite any prayer or to explain any religious problem during *Khutba* are all prohibited. It is, however, permissible for the deliverer of the *Khutba* to explain some religious problem during the *Khutba*.

3—If the *Khutba* begins while one is offering *Sunna* or *Nafl* prayer, then the *Sunna* should be completed and the *Nafl* should be concluded after two *Raka'ats* only.

4—It is highly execrable for the *Imam* or the followers to pray with raised hands during the sitting of the *Imam* between the two *Khutbas* but praying within oneself is permissible provided no words are spoken neither loudly nor in a low voice. To recite items of farewell or separation in the *Khutba* of the last Friday of *Ramadan* is not reported from the Holy Prophet (SAW) or his Companions.

5—It is permissible to read the *Khutba* from a book.

6—It is permissible for the listeners to recite *Darood Sharif* within themselves on hearing the holy names of the Prophet (SAW) occurring in the *Khutba*.

**Injunctions for Juma Prayer**

1—It is preferable that one who delivers the *Khutba* should also lead the prayer, but it is also permissible if another one leads it.

2—It is *Sunna* to begin the prayer immediately after the *Khutba* by saying *Iqamat*. It is highly execrable to do any worldly business between the *Khutba* and the prayer. But it is not execrable if one feels the need of ablution and goes for it or reminded the need of bath after the sermon and goes for it. If the delay between the *Khutba* and the prayer is substantial, then the *Khutba* should be repeated. If the *Imam*, after delivering the *Khutba*, feels some such need as described above and goes for it, then repetition of the *Khutba* is not necessary.

3—The intent for *Juma* prayer is :—

نَوَيْتُ اَنْ اُصَلِّى رَكْعَتَىِ الْفَرْضِ صَلٰوةِ الْجُمْعَةِ

(*Navaito an ossalli raka'til-farde min salatil Jum'ate*)
"I intend to offer two *Raka'ats Fard* of *Juma* prayer."

4—It is preferable that all men of one area should assemble at one place (mosque) to offer *Juma* prayer though this prayer in several mosques of the area is also permissible.

5—If *masbuq* of *Juma* prayer joins its congregation in the sitting posture or after *Sajda-e-Sahav*, then his prayer will be proper and he should complete the remaining prayer of *Juma* and need not offer *Zuhr* prayer.

6—Some people after offering *Juma* prayer offer *Zuhr* prayer as a precaution. This practice has very much disrupted the belief of common people. It should be prohibited strictly. However if any learned man on account of some doubt offers *Zuhr* prayer, he may do so but he should not tell other about it.

# EID PRAYERS

بِسْمِنَا بَيِّدْ قَلْبَهُ يَحْفَظُنَا رَبَّنَا أَنْ تَسْبَي

### Eid-ul-Fitr and Eid-ul-Azha

1—The first day of the month of Shawwal is called *Eid-ul-Fitr* and the tenth day of the month of *Zilhijja* is called *Eid-ul-Azha*. These two days are of great rejoicings in Islam.

2—The requisites for accuracy and essentiality of *Juma* prayer, as described above, are also applicable to the prayers of both the *Eids*, except the *Khutba* which is obligatory and imperative in *Juma* prayer and is delivered before the prayer. But it is not obligatory in the prayers of *Eids*, but is *Sunna*, and is delivered after offering the prayer. The listening of the sermons of both the *Eids* is as essential as that of *Juma Khutba*, that is, talking, praying etc. during the *Khutba* is prohibited.

3—On *Eid-ul-Fitr* day thirteen things are *Sunna*:

(1) To adorn oneself as permitted by *Shariat*. (2) To take a bath. (3) To clean teeth with *miswak*. (4) To wear best clothes that one has. (5) To use perfume. (6) To rise very early in the morning. (7) To go to *Eidgah* very early. (8) To eat some sweet thing like dates before going to *Eidgah*, (9) To give away *Sadqa-e-Fitr* before going to *Eidgah*. (10) To offer *Eid* prayer in *Eidgah*, that is, not to offer it in the mosque of the locality without any legitimate excuse. (11) To go to *Eidgah* by one way and to come back by the other (12) To go on foot. (13) To recite on way to *Eidgah* slowly:

اَللهُ اَكْبَرُ اَللهُ اَكْبَرُ لاَ اِلٰهَ اِلَّا اللهُ وَاللهُ اَكْبَرُ

اَللهُ اَكْبَرُ وَ لِلّٰهِ الْحَمْدُ

(*Allaho-Akbar, Allaho Akbar, La ilaha-Illallaho-Wallaho-*

Akbar, Allaho-Akbar, Walillahilhamd).

**Method of Eid Prayer**

4—First intend in the following words:

نَوَيْتُ اَنْ اُصَلِّيَ رَكْعَتَىِ الْوَاجِبِ صَلٰوةَ عِيْدِ الْفِطْرِ

مَعَ سِتَّةَ تَكْبِيْرَاتٍ وَاجِبَةٍ

(Navaito-an-osalli rakatil wajibe salata Eid il fitre ma'a sitta Takbiratin wajibatin).

After intending one should fold hands in front in the prescribed manner and recite *Subhanakallahumma* till end and say *Allaho-Akbar* three times and each time raise both the hands upto the ears and drop them. After each *Takbir* there should be a pause in which *Subhanallah* may be recited three times. After the third *Takbir* the hands should not be dropped but folded in front and recite *A'oodhobillah*, *Bismillah*, *Sura Fateha* and some other *Sura* and then perform the *Ruku* and *Sajda* as usual. The recitation by the *Imam* should be done loudly. Thus one *Raka'at* is complete. In the second *Raka'at* after recitation of *Sura Fateha* and some other *Sura*, the three *Takbirs* are said in the first *Raka'at*. In all these three *Takbirs* hands are not to be folded but dropped after each *Takbir* and go in *Ruku* just after the fourth *Takbir*.

5—Two sermons (*Khutba*) are to be delivered by the *Imam* sitting on the pulpit after the prayer and sit between the two *Khutbas* for the same period as in *Juma* sermon.

6—In *Eid* prayers six extra *Takbirs* are essential.

7—To pray after *Eid* prayers has not been reported from the Holy Prophet or his companions or respected followers, but because to pray after prayer is *Sunna*, it would also be *Sunna* to pray after *Eid* prayers.

8—The *Khutbas* of both the *Eids* should be begun with *Takbir*. *Takbirs* should be called nine times in the first *Khutba* and seven times in the second *Khutba*.

## EID PRAYERS

9—The method of offering the prayer of *Eid-ul-Azha* is also the same with the difference that in its intent the words *Eid-ul-Azha* should be substituted for *Eid-ul-Fitr*. It is *Sunna* to eat something before going to *Eidgah* in *Eid-ul-Fitr* but not so in *Eid-ul-Azha*. In *Eid-ul-Fitr* the *Takbirs* are called in low tone, but in *Eid-ul-Azha* they are called loudly. It is *Sunna* to delay the prayer in *Eid-ul-Fitr*, but it should be expedited in *Eid-ul-Azha*. In *Eid-ul-Azha* no *Sadqa-e-Fitr* is given, but sacrifice for those who can afford and it is offered after the prayer. There is no *Adhan* or *Iqamat* in both.

10—At the place where *Eid* prayer has been offered, it is execrable to offer any other prayer at that place on the same day, whether before or after the prayer. It is permissible to offer any prayer after returning home, but before *Eid* prayer it is also execrable.

11—It is execrable for women and those who cannot participate in the *Eid* prayers due to some legitimate excuse, to offer *Nafl* or any other prayer before the *Eid* prayers.

12—In both the *Khutbas* of *Eid-ul-Fitr* the instructions and importance of *Sadqa-e-Fitr* and in the *Khutba* of *Eid-ul-Azha* of sacrifice and *Takbir Tashriq* should be described and explained, *Takbir Tashriq* is :

اَللهُ اَکْبَرُ اَللهُ اَکْبَرُ لَا اِلٰهَ اِلَّا اللهُ وَاللهُ اَکْبَرُ

اَللهُ اَکْبَرُ وَلِلّٰهِ الْحَمْدُ

(*Allah-o-Akbar, Allah-o-Akbar, La-ilaha-illallaha-wallah-o-Akbar, Allah-o-Akbar-walillahilhamd*)

*Takbir Tashriq* should essentially be recited after every *Fard* prayer, provided that is offered in congregation and in the city. This *Takbir* is not essential for women and those in journey. But if these are following in congregation someone for whom this *Takbir* is essential, then it will become essential for them also. It is better if the women and the traveller also recite it as according to the two *Imams* it is essential for all Muslims.

13—*Takbir Tashriq* should be recited from the *Fajr* prayer of *Arafa* i.e. 9th of *Zilhijja* upto the *Asr* prayer of the 13th *Zilhijja*. In all these are 23 prayers in which this *Takbir* should be recited aloud.

14—It is essential to recite *Takbir Tashriq* aloud, but women may recite it in a low tone.

15—The *Takbir* should be recited immediately after concluding the prayer.

16—If the *Imam* forgets to recite the *Takbir*, the followers should say it without waiting for the *Imam*.

17—According to some jurists it is also essential to recite the *Takbir* after the prayer of *Eid-ul-Azha*.

18—It is consensus that prayers of *Eid* are permissible in several mosques.

19—If anyone has missed the *Eid* prayer and the congregation has ended then he cannot offer it individually as congregation is essential for this prayer. In the same way if any one is in the congregation but his *Eid* prayer is disrupted due to some reason, then he cannot offer it as a postponed prayer even nor its postponed prayer is essential for him. But if there are several such persons then it becomes essential for them to offer it.

20—If on account of some reason *Eid* prayer could not be offered on first day, then *Eid-ul-Fitr* prayer can be offered the next day and *Eid-ul-Azha* prayer upto the 12th of *Zilhijja*.

21—The *Eid-ul-Azha* prayer may be delayed without any cause upto 12th of *Zilhijja* ; but it would be execrable if the prayer of *Eid-ul Fitr* is delayed without any cause and in such case it would not be offered at all. The legitimate causes may be :—The absence of the Imam ; It is raining heavily ; The date of moon is not confirmed or it was confirmed after midday etc.

22—If anyone joins the *Eid* congregation when the *Imam* has said his first three *Takbirs* and is still standing, then he should immediately join and say his three *Takbirs*. If the *Imam* has begun recitation or his bowing, then if this man has strong hope that he will join the *Imam* in *Ruku* he should say the three *Takbirs* after folding hands and then go to *Ruku* But if it is feared that he will not join the *Imam* in *Ruku* he should immediately go to *Ruku* and recite the *Takbirs* in *Ruku* instead of its phrases. He should not raise his hands with *Takbirs* while in *Ruku*. But if the *Imam* stands up from the *Ruku* he should also stand up with the *Imam* and the remaining *Takbirs* are remitted for him.

23—If anyone missed the first *Raka'at* of *Eid* congregation and he offers it, then he should say the three *Takbirs* after the recitation. If the *Imam* forgets to say the *Takbir* he should say them in *Ruku‘* and should not stand up. But if he stands up, it is not prohibited and the prayer will not be impaired. But no prostration of forgetfulness (*Sajda-e-Sahav*) should be offered by him due to the large congregation as it would be embarrassing for the followers.

# THE FAST
## (SAUM)

Great merit and credit has been ascribed to fasts in the Traditions and one who keeps fast is in great esteem to Allah. The Holy Prophet (SAW) has said that one who keeps fast in the month of *Ramadan* for the sake of Allah, all of his sins of the past are forgiven by Him and that the odour of the mouth of one who fasts is most appreciable to Allah than the smell of musk. Unlimited reward for fasting shall be given by Allah on the Day of Judgment. Tradition says that on the Day of Judgment a very long cloth shall be spread under the Seat (*Arsh*) of Allah for those who used to keep fasts in the world and they will eat thereon, while others will remain engaged in their statement of account. They will ask as to who are those persons eating there while they themselves are yet engaged in their account. They will be told that these people used to keep fasts. Fast is one of the tenets of Islam and one who will not keep fasts shall commit a sin and his *Deen* (Faith) will become weak.

1—Keeping of fasts is obligatory for every Muslim who is not insane or minor. It is not proper to give up fasts without legitimate cause. One who vows to fast then it becomes obligatory for him and keeping of missed or compensatory fasts is also obligatory.

2—Besides the abovementioned ones other fasts are *Nafl* and keeping them would be rewarded but it is not a sin not to keep them. But fasting on *Eid* days or three days after *Eid-ul-Azha* are prohibited.

3—According to *Shariah* to abstain from eating, drinking and sexual intercourse from the time of *Fajr* till sun-set with an

## THE FAST

intent, is called fast.

4—It is not essential to express the intent in words, but merely a resolve to keep a fast and not eat or drink anything or indulge in sexual intercourse for the whole day, completes a fast. It is better to say :

وَبِصَوْمِ غَدٍ نَوَيْتُ

"O Allah I will keep fast tomorrow for Thy sake."

5—If anyone did not eat or drink and remained thirsty and hungry throughout the whole day but did not resolve for a fast in the heart, then it will not be a fast. Had there been an intent, then it would have been a fast.

6—According to *Shariah* the time of fast begins from early dawn and upto that time eating, drinking etc. is allowed. Some persons take *Sehri* (eat something) in the later part of night and go to sleep and think that nothing should be eaten or drunk after the resolve or intent. This is not correct. They may eat or drink upto early dawn whether resolved or not.

### Instructions About Ramadan Fast

1—If intent was made in the previous night then the fast of Ramadan on the following morning would be in order. If it was not resolved in the night to keep fast nor in the morning had any intention but when the day had advanced it struck to him that not keeping an obligatory fast would be a sin and so resolved then, even then the fast is in order provided nothing was eaten or drunk.

2—If nothing has been eaten or drunk in the morning, then the intent made an hour before mid-day would be in order.

3—To keep the fast of the month of Ramadan only so much resolve is enough that one is fasting that day or if went to sleep in the previous night intending to keep fast next day, the fast would be in order. The fast would also be in order even if the idea that it was the fast of *Ramadan* or an obligatory fast was not in mind.

4—If during the *Ramadan* anyone intended that next day

he or she would keep a *Nafl* fast instead of an obligatory, even then it would be counted as *Ramadan* fast.

5—If anyone had omitted fast in the last *Ramadan* and could not observe it till the next *Ramadan* came and kept with the intent of omitted fast, even then it would be a *Ramadan* fast and not an omitted one. The omitted fast should be kept after the *Ramadan*.

6—One had vowed that if he succeeds in certain aim, he will keep fast for Allah and during the month of *Ramadan* resolved to keep the fast of vow and not of *Ramadan*, then it would be *Ramadan* fast and the fast of vow would remain due which should be observed after *Ramadan*. During the month of *Ramadan* whatever other kind of fast is resolved, it will always remain a fast of the *Ramadan*.

7—If the new moon is visible on 29th of *Sha'ban*, then fast should be observed next day. But if it is not visible on 29th then no fast should be kept next day as it is prohibited according to Traditions. Fasting should begin after completing the thirty days of *Sha'ban*.

8—If the moon was not visible on 29th of *Sha'ban* on account of clouds then even *Nafl* fast should not be kept next day. But if one is used to keep fast on certain fixed days and the next day happens to be the same day, then a fast with intent of *Nafl* fast may be observed and if during the day the visibility of moon confirmed from somewhere else, then this fast will become a *Ramadan* fast.

9—If the moon was not visible on 29th of *Sha'ban* due to clouds, then nothing should be eaten or drunk till an hour before mid-day and if the visibility of moon is confirmed from somewhere else, then the fast should be resolved. But if it is not confirmed then eating etc. is allowed.

10—If the new moon was not visible on the 29th of *Sha'ban* then it should not be taken that as there will be no *Ramadan* next day and a postponed fast may be kept or a fast of a vow be kept. To observe a postponed fast or a vow on that day is execrable. But if anyone keeps such a fast and the visibility of moon is confirmed, then the fast would be counted as *Ramadan* fast and the postponed or the fast of a vow should be kept after *Ramadan*. If the appearance of moon is not confirmed then fast will be as it was intended.

**Visibility of Moon**

1—If due to cloud or dust the moon of *Ramadan* was not visible but a reliable and pious man gave evidence of having seen the moon, then the visibility of moon is proved whether the person is a man or woman.

2—But if the moon of *Eid* is not visible due to cloud, then the evidence of one man, however pious or reliable he may be, will not be counted till two reliable and pious men or one pious man and two pious women give evidence of their having seen the moon. The evidence of four women even will not be counted.

3—Anyone who does not observe the religious code i.e. does not pray or keep fast and always tells a lie or is guilty of other sins against religious law, then his evidence should not be believed as reliable despite his swearing. Even if two or three such persons give evidence, it will not be counted or relied upon.

4—It is generally said that on the day which was fourth of *Rajab* (month) the first of *Ramadan* will fall on that day. This is not correct according to *Shariah*. No fast should be observed if there is no moon.

5—On visibility of new moon it is bad to say that it is very big or appears to be of the day before. It has been said in the Traditions that people would say so near the Dooms day. Nor the *dooj* of Hindus should be believed that the visibility of moon is certain as it is *dooj* that day. All these thoughts are irrelevant according to *Shariah*.

6. If the sky is quite clear, then the evidence of two or three men would not suffice either for *Ramadan* or *Eid* moon till the number of witnesses is large enough to establish that such large number of men could not have conspired and that they cannot tell a lie.

7—If it is rumoured in the entire population that the new moon has appeared and many persons have seen it, but in spite of all efforts not a single person could be found who had actually seen the moon, then such a rumour would not be relied or taken account of.

8—If a single person has seen the moon of *Ramadan* and none else, but he does not observe the religious laws, then upon his evidence others should not keep fast. But if this man has completed thirty fasts and the *Eid* moon is not visible, then he should observe the 31st fast also and celebrate *Eid* with others.

9—If only one man has seen the *Eid* moon and his evidence was not relied upon, then it is not proper for him to celebrate *Eid*. He should keep a fast next day and should not rely upon his own seeing of moon.

10—If the residents of a city have seen the new moon, it would be binding and a proof for the people of other city, whatever the distance between them may be — so if this moon was visible at one end of the West and its evidence reached through a reliable source to the other end of East will become obligatory for the people of East.

11—If upon the evidence of two reliable persons the visibility of new moon was established and people observed fast accordingly but after 30 days the *Eid* moon was not visible whether the sky was clear or not, fast should not be kept on 31st day and that day will be counted as the first day of *Shawwal*.

12—If the moon was seen at day time on the 30th, it will be regarded as that of coming night and not of last night and that day will not be counted as that of the next month, whether the moon was seen before mid-day or after that.

13—If any one sees the moon of *Ramadan* or *Eid* and due to some reasons his evidence is not relied upon, then it is essential for him to keep fasts of both the days i e. if he saw the moon of *Ramadan*, then next day he should keep a fast and in the same way if it was *Eid* moon he should keep a fast next day.

## Breaches of Fast

14—If anyone ate something in forgetfulness or indulged in sexual intercourse and thinking that his fast is disrupted ate deliberately then his fast is disrupted and only compensatory fast and not recompensation will be due. But if one knows the rule and after eating something in forgetfulness deliberately breaks his fast, then in case of sexual intercourse recompensation will be due and a compensatory fast in case of eating only.

15—If any one vomits without intention or has a wet dream or is discharged on seeing a woman and due to ignorance of law presumes that his fast is broken and eats something deliberately then only compensatory fast will be due and not recompensation. But if one knows the law that fast is not disrupted by an involuntary act and still breaks his fast, then recompensation will also be due.

16—If a man inserts something in his penis and as it does not reach the root, then the fast will not be disrupted.

17—If any one committed sexual intercourse with a dead woman or with a minor girl who does not excite passion or with an animal or embraced or kissed anyone or masterbated and in all these instances semen came out, the fast will be disrupted but recompensation will not be due.

18—If any one committed inter-course with a woman forcibly or in madness or when she was asleep, then her fast is disrupted and no recompensation is due, while on the man recompensation is also due.

19—If any person who is liable to fast in all respects after resolving to fast in the morning, deliberately puts something in his mouth which is used as food or medicine and it goes to the stomach even if it is equal to a linseed or commits or agrees to be subjected to intercourse or commits sodomy, then in all such cases both compensatory fast and recompensation are due. In sexual intercourse entering of the top of the penis is sufficient, coming out of semen is not essential.

20—If anyone oils his hair or uses *Kuhl* in eyes or a man inserts something dry in his excretion hole and its end remains out, then because these things do not reach the stomach the fast will not be disrupted and neither compensatory fast nor recompense will be due.

21—Those who smoke *Huqqa* habitually or for some benefit during a fast, then compensatory fast and recompensation both will be due.

22—If a woman subjects herself to sexual inter course with a minor or an insane, then compensatory fast and recompensation both will be due on her.

23—In sexual inter course it is not necessary that man and woman both should be sane. If one of them is sane and the other insane, then compensatory fast and recompensation both will be due on the sane person.

24—Fast will not be disrupted due to a wet dream and if the fast is kept without bathing. In the same way it will not be disrupted if semen came out on seeing the private part of a woman or just by thinking.

25—Fast is not disrupted if a man enters some oil or water with a syringe or otherwise in his penis though it may reach the bladder.

26—No harm occurs in a fast if one cleans the teeth with a wet or dry *Miswak* (tooth-stick).

27—It is execrable to embrace or kiss a woman if there is apprehension of discharge of semen or may commit sexual inter course under force of passions. If there is no such apprehension then it is not execrable.

28—It is execrable to suck the lips of a woman or to bring together the private organs in a naked state without indulging in sexual inter-course whether there is an apprehension of semen discharge or not.

29—If a resident person starts on a journey after resolving to fast and after a while comes back to home to take something left behind and breaks his fast there, then recompensation will be due on him as at that time he was not in journey although he did not go back to stay or did stay.

30—If recompensation was due for any cause other than sexual inter course and while one recompensation was not discharged when another became due, then one recompensation would be enough for both though they be of two different *Ramadan*. But in case of disruptions of fasts due to sexual inter-course then if they are of one *Ramadan* only one recompensation will be enough, but if they relate to two different *Ramadan*, then recompensation for each would be essential even if the first recompensation has not been met.

**Missed Fasts**

1—If some fasts have been missed for some reasons, they should be kept after the *Ramadan* as soon as possible otherwise it would be a sin to delay them without any legitimate cause.

2—While intending for missed fast it is not necessary to specify the day and date of missed fasts, but only as many fasts should be observed as have been missed. But if fasts of two *Ramadan* have been missed, then it should have been missed, then it should be specified of which *Ramadan* it is the missed fast and should intend that the missed fast of that year is being kept.

3—It is essential to resolve for a missed fast in the previous night. If it is not resolved till morning then the fast would be a *Nafl* fast and the missed fast will remain due and should be observed.

4—The above rule applies to a compensatory fast also that is unless it is resolved from the last night it will not be accomplished.

5—All the missed fasts may be kept in continuation or in instalments—both ways are correct.

6—If the missed fasts of one *Ramadan* were not kept yet and the next *Ramadan* came, then the fasts of this *Ramadan* should be observed and the missed fasts of the previous *Ramadan* should be observed after *Eid*. But it is bad to delay them so long.

7—If during *Ramadan* anyone became unconscious in the day and remained so for three days, then only two missed fasts should be observed and the fast of the first day is not necessary as that day's fast has been accomplished because of the resolve. But if he was not fasting that day or some medicine was given to him which went down the throat, then the fast of that day will also become due.

8—If one became unconscious at night, then fast of the day is not missed but only the fasts of the days on which he remained unconscious thereafter will be due. But if it was intended to fast that day or some medicine has been taken, then the fast of that day, too, will become due.

9—If one remained unconscious throughout the whole of *Ramadan*, then all the missed fasts should be kept and it should not be presumed that these fasts have been remitted. But if anyone became insane and remained so during the whole month of *Ramadan* then no compensatory fast will be due and if he regained sanity on any day during *Ramadan*. Then he should begin to keep fast from that day and should also offer the missed fasts later on.

**Vowed Fasts**

1—If anyone vows to keep a fast, then it is essential for him to observe it and non-observance would be a sin.

2—The vow is of two kinds—one is specification of day and date as to say that if Allah accomplishes his desire today then he will keep a fast tomorrow. Or to say that if his business is accomplished by Allah he will keep a fast on the day after or on Friday. In such a vow if the resolve of the fast is made in the previous night or on the very day one hour before mid-day, then it would be proper in both the cases.

3—If one vowed to keep a fast on Friday and on Friday he only resolved to keep fast without specification whether it is the fast of the vow or a *Nafl* fast, even then the obligation of the vow would be discharged. But if on that Friday he resolved to keep a compensatory missed fast and forgot the vowed fast or deliberately resolved for a missed fast, then the fast of the vow would remain due and only the compensatory missed would be observed.

4—The other kind of vow is that no day or date is specified and only vowed that if such and such business is accomplished by Allah, he will fast for one day or did not name any business and only resolved to keep five fasts, then in such vow making of resolve in the previous night, is essential. If resolved in the morning then it would be treated as a *Nafl* fast and the fast of the vow would remain due.

### Nafl Fasts.

1—In an intent for a *Nafl* fast whether it is specified as a *Nafl* fast or merely a fast, then the intent would be in order in either case.

2—To resolve for a *Nafl* fast till one hour before mid-day is in order. If there was no intent to keep a fast till 10 a.m, and up to that time nothing was eaten or drunk and now resolved to keep a fast and kept it, then the fast is in order.

3—Other than the month of *Ramzan* any number of *Nafl* fast may be kept on other days. They will be rewarded according to their number. Fasting on *Eid* day and the tenth, eleventh twelfth and thirteenth of *Zilhijja*, i.e. five days in the whole year, is prohibited.

4—If anyone vows to keep a fast on Eid day even then the fast of that day is not proper and it should be kept on some other day.

5—If any one vowed to keep fasts for the whole year and that he would not leave any day, even then the fast should not be kept on the five prohibited days and compensatory fasts for these five days should be kept.

6—A *Nafl* fast becomes essential after resolve. If one resolved in the morning to keep a *Nafl* fast on that day but broke it later, than compensatory fast is neeessary for him.

7–If one resolved in the night to keep a fast next day but before morning changed his mind and did not observe a fast, the compensatory fast is not essential.

8—A wife should not keep a Nafl fast without the permission of her husband. If she has kept a fast, then she should break it if the husband asks her to do so and she may fast later when the husband allows her.

9—If any one went as a guest somewhere or was invited to dinner and there is apprehension that if he would not dine, the host would be displeased, then *Nafl* fast may be broken. In the same way, for the sake of a guest, the host and other members of his family may break their fast.

10—If any one resolved and kept *Nafl* fast on Eid day even then he should break it and no compensatory fast would be due.

11—It is highly appreciable to keep a fast on the tenth of **Muharram**. It has been reported in the Traditions that one who keeps a fast on this day, his sins of last year are forgiven.

12—The fast on 9th of *Zilhijja* has great merit and on account of it the sins of past one year and future year are forgiven. It is appreciable if the fasts are kept from the 1st to tenth of *Zilhijja*.

13—To keep fast on the 15th of *Sha'ban* and the six *Nafl* fasts after *Eid* have great merit.

14—If any one fasts on the 13th 14th & 15th of each month, it would be as if he has kept the fasts for the whole year. The Holy Prophet (SAW) used to keep these fasts and also on every Monday and Thursday, it is of great merit if anyone has the courage to keep these fasts.

**When A Compensatory or Recompensatory Fast Becomes Due.**

1—If any one, keeping a fast, eats or drinks in forgetfulness or commits sexual intercourse, then the fast is not breached even if it is full meal.

2—If any one is found eating or drinking in forgetfulness, then if such a person is strong enough to bear the fast he may be reminded about the fast. But if he is weak and unable to bear the fast, he may not be reminded and allowed to eat.

3—One slept during the day and had a dream which necessitated a bath, the fast is not broken.

4—The use of *kuhl* (Surma) in the eyes or oiling of hair and smeling of perfume is permissible in a fast and no harm is done to it. Even if the colour of *kuhl* is found in the saliva or in the nose, it is not execrable and also does not breach the fast.

5—Coherence of husband and wife and kissing in a fast is permissible and in order. But if it may excite passions and they may indulge in intercourse, then it is execrable.

6—If a fly or smoke or dust enters the throat without any intention, then the fast is not broken. But if it is done deliberately then the fast is lost.

7—If anyone burnt an incense near him and smelt it then the fast is lost in the same way the fast is broken by smoking Huqqa, cigarette or tobacco. It is permissible to smell perfumes of rose etc. in which there is no smoke.

8—If a bit of flesh or betel nut or anything else was sticking in the teeth and was removed with a tooth-pick and swallowed without taking it out or went of its own in the throat, then if it was less than a gram the fast is not lost, but if it was equal to or larger than a gram then the fast is breached. But if the article is taken out of the mouth and then swallowed the fast is broken whether it was equal to or less than a gram.

9—The fast is not broken by swallowing any quantity of one's own saliva.

10—After chewing betel leaf if the mouth has been properly cleaned and gargled but the redness of the saliva was not removed, then there is no harm and the fast is not broken.

11—If bath became essential in the night but did not bathe or bathed in the day, then the fast is complete. Even if one did not bathe in the day, the fast is not lost but it is a sin in its own place.

12—If anyone sucked the nose or water of the mouth and it went into the throat, the fast is not lost.

13—Anyone slept in the night with a betel-leaf in his mouth and got up in the morning, then the fast is lost. A compensatory fast only is due and no recompensation.

14—While gargling water entered the throat of anyone having knowledge of the fast, then it is lost. A compensatory fast only is due and no recompensation.

15—If anyone vomitted involuntarily, then the fast is not lost whether it be small or large in quantity. But if one vomitted intentionally and it was mouthful then the fast is lost and it was less than mouthful then the fast is not lost.

16—If a bit vomit came and returned to the throat of its own, then the fast is not lost. But it will be lost if returned intentionally by the person.

17—If anyone swallowed a pebble or a piece of iron or any such thing which is not usually eaten or used as a medicine, then the fast is broken but no recompense is essential. But if any such thing is swallowed which is used as food, drink or medicine, the fast is broken and both compensatory fast and recompense is due.

18—Sexual intercourse disrupts the fast and both compensatory fast and recompense become due. The fast is broken when the top of the penis enters the vagina whether semen is discharged or not.

19—If a man enters his penis in back part (hole) and its top has entered, then fast of both is lost and compensatory fast and recompense becomes due on both.

20—Recompense is due only on breaking the obligatory fast of the month of Ramazan and not of any other fast in whatever way it may be broken even if it is compensatory fast of Ramazan if it was not intended in the previous night

21—If anyone put some smelling powder in his nose or oil in the ear or used something in the back hole to facilitate motion though did not drink any medicine, then the fast is lost. But only compensatory fast and no recompense is due. The fast is not lost by pouring water in the ear.

22 – It is not proper for women to put any medicine or oil in their private part. It disrupts their fast and if done, only compensatory fast is due and no recompense. Men can use medicine or oil in their penis.

23—If the mid-wife put the finger in the vagina or the woman herself did it and after taking out the entire or part of the finger inserted it again, then the fast is broken, but no recompense will be due. The fast will not be disrupted if the finger was not put again after taking it out. But if the finger is already wet with water or any thing else then the fast will be disrupted at its first entry.

24—If the blood coming out of mouth is swallowed with the saliva, then the fast is broken. But if the quantity of blood is less than the saliva and its taste is not felt in the throat, then the fast is not broken.

25—The fast is not breached if anyone spat out anything just after tasting it but it is execrable to do so. But it is permissible for a woman whose husband is short-tempered and there is apprehension that if the salt etc. are not proper in the food he is likely to be angry. It is not execrable for her to do so.

26—It is execrable to crush anything in mouth to feed a baby. But if it is necessary and unavoidable then it is not execrable.

27—To clean the mouth by crushing coal with teeth or with tooth-powder is execrable and if any portion of it goes to the throat, the fast is broken. But it is permissible to clean the mouth with a Miswak (tooth-stick) whether it is dry or fresh. It the Miswak is of Neem (margo) and its bitterness is also felt in the mouth, even then it is not execrable.

28—If a woman was sleeping soundly or was unconscious and someone has had intercourse with her, then her fast is broken and only a compensatory fast is due but for the man both compensatory fast and recompense is due.

29—If anyone ate something in forgetfulness and thought that the fast is broken and then ate deliberately then the fast is lost and only compensatory fast is due and no recompense.

30—If anyone vomitted and thinking that the fast is broken and then ate deliberately, then the fast is lost and only compensatory fast is due.

31—If nayone used kuhl or oil or got himself bleeded and presumed that the fast is broken and then ate deliberately, then both compensatory and recompense become due.

32—If during the Ramazan anyone's fast is broken accidentally, it is not proper to eat or drink anything for the rest of the day. He should behave as those who are fasting.

33—If anyone did not resolve to fast in Ramazan and continued to eat and drink, then no recompense will be due. It is due only on breaking a fast without a legitimate cause after making a resolve.

### About Sehri and Iftar

*(Eating something before dawn and breaking of fast)*

1—Taking of *Sehri* is *Sunna*. If one is not hungry and has no desire to eat, then two or three dates or some other light food may be taken or some water at least should be drunk.

2—If anyone woke up and did not eat anything as *Sehri* but only chewed a betel-leaf, then he will get the credit of *Sehri*.

3—As far as possible the taking of *Sehri* should be delayed but not so much that the dawn may appear and put the fast in doubt.

4—If *Sehri* is taken early but continued to take tea etc. for long and gargled near dawn, then the credit of delayed *Sehri* is gained.

5—If anyone did not wake up for *Sehri* and all remained asleep, then fast should be observed without it. It is a sin and also cowardice not to keep a fast because of not eating *Sehri*.

6—It is permissible to take *Sehri* till *Fajr* time and not after that. Time of *Fajr* and dawn have already been described in the chapter of Timings of *Namaz*.

7—If any one woke up late for *Sehri* and under the impression that it was still night took *Sehri* but it revealed later that it was after dawn, then the fast was not accomplished and it should be kept as a missed fast but recompense is not due. But even then nothing should be eaten or drunk and one should behave like fasting ones. In the same way if fast is broken thinking that the sun had set but the sun appeared after a while, then the fast is breached and should be kept as a postponed fast but no recompense is due, and it is also not proper now to eat or drink till the sun has actually set.

8—If the waking up was so much delayed that it was suspected to be dawn, then to eat or drink anything now is execrable and it would be a sin to do so. If after eating something it was confirmed that it was dawn, then a missed fast should be kept and if it is still doubt then a postponed fast is not essential. But as a precaution a postponed fast may be kept.

9—It is appreciable to break the fast as soon as the sun has definitely set. To delay after that is execrable.

10- On cloudy days the fast should be broken with some delay till it is definite that the sun would have set. The watches or clocks should not be relied upon as they may go wrong. Even if someone has called the *Adhan* and the setting of sun is doubtful, fast should not be opened till you are yourself satisfied about the time.

11—It is appreciable to break the fast with dates or with some other sweet thing, but if any of these is not available, then with water. Some men and women open fast with a bit of salt and think it is to be creditable. It is a wrong belief.

**Recompensation of Fast** : *Kaffara*

1—The compensation (*Kaffara*) of breaking a fast of Ramazan is to fast continuously for two months—keeping in instalments is not proper. If due to some reason a fast is missed in the middle then it should be started again for full two months. But if a woman's fasts are missed during the recompense period due to menses, then recompense will not be affected by it and after being clean she should start again to complete sixty fasts in all.

2—If some fasts of a woman during this period were missed due to after-birth discharge and could not keep the sixty fasts then the recompense is disturbed and she should fast again for full two months.

3—If same fasts of recompense were missed due to some illness, even then one should begin again after recovery and keep fast for sixty days.

4—If the month of Ramazan came during the period of recompense, even then it would be disturbed.

5—If anyone is weak and does not possess the strength to keep sixty fasts at a stretch, then he should feed sixty poor persons morning and evening to their full satisfaction i.e. as much as they can eat.

6—If there are small children among those sixty people it is not proper. Others should be fed instead of them to make up the number.

7—If the food consists of wheat bread, then mere bread can be given, but if it is of barley, millet etc. then some curry should also be given with it.

8—Instead of feeding, it is also permissible to give grain to the poor but its quantity for each person should be equal to *Sadqa-e-Fitr* which will be described in the chapter of *Zakat*.

9—It is also permissible to give the price of so much of grain.

10—If anyone asked someone else to give recompense on his behalf and that person fed the poor or gave them grain, then the recompense will be discharged. But it will not be met if it is given by someone else without his instruction.

11—If one poor was fed for sixty days morning and evening or grain or its price was given to him for sixty days, then the recompensation is discharged.

12—If the poor were not fed continuously for sixty days and some days were missed in between, then there is no harm and it is in order.

13—Giving of sixty days' grain to poor man at a time, is not proper and in order. In the same way if one poor is given sixty meals the same day, it would not be in order and proper and same is the case of price of grain—it will be counted as one and fifty nine poors should be fed or paid again. It is not proper to give more than one day's meal, grain or price to one poor.

14—If any poor man is given less than the *Sadqa-e-Fitr*,

# THE FAST

then the compensation will not be wet.

15—If more than one fast have been missed of the same Ramazan, then one recompensation is enough for all, but if they relate to two different Ramazan, then recompensation for each Ramazan should be given separately.

## When breaking of fast is permissible

1—If anyone fell so ill suddenly that the fast may endanger his life or will aggravate the illness, then it is permissible for him to break the fast on this excuse. Or such as there was severe pain in the stomach or was bitten by a snake, then it is permissible to take medicine and break the fast. In the same way if the thirst became so severe that life is endangered, then breaking of fast is permissible.

2—If any such thing happens to a pregnant woman that her life or that of the child is in danger, then she may break the fast.

3—If on account of cooking food thirst became so severe and unbearable that one's life was in danger, then it is permissible for such a person to break the fast. But if the person was himself responsible to bring about such condition by working excessives deliberately, then it would be a sin.

## Conditions for not keeping fast

1—If any one is so ill that fasting will be injurious or there is fear of aggravation or it may prolong, then such a person may not keep fast and should offer compensatory fast after recovery. But it is not proper to give up fasting merely upon one's own guess unless some pious Muslim Hakim or Doctor advises.

2—If the Hakim or Doctor is a non-believer or does not follow the religious code, his advice should not be trusted and fast should not be given up.

3—If on personal experience some symptoms convince one that fasting will be harmful, then such a person may give up fast. But if one has no personal experience and is not aware of the condition of the illness, then fast should not be given up on own guess. If not on the advice of a pious Hakim but on ones own experience a fast is given up, then recompensation shall have to be given and it will be a sin to give up the fast.

4—A person has recovered from illness but is still weak and it is feared that the illness will revive if he fasts, then it is allowed for him not to keep it.

5—If any one is in journey, then it is permissible for him not to keep a fast and keep compensatory fast after returning from the journey. Traveller has already been discussed. The same rules apply here.

6—If there is no inconvenience in fasting during a journey. For instance he is travelling by train and hopes to reach home by the evening or has every thing of comfort, then it is better to keep a fast in the journey and if no fast is kept then there is no sin. A missed fast should be observed. In case fasting in a journey causes discomfort of inconvenience, then it is better not to keep a fast.

7—If any one did not recover from illness but died in it or died while in journey, then for the period that he did not fast in illness or journey, then he will not be held responsible for those on the Day of Judgement as he did not have time to keep the missed fasts.

8—If any one missed ten fasts in illness and then was well for five days but did not keep missed fasts in this period, he will be held responsible for these five fasts which he did not keep and the rest fasts will be remitted by Allah. But if he was well for full ten days and did not keep the ten missed fasts, then he will be held responsible for ten days. So it is essential for such a person, if he has the means, to make a will before dying for recompensation (*Fidya*) to be given for the days he is likely to be held responsible.

9—The same rule applies to the fasts missed in a journey. A Will should be made for recompensation of the missed fasts.

10—If any one in a journey stays at a place with the intention of staying for fifteen days, then he should not give up fast as according to *Shara'* now he will not be treated as a traveller. But if the intention is to stay for less than fifteen days, then it is permissible not to keep fast.

11—A pregnant woman or one with a suckling baby may not fast for the fear of her own-self or of the baby and should keep the missed fast later. But if her husband has the means he may engage a wet nurse and relieve the wife and then it would not be permissible for the wife to give up fasts. But if the child is of such nature that it will not take milk from anyone else except the mother then it is permissible for her to give up fast.

12—If a wet-nurse took employment for a suckling baby and Ramazan came and the child's life will be at risk if she fasts, then nurse may also not keep fast.

13—If during Ramazan a woman has monthly course or gave birth to a child, then for period of menses and after birth discharge she may not keep fasts.

14—If a woman was relieved of the discharge at night then she should fast next morning. If she did not bathe in the night even then she should keep a fast and bathe in the morning. But if she relieved in the morning then she should not fast that day but it is not proper for her now to eat or drink but should remain like the fasting ones.

15—If any one accepts Islam during day or attained maturity in the day then it is not permissible for such person to eat or drink for rest of the day. But he did eat, then compensatory fast for such person is not essential.

16—Being in journey one had no intention of keeping a fast, but reached home an hour, before mid-day or stayed some where with an intention of staying for fifteen days and nothing was eaten or drunk upto this time, then he should now resolve for a fast.

17—It is not proper to give up the Ramazan fast without any legitimate cause, it is a major sin. It should not be thought, he will keep a postponed fast for each missed fast as it has been described in the Tradition that even if fast is kept one whole year for one missed fast even then it cannot be equal to the reward of one fast of Ramazan.

18—If one has the misfortune of not keeping a fast then he should not eat or drink in presence of others and should neither declare that he is not fasting as publicising a sin is also a sin and if declared it would be a double sin—one of not keeping a fast, and the other of publishing it. One who is not keeping a fast due to some reason, he too, should not declare it before others.

19—When boys and girls are capable of keeping fast they should be made to keep fast and should be compelled to keep fast when they attain the age of ten years. If fast of one month are not possible for them to keep then as many as possible should be kept by them.

20—If a minor boy or girl breaks a resolved fast then he or she should not be forced to observe a postponed fast but if prayer is disrupted after making intent, then they should be made to repeat it.

### Recompensation in Cash or Kind (*Fidiya*)

1—If one is too old and has no strength to fast, or is so ill that there is no hope of recovery or has not the strength to fast, then he may not fast and for each fast he may give *Fidiya* (recompensation) equal to *Sadqa-e-Fitr* to the poor or feed sufficiently in the morning and evening. This is called *Fidiya* in *Shara'*. Price of grain may also be given.

2—It is also permissible to distribute the grain of *Fidiya* to several poor.

3—If the ailing person who has already given *Fidiya*, recovers from his illness or gains enough strength, he shall have to keep all the missed fasts and the recompensation already given shall have its own reward.

4—If several missed fasts were due to some one and he made a will before death that recompensation be given for his missed fasts, then his heirs should give the *Fidiya* out of his property and it is essential. If after meeting the funeral expenses and discharge of debts so much property is left that one-third of it may be given as *Fidiya*, then it should be given.

5—If one has not willed but his heir gave the *Fidiya*, out of his property, then also it should be hoped that Allah may accept it and may not hold the deceased responsible for the missed fasts. Without one's Will it is not permissible to give recompensation *Fidiya* out of the property of the deceased. If the recompensation exceeds one-third of the whole property even then it is not allowed to give more than 1/3 in recompensation without the consent of all the heirs. The consent of a minor heir has no value according to *Shara'*. After separating the share of minor, it is permissible for the major heirs to give willingly.

6—If any who has missed prayers dies with a Will that recompensation be given for the missed prayers, then the rule described at No. 5 above shall apply.

7—The recompensation for each time of prayer is the same as for one fast. So the *Fidiya* of one day's five due prayers and one witr prayer i.e. six prayers is equal to 10 Kg of wheat.

8—If *Zakat* is due and has not been paid, then he should make a Will and it is essential for heirs to pay it. But if it is not willed and the heirs paid it of their own free will, then *Zakat* has not been settled and it shall remain due to the deceased.

9—It is not proper for the heir to offer missed prayers or to keep missed fasts on behalf of a deceased as these shall remain due on the deceased.

### Aitikaf or Seclusion.

*Definition* : To retire to mosque from a little before sun-set on the 20th Ramazan upto the sun-set of 29th or 30th i.e. till the appearance of new moon is called *Aitikaf*. It has great merit. Women, if desirous of sitting in *Aitikaf*, may retire to the place in the house which is fixed for usual offering of prayers. If one sits in *Aitikaf*, then save for calls of nature or meals, he should not move from that place. If there is some one to bring meals, then, too, one should not move from there for the meals. He should remain there for all the time and should sleep there. It is better not to sit idle but should continue to recite the Holy Quran or offer *Nafl* prayers or remain engaged in other prayers. For a woman it is essential to give up *Aitikaf* in case of menses or after-birth discharge and it is also not permissible to embrace the husband or indulge in sexual intercourse during *Aitikaf*.

1—Three things are essential in *Aitlkaf* :

(1) To retire to a mosque (for men) in which congregational prayers are held.

(2) To resolve for *Aitikaf* as it will not be an *Aitikaf* if one retires to a mosque without an intent, since for the intent to be in order it is essential that the person should be a Muslim and sane. Therefore the condition of being a sane Muslim also comes under resolve.

(3) For a woman to be free from menses and afterbirth discharge and not be in need of bath.

2—The best of all *Aitikaf* is one which is observed in Ka'aba and the next best is in the mosque of the Holy Prophet (peace be upon him) at Medina and then at Jerusalem and in Juma Masjid where congregational prayers are held daily and then the mosque of the locality in which congregational prayers are held mostly.

3—There are three kinds of *Aitikaf*—(1) Essential (2) *Mo'akkeda* (Emphasised) and (3) *Mustahab* (appreciable).

*Essential Aitikaf*—Is one which is vowed, whether conditional or unconditional, as one vows that he will perform *Aitikaf* if certain wish or business is accomplished.

*Mo'akkedaAitikaf* (Emphasised) is of the last ten days of Ramazan. Authentic Traditions say the Holy Prophet (SAW) regularly performed *Aitikaf*. But this *Mo'akkeda* is accomplished for all if some persons perform it.

*Mustahab (Apperciable) Aitikaf* is of some time, other than the last ten days of Ramazan, it may be the first or second ten days of Ramazan or any other month.

4—For Essential (*wajib*) *Atikaf* fast is necessary. If any one sits for *Aitikaf* he shall have to keep fast. If one resolves not to fast even then fast is essential for him. Therefore if any one intends for *Aitkaf* at night, it would be useless because night is no time of fasting. But if he resolves for *Aitikaf* for several days or day and night, then night will be included in it and it will be necessary to remain in *Aitikaf* for night also. It is not necessary to intend fast for *Aitikaf* as fasting for any purpose is enough for *Aitikaf*. For instance if any one intends to sit for *Aitikaf* in Ramazan, then the fast of Ramazan, will be enough for the *Aitikaf*. But it is necessary that fast should be an essential fast as *Nafl* fast is not enough for this *Aitikaf*. For example if any one resolves for a *Nafl* fast and then sits in *Aitikaf* the same day, then it will not be in order.

If any one vowed to sit in *Aitikaf* for the whole month of Ramazan and due to some reason could not do so in Ramazan, then he may do it in any other month and his vow would be accomplished but continuous fasting and sitting is essential.

5—In the *Sunna Aitikaf* the fast is already there, hence its condition is not necessary.

6—In *Mustahab* (appreciable) *Aitikaf* as a precaution fast is a condition but condition is not trustable.

7—*The Essential Aitikaf* can be at least for one day and more for as many days as resolved.

The *Sunna* (*Mo'akkeda*) *Aitikaf* is for ten days i.e. the last ten days of Ramazan.

For *Mustahab* (appreciable) *Aitikaf* there is no time limit. It may be for one minute or even less.

8—Two actions are prohibited during *Aitikaf* and committing them would vitiate the *Sunna* (*Mo'akkeda*) and essential. *Aitikaf* and should be observed again. If it is a *Mustahab Aitikaf* it will be disrupted and would end. The first is to go out of the place of *Aitikaf* without necessity. The necessity may be natural or religious. Natural necessity to make water or ease oneself or to go for the essential bath. Food is also a necessity if there is no one to bring it and religious need is such as to go for Friday prayer.

9—If anyone in *Aitikaf* goes out of his mosque due to some necessity, then he should not stay after the need is fulfilled and as far as possible he should try to meet the need at a place nearest to the mosque. If he goes to a mosque for Friday prayer and stays there to complete the *Aitikaf*, though permissible, but is execrable.

10—To leave the *Aitikaf* mosque for a minute even in forgetfulness, is not permissible.

11 - It is against the spirit of *Aitikaf* to leave its place for such needs which are not of frequent occurrence. For example it is not sinful but essential to go to save life, to visit a patient or to save a drowning man or to go out of the mosque for fear of its falling down, but in such cases the *Aitikaf* shall no longer remain. There is however, no harm if one goes out for any natural or religious need and either before or after the fulfilment of the need visits a patient or joins a funeral prayer.

12—One sitting in *Aitikaf* should go out for Friday prayers with such provision of time so that he may be able to offer prayer *Tahiyatul-Masjid* (greeting to mosque) and the *Sunna* prayer of Friday and it is also permissible for him to stay after Friday prayer to offer *Sunna* prayer. The determination of the time that it will take is left to the discretion of the person. There is no harm if he reaches a bit earlier due to wrong estimate.

13— If a person in *Aitikaf* is forced out of the place of *Aitikaf*, then *Aitikaf* will be disturbed. For instance one is implicated in some crime and warrant is issued against him and he is arrested by the police and taken out of the *Aitikaf* place or he is indebted to someone and he pulls him out.

14—Also if one goes out on account of any natural or religious need and on way some creditor detains him or falls ill and is delayed in returning, then *Aitkif* shall be disrupted.

15—The second kind of acts which are not permissible in *Aitikaf*, are sexual intercourse etc. whether done deliberately or in forgetfulness—committed in the mosque or outside— shall vitiate the *Aitikaf*. The acts which lead to sexual inter-

# THE FAST

course i e. kissing, embracing etc. are also not permissible in *Aitikaf*, but *Aitikaf* is not disrupted by these acts if semen is not discharged. But if semen is discharged by mere thinking then also the *Aitikaf* will not be disrupted.

16—It is highly execrable to engage in any type of worldly business i.e. buying or selling or any other commercial act. But in case there is no food in the house and also there is no reliable person to purchase it, then it is permissible for the person in *Aitikaf* to purchase. But in no case the purchased goods should be brought to the mosque when there is fear of polluting the mosque or obstructing the space. It is also permissible if there is no such risk.

17—It is also highly execrable to sit silent in *Aitikaf*, but objectionable things should not be uttered i.e. one should not lie or back-bite. Instead all the time should be devoted in recitation of Holy Quran or teaching and learning religious knowledge or should remain engaged in other religious prayers. In short, to sit silent in *Aitikaf* is no worship or prayer.

## ZAKAT

One who has the means and saves wealth following the instructions of religion and it remains spare and more than one's needs during the year, then an amount is to be paid according to the ratio of this spare wealth. It is called *Zakat*.

One who possesses such money and does not give *Zakat* out of it according to *Shari'ah*, is a sinner and will be punishable very severely on the Day of Judgement.

The Holy Prophet (peace be upon him) is reported to have said that whosoever possesses silver and gold (wealth) and does not pay *Zakat* for the same, on the Day of Judgement plates of silver and gold will be prepared for him and after heating them with the fire of Hell, his both sides, forehead and back shall be stigmatised (branded) with them. On turning cold, the plates will be heated again.

The Holy Prophet (peace be upon him) has said that one who was favoured with wealth by Allah and he did not give *Zakat* out of it, then on the Day of Judgement his wealth will be turned into a very poisonous and bold snake. That snake will coil round the neck of this man and will pick both of his jaws and would say, "I am your wealth, I am your treasure." May Allah save us all ! Who can bear such a punishment ? To beget such a severe punishment for the sake of little greed, is sheer foolishness. How improper and unjustified it is not to spend the wealth bestowed by Allah in His way ? Wealth given by Allah is to be shared with poor and the needy. That is its proper use.

1—*Zakat* is essential and compulsory for one who possesses 612 grams of silver or about 88 grams of gold and one year has passed over it and remains with him unused or consumed. If the quantity is less than this, then *Zakat* will not be compulsory.

2—If one had 90 grams of gold for four or six months and then the quantity was reduced below the prescribed quantity and again regained after two or three months then also *Zakat* will be essential. Thus if in the beginning or at the end of year one was rich and possessed the prescribed wealth and in the middle had less than that for some time, then *Zakat* is essential and one is not excused from its payment. But if the whole wealth is lost and again he gets it, then the period of one shall be counted from the day of regaining it.

3 – One had wealth more than the prescribed limit, but one full year did not pass over it and was consumed before the end of the year, then payment of *Zakat* will not be due.

4—If one has Rs. 4000/- upon which *Zakat* is essential and he is also indebted for Rs. 4000/-, then *Zakat* is not due upon him whether the amount remains with him for full one year or not.

5—If one has Rs. 4000/- and is indebted for Rs. 2000/- then *Zakat* will be due and essential for the remaining Rs. 2000/-.

6—*Zakat* is also essential and due upon gold or silver ornaments, utensils and silver or gold laces etc. whether they are in use or kept in a safe and are never used. Thus on everything of gold or silver *Zakat* is essential provided that it is not less than the prescribed quantity.

7—If gold and silver is not pure but alloyed, that is if lead is mixed with silver or brass with gold, then it should be judged whether the quantity of silver or gold is greater than lead or brass in the alloy. If the silver or gold is more, then the alloy will be treated as silver or gold and *Zakat* will be essential if it is in the prescribed quantity.

8—If one possesses some gold and some silver and neither of them is in the prescribed quantity, but if the total price of both is equal to the price of 612 grams of silver or 88 grams of gold, then *Zakat* will be essential, not due if less. But if both gold and silver are in prescribed quantity then there is no need to assess their value as *Zakat* is due upon it.

9—Suppose the rate of gold is Rs. 600/- per 10 grams and of silver Rs. 20/- per 10 grams and one possesses 25 grams of gold and it remains with him for full one year, then *Zakat* is due and essential on this gold because with the price of this gold i. e. Rs. 15000/- 750 grams of silver can be purchased and the prescribed limit of silver is 612 grams.

10—If one had few hundred rupees with him more than his requirement and before the end of the year he received some more, then the additional money will not be counted separately and at the end of the year *Zakat* on the entire sum will be due and essential as if he had the entire amount for the whole year.

11—If one had 1 kg. of silver and before the end he received some gold also, then the gold will not be counted separately but jointly with the silver and *Zakat* will be essential on both at the end of one year.

12—Besides gold and silver, other goods like copper, iron, brass etc. and vessels made of them, clothes, shoes, etc if are meant for sale, then their cost should be valued and if it comes equal to the price of 612 grams silver or 88 grams of gold, then at the end of year *Zakat* will be due on these. But if their value is less than that, *Zakat* will not be due. But if these goods are not for sale, *Zakat* will not be due of whatever value the goods may be.

13—The household goods are exempted from *Zakat*. There is no *Zakat* on vessels—large or small, residential house, clothes, necklaces of real pearls – whatever their quantity may be. In short, with the exception of silver and gold, every other thing (if not for sale) is exempted from *Zakat*.

14—If one owns several houses and they are let out on rent, there is no *Zakat* on them whatever their value may be. In the same way someone purchased some utensils and lets them out on hire, then no *Zakat* is due on them.

15—Clothes, however costly, are exempted from *Zakat* but if they are embroidered with gold or silver thread and its cost, if removed, will be more than 612 grams of silver, then *Zakat* will be due otherwise not.

16—If anyone, is in possession of some gold or silver and some merchandise goods also, then the value of all should be calculated and if it is equal to the price of 612 grams of silver or 88 grams of gold, then *Zakat* is due on all otherwise not.

17—The merchandise goods are those which are purchased with the intention of trade; but if one purchased some rice for domestic use or for wedding purpose and later on sold it then *Zakat* will not be due on this rice.

18—If some meney has been given as loan to some one, then *Zakat* is due on this amount and must be paid by the lender. Loan is of three kinds i. e. gold and silver, cash or sold something and its price is due and was realised after two or three years. If it is equal to the amount on which *Zakat* is essential, then it is compulsory on the whole amount. If the amount was not realised in lump sum, then whenever eleven rupees are realised, *Zakat* will be due and on subsequent instalments of that amount but not on less than that. Whenever eleven rupees are realised, *Zakat* should be paid and for all the two or three years.

But if the amount loaned out is less than the prescribed limit, no *Zakat* will be due.

But if he possesses some other trade goods also besides this, then its value should be calculated and if both exceed the limit the *Zakat* will be due.

19—The second kind of loan is when neither cash is lent nor anything of trade is sold, but sold wearing clothes or some of the domestic goods and their price was realised after several years and its amount is such on which *Zakat* is due, then whenever it is realised *Zakat* is essential for all the years. But if the whole amount is not realised at a time but is paid in instalments, then so long as Rs. 54/75 paise are not realised *Zakat* will not be due and whenever this amount is received, *Zakat* for all the years is essential.

20—The third kind of loan is that a wife's dowry is due towards the husband and it was paid after several years. Then its *Zakat* will be due from the time it is realised but not of earlier when it was not paid by the husband, provided that it remains with her for one full year.

21—If a wealthy man liable for *Zakat* pays *Zakat* before the end of year, then the payment is in order and the obligation will be discharged. But if a person has no wealth but in the expectation of receiving some wealth pays *Zakat* in advance for that wealth, then the *Zakat* will not be in order. When he gets the wealth and one full year passes over it, he should again pay *Zakat*.

22—If a wealthy person pays *Zakat* in advance for several years, then it is permissible. But if any year the wealth increases than the estimate for that year, then extra *Zakat* shall have to be paid.

23—One has one hundred rupees more than his need and expects to receive one hundred rupees more and paid *Zakat* for Rs. 175/- before receiving the amount. It is in order. But if at the end of year the amount remains less than the prescribed limit (*Nisab*) then *Zakat* is remitted and the amount paid will be treated as *Sadqa-e-Nafla* i.e. an amount paid over and above the obligation.

24—A whole year passed over a man's wealth and before its *Zakat* was paid, the wealth was stolen, then *Zakat* is also excused. But if he himself gave it away to someone or destroyed it intentionally, then the due *Zakat* shall have to be paid and it will not be remitted.

25—If at the end of one year, anyone gave away all of his wealth as charity, then *Zakat* is also remitted.

26—One had two hundred rupees, but at the end of the year one hundred rupees were stolen or he gave away as charity, the *Zakat* for one hundred rupees only will be due.

27—When one full year has passed over anyone's wealth, *Zakat* should be paid immediately as it is not appreciable to delay it as it is possible that one may die suddenly and the responsibility will remain upon his shoulders. If anyone did pay *Zakat* for one year and the next year also passed, even then he should repent and pay *Zakat* for both the years, otherwise he would be a sinner. In short *Zakat* should be paid within lifetime and should not allow to remain due.

28—It is essential to pay fortieth part of the wealth as *Zakat* or two and a half per cent of the money.

29—When the *Zakat* is given to a poor it should be the intent in mind that he is giving *Zakat*. If the intent was not there, then *Zakat* is not paid and it should be paid again.

30—The whole amount of *Zakat* may be given to one or several persons either at a time or in several days or months. It is better to give it to a poor in such quantity which may be sufficient for him for that day

31—It is execrable to give to one person so much amount upon which *Zakat* is due. But if given, the obligation will be discharged. To give less than that is permissible and not execrable.

32—If anyone asks for loan and it is known that he is in poor circumstances or not good in repayment of loan and will never pay, and loan was given to him out of *Zakat* money with the intent of *Zakat* then *Zakat* is paid even though the other person thinks it to be loan.

33—If an amount was given as reward to some one but with the intent of *Zakat* in mind, even then *Zakat* is paid.

34—If ten rupees are due towards anyone and the amount to be paid as *Zakat* is also ten rupees, then the due amount cannot be remitted thinking that it would be *Zakat*. But if ten rupees are given to him with the intention of *Zakat* then the obligation of *Zakat* will be fulfilled and this money may be taken back in settlement of the loan.

35—If anyone did not pay *Zakat* himself and gave it to someone else to pay, then it is permissible, even if the other person does not intend while paying that it is *Zakat*, the *Zakat* will be settled.

36—If anyone instructs another person to pay *Zakat* on his behalf and he pays it, then the obligation of *Zakat* is fulfilled and he can take back the amount spent by him in payment of

*Zakat.*

37—If anyone was not asked to pay *Zakat* on behalf of someone and he paid without his permission, then *Zakat* is not settled, even if now the other person recognises it to have been paid on his behalf. It should be paid again.

### Zakat on Produce of Land

1—If a certain place or town was in possession of non-believers who lived there. It was taken over by Muslims after battle and Islam was propagated there. The Muslim ruler appropriating the lands of non-believers distributed it among the Muslims, then such lands will be called *Ushri* according to religious code. If the residents of that place accept Islam voluntarily even then its lands will be called *Ushri*. All the land in Arabia is *Ushri*.

2—If anyone inherits such *Ushri* land from his ancestors or purchases it from a Muslim who held it as *Ushri*, then *Zakat* is essential on whatever is produced in the land in the following way :—

If the produce in land is without irrigation and with rain water only or anything was produced in wet land on the bank of a river without being irrigated with its water, then it is essential to give one-tenth of the produce as *Zakat* or charity i.e one kg. out of ten kg. But if the land is irrigated, then one-twentieth of its total produce should be given away in charity.

The same rule applies to orchards and such other lands, howsoever small the produce may be, this charity is essential and the large or small quantity of produce makes no difference.

3—The same rule applies to all kinds of produce like grain, vegetables, fruits and flowers etc.

4—If honey is obtained from *Ushri* land, hills or forests the same charity is also due on it.

5—If *Ushri* land is purchased by a non-believer, then it no longer remains an *Ushri* land, but if it is purchased again by a Muslim from this non-Muslim or acquires it somehow or other, even then it will not be *Ushri* and shall remain non-*Ushri*.

6—The quantity of one-tenth or one-twentieth of the produce to be given in charity, is to be given by the person who produces it. But if the land has been let out on the share of produce, then both the parties should give out of their respective shares.

### Who is entitled to Receive Zakat ?

1—Anyone who possesses the prescribed quantity of wealth as explained above, is wealthy man according to religious code- For such a person it is not permissible to receive *Zakat*.

Also if anyone possesses property of the value of prescribed limit though it is not meant for business but more than his need, then such a person is also not entitled to receive *Zakat*, though he himself is not liable to pay *Zakat*.

2—One who does not possess so much of wealth or has very little even to be sufficient for one day, he is called a poor. Paying to and receiving by such persons of *Zakat* money is in order and permissible.

3—Large vessels, carpets, shamiyanas etc. which are needed in certain ceremonies and not in daily use are not included in necessary goods.

4—The house, wearing apparel and other things of daily use are all necessary possessions and anyone possessing these will not be counted as wealth whatever may be their value and it is permissible to give him *Zakat*. Also books and other necessities of an educated person are included among his necessary possessions.

5—If anyone possesses several houses which he has lent out on rent and lives on their income or someone owns a village or two and has income from them, but he has such a large family and dependents that the income does not suffice and lives in strain and also does not possess any such thing upon which *Zakat* is essential, then to pay *Zakat* to sach a person is permissible.

6—If anyone possesses one thousand rupees, but is also

indebted equal to the same amount, then it is permissible to give *Zakat* to him. But if he is indebted for less than one thousand rupees and after deducting the amount of debt so much is left on which *Zakat* is due, then it is not permissible to give him *Zakat* but if the remaining amount is less, then it is permissible.

7—If a person is very wealthy, but while travelling it so happened that everything was stolen and was left with nothing to return home. Then it is permissible for such a person to receive *Zakat*. So if a *Haj* pilgrim spent all his money and was left with no money to return home, though he may be possessing wealth at home, then it is permissible to give him *Zakat*.

8—It is not permissible to give *Zakat* to a non-believer. It should be given to Muslims only. But other charity, besides *Zakat*, *Ushr*, *Sadqa-e-Fitr* and *Kaffara* (recompensation money), is permissible to be given to non-believers.

9—It is not proper and permissible to build a mosque with *Zakat* money, or to arrange funeral and burial of an unclaimed dead body or to pay the debt of a deceased or to spend it in any other item of charity. The obligation of *Zakat* will not be discharged unless given to the needy.

10—It is not proper and permissible to give *Zakat* to one's parents or grand-parents etc. (from whom he was born) or to his children or grand children, great-grandsons and maternal grand children, i e. those who are included in his issues. The husband also cannot give it to his wife or the wife to the husband.

11—With the exception of the above-mentioned relatives, it is permissible to give *Zakat* to other relatives such as, brother, sister, niece, maternal niece, uncle, father's sister, mother's sister, maternal uncle, step-mother, step-father, step-grand-father, mother-in-law and father-in-law etc.

12—It is not permissible to give *Zakat* to a minor child whose father is wealthy. But if the child, male or female is matured and is himself not wealthy but his father is, then it is permissible to give him or her *Zakat*.

13—If the father of a minor child is poor but his mother is wealthy, then it is permissible to give him *Zakat*.

14—It is not permissible to give *Zakat* to Syeds, Alvis, the descendents of Hazrat Abbas, Hazrat Jafer, Hazrat Aqeel or Hazrat Haris Bin Abdul Muttalib. But besides *Zakat, Ushr, Nazar, Kaffara* and *Sadqa-e-Fitr,* other charities may be given to them.

15—It is permissible to give *Zakat* to domestic servants, maid-servants, nurses etc. but it should not be counted in their wages. It may be given as reward intending it as *Zakat*.

16—It is permissible to give *Zakat* to a woman who suckled him as a child or by a woman to a child who was suckled by her.

17—If a woman's *Mehr* (Dower) is one thousand rupees but her husband is very poor and cannot pay, then it is permissible to give her *Zakat* It is also permissible to give *Zakat* to a woman whose husband, though wealthy, does not pay her dower or she has remitted it. But not to a woman who is convinced that her husband will pay the dower whether it is demanded.

18—If *Zakat* was given to someone thinking him to be a poor and later on it was discovered that he was wealthy or Syed, or it was given in darkness and later on it revealed that the person was such a relative to whom it is not permissible, then in all such cases the obligation of *Zakat* is met and it is not necessary to give it again. But if that who received it, finds that it was *Zakat* for which he is not entitled, then he should return it. If after giving *Zakat* to someone it was confirmed that he was a non-believer, then *Zakat* is not paid and it should be paid again.

19—If there is doubt about a person whether he is rich or poor, then without ascertaining the correct position *Zakat* should not be given. If it was given without enquiry, then it should be judged in mind as to which side is weighty. If it is felt that the man is poor, then the *Zakat* is proper, and settled and should not be given again. But if after giving *Zakat* it was found that the man was rich, then it should be paid again and it is not settled.

20—In giving *Zakat* and all other charities, greatest consideration should be kept for relatives and they should be given preference over others, but without telling them that it was charity lest they may feel it. It has been reported in Traditions that giving of charity to relatives has double reward—one of giving charity and the other for doing good to relatives. Whatever is left after giving them, be given to others.

21—It is execrable to send *Zakat* of one city to the other. But if one's relatives are living in another city it may be sent to them, or the people of the other city more needy than this city or they are engaged in religious work, then sending *Zakat* for them is not execrable. Its giving to students, religious teachers, scholars and men of piety is of great merit.

## SADQA-E-FITR

1—Any Muslim who has so much that *Zakat* is due on him or on whom *Zakat* is not essential but has goods more than his need on whose value *Zakat* could be due, whether the property is for trade or not and whether a year has passed on it or not, it is essential for him to give *Sadqa* on *Eid* day and this charity is called *Sadqa-e-Fitr*.

2—If one possesses a large house of substantial value and also has costly clothes and other goods of necessity, but no ornaments, or in such quantity upon which *Zakat* is not due, then *Sadqa-e-Fitr* is not essential for him.

3—If a person has two houses, in one of them he resides and the other is vacant or is let out on rent, then the other house is more than his need and if its price is such on which *Zakat* becomes due for him, the *Sadqa-e-Fitr* is essential for him and giving of *Zakat* to him is also not proper. But if he depends upon the income of this house, then it will also be counted in his necessary goods and then *Sadqa-e-Fitr* will not be essential for him and it will also be permissible for him to take *Zakat*.

In short, one for whom it is permissible to take *Zakat* and *Sadqa-e-Fitr*, then *Sadqa-e-Fitr* is not due and essential for him. But it is essential for those who are not entitled to take *Zakat* or *Sadqa-e-Fitr*.

4—If anyone possesses more property than his need but he is indebted also, then if after deducting the amount of debt so much is left on which *Zakat* is due, *Sadqa-e-Fitr* will also be due, but not if it is less.

5—On *Eid* day at the time of *Fajr* prayer, *Sadqa-e-Fitr* becomes due, but if one dies before *Fajr* prayer, then *Sadqa-e-Fitr* is not due on him and it should not be paid out of his left over property.

6—It is better to give *Sadqa-e-Fitr* before going for *Eid* prayer, but if not offered before, then it may be paid afterwards.

7—If anyone paid *Sadqa-e-Fitr* in Ramazan before *Eid*, then it is discharged and need not pay it again.

8—If anyone did not pay *Sadqa-e-Fitr* on *Eid* day, then it is not remitted and it should be paid on any day.

9—*Sadqa-e-Fitr* is due for oneself and on behalf of minor children but not for major children. It may be paid on behalf of an insane. The major children should pay their own.

10—If a minor child possesses so much property on which *Sadqa-e-Fitr* is due, then it should be paid out of it.

11—*Sadqa-e-Fitr* is essential for both—one who observed fasts in Ramazan and one who did not due to any reason.

12—If wheat or its flour or powder of parched wheat is given as *Sadqa-e-Fitr*, then it should be one kg and 667 grams in weight, but as a precaution full two kg. of these be given. But if barley or its flour is given, then it should be double of this quantity.

13—If some other grain, other than wheat and barley, is given (grain or millet) then its value should be equal to the value of above mentioned quantity of wheat or barley.

14—If no wheat or barley etc. was given, but the cost of the presented quantity was given, then it is much better.

15—The *Sadqa-e-Fitr* of one person may be given to one poor or be distributed among several. Both procedures are correct.

16—It is also permissible if *Sadqa-e-Fitr* of several persons is given to one poor only.

17—Those entitled to take *Zakat* are also eligible to take *Sadqa-e-Fitr*.

# SACRIFICE
## (QURBANI)

Offering of *Qurbani* (Sacrifice) is of very great credit. The Holy Prophet (peace be upon him) is reported to have said that during its days no other thing is dearer to Allah than *Qurbani* and during these days this good act is better than all virtues.

While sacrificing an animal every drop of blood which falls on the ground is accepted by Allah before it actually reaches the ground. Therefore sacrifice should be given with pleasure and with an open heart. The Holy Prophet (peace be upon him) is reported to have said that for each hair of the sacrificial animal one virtue is recorded for one who offers the sacrifice. Allah be praised! what more credit can be than the unlimited virtues to be obtained by a sacrifice? It would be highly virtuous if one, for whom offering of sacrifice is not essential, offers sacrifice in the expectation of this unlimited reward. If the days of sacrifice are missed, how would one get the reward.

If one has been favoured with wealth by Allah, then it is better for him to offer sacrifice for his deceased relatives — father, mother etc. — so that their souls may get the great reward. Sacrifice should also be offered for the Holy Prophet (peace be upon him), his consorts and one's spiritual preceptor etc. At least sacrifice should be offered for one's ownself. It is essential for a rich person and such a man would be more unlucky and miserable if he does not offer sacrifice and the sin for not offering would be an additional burden on his shoulders.

When the sacrificial animal is laid on the ground facing the Ka'aba, then the following prayer should be recited :

اِنِّىْ وَجَّهْتُ وَجْهِىَ لِلَّذِىْ فَطَرَ السَّمٰوٰتِ وَالْأَرْضَ
حَنِيْفًا وَّمَا اَنَا مِنَ الْمُشْرِكِيْنَ ط اِنَّ صَلَاتِىْ وَ نُسُكِىْ
وَ مَحْيَاىَ وَمَمَاتِىْ لِلهِ رَبِّ الْعَالَمِيْنَ ٥ لَا شَرِيْكَ لَهٗ وَبِذٰلِكَ
اُمِرْتُ وَ اَنَا اَوَّلُ الْمُسْلِمِيْنَ ٥ اَللّٰهُمَّ مِنْكَ وَلَكَ
بِسْمِ اللهِ اللهُ اَكْبَرُ

and then saying *Bismillah-e-Allah-o-Akbar*, cut the throat of the animal and then recite this prayer :

اَللّٰهُمَّ تَقَبَّلْهُ مِنِّىْ كَمَا تَقَبَّلْتَ مِنْ حَبِيْبِكَ مُحَمَّدٍ
وَ خَلِيْلِكَ اِبْرَاهِيْمَ عَلَيْهِمَا الصَّلٰوةُ وَ السَّلَامُ ۔
يَغْفِرُ اللهُ لَنَا وَ لَكُمْ

### Injunctions

1—Anyone on whom *Sadqa-e-Fitr* is essential, sacrifice is also essential for him. But if he does not possess so much as to make *Sadqa-e-Fitr* essential for him, even then if he offers sacrifice, he will get great credit for the same.

2—Sacrifice is not essential for a traveller.

3—The time of sacrifice is from 10th of Zilhijja upto the evening of 12th of that month and may be offered on any of these days. But the best time for the sacrifice is on the day of *Eid-ul-Azha* and then 11th and then 12th in their order.

4—It is not proper to offer sacrifice before the prayer of *Eid-ul-Azha*. It should be done when people have offered prayer. Villagers can offer sacrifice after *Fajr* prayer. But those living in cities and towns should do it after *Eid-ul-Azha* prayer.

5 – If anyone resident in a city sends his animal to a village, then its sacrifice is permissible before *Eid* prayer and then he may bring its meat to the city for consumption and distribution.

6—To offer sacrifice on 12th Zilhijja is proper before sun-set but not permissible after sun-set.

7—Sacrifice may be offered at any time from 10th to 12th Zilhijja whether in the day or night, but it is not good to do it at night lest some vein may be left uncut and the sacrifice may not be done properly.

8—If anyone was in journey on 10th and 11th but came back home on 12th before sun-set, then sacrifice becomes essential for him. If he intended to stay for fifteen days even, sacrifice is essential for him. If one did not possess the required wealth on which sacrifice becomes essential, but got it from somewhere before sun-set on 12th, then sacrifice becomes essential for him.

9—It is better if one sacrifices the animal with his own hands, but if one does not know how to do it, he may get it done by someone else, but one must stand before the sacrificial animal at that time. But if one cannot do so even, then there is no harm.

10—It is not necessary to make the intent or recite the prayer and it would be sufficient if one thinks in his mind that he is making the sacrifice and cuts the throat of the animal just reciting *Bismillah-e-Allah-o-Akbar*. If one remembers it is better to recite the abovementioned prayer.

11—Sacrifice (*Qurbani*) is essential for one's ownself and not on behalf of his children even. If minor children possess the means even then it is not essential to offer the sacrifice either from their money or from one's own. If done, it would be treated as *Nafl*.

12—The sacrifice of goat—male or female, sheep of all species, cow, bull, buffalo—male or female, camel and she-camel is permissible and of any other animal is not in order.

13—It is permissible for seven persons to share the sacrifice of cow, buffalo and camel with the condition that no one's share is less than one-seventh and intent of all is to sacrifice and not merely to eat meat. The whole sacrifice will not be in order if anyone's share is less than one-seventh

14—If any animal's sacrifice is shared by less than seven persons, four or five, and none's share is less than one-seventh, then the sacrifice would be in order. If eight persons share it, then the sacrifice itself would not be in order.

15—If one intended at the time of purchasing an animal that if any other person is found he will make him a partner and actually some persons joined him, then it is permissible. But if at the time of purchase his intention was to sacrifice the animal on his behalf alone and not to share it with others, then it is not good to share it with others But if it is done then it should be seen if the person desiring to become a partner is such on whom sacrifice is essential or is a poor. If he is a man of means then sharing with him would be in order but not if he is poor.

16—If sacrificial animal is lost and another was purchased and then the first one is also found, if it was in the case of a poor man, then sacrifice of one animal is essential and in the case of a rich man, of both the animal will be essential.

17—If the sacrifice of a buffalo is shared by seven persons, its meat should not be distributed by guess only, but should be weighed exactly and if anyone's share is more or less than one seventh, then it would be counted as interest.

18—The sacrifice of a goat less than one year old is not in order. Cow and buffalo should be two years old at least and camel should not be less than five years. But if sheep (of all kinds) is so strong and fat that it appears to be of one full year, then its sacrifice would be in order, otherwise it should be of one full year.

19—The sacrifice of such an animal will not be in order if it is blind or one-eyed or has lost one-third or more of its eye-sight or one-third or more of its tail or ear has been cut off.

20—The sacrifice of an animal will not be in order whose

## SACRIFICE

one leg is lame and walks with three legs only or can put its fourth leg on the ground but cannot use it.

But if puts fourth leg on the ground and walks with its support but limps, then its sacrifice is permissible.

21—If an animal is so lean and thin that its bones have no marrow, then its sacrifice is not in order. But if it is not so lean and thin, then it would be in order. But it is better to sacrifice a strong and fat animal.

22—The animal which has no teeth at all, its sacrifice is not in order. But if only some of the teeth have fallen and more than those are still in tact, then its sacrifice would be in order.

23—The sacrifice of such an animal is also not in order which has no ears from its very birth. But it would be in order if it has very small ears.

24—The sacrifice of that animal is in order which has no horns from its birth or they have been broken if he had. But it would not be in order if the horns have been broken from their roots.

25—The sacrifice of a castrated goat, sheep or ram is in order. So also the sacrifice of an animal suffering from Scabies is in order, but if made too lean and thin by the disease, then it would not be in order.

26—If an animal was purchased for sacrifice and later on some such defect developed in it for which its sacrifice is not permissible, then another animal should be purchased for sacrifice. But if the owner is a poor man for whom sacrifice is not essential, then he may sacrifice the same animal.

27—One should eat the meat of sacrifice, give to his relatives and friends and also to the poor as charity. One-third share should be given in charity. But if given less, then it will not be a sin.

28—The skin of sacrificed animal, if sold, then its price be given as charity. This should be given to such persons to whom giving of *Zakat* is allowed. In case of price the same money should be given which is realised in price and it should not be changed.

29—The skin may also be used for one's ownself i.e. in making buckets or prayer-mat with it.

30—It is not permissible to give meat, fat etc. of the sacrifice to the butcher as his wages. It should be paid to him in cash.

31—The rope, cover etc. of sacrificed animal should also be given in charity.

32—If anyone for whom sacrifice was not essential purchased an animal for sacrifice, then sacrifice of that animal becomes essential for him.

33—Sacrifice was due on someone, but he did not offer and the three days of sacrifice passed, he should then give in charity the price of an animal or the animal itself.

34—If anyone pledged to sacrifice for certain work, then upon its acccomplishment sacrifice is essential whether the person is rich or poor. The whole flesh of such a sacrifice should be given to the poor as charity and should not be used in one's own consumption.

35—If anyone willingly offers sacrifice for the benefit of some dead person, then it is permissible to eat or distribute its meat as in one's own sacrifice.

36—Someone willed before his death that sacrifice should be offered out of his legacy and in fulfilment of his Will sacrifice was done then it is essential that its entire meat should be given in charity.

37—In the absence of a person sacrifice was offered by someone without his permission, then the sacrifice would not be in order. If the shares of an absent person is assigned in a sacrifice without his consent, then the sacrifice of other shares will also be spoiled.

38—If there are several partners in a sacrifice but they do not distribute the meat among themselves and distribute it to relatives, friends and poormen or cook it jointly to feed, then it is permissible.

39—It is not permissible to give the skin or its price as wages but it is necessary to give it in charity.

## SACRIFICE

40—The meat of sacrifice may be given to non-believers also provided it is not in their wages.

41—The sacrifice of a pregnant animal is also permissible and if its kid comes out alive, then it should also be sacrificed.

42—The price of a skin of sacrificed animal should not be used in the repair of a mosque.

# REMOVAL OF HAIR OF A NEWLY BORN CHILD
## (AQUEEQA)

1—When a baby is born, male or female, he or she should be given a name on the seventh day of birth. When the head of the baby is shaved, a sacrifice is also offered, which is called *Aqueeqa*. By *Aqueeqa* all impurities of the child are removed and the child is saved from all calamities by Allah.

2—The method of performing *Aqueeqa* is that for a boy two goats or two sheep and for a girl one goat or sheep is sacrificed or in buffalo of Eid-ul Azha sacrifice, two shares for boy and one share for a girl is taken and of the head of the child shaved. Silver equal to the weight of shaved hair is also given in charity.

3—*Aqueeqa* is performed on the seventh day of the birth of a child and if not done on the seventh day, then whenever it is done, it should be seventh day i.e. if the child was born on Friday, then *Aqueeqa* should be done on Thursday and so on. In short whenever *Aqueeqa* is done, it should be the day on which the child had become seven days old.

4—There is no restriction that the razor of the barber on the head of the child and the knife on the throat of the animal should move simultaneously. To behave in this manner is superstitious. According to religious code it is permissible whether the sacrifice is offered before or after the shaving of the head.

5—The animal whose sacrifice is not permissible is also not fit for *Aqueeqa*. Only those animals who are fit and permissible for sacrifice should be sacrificed in *Aqueeqa*.

6—It is permissible to distribute the meat of such animal

## AQUEEQA

either in raw or cooked shape and served to the guests.

7—It is permissible for all the relatives to eat the meat of *Aqeeqa* i.e. father, mother, grand-father, grand-mother, maternal grand-father and mother and there is no restriction upon anyone.

8—If one does not possess sufficient money, then for such a person it is permissible to sacrifice one goat for a male child. There is no harm if *Aqeeqa* is not performed provided that one has no means for the same.

# HAJ (PILGRIMAGE)

One who has substantial money to spare with which he can undertake the journey to Mecca moderately and return after performing *Haj*, then performance of *Haj* is obligatory for such person.

Great merit has been attributed to *Haj* and the Holy Prophet (peace be upon him) is reported to have said that '*Haj* which is free from sins and defects, is rewarded with nothing less than Paradise.' In the same way very great reward has been promised for *Umra* also and the Holy Prophet (peace be upon him) has said that both *Haj* and *Umra* absolve sins as a furance purifies the iron.

One for whom *Haj* is obligatory and he does not perform it, great warnings have come for him. So the Holy Prophet (peace be upon him) has said that one who possesses sufficient money to meet the expenses of *Haj*, that is, to go to Mecca, and he does not perfrom *Haj*, he will die as a Jew or Christian and Allah does not care for him. The Prophet (peace be upon him) further said that to avoid or abandon the performance of *Haj* is not the way of Islam.

1—To perform *Haj* once in the whole life is obligatory for one who possesses the means and if anyone performed several *Haj* then only one of them is obligatory and the rest are *Nafl Haj* which also carry very great reward and merit.

2—If anyone performed *Haj* in childhood when he was not mature, then it will not be counted. If he has the means he should perform it again after getting matured and the first *Haj* will be treated as *Nafl Haj*.

3—*Haj* is not obligatory for blind person howsoever wealthy he may be.

## HAJ PILGRIMAGE

4—When *Haj* becomes obligatory for any one, then it should be performed in the same year. It is not proper to delay it without any legitimate cause under the impression that still there is enough time in life and it may be performed in any year. If it was performed with delay, the obligation would be discharged but would be a sinner for the delay.

5—For a woman, when going for *Haj*, it is essential to be accompanied by a *Mehram* and it would not be proper for her to go without a *Mehram*.

6—If the *Mehram* is a minor or such who is so irreligious that even mother and sister cannot trust him, then it is not proper to go with such a person.

7—When a trustworthy *Mehram* is available, then it is not permissible for the husband to refuse her to go and if he does, then she should not obey him and should go to perform *Haj*.

8—If a girl is near maturity she should also not go without a *Mehram*. It is also not permissible for her to go with some body who is not *Mehram*.

9—The woman going for *Haj* should bear all the expenses of the *Mehram* who is accompanying her.

10—If no *Mehram* is found by a woman all her life, then she will not be a sinner for not performing *Haj*. But such a woman should make a Will before her death that some one be sent for *Haj* on her behalf and heirs should send someone to perform *Haj* on her behalf after her death. Thus her obligation will be discharged. *Haj* performed on behalf of someone else is called *Hajj-e-badal* (Substituted *Haj*).

11—*Haj* had become obligatory for one and he delayed it due to laziness and then became blind or so ill as to be unable to undertake the journey, then such a person should make a Will for *Hajj-e-badal* after his death.

12—If one has left so much wealth after death that after discharging his liabilities *Hajj-e-badal* may be performed out of one-third of the remaining wealth, then it is essential for the heirs of the deceased to carry out the Will. But if one-third is not sufficient for the expenses of *Haj*, then heirs may not do it.

But if they willingly make up the deficiency, then some one may be sent for *Hajj-e-badal.*

13—One died after making a Will for *Hajj-e badal* but the one-third of the legacy was not sufficient and the heirs also did not agree to part with their share for the purpose and *Hajj-e-badal* was not performed, then there is no sin upon the deceased.

14—The same rule applies to other Wills also. If one had missed fasts, prescribed prayers or *Zakat* due towards him and made a Will, it will be made good out of one-third of his legacy. To spend more than one-third without the willing consent of the heirs is not permissible.

15—If a woman is in *Iddat*, being widowed or divorced then it is proper for her to disrupt *Iddat* and go for *Haj.*

16—If one has the means to meet expenses upto Mecca only and not for Medina, then, *Haj* is obligatory for him. It is wrong to think that unless he has expenses for Medina also *Haj* will not be obligatory.

19—While in *Ehram* a woman should not cover her face with cloth. There is a net for this purpose. It should be tied on the face.

The other problems of *Haj* are available in other books which should be consulted before going for *Haj* or guidance be taken from the Muslims who are appointed for this purpose by the Saudi Government.

## Visit to Medina Munawwara

One who can afford should also visit Medina before or after *Haj* and gain blessings by visiting the sacred Tomb of the Holy Prophet (peace be upon him) and his mosque—Masjid-e-Nabvi (Prophet's Mosque). In this connection the Holy Prophet (peace be upon him) has said that one who will visit his grave after his death will gain the same blessings as if he has seen him (Prophet—peace be upon him) in his life, and further said that one who performed mere *Haj* only and did not visit his grave, has done great injustice to him (Prophet—peace be upon him).

About the Masjid-e-Nabvi the Holy Prophet (peace be upon him) has said that one who offers one prayer in this mosque, he

~~Vellard~~
~~Vestacd~~
~~Cushan~~
~~Prof~~
~~Aween~~
Rajni
Do Mohamed As
~~Aset~~
Amin Qured

shall get reward of fifty thousand prayers. May all of us have this fortune.

**Traditions About Masjid Nabvi**

1—The Holy Prophet (peace be upon him) is reported to have said that anyone who offered forty prayers in his mosque without missing any, then he is absolved of falsity and punishment of Hell.

2—The Holy Prophet (peace be upon him) has said that of all the mosque there are only three such mosques to visit which one should undertake journey. The first of them is the mosque of Ka'aba, next his mosque at Medina and the third the mosque of Aqsa in Jerusalem.

3—The Holy Prophet (peace be upon him) has said that if anyone can die then he should die there as he (Prophet—peace be upon him) will intercede for all those who die in Medina Munawwara on the Day of Judgement.

# NIKAH (MARRIAGE)

1—*Nikah* (marriage) is a great boon of Allah for this world and the next. It corrects the religious as well as worldly affairs. There are many benefits and good things in it. Man is saved from the sins, heart and mind are settled and his intention does not waver.

2—It is credit as well as benefit. *Nikah* is performed just by two words such as anyone said in the presence of two witnesses that he gave his daughter, say Rabia to Mehmood in marriage and the other said that he accepts it. So marriage (*Nikah*) is performed and the two become husband and wife.

3—If one asked someone, "Give this daughter of yours to me in marriage " and the other said that he gave, then marriage is accomplished and now it is not necessary for the first person to say that he accepts her.

4—If the girl herself is present there and the father pointing towards her says, "I give her in your marriage," and the other accepts it, then marriage is performed. In such case there is no need of calling her by name. It she is not present, then her name, father's name and if needed for specifying, her grand-father's name should be called with such clarity that all present may know as to whose marriage is being solemnised.

5—For *Nikah* to be valid there is the condition that there should be at least two male witnesses or one male and two female witnesses and they should be listening the words of offer and acceptance clearly. If in seclusion one said that I gave my daughter to you in marriage and the other said that he accepts, then the marriage will not be correct and in order.

6—The witnesses—men and women—should be Muslims, mature and sensible.

## NIKAH (MARRIAGE)

7—If there is no male witness but all are women the marriage will not be in order even if the women witnesses are ten or twelve. One male witness is necessary with two females for the evidence to be valid.

8—It is better that the marrige should be held in a large gethering such as after Juma prayer in Juma Masjid so that the marriage is widely publicised and should not be done secretly. If a large number of men cannot be collected due to some reason, then there should be at least two men or one man and two women who may themselves hear and witness the performance of marriage.

9—If the man and the woman both are mature, they can marry themselves in presence of the required number of witnesses when the woman says, "I marry you," and man accepts it.

10—If one woman did not herself marry but authorised someone to marry her with someone or some particular person and that man did so in the presence of two witnesses, the marriage is accomplished and now it cannot be negated.

**Prohibited Matrimonials**

1—Marriage is not permissible with one's own children, grand-children and great-grand-children as well as daughter's daughter, father, mother, grand-father and grand-mother.

2—Marriage is not permissible with one's brother, sister, uncle, maternal uncle, aunt, maternal aunt, nephew, niece, sister's son or daughter. Brother, according to religious code is one who is from the same father and mother or whose mother is one and fathers are different.

3—A woman's marriage with son-in-law is not permissible and so the marriage of one with his daugher-in-law is also not permissible.

4—Any girl's father died and her mother married another person but she died or was divorced before she lived with him, then it is permissible for the girl to marry with the step-father.

5—It is not permissible for a woman to marry with step-sons or a man with his step-daughters. Such as a man has several wives—more than one—then it is not permissible for any of his wives to marry with the son of her co-wife, whether she lived with her husband or not. It is prohibited.

6—Marriage is also not permissible for a woman with her father-in-law, his father or grand-father. So for a man with his mother-in-law, his mother or grand-mother.

7—So long as one sister is in his marriage, marriage with other sister of wife is not permissible But it is permitted if the first sister is dead or divorced. In case of divorce the other sister cannot marry her brother-in-law before the expiry of the period of *Iddat* of her sister.

8—If two sisters marry one man, then the *Nikah* of the one who marries first is valid and that of the other is invalid.

9—So long as a woman remains in marriage of a man, then her father's sister, mother's sister, niece, or sister's daughter cannot be married with this man.

10—If two women are so related that had one of them been a male, marriage between them would not have been permissible, then such two women cannot be married to one man at the same time. But in case of death or divorce of one, then the other woman can be married with him. In case of divorce, after the expiry of the period of *Iddat* and not before.

11—One can marry a woman and her step-daughter at the same time.

12—Adoption of a child is of no account according to Islamic *Sharia'*. By treating anyone as son or daughter he does not actually become a son or a daughter. So marriage with an adopted child is permissible.

13—If one is not real maternal uncle, but is a related maternal uncle somehow, then marriage of the girl is permissible with him. Similarly if one is distantly related as paternal uncle or nephew, marriage with him is in order. So marriage between cousin brothers and sisters is permissible provided they are not real brothers and sisters.

14—If two women are not real sisters but are cousin sisters that is, daughters of uncle, maternal uncle, aunt or maternal aunt, they can marry the same person at a time. The same rule applies to distantly related aunts—maternal or paternal and nieces etc. They can be married to the same man at a time.

15—Marriages between all relations of birth are prohibited. In the same way marriages between relations by milk-feeding are also prohibited. Marriage of a woman with the husband of her wet-nurse is not permissible as he amounts to be her father. Marriage between a man and woman who shared milk of the same woman is also not permissible. One who was fed milk by her, marriage with him or his sons is not permissible for the woman as he amounts to be her son. In respect of sharing milk, marriage is prohibited with maternal uncle, son of sister, uncle or nephew.

16—Two girls who have shared milk of the same woman cannot remain in marriage with the same man at a time as they amount to be sisters with each other.

17—If any man committed illegal sexual inter-course with a woman, then it is not permissible for her mother or her daughters to marry this man.

18—If a woman in her passion of youth touched a man with evil motive, then it is not permissible for her mother or her daughter to marry this man. If a man touched a woman in the same way, then his marrying her mother or her daughter is prohibited.

19—In darkness of night a husband woke up to awaken his wife, but mistakenly touched his daughter or mother-in-law in youthful passion, then in such case his wife has become prohibited for him for ever and there is no way now to legitimatise it. It is essential for him to divorce his wife.

20—If a boy touched his step-mother with evil motive, then she became absolutely prohibited for her husband and there is no way to legitimatise it. The same applies to the step-mother if she touches her step-son with such intention.

21—The marriage of a Muslim woman is not permissible with a man of another religion.

22—If a woman is divorced or her husband dies, then it is not permissible for her to re-marry unless the period of *Iddat* has expired in both the cases.

23—If a woman has been married, then it is not permissible for her to marry someone without obtaining divorce and observing *Iddat*.

24—If an unmarried girl conceived by illegal sexual intercourse, her marriage is permissible. But it is not permissible for her husband to have sexual intercourse with her till her child is born. If she is married with the person who committed illegitimate intercourse, then it is permissible for him to have sexual intercourse with her.

25—One who already has four wives, it is not permissible for him to marry the fifth. If he has divorced one of them then so long as the *Iddat* period of the divorced woman does not pass, no woman can marry him.

26—According to some scholars and jurists the marriage of a *Sunni* girl is not permissible with a *Shia* male.

### Wali—Guardian

The person who is authorised to give a girl or boy in marriage is called *Wali* (guardian).

1—The guardian (*wali*) of a boy or girl in order of their merits are as under :

(*i*) Is the father of child, then grand-father or great-grand-father.

(*ii*) In the absence of above, real brother, then step-brother (of the same father), then nephew, son of nephew or grand-son of nephew.

(*iii*) In the absence of all of above, real uncle, son of uncle, grand-son of uncle. Then step-uncle (step-brother of father), son of step uncle and grand-son of step uncle.

(*v*) In the absence of above three categories of relatives, uncle of father and his sons.

(*vi*) In the absence of all of abovementioned relatives, uncle of grand-father and his sons.

## NIKAH (MARRIAGE)

(*vi*)—If none of the abovementioned relatives is there, mother is the guardian of the child.

(*vii*)—After the mother, grand-mother, then maternal grand-mother, then real sister, then step-sister from the same father, then brother or sister from the same mother, then father's sister, mother's brother and sister etc. may be the guardian.

2—A minor, or an insane cannot be the *Wali* and so a non-Muslim cannot be a *Wali* of Muslim.

3—If a *Wali* got a mature girl married without asking her or her consent, then it depends upon the girl to accept it or reject it. If she accepts it then the marriage is in order otherwise not.

4—If a *Wali* informed a mature girl that he is giving or has given her in marriage to such and such person and the girl remains silent on hearing it or just smiled or began to weep, then this amounts to consent and the marriage will be in order. The expression of consent in words by the girl is not essential.

5—While seeking the girl's consent, the guardian did not mention the name of the would-be husband nor she herself knows him, then the girl's silence will not amount to consent. It is necessary to mention the name etc. of the proposed husband so that the girl may know him. Similarly if the amount of *Mehr* (dowry) was not told to her and the *Wali* married her on less than usual amount in her family then the marriage will not be in order without her consent which should be taken again.

6—If it is the second marriage of woman and she is not virgin, then her silence will not be enough seeking her consent by her guardian. She must express her consent in words and if the marriage is performed without expressed consent, it will remain suspended. If later on she expresses her consent in words, then the marriage will be in order and if she does not give her consent, then it will not amount to marriage.

7—When father is present but uncle, brother etc. went to seek the girl's consent, then her silence should not be taken as her consent. It must be expressed in words. But if they were sent by the father for this purpose, then her silence will amount to her consent. In short according to *Sharia*' only the nearest *Wali* has the right to seek consent, but if anyone was deputed by him for this purpose, then her silence will mean her consent. But if the grand-father had the right, but the brother asked her; or the brother had the right but the uncle asked her, then her silence will not mean her consent and in such case it should be expressed in words.

8—If a *Wali* gave a girl in marriage to someone without asking the consent of the girl and then the *Wali* himself or someone deputed by him for this purpose came to inform her that she has been married with such and such man, and she remains silent on hearing it, then the marriage will be in order. If someone else other than these comes to inform her and he is a reliable person or are two men, even then the marriage will be in order if she remains silent. If the informant is one man and he is unreliable, then the marriage will not be in order and shall remain suspended till she consents or some such thing happens which may amount to consent.

9—When it is essential to express consent in words and the woman did not, but when the husband came to her in privacy and she did not refuse sexual intercourse, then the marriage will be in order.

10—A major boy cannot be forced to marry against his will to marry. He cannot be married against his will by the guardian and if done it will remain in suspense. If he agrees to it then it will become in order otherwise not. Mere silence of the boy will not amount to his consent. It should be expressed in words.

11—The marriage of a minor boy or girl, being dependents, will not be in order without the consent of the guardian. If he or she contracts a marriage or someone else gets it done without the consent of the guardian, then for it to be in order depends upon the consent of the *Wali*. If he agrees to it the marriage will be in order otherwise not. The *Wali* has full right to marry or not to marry him or her with anyone. Minor boys or girls cannot reject that marriage at that time. The

## NIKAH (MARRIAGE)

minor boys and girls cannot repudiate the marriage whether they had been married once and this be their second marriage. In both cases the same rule applies.

12—If the father or grand-father gave the minor boy or girl in marriage, they cannot repudiate the marriage on attaining maturity whether the marriage was in their class or in a lower class and whether the dowry was according to family tradition or less than that. The marriage cannot be repudiated in any case after attaining maturity.

13—If the minor was given in marriage by some *Wali* other than the father or grand-father quite in accordance with all the conditions and requirements then the marriage is in order, but on attaining maturity the minor has the right to repudiate the marriage. But it can be done in the court of a Muslim Officer.

14—A minor girl was given in marriage by some *Wali* other than father or grand-father and it was in her knowledge also. Thereafter she matured but did not have privacy with her husband and she does not agree with the marriage now. Then it is essential that she should express her disagreement immediately on attaining maturity or should say that she does not wish to keep the marriage whether in presence of anyone or when quite alone. It should be expressed so. But mere such expression would not annul the marriage. She should approach a Muslim Judge for this purpose and with his permission it would be done. But the explicit condition for such annulment is that the disagreement should be expressed immediately after attaining maturity and even if for a moment after that she remains silent, the marriage cannot be repudiated. But if she had no knowledge of her marriage, then he should declare her disagreement with it immediately on hearing about it and if she remains silent even for a moment after the information, then she will not have the right to repudiate it.

15—If a girl matured when her husband has had sexual intercourse with her, then it is not necessary that she should refuse to accept the *Nikah* immediately. So long as she does not express her intention, she will have the option of either accepting or rejecting the marriage however long a period may pass thus. If she expresses to accept it some such thing happens which betoken it i.e. she remained as wife with her husband in privacy, then the marriage is final.

16—If the guardian who has the right to give away the girl in marriage is out and there is an offer for the girl. The guardian is so far away that the opportunity may be lost by waiting for him to get his consent and the other party may not wait, then the person next in guardianship can give her in marriage and it would be in order.

But if the first guardian is not so far away and his consent may be obtained easily, then the second guardian cannot give her in marriage and if did, then the marriage shall remain suspended till the consent of the first guardian and shall be finalised only upon his consent.

17—If in the presence of the rightful *Wali* the second guardian gave away a minor in marriage, such as, the father had the right but it was done by the grand-father without consulting the father, then that marriage shall remain suspended upon the consent of the father.

18—If major woman is independent and it is upon her to marry or not or to marry anyone she likes. No one should force her against her Will. If she marries someone of her own Will, then it would be in order whether the guardian was informed about it or not and whether he is pleased of displeased, in every case the marriage is in order.

If she married outside her class with a male of unequal status and the guardian is displeased with it, then the marriage will not be right. But if she marries in her own class but the *Mehr* was less than the *Mehr-Misl* (dowry is usage in her father's family) the marriage will be in order but the *Wali* can get it rescinded. The guardian should lodge the complaint with a Muslim authority in this respect. But the right of this complaint is to the persons who are in the list of guardians before the mother i.e. from father to the sons of grand-father's uncle.

## Mehr—Dowry

1—*Mehr* (dowry) is an essential requisite of *Nikah*. The

marriage will be in order even if no mention of dowry is made in *Nikah*, but it will have to be given. Even if one makes it a condition that he will not pay any dowry, he is still bound to pay it.

2—The minimum amount of dowry (*Mehr*) is the value of silver of about 32 grams in weight, but for more there is no limit. To fix excessive dowry is not good. If anyone fixed *Mehr* even less than this minimum, even he shall have to pay this minimum as according to *Sharia* there can be no dowry less than that. But in case of divorce before company and privacy between husband and wife, he shall have to pay half of it.

3—Someone fixed *Mehr* according to his financial position, say one thousand rupees, and brought his wife to his home and had sexual inter-course or did not but remained with her in such privacy where nothing could obstruct it, then payment of the whole *Mehr* money has become due. If there has been no such privacy and the husband or wife died before that, even then full *Mehr* is due. But if the husband divorced his wife before company and privacy, the only half of the fixed *Mehr* will be due.

4—If the husband is impotent but there has been such company and privacy between them, even then the wife is entitled to full *Mehr*. Similarly if an eunuch marries a girl and after company and privacy was divorced, even then the girl is entitled to full dowry.

5—The husband and wife lived in company and privacy but the wife or the husband is so minor that cannot perform the obligation of sexual intercourse and consequently there was divorce, then the wife is entitled for the half of the dowry.

6—If the amount of dowry was not mentioned at the time of *Nikah* or the marriage was contracted on the basis that the husband will pay no dowry, then anyone of them died or there has been such company and privacy as is accountable in *Shariah* even then dowry shall have to be paid and this dowry shall be *Mehr-Misl* i.e. as is in usage in the family. But if the husband divorced her before seclusion and privacy, then the wife will not be entitled to any *Mehr*. In that case only one suit of clothes shall be given by the husband to her and it is essential, if not given he will be a sinner.

7—In such suit four pieces only are essential for the husband to give, that is, one shirt, one scarf (dupatta) for head, one trouser or saree whichever is in use and one large sheet with which she can cover herself from head to feet. Besides these no other cloth is essential.

The clothes to be given should be according to the status of the husband. An ordinarily poor man should give cotton clothes. A middle class man of tusser and a wealthy person should give silken clothes but in any case the cost of the clothes should not exceed half of *Mehr-Misl* of the family and should also not be less than that.

8—No *Mehr* was fixed at the time of marriage but later on both the husband and wife mutually agreed and fixed some dowry, then the current dowry (*Mehr-Misl*) will not be due but that which has been agreed between them. But before company and privacy she was divorced by the husband then she will not be entitled to get the agreed or current family dowry but just one suit of clothes as explained above.

9—Dowry of certain amount was fixed at the time of marriage according to the status of the husband but later on the husband at his own free Will increased it, then this later amount will become essential and the husband will commit a sin if he does not pay this increased amount. But if the wife was divorced before seclusion and privacy, then of the amount fixed originally shall have to be given and the increased amount will be of no account. If the wife of her own free Will had forgone full or any part of the dowry then she will not be entitled to he amount she had remitted.

10—If the remission of dowry was obtained by the husband by threats, harassment and coercion, then the remission will not be valid and the entire dowry shall be due from him.

11—If a village, groove or some land instead of gold, silver or money is fixed as dowry, then it is also proper and the same should be given.

12—Someone had contracted marriage against the rules and so they were separated, such as, one had done the marriage secretly and not in the presence of the valid witnesses, or a woman was divorced or her husband died and before completing the period of *Iddat* she married someone ; then in such case if there has been no privacy or seclusion, no dowry will be due. But if sexual intercourse was done, then the fixed dowry shall have to be given.

13—If anyone mistakenly committed sexual inter-course with a woman thinking her to be his wife, then he will have to give her *Mehr-Misl* and such inter-course will not amount to adultery or a sin. If she is impregnated and the child is to be born will be of proper descent and it would not be right to call him illegitimate. When it is known that she was not his wife, then he should not go to her again and for that woman it is essential to observe *Iddat* and without completing its period it is not permissible for her to live with her husband and for the husband not to have sexual intercourse with her.

14—Where there is custom to pay the whole dowry on the first night of marriage, then the wife has a right to claim it on that night and if she did not demand it, then whenever she demands it must be given without delay.

15—In India it is a custom that giving or taking of the *Mehr* is done after death or divorce and the woman claims dowry after divorce or if the husband dies, she takes it from the property left by the husband. If the wife dies then her heirs claim the dowry. So long as both live together neither the husband gives nor the wife demands. Then in such case the woman cannot prefer a claim for her dowry before divorce.

16—If there is a custom of giving certain parts of the dowry in advance and if it is not given, then the wife has the right not to allow the husband to have sexual intercourse with her till the amount is not paid. If the husband has done intercourse with her once, she has the right not to allow him to do it for the second or third time and refuse to go with him if he wants to take her somewhere without taking the amount.

Similarly if she wants to go to her father's house, then the husband cannot stop her.

17—If the husband gave something to wife with the intent of dowry, then it is in order and paid up to that extent. It is not necessary to tell the wife at the time of giving that it is part of the dowry.

18—If the husband gave something to the wife and now there is difference between them over it. The wife says that it is a gift and not part of dowry, but the husband says that it was part of dowry then the husband's claim will prevail and it will be taken into account. Eatables will not be counted as dowry.

**Family or Model Dowry (Mehr-i-Misl)**

The family dowry or *Mehr-Misl* means that in the family of the girl (father's lineage), observe a girl like her, that she is as young as this one, as handsome as this one, like this she was also maiden at the time of her marriage, she had as much property as this one has, both belong to the same place (country), are equal in religiousness, sensibility, both are clever and equally educated. To sum up at the time of her marriage that girl was in all respects like this girl now to be married, then the dowry that was fixed for that girl has become the current dowry (*Mehr-Misl*) for this girl also.

**Marriage of New Converts to Islam**

1—The Islamic Law recognises, the marriages of non-believers performed according to their customs and rites as reliable. If husband and wife both accept Islam together at the same time, then there is no need for their marriage to be performed again. Their previous marriage remains valid.

2—If either of the two accepts Islam—husband or wife—and the other does not, then their previous marriage is revoked. They cannot now live as husband and wife.

3—If only the wife accepts Islam, then so long three monthly courses are not completed, she cannot marry a man.

**Equality Among Wives**

1—If anyone has more than one wife, then it is essential

## NIKAH (MARRIAGE)

for him to keep all of them on equal level and whatever he gives to one wife, the other has equal claim for that. If he stays for one night with one, he should stay for one night with the other also. Clothes and ornaments which he gave to one wife, the other also has the right to claim the same.

2—There is no difference between the new and old wife. Both have equal rights.

3—Equality is in night stay only and equality in stay during the day is not essential. If one stayed more with one wife during the day and less with the other, then there is no harm as it is essential only for stay in night. If he went to one wife immediately after Maghrib in one night and went to the other after Isha next night, then it would be a sin. But one who remains engaged in his duty at night and remains at home during the day, them for him to maintain equality during the day is essential.

4—Equality in sexual intercourse is not essential, that is, it is not necessary if he has had intercourse with one wife on her turn he should also do it with the other on her turn.

5—The equality in stay should be observed by the husband whether sick or not.

6—It is not a sin if the husband has greater love for one than the other as the heart and its feelings are beyond one's control.

7—There is no equality while going on a journey and the husband may take either of the wives with him. It is better to draw lots so that none may have a cause for complaint.

### Considerations in Nikah

1—While marrying his children one should have greater regard than the person whom he is giving his child in marriage is pious. Wealth should not be considered much. Now-a-days there are such rich and educated men who commit apostasy and talk blasphemy. Marriage is not proper with such person as with such person the entire life will be spent in the sin of adultery.

2—Some women praise the beauty of other women before

their husbands. It is very bad and improper. If the husband is attracted towards such a woman, it will bring misfortune for her.

3—If somewhere an offer of marriage has come and negotiations between the two parties are going on, then third person should not interfere there to seek that boy or girl for his ward. But if the previous offer has been rejected by one party, then one can send his child's offer.

4—To talk about and discuss the private affairs of husband and wife among friends and companions is unmodesty and disliked by Allah. Some wives and husbands do not care about it.

5—If anyone seeks someone's advice in matrimonial matters, then he should frankly tell him of any defect or evil that he knows in that matter. Though this is back-biting (*gheebat*) but it is not prohibited.

6—If the husband having means does not provide enough to his wife to meet her expenses of house-hold, then the wife can take by stealing. But it is not proper to take anything in this way for wastefulness or for worldly ceremonies.

**Divorce—Talaq**

1—If divorce is pronounced by a husband, who is major and not an insane, it will be valid. Divorce by an insane, whose mind is not in order, will not be valid.

2—If man while in his sleep said to his wife that he has divorced her or said that he divorced his wife, then this grumbling in sleep will not be taken into account and divorce will not take effect.

3—If the husband was forced to divorce his wife by being beaten or threat of being killed and he pronounced divorce, even then it will be valid.

4—If anyone divorced his wife when he was drunk and repented when regained his senses, but it would be of no avail as divorce has become valid. Divorcing in anger is also valid.

5—None except the husband is authorised to give *Talaq*

(divorce), but if he asks someone else to pronounce divorce on his behalf, then it would be valid.

6—Man alone is competent or has the right to divorce. When he has pronounced it, the woman is helpless as it has become effective immediately. Whether the woman agrees with it or not the divorce is valid in any case. A wife cannot divorce her husband.

7—Man is entitled to call divorce thrice only and not more than that. If he calls four or five divorces even then only three will be regarded.

8—When a man said in words that he has divorced his wife so distinctly that he heard his own voice then divorce becomes valid whether he said it in the presence of some one or alone and whether the wife heard it or not. In every respect the divorce is valid and complete.

9—Divorce is of three kinds :

(1) One divorce is such in which marriage is completely revoked and rescinded and it is not permissible for the wife to live with her husband without marrying him again. If they both wish to live again with each other, then they will have to marry again. This is called *Talaq-e-Bayyin* (Distinct Divorce).

(2) The other divorce is such in which the marriage is so revoked and rescinded that if they both wish to live again as husband and wife it will not be possible unless and until the woman marries some other man and when this man divorces her and after completion of *Iddat*, the first husband may remarry her. This is called *Talaq-e-Mughalliza* (Severe Divorce).

(3) The third kind is one in which the marriage is not revoked or rescinded and if the husband repents after pronouncing divorce once or twice then there is no need of marrying again and the husband can keep her. This is called *Talaq-e-Rajaie*. But if the husband after pronouncing the divorce sticks to it and does not repent during the period of *Iddat*, the marri-

age shall be rescinded. But during the period of *Iddat* it is permissible for husband to retain her or not. If the divorce was pronounced three times then there is no alternative.

10—There are two ways of giving *talaq* : The first is that the husband clearly says that he divorces his wife or 'I divorce you.' This cannot be interpreted other than divorce. This is called *Sarih Talaq* (definite divorce). The other way is in which divorce is not pronounced so clearly and distinctly but in some ambiguous words which can be interpreted for divorce and otherwise also, such as one says. "I have parted with you," which may mean that he has divorced her and also that though not divorced but he does not wish to keep her with him. She may go to her father's house for ever and he will not care for her. Or says that he has no concern with her and she must leave his house immediately or says "Be away. I cannot endure you" or such words which may be interpreted in both ways. This is called *Talaq-e-Kinaya* or indirect divorce.

11—If divorce is pronounced distinctly then as soon as the words of divorce come out of the lips the divorce becomes effective, whether it was intended or not, or it was uttered in mere joke only. In such case it would be the third kind of *Talaq* i.e. *Talaq-e-Rajaie* and till the expiry of *Iddat* period, the husband has the option of retaining her or not. If the divorce is said once, it would be one *Talaq* but not two or three. But if it is called thrice, then there will be three divorces. *Rajaie* is derived from the Arabic word *Ruju* which means, "To turn, to return, to incline" etc.

12—If anyone pronounced one divorce, then till the expiry of the *Iddat* period he may also give the second and third divorce and if he does so the divorce shall become final and complete.

13—If one says to his wife, "I will divorce you," then it will not amount to divorce, nor will be a divorce if he says that if she did some such and such thing he will divorce her, whether she does that or not. But if the husband says that if

## NIKAH (MARRIAGE)

she does something then it will be divorce and she did that thing, then the divorce is valid.

14—If any one while pronouncing *Talaq* says *Insha-Allah* also with it, then it will not be a valid divorce and if said so, "If Allah wills you are divorced," even then it is not divorce. But if after pronouncing *Talaq*, he pauses for a while and then says *Insha-Allah*, then *Talaq* is complete.

15—If anyone addressed his wife with the words *Talaqan* (divorced), then it will be a divorce even if he said in mere joke.

16—If anyone says to his wife that if she will go to a certain place, it will be a divorce on her and if she goes there then it will be divorce.

17—If anyone did not pronounce divorce clearly—but in ambiguous words, then if at the time of uttering those words divorce was intended, then it will be divorce of first—*Bayyan*—Distinct. Now he cannot retain her without re-marriage. But if divorce was not intended but the words were spoken in other meaning, then it will not be divorce. But by context it is found that actually divorce was intended and now he is telling a lie then the woman should not live with him and take it as divorce.

Similarly if a woman in anger says that they cannot live together and he should divorce her and the husband in the same temper replies that he has left her, then the woman should take it as divorce.

18—If the husband called, *Talaq, Talaq, Talaq* three times, then all the three divorces are justified even if pronounced in ambiguous words.

### Divorce Before Joining After Nikah

1—The wife had not yet gone, to live with her husband and was divorced or had gone, but there was no seclusion and company between them which is recognised in *Shariah* and divorce was pronounced before such privacy, then it will amount to distinct divorce of the first kind whether pronounced in clear words or not. In such conditions it is always a distinct divorce for such woman and there is no restriction of observing *Iddat* for her. She can marry another person immediately after divorce.

2—To such a woman the husband said that if she will do such and such thing, she is divorced and she did that thing then the divorce is complete.

3—If there has been privacy and company between the husband and wife whether there has been sexual intercourse or not and he divorced her once or thrice in distinct words. Then this would be revocable (*Rajaie*) and it is permissible for husband to retain her without remarriage. But if pronounced in vague and ambiguous words, then it is distinct divorce (*Bayyan*) and he has no right to retain her. But if the three divorces were not pronounced and both husband and wife are willing, then they re-marry within *Iddat* period.

### Talaq-e-Mughallaza—the three Talaqs

1—If a husband pronounces three divorces to her wife, the woman becomes totally prohibited for him. The divorce whether given in clear or vague words both have the same force. Now if she wants to re-marry the same person, then it is possible in one condition only and that is, that she should first marry another man and have sexual intercourse with him and when the second husband dies or divorces her after sexual intercourse, then after completing the *Iddat* period she can re-marry the first person. But if the second husband died or divorced her before sexual intercourse then it will be of no account and she cannot marry the first husband in this condition.

2—The three divorces may be pronounced together at a time or after intervals as one today, the next tomorrow and the third on the day after, or one in this month, second in the next month and the third in the third month i.e. within the *Iddat* period and all are covered by the same order. After pronouncing three divorces in clear words to retain the wife is not permissible and nothing is possible after that.

3—If a husband pronounces one divorce to his wife, it is *Rajaie* (revocable) and the husband can retain her. But again after some time, say two or three years, being angry gave another revocable divorce in which retaining the wife is permissible and retained her again. Then there are two divorces now. If in future he again divorces her, then the three divorces will be completed and he cannot retain her now unless she marries another person as already explained above.

4—If one pronounced clear divorce (*Bayyan*) in which there is no option to retain the wife, then the marriage is dissolved, but if he repents he can re-marry her with her consent. After some time he again gave her a clear divorce and again repented and both husband and wife willingly re-married, then these are two divorces now and if he will divorce her for the third time, the wife cannot return to him unless she marries another man and is released by him after sexual intercourse.

5—If the marriage with the second husband was conditional that he will divorce her after having sexual intercourse with her, then such a marriage is forbidden. It is at his discretion to release her or not and may release her whenever he likes. To re-marry with this condition is not only forbidden but a sin also and wrought with curse of Allah. If the second husband dies after sexual intercourse or divorces her after it, then she becomes permissible for her first husband.

6—Man has a right for giving three divorces only. He can pronounce them either together at a time or at intervals.

But it must be remembered that of all the permissible acts divorce is the most undesirable act to Allah.

## Conditional Divorce

1—If anyone said that any woman that he marries will have divorce, then divorce will be effective on every marriage that he contracts. But if re-marries the same woman then the divorce shall lose its force.

2—If any one said to his wife that if she does certain thing she will have divorce or if she goes away from him she will have divorce or that on the happening of certain thing she will have *Talaq* : then if she does that thing, it will be revocable divorce in which there is option of retaining her after divorce without re-marriage. But if it is said in vague and ambiguous words such as that if she does something, he shall have no concern with her and she does that, then the divorce will be distinct (*Bayyan*) provided the man meant it when he said so.

3—If the husband said to his wife that if she does such and such thing she will have two divorces or three divorces and she did that thing then as many divorces as he said will become effective.

4—If anyone said to his wife that if she keeps a fast she will have divorce. Then divorce will become effective just on keeping the fast. If he has said that if she keeps one fast then she will have divorce. So if she breaks the fast then the divorce shall not be due.

5—If a woman intended to go out and the husband said that she should not go 'now' but she did not obey and the husband said that if she will go she will have divorce. Since the man had said that she should not go 'now' and if she went she will have divorce, so if she goes after some time, the divorce will not be effective as he intended to stop her from going just then and not for the whole life.

**Divorce by Patient**

1—If anyone divorced his wife in his sickness and before the expiry of her *Iddat* he died in the same sickness, then the woman will get her prescribed share in his property irrespective of the number of divorces, whether it was revocable or not, the same rule shall apply in all cases. But if the man died after expiry of her period of *Iddat*, she will not be entitled to any share. If the man recovered from that sickness and then died the woman shall have no share whether the *Iddat* period had expired or not.

2—If the woman had demanded divorce and the man gave it, then the woman will have no claim of her share in his property whether the man dies before or after the expiry of *Iddat* period.

3—In his illness the husband said to his wife that if she goes out of the house she will have distinct (*Bayyan*) divorce and she goes out, then she will not be entitled to any share as she herself did such thing which resulted in divorce. But if the man said that if she took food or offered prayer then it will be distinct (*Bayyan*) divorce for her and she did it and the man dies during her *Iddat* period, then she will have her share in his property as the divorce was not of her choice as eating food and offering of prayer are essential. In short in case of distinct (*Bayyan*) divorce given in illness the woman is entitled for her share.

4—If a man in his good health said to his wife that if she goes out of the house it will be distinct (*Bayyan*) divorce for her and when she went he fell ill and died in the same sickness within the period of her *Iddat*, the woman will have no share.

5—If a man in his perfect health said to his wife that when her father returned from abroad it will be distinct divorce for her. When her father returned the husband was ill and died in the same sickness, then the woman will not claim her share in his property. If he said this in his sickness and died in the same before the expiry of her *Iddat*, then she will get her share.

**Rejoining in Revocable Divorce—Talaq-e-Rajaie**

1—If anyone gave one or two revocable divorces to his wife then he has the right to retain her before the expiry of her *Iddat* and there is no need of re-marriage whether the woman consents or not as she has no choice. But if he has given all the three divorces, then he has no authority to retain her and in such case the injunction of marriage with some other person will apply as explained before.

2—The method of revoking the divorce or retaining the wife that either he should say clearly that he retains her and would not give her up or says that he takes her back in marriage or tells someone else that he has retained his wife and rescinded the divorce and just saying this she became his wife again. Or said nothing in words but had sexual intercourse with her or kissed her or touched her in youthful passion, then also she will become his wife and there would be no need of re-marriage.

3—If one intends to retain a woman in such circumstances,

it is better to do so in the presence of several witnesses so that there may be no difference over this issue in future and none of them may go back on his words. But it is also in order if he did it alone.

4—If the period of woman's *Iddat* has passed, then revocation will not be in order and the husband is helpless. Now if the woman agrees there can be re-marriage between them. Without re-marriage she cannot be retained, even if he wants her retaining is not permissible.

5—The woman with whom sexual intercourse has not been done by her husband nor there has been such privacy and seclusion between them and she is given one divorce by her husband, then he has no right to retain her because the divorce which is given is distinct (*Bayyan*). It has already been explained.

6—If husband and wife both have remained in seclusion and the husband says that he has had no sexual intercourse with her and divorce her. After his confession the husband has no right to retain her or revoke the divorce.

7—If a woman who has been given one or two revocable divorce in which the husband has a right to retain her, the woman should remain well dressed groomed so that the man may be inclined towards her and may retain her. But if the man has no intention to revoke, then it is proper for the man that whenever he enters the house, he should announce his coming by some sign so that the woman may cover herself properly and his eyes does not fall at any part of her body which is essential for her to hide. When the period of *Iddat* expires the woman should go from that house and live somewhere else.

8—If the husband has not yet revoked the divorce then it is not permissible for him to take her somewhere with him and neither the woman should go with him on a journey.

9—If a woman has been given one or two distinct (*Bayyan*) divorces in which the man has no right to retain her, and she wants to marry another man then she can do so after expiry of *Iddat*. But if she wants to re-marry her first husband, she can re-marry him even within *Iddat* period.

## NIKAH (MARRIAGE)

10—A woman who is in her menses, then the period of her *Iddat* is three monthly courses and with the end of three monthly courses the period of *Iddat* will also expire. If the third monthly course has lasted for full ten days, then when discharge stops, the period of *Iddat* shall expire with it and the option for the man to retain her, if not exercised, will no longer remain. But if the third monthly course lasted for less than ten days but the woman had not yet taken her bath nor any obligatory prayer became due to her, then man's option still remains and even now he can revoke and the woman will become his wife. But if after the monthly course she has bathed or if not bathed then one time's obligatory prayer is missed and became due on her, then in both cases he cannot retain her without re-marriage.

### Oath Not To Go To Wife (Eila)

1—If anyone swore or said to his wife that by Allah he will not have sexual intercourse, or by Allah he will never do sexual intercourse with her or something else in this respect, then its order is that if he actually did not have sexual intercourse then at the end of four months it will have the effect of distinct divorce (*Bayyan*) and now they cannot live as husband and wife without re-marriage. But if before the end of four months he breaks his oath and did sexual intercourse, then there will be no divorce but he shall have to give recompensation for breach of oath. According to Islamic Law such oath is called *Eila*.

2—If one did not swear to abstain from sexual intercourse for ever but just for four months saying that by Allah he shall not have sexual intercourse with her for four months, then it is *Eila* and if he actually did not do sexual intercourse with her for four months, then it will be a distinct (*Bayyan*) divorce. But if he did sexual intercourse before the end of four months, then re-compense for breach of oath shall be due.

3—If he swore to refrain for less than four months then it is immaterial. If the oath is for even one day less than four months it will not be *Eila*. If he did sexual intercourse before the end of specified time, then recompense for breach of oath will be due. But he did no intercourse then there will be neither divorce nor breach of oath.

4—If anyone swore not to have sexual intercourse just for four months and kept his oath and so divorce became effective after four months and re-married the same woman and he does not have sexual intercourse with her for four months after re-marriaye, then there is no harm.

5—If one gave distinct divorce to his wife and then swore not to have sexual intercourse with her, then it is not *Eila* and after re-marrying her he does not have intercourse with her, then it will not be a divorce to her. But if he does, he shall have to give recompensation for breach of oath. But if he took such an oath after giving a revocable divorce, then it will become *Eila* and if he revokes and does not do sexual intercourse, then divorce will be effective after four months and if he does then he shall have to give recompensation for breach of oath.

6—One did not swear but said if he did sexual intercourse with her, it would be her divorce, then it would be *Eila*. If he does sexual intercourse then it will be a revocable divorce and there will be no recompense for breach of oath ; and if he did not do sexual intercourse then it will be a distinct divorce after the expiry of four months.

7—If anyone said to his wife that if he would do sexual intercourse with her, then one Haj or a fast or charity of one rupee or one sacrifice would be due towards him. Then it is *Eila* in all cases. If he will do sexual intercourse then he will have to fulfil the promised thing and recompensation for breach of oath shall also be due. If he did not do sexual intercourse then a distinct divorce will be effective after four months.

**Release From Marriage (Khula)**

1—If husband and wife cannot pull on together in any way and the husband refuses to divorce, then it is permissible for the wife to offer certain amount to the husband to release her or by foregoing her dowry (*Mehr*) may seek her release from marriage. She would say, she forgoes her dowry which is due on him and he may release her. The man says in reply that he did release her, then it is one distinct divorce (*Bayyan*) and now the man has no right to detain her. But if the man did not reply on the spot but left the place or the woman went away and afterwards he said that he released her, then it is of account. The offer and acceptance both should be on the spot. Such release is called *Khula*, that is, release from marriage.

2—If the husband said to his wife that he has released her and the wife agreed, then *Khula* is accomplished. But if the woman did not reply on the spot but left the place or she did not agree to it, then it will not be accomplished. But if the woman remained sitting silently on the spot and the man stood up saying it and left the place and the woman accepted it afterwards, then also the release (*Khula*) is accomplished.

3—If the husband just said that he has released her and the woman accepted it and nothing was mentioned about money by either of them, then all that is due from the man or the woman is remitted. If dowry is due towards the man it is also remitted and if the woman had already received it, it is not essential to return it. But the man shall have to give her maintenance and a house to live during *Iddat*. But if the woman gives up that claim also, then that too, will be remitted.

4—If in the offer or acceptance payment of some money was also mentioned, such as the man said that he is releasing her for one thousand rupees and the woman agreed, then this amount is due towards her and it is essential for her to pay it whether she had already received the dowry or not. If she has already received the dowry, then it will not be returned and if she has not received it, then it will be remitted and will not remain due on the husband as it is a condition of *Khula*.

5—In case of *Khula* (release) if the husband is at fault, then it is a great sin and also prohibited for him to release his wife in return for some money or property or dowry. If some money has been taken, it is prohibited for him to use it. But if the wife is at fault, then nothing more than the dowry, if paid, should be taken. If not paid, then she should be released in return for the dowry and nothing more should be taken. If more than that is taken it would be improper but not sinful.

6—If the woman did not agree to the release and the husband got it accepted by beating or threat or force, then it is divorce, but nothing is due towards the woman and the dowry, if due towards the husband, shall also not be remitted.

7—All of the above instances are when the word *Khula* was expressed and not divorce was demanded. For instance, if the woman said to her husband to divorce her in return for some money. Then it will not be called *Khula*. If the man accepts that offer and divorces her then it will be one distinct (*Bayyan*) divorce and in such case no right of either party shall be remitted—neither those which are due on the husband nor those which are due on the woman. She is entitled to her *Mehr* (dowry) and the man for the money she promised to give in return of divorce.

8—If the man said to his wife that he is divorcing her in return for one thousand rupees, then its accomplishment depends upon the acceptance of the woman. She may accept it or not. In case of acceptance it will be one distinct (*Bayyan*) divorce. If the woman accepts after changing her place then there will be no divorce.

9—If the husband promised to divorce his wife in return for her dowry and other rights and the wife said that she gave up all; but the husband did not divorce her. In this case no right or claim of the wife shall be remitted and all of them shall remain due towards him.

10—If the wife asked her husband to give her three divorces in return for three hundred rupees and after agreeing the husband gave one divorce only, then he will get one hundred rupees only. If he gave two divorces, then two hundred rupees. But if he gave all the three divorces then the woman shall have to pay three hundred rupees and in such case the divorce is *Bayyan* (distinct) as it is in return for money.

11—A minor or insane cannot agree to *Khula* with his wife.

## Declare Wife Equal to Mother (Zihar)

1—If anyone said to his wife that she was equal to his mother or like his mother etc. then it should be judged as to what he meant by it. If he meant that in respectability, age or appearance she is equal to his mother, then it is immaterial and of no account. But if while saying he did not mean this nor did intend anything but merely said without any aim or purpose, then also it is of no account and no harm is done. But if saying this he meant divorce, then it is one distinct (*Bayyan*) divorce. If he did not intend divorce even, but just meant that though she is his wife but he has forbidden on himself to do sexual intercourse with her and she shall receive her maintenance. Then according to Islamic Law it is called *Zihar*.

2—The religious decree for such position is that the woman will continue to be his wife, but the husband cannot do sexual intercourse with her or kiss her or embrace her with passion etc. and she will remain forbidden for him howsoever long a period may pass. But after giving recompensation, they can live as husband and wife and there is no need for re-marriage. Recompensation for *Zihar* is the same as for breach of fast.

3—If the husband did sexual intercourse with her without giving recompensation (*Kaffara*), then it would be a major sin. He should repent and pray Allah for His forgiveness and should resolve firmly not to do sexual intercourse with her without giving recompensation. The woman should also not allow him to come near her without giving recompensation.

4—The same rule will apply in case the husband said to his wife that she was equal to his sister or daughter such relation with whom marriage is forbidden for ever.

5—If a husband said to his wife that to him she is as a wine, then if the intent was for divorce, then it is a divorce, but if the intent was for *Zihar*, then it is immaterial and of no account. If he meant nothing at all, then also it is of no account.

6—If during *Zihar* the husband neither did sexual intercouse for more than four months nor gave recompensation, it will neither be divorce nor *Eila*.

7—Looking at or talking with the wife during *Zihar* and before giving recompensation is not prohibited. But it is not permissible to look at her private parts.

8—If *Zihar* was not intended for ever but for a limited time, such as, he said that she was equal to his mother for four months, then *Zihar* will last for that specified period. If one wants to have sexual intercouse with her during this period, he should first give recompensation. But if he does it after the expiry of the specified period, then it is permissible and no recompensation shall have to be paid.

9—A minor or an insane cannot practice *Zihar* and if he does it would be of no account.

10—If the words of *Zihar* are spoken more than once, then he has to give recompensation as many times as he spoke the words. But if by repeating the words of *Zihar* twice or thrice he just meant to emphasise, then he may give one recompensation only.

11—If the husband said words of *Zihar* to more than one of his wives, then he has to give recompensations according to the number of wives to whom he said the words.

12—If the husband did not use the words 'equal' or 'like' but just said that she was his mother or sister, then it is of no account. But to say like that is very bad and a sin also.

13—If anyone said to his wife that she is prohibited for him like his mother, then if the intent was for divorce, then it is divorce. If the intent was for *Zihar* or there was no intent at all, then it will be *Zihar* and sexual intercourse with her will be permissible after giving recompensation.

### Recompensation for Zihar

1—The recompensation of *Zihar* is the same as that of breach of fast and there is no difference.

2—If the man has capacity and strength he should keep fasts for sixty days continuously without any gap and should not have sexual intercourse with his wife before the end of sixty fasts. If he does during the fasts, he shall have to keep the sixty fasts afresh whether the intercourse was done during the day or night, intentionally or otherwise.

3 – If he started to keep fasts from the 1st date of a month, then he should complete two months. Some of the lunar months are short of thirty days, even then the recompensation would be met—that is the months may be either of 30 or 29 days each.

4—If one is not strong enough to keep sixty fasts continuously, then he should feed sixty poor people in the morning and evening with full meal or give foodgrain instead in the same quantity as already explained. If before completing the feeding of poor for two times, he committed sexual intercourse, then it would be a sin, but recompensation will be accomplished and should not be given again.

5—If two recompensations of *Zihar* were due on anyone and he gave four kg. of wheat to sixty poor persons presuming that both recompensations are accomplished, even then only one shall be fulfilled and not both and should give one more. But if the recompensations were for *Zihar* and breach of fast, then both have been met.

### Allegation of Adultery (Li'aan)

1—If any husband accuses his wife of adultery or says that the child born to her is not from him, then she should appear before Qazi or an officer of religious order and he shall put both to oath. First the husband should be made to say that he makes Allah witness and repeat it four times and on the fifth should say that the curse of Allah be on him if he is false. Then the woman should say four times that the husband's accusation is false and unjust and on the fifth time should say that curse of Allah be on her if the accusation of the husband is just and correct. Upon taking this oath the officer will order separation between them and the child born will not be treated as from him and will be given over to the woman. This separation will be a distinct (*Bayyan*) divorce. This kind of oath taking is called *Li'aan* (Slander)

### Absconding of Husband

If a woman's husband is absconding and it is also not known whether he is dead or alive, then the woman cannot marry any other man immediately, but should remain waiting for him in the hope that he may return. When she has waited so long that the age of the man is presumed to be ninety years and might have died during this period. So if the woman is still young and also wants to marry, then after the presumption that her husband might have attained the age of ninety years, she can do so after observing *Iddat* provided that the absconding person has been declared as dead by an officer of religious order.

### Wife's Confinement on Husband's Death or Divorce (*Iddat*)

1—If a woman's husband divorces her or the marriage is revoked by *Khula* (release) or *Eila* etc. or he dies, then in all such cases she has to live in the house for the specified period and cannot go out or re-marry another man immediately. After the end of this period she is at liberty. This waiting period is called *Iddat*.

2—If a man divorces his wife, then she will have to remain in the same house till she has had three monthly courses and should not go out of the house at any time during this period. Also she cannot marry another man during the period. With the end of the third monthly course the period of *Iddat* also expires. It is immaterial whether the man has given one divorce or two or three and whether the divorce is distinct (*Bayyan*) or revocable as the same rule will apply to all in *Iddat* performance.

3—If a minor girl who does not have monthly course or an old woman whose monthly courses have stopped, is divorced then in both cases the period of *Iddat* shall be three months and after that she will be at liberty to marry or not.

4—If a minor girl after being divorced began to count the *Iddat* period by months and then after one or two months she has monthly course, then she should complete three continuous monthly courses to complete the *Iddat* period.

5—If a pregnant woman is divorced then she will have to observe *Iddat* till the child is born and that is her limit of *Iddat*.

# NIKAH (MARRIAGE)

Even if the child is born just after being divorced.

6—If a woman was divorced during the monthly course then that course will not be counted but three monthly courses after that will be the period of *Iddat*.

7—To observe *Iddat* is essential for the woman who has had sexual intercourse with her husband and then was divorced or there was no sexual intercourse but they have remained in such seclusion. If there has been none of the two, then it is not essential to observe *Iddat*.

8—If anyone had given distinct (*Bayyan*) divorce to his wife or three divorces but during *Iddat* has had sexual intercourse with her in forgetfulness, then another *Iddat* has become due and she will have to wait for three more monthly courses after the incident and only then her *Iddat* will be complete.

9—If the divorced woman is living in the same house where the husband is living, then she should remain away and in seclusion from him.

10—The maintenance of the divorced wife is the responsibility of the divorcing husband during the period of her *Iddat*

11—If any woman's husband is dead, then she shall have to observe *Iddat* for four months and ten days in the same house where she was living at the time of her husband's death. Whether she has had sexual intercourse or not, and whether she was having monthly courses or not, the same rule shall apply. But if she was pregnant when her husband died, then the period of *Iddat* will end with the birth of the child and such months will not be counted. The birth of the child may be immediately after the death of the man or it may take more than four months.

12—Such woman can live in any part of the house where she likes. No particular spot should be specified for the bereaved woman.

13—If any woman's husband died on the first date of the lunar month and she is not pregnant, then she should count four months and ten days according to the lunar month, but if he died on any other date, then counting each month to be of thirty days she should complete four months and ten days. The same rule applies to the *Iddat* of divorce if the woman is not pregnant or in her monthly course.

14—If anyone gave distinct (*Bayyan*) divorce in his illness and he died before the expiry of *Iddat*, then it should be seen whether days of divorce *Iddat* are more or of death *Iddat* and whichever is more should be observed. But in case of revocable divorce in illness and death, the period of *Iddat* of death is valid.

15—If a husband died and his wife remained unaware of his death for full four months and ten days or more then she has completed the period and now it is not necessary for her to observe *Iddat* on learning his death. Similarly if a husband divorced his wife and she learnt about it after a long time when period of *Iddat* had already passed, then her period of *Iddat* is complete and now she should not sit in *Iddat*.

16—The woman had gone out of the house on some business or to her neighbour's house and during this period her husband died, then she should immediately return and observe *Iddat* in that house.

17—There is a custom at some places that woman sit in *Iddat* for one full year. This is not permissible.

18—The maintenance of a widow is not due on the dead husband during *Iddat*. She should manage her maintenance.

**Mourning for the Dead**

1—If a woman is observing *Iddat* on account of death of her husband or a distinct divoce or on breach of marriage, then she should not go out of the house or re-marry or put on fine clothes and ornaments. This abstaining from make up and toilet and putting on coarse clothes is called mourning.

2—So long as a woman is in *Iddat* it is not permissible for her to use perfume, wear ornaments and flowers, use *Kuhl* in her eyes, to use any type of lip paint, anoint her head, comb her hair, use myrtle, wear fine or silken clothes of gaudy colours.

3—In case of head-ache it is permitted ordinary and unperfumed oil in hair. Use of *Kuhl* is permissible as medicine at night only. To wash head when necessary and to comb hair to remove lice is permitted, but the hair should not be dressed ornately.

4—This type of mourning is essential for mature women only and not for minor girls. A minor widow should not go out of the house only and also should not marry during *Iddat* period.

5—Mourning is not permissible on the death of anyone else except the husband. But if permitted by the husband mourning may be observed on the death of some near relative but for more than three days is strictly prohibited.

**Maintenance of Wife**

1—The husband is responsible for the maintenance of his wife, howsoever rich she may be. He also has to provide a place for her residence.

2—Marriage (*Nikah*) has been solemnised, but she has not yet gone to live with the husband and is living with her parents, even then she can claim her maintenance from the husband. But if the husband desired to take her to his house and she did not go, then see cannot claim her maintenance from him.

3—If the customary advance *Mehr* has not been paid by the husband and so she did not go to her husband's house, then she is entitled to get maintenance from the husband. But if she does not go without any reason, then she is not entitled for her maintenance.

4—The period for which a wife lives with her parents with the permission of her husband, the husband can pay her maintenance for that period.

5—If the wife falls ill, she has the right to get maintenance from the husband whether she is living with her husband or with her parents. But if the husband called her to his house during the illness and she did not go, then the husband will not be responsible for treatment and only maintenance i.e. food and clothes will be due.

6—The husband is not responsible to arrange for the maintenance of his wife when she goes for Haj. But if he also accompanies her then he will be responsible for her maintenance. But he is not responsible for her Haj expenses and if he bears then it is his kindness.

7—In the matter of maintenance the position and status of both shall be taken into account. If both husband and wife are rich then food and clothing of the wife shall be of the same standard if both are poor, then it should be of that standard. If one of them is rich and the other poor, then the food and clothing should be average of both, that is, below rich level and higher than the poor.

8—If the woman is sick and cannot perform her house-hold duties or she belongs to a rich family and domestic works are beyond her or she regards it to be below her dignity, then she may be provided with cooked food. But it is better to do her domestic work with her own hands and as a house wife it is her responsibility. The duty of the husband is to provide the means and the wife should manage and run the house.

9—If the maintenance of wife has been provided by the husband for an year in lump-sum then it is permissible. Now he cannot take it back.

**Residence**

1—Husband is also responsible to provide for her such place to live in which no other relative of the husband resides so that both husband and wife may reside there freely. But if the wife herself agrees to live with others, then it is permissible.

2—If a specific part of the house is given exclusively to the wife where she can keep her goods under lock and key and it is in her charge, even then the responsibility of the husband is fulfilled.

3—Just as the wife has a right to claim a house exclusively for her in which no relative of the husband can live. Similarly the husband has the right to prevent the relatives of his wife to come to the house in which she lives, not even her parents, brothers or other relatives.

4—The wife is allowed to go to see her parents once a week

and other *Mehram* relatives once a year. More than that she cannot claim. Her parents also can visit her once a week only.

5—If the father of a woman is seriously ill and there is no one else to look after him, then she can go to see him daily, even if her father is irreligious or a non-believer. Even if the husband prevents her to go, she may go, but in such case she will not be entitled for her maintenance during her stay at her father's house.

6—Even a divorced wife is entitled for her maintenance and a house to live during the period of *Iddat* as a result of divorce. But in case of death of husband she is not entitled for it during the *Iddat*.

**Legitimate Issues**

1—When child is born to a married woman, then it would be preserved to be from the husband and it is not proper to say that the child is not from her husband but from someone else. Nor is it right to call the child illegitimate. In Islamic State such an accused will be flogged.

2—The period of pregnancy is six months at least and maximum two years. No child is born before six months nor can it remain in the womb for more than two years.

3—According to Islamic Law no child should be declared as illegitimate, unless it is inevitable to say so and then its mother shall be accused of adultery and a sinner.

4—If husband gave revocable divorce to his wife and then within two years from that, a child was born to her, then the child is not illegitimate but from the same husband.

5—If the husband of a woman dies and a child is born to her within two years of his death, then the child is legitimate and from her husband.

6—If a child is born to a woman in less than six months after marriage, then it is illegitimate. But if born after six months or more, then the child is from the husband and it is a sin to doubt him. But if the husband alleges that the child is not from him, then it would be a case of *Li'aan* (slander) and will be decided accordingly.

7—The *Nikah* was performed and a child is born to the wife before she joined her husband after her marriage, then the child is from her husband and not illegitimate. But if it is not from her husband, then he should refuse and after his refusal, it will be declared a case of *Li'aan* and will be decided accordingly.

8—The above rule also applies to a child born in the absence of the husband who was abroad since years. If the husband accepts the child to be from him, it would be a legitimate child, otherwise it would be a case of *Li'aan*.

**Right of Fostering a Child**

1—If separation and divorce have become final between husband and wife and there is a child yet in arms, then the mother has the right to foster the child. Father cannot take the child by force, but all the expenses of the child shall be borne by him. But if the mother does not agree to foster the child and gives it to the father, then he cannot refuse to have the child and also cannot force the mother to foster him.

2—If a child has no mother or if she refuses to take the child, the right to foster the child shall devolve in this order; the maternal grand-mother, and great grand-mother, then grand-mother, then her real sisters, step sisters whose and child's mother is the same, then step sisters whose and child's father is the same then mother's sister and lastly father's sister.

3—If there is no female among the child relatives, then the father of the child has the greatest right and then the grand-father etc. to foster the child in the same order as mentioned above in case of female relatives of the child.

4—The right of fostering a child is upto its age of seven years and when the child is upto its age of seven and when the child has attained his age the father can take the child even forcibly and the mother has no right to detain the child after that age.

**Mother's Milk—Sucking and Suckling**

1—When a child is born it is essential for the mother to suckle the baby. If the husband has means he can, of course, engage a wet nurse to the child, then it would not be a sin for the mother not to suckle the child.

2—It is not permissible for a woman to suckle someone's child without the permission of her husband, but if any baby is extremely hungry and there is risk of its dying if not suckled, then the woman may suckle the child without the consent of her husband.

3—The maximum period of suckling a baby is two years. It is prohibited and not proper to suckle a child after two years.

4—There is no harm if suckle is discontinued even before two years if the baby has begun to take solid food.

5—When a child suckled the milk of another woman, then she becomes its mother and her husband becomes father of the child. Thus the issues of this pair become sisters and brothers of that child and marriage betwen them is prohibited and relatives banned on account of descent are also banned on milk sharing. This restriction is appreciable if the suckling was upto the age of two years of the child. But not applicable if the child was suckled after the age of two-and-a half years. In this case marriage between them is permissible. Suckling of a child after his being more than two-and-a half years is of no account.

6—Once the milk of another woman has gone into the throat of the child, the ban is established whether the milk was substantial or small in quantity.

7—If the baby was not suckled by breast, but the milk was taken out and put into the mouth of the child, even then the ban will come into being. The same applies to putting of milk into the nose of the child. But if the milk was poured in the ear, then it is of no account and also not reliable.

8—If the milk of a woman was mixed with water or medicine and given to a child, then it should be seen whether the quantity of milk is greater or equal to the water or medicine. If the quantity of milk is larger or even equal to the water or medicine then the woman will become mother of the child and the ban will apply and if the quantity of milk is lesser than the water or medicine then the ban will not apply and the woman would not become mother of the child.

9—If the milk of a woman was mixed with the milk of a cow or goat and given to a child, then the above rule will apply to it also.

10—If somehow milk comes in the breasts of a maiden girl and it is sucked by a child, even then the ban will apply.

11—If a dead woman's milk is given to a child then the ban will become operative and marriage between the relatives of the woman and the baby will be prohibited.

12—If two babies were fed on the milk of the same cow or goat, they will not become sister and brother on this account.

13—If a man sucked the milk of his wife, then she will *not* become prohibited for him but it would be a major sin because it is prohibited to suck the milk of a woman after the age of two years.

14—If a boy and a girl have sucked the milk of the same woman, then marriage between them is prohibited whether they sucked together or at interval.

15—If a girl has sucked the milk of Baqar's wife, then this girl cannot marry Baqar, his father or grand-father or his sons and not even his sons from second wife.

16—If Abbas sucked the milk of Khadija and Qadar (husband of Khadija) had another wife named Zenab whom he had divorced. Now Zenab cannot marry Abbas as he is the son of Qadar. Marriage with husband's son is prohibited. In the same way Qadar cannot marry the divorced wife of Abbas because Qadar is her father-in-law. Qadar's sister cannot marry Abbas as she is his aunt, but sister of Abbas can be married with Qadar.

17—The sister of Abbas sucked the milk of a woman and not Abbas, then Abbas can marry that woman.

18—Zahid has sucked the milk of a woman, then Zahid's father can marry that woman.

19—Qadir and Zakir are two real brothers and Zakir has

a milk sharing sister. She can be married to Qadir but not to Zakir.

20—It is not permissible to mix medicine in the milk of woman, if done its use is prohibited. It is not proper to use this milk in any other personal use or for benefit.

## OATH—VOW AND PLEDGE
### (MANNAT)

1—It is very bad and improper to swear unnecessarily because in this way there is (Allah Forbid) disrespect and disgrace of the name of Allah.

2—It is prohibited to swear, in the name of any other except Allah i.e. in the name of one's child, health or eyes etc. It is a sin. If any such oath is uttered unintentionally, then *Kalima* should be recited immediately.

3—One should never swear by saying that if he is wrong, he may lose his faith even if the fact is correct.

4—If anyone took such an oath in anger the accomplishment of which is a sin, then it should be broken and give recompensation i.e. one swore that he will not speak with his parents. Such oath is a sin.

5—As far as possible one should not swear even for a true fact.

6—If anyone swore by Allah and said that by His Greatness, by His Dignity, by His Honour, then the oath becomes a pledge and it will not be proper to violate it. But in the oath the name of Allah was not mentioned and he said that he "Swears to do such thing," even then it is a pledge and its fulfilment is essential.

7—If anyone said "Allah is witness or I make Allah a witness and knowing Him to be Omnipresent" even then it is pledge.

8—If anyone took an oath by Holy Quran or the name of Allah, then it is a pledge, But if one said anything by putting hand on Holy Quran and did not swear by it, then it is not a pledge.

9—If anyone swore by saying that if he would do any particular thing, he would die as a faithless or will not be a Muslim then it is a pledge. To violate it would destroy his faith. In case of violation recompensation is essential.

10—To swear by saying that if he will do certain thing, he may lose his hands, eyes or may become a pauper or be cursed by Allah, or be ashamed before Allah and Holy Prophet on the Day of Judgement or may not be able to recite *Kalima* at the time of death, then in all such cases it is not a pledge and no recompensation is essential upon its violation.

11—Taking an oath i.e. the name of anyone else except Allah, is not a 'pledge or oath i.e. swearing "By the Prophet (SAW) by Ka'aba, or by one's eyes, hands, youth, or by father, children or by one's head etc. There is no recompensation for violation of such oath. But such oath has been strictly prohibited by the Traditions. It amounts to *Shirk* and should be avoided.

12—If anyone swore not to eat food of some other person's house, or said that a certain thing has become forbidden for him, that food or thing will not become forbidden (*Haraam*) but it is a pledge and its violation entails recompensation.

13—Oath given to someone else is not binding i.e. Baqir said to Zakir that he give him Allah's pledge (oath) to do a certain act, then it is not binding on Zakir and there will be no recompensation for its violation.

14—If anyone said "By Allah I will do that thing *Insha Allah*" then it is not a pledge.

15—To take a false oath about anything is a major sin, i.e. one did not offer prayer and when asked about it he said by Allah he has offered it. The limit of such a sin cannot be measured. It cannot be rectified by giving recompensation even. So one should repent day and night and seek Allah's forgiveness.

16—If anyone swore for such a thing which has not as yet happened i.e. said 'by Allah it will rain today' or 'by Allah his brother would come that day,' but it did not rain or his brother did not come, then recompensation will be essential.

17—If anyone swore to commit a sin, then it is essential

to break such an oath and give recompense.

18—If anyone swore not to eat a particular thing that day and ate it in forgetfulness, then recompensation is due.

19—If one swore not to go to house, if he stands at the thresh-hold or under its balcony, the oath will not be broken. Only on entering the house it will be broken.

20—If anyone swore not to go to a certain house. The house fell and was ruined and he went there, then the pledge is broken. But if the house was levelled to the ground and no trace of it was left or it was turned into a mosque and now he goes there, then the oath will not be broken.

21—If anyone swore not to go to a certain house. It fell down and was rebuilt and if he goes there now it will breach his pledge.

22—If anyone swore not to live in a certain house and immediately began to arrange to shift his goods, then the oath will remain. But if he waited for some time after taking oath and did not start packing immediately, then oath is breached.

23—If anyone swore not to drink certain milk but it was later on turned into curd, then eating of this curd will not breach his oath.

24—If anyone swore not to eat meat, but ate fish or liver etc. then oath is not breached.

25—If anyone swore not to eat bread, then he should not eat any such stuff which is used in preparing a bread otherwise his oath will be breached.

26—If anyone took an oath not to speak with a boy, but when he became matured or old, then speaking with him at that stage will not breach the oath.

27—If anyone swore not to see any particular person's face meaning thereby not to have any company with him, then the oath will not be breached if he by chance sees his face from a distance.

28—If anyone swore not to beat his child and then got him beaten by some one else, then the oath will not be breached.

29—If anyone swore to offer some prayer for success in any matter, upon its accomplishment it is essential to fulfill the oath and it would be a sin if not done. But if the oath is for some absurd and superstitious thing which is not according to Islamic Law, then its fulfilment is not essential.

30—If anyone prayed to Allah that if his object or aim is granted, he will keep fast for five days. Then it is essential to keep the fasts upon its accomplishment according to words of pledge whether continuously or in instalments.

31—If anyone swore to keep a fast on Friday or for ten days from 1st to 10th of Muharram, then it is not essential for him to keep fast just on Friday or on the same dates of Muharram. He may keep the fast on anyday, and the ten fasts of Muharram can also be observed at any time, but they shall have to be kept continuously.

32—If anyone vowed to offer eight *Raka'ats* of prayer on finding his lost thing or person, then the *Raka'ats* should be offered either at a time or by fours or twos.

33—If anyone vowed to feed ten poor or orphans on the accomphsliment of certain aim, then if he had in mind to feed one or two meals, he should do accordingly. But if he had no such idea in mind, then he should feed ten poor people two times. He can give food grains also to the poor in lieu of cooked food. But it shall also be governed by the same rule (of one or two times) and should be equal to *Sadqa-e-Fitr* in weight.

34—If anyone vowed to pray in *Juma Masjid* he can offer prayers in any mosque after the accomplishment of his aim.

35—If some one vowed for a certain thing to be accomplished i.e. for success in litigation, or for recovery from illness or for getting service, then it is essential to fulfil it upon the accomplishment of the desire.

36—If anyone vowed to hold a meeting of sermon (*Milad*) on Prophet's (SAW) birthday on accomplishment of his aim or that he will offer a covering for a saint's grave, then it is improper and its fulfilment is not essential.

37—If anyone vowed to rebuild a rescinded mosque upon accomplishment of his aim, then it is not proper and nothing will be due upon him.

38—It is not permissible to vow or take oath about not keeping fast or not offering of prayers etc. If foolishly someone takes such an oath or vow it should be broken and recompensation should be given.

### Recompensation (Kaffarah) of Oath

1—If anyone breaks his oath, then its recompensation is to feed ten poor men for two times with full meal, or may give foodgrain in lieu thereof and its weight shall be equal to *Sadqa-e-Fitr* and it is better to give two kg. of wheat per head per day and if barley is given then it should be double in weight than wheat. The method of feeding the poor is the same as already described in the recompensation of fast.

Clothes can also be given as recompensation to ten poor people but it should be sufficient to cover greater parts of body. But the clothes should not be too old. In case of women the clothes should be such which may cover her body so that she may offer prayer with them. If given less, then the recompensation will not be met.

2—If anyone is so poor that he can neither feed ten poor people nor give clothes to them, then he should keep three fasts continuously. These fasts cannot be kept at intervals. If one missed any of these fasts, he shall have to keep three fasts continuously again otherwise recompensation will not be met.

3—If anyone gave recompensation before breaking an oath, then it is not met. He will have to give it again after breaking the oath. What has already been given to the poor cannot be taken back from the poor.

4—If several recompensations are due towards anyone, then separate recompensation for each should be given. If it could not be given during lifetime, then he should leave a Will in this respect for his heirs to give the due recompensation. Such Will is essential.

5—Recompensation should be given only to those persons who are eligible to receive *Zakat*.

# APOSTASY
## (DENOUNCING FAITH)

1—If anyone, Allah Forbid, denounces faith and religion then such a person be given three days to reconsider and if he or she has any doubts, the same should be removed. If within this period he or she returns to faith, so far so good. If not, then in case of a woman she should be put to prison for her life and should be released only when she repents and recants. In case of a man he should be killed after three days.

2—If anyone utters a word of disbelief and blasphemy, then he loses his faith (*Iman*) and all of his good acts and devotion which he had done so far are also wasted. His marriage is also breached. If he has performed Haj then it also remains of no avail. If such a person repents and recants, then he should re-marry and perform Haj again.

3—If a woman's husband becomes apostate and abandons his faith, then the marriage is breached and till he repents and recants and remarry her she should have nothing to do with him. If they indulge in sexual intercourse, it would be a sin. If the man does it by force, then the woman should make it public and should not feel shy in doing so.

4—As soon as one utters a word of blasphemy and disbelief, his faith (*Iman*) is lost even if such word was said in joke. For instance if one said "Does Allah not possess so much power to accomplish certain business?" and some other person replied in the affirmative, then the other person becomes a non-believer.

5—If anyone asked someone to get up and offer prayer and he replied, "What is there in doing this exercise." Or anyone asked the other to observe fasts and he replied, "Why one should starve ?" or said "Fasts are for those who have nothing to eat." All these are words of apostasy and blasphemy.

6—On seeing someone committing a sin one said, "Are you not afraid of Allah," and the other replied, "No", then it amounts to apostasy.

7—While offering prayer some calamity befell him and if he says that this bad presage is on account of prayer, then he will become apostate.

8—If any worldly good is seen in a non-believer and someone wished to be a non-believer to get that benefit, then he becomes an apostate.

9—If anyone's child died and in agony he or she cried saying "O' Allah ! why this tyranny upon me ?" then he will become an apostate.

10—If anyone says that he will not do certain thing even if ordered by Allah or even if Angel Gibrail comes from Heaven, then he becomes an apostate.

11—If Allah or His Holy Prophet (SAW) is insulted or debased by someone or found fault with the injunctions of religious code, then in such cases he loses his *Iman* (faith). May Allah preserve us all and keep our faith secure and may all of us die on faith. Aameen.

# SLAUGHTERING OF ANIMALS
## (DHABIHA)

1—The method of slaughtering permitted animals for food is to lay the animal on the ground with its face towards Ka'aba and then reciting:

*Bismillah-e-Allah-o-Akbar*

Cut its throat in such a way that four of its arteries are cut fully i.e. one of food passage, second respiratory and two arteries on either side of the food passage. The slaughtering will also be in order if only three arteries are cut. If only two have been cut, then the animal would become banned and its flesh will not be permissible.

2—While slaughtering if reciting of Bismillah was omitted deliberately, then the animal becomes polluted and banned and its flesh is prohibited. But if the omission was inadvertent, then it is permissible to eat the flesh.

3—To slaughter an animal with a blunt knife is execrable and not permissible because the animal feels extreme pain in this way. So it is also execrable to remove its skin or break its bones before it is quite cold.

4—While slaughtering a hen if its head is separated, then its flesh is permissible and not execrable. But the action of cutting it to such extent is execrable.

5—The slaughtering of an animal is in order by a Muslim whether by man or woman, clean or unclean. But it is prohibited to eat meat of an animal slaughtered by a non-believer.

6—The implement of slaughtering should be sharp edged, it may be a knife or a stone or even skin of sugar cane.

## Permissible and Prohibited Things

1—The animals or birds which live by hunting other animals or whose food is filth and dirt, their flesh is prohibited i.e. lions, wolves etc. vultures, foxes, kites, crows and falcons etc. and those which are not of their category; such as, parrots, doves, sparrows, partridges, ducks, pigeons, neelgao, bucks, rabbits etc. their flesh is permissible.

2—The flesh of wild cat, lizard, wasp, mule, donkey etc. is not permissible. So also the milk of female donkey is not permissible. The flesh of horse is permissible but not preferable. Among the sea or river animals, only fish is permissible and all other animals are prohibited.

3—Only fish and locusts are permitted to be eaten without proper slaughtering as explained above. The dead animal's flesh is prohibited.

4—If a fish dies and floats on the water, its flesh is not permissible.

5—The eating of entrails is neither right nor wrong nor execrable.

6—If ants die in anything, it is not permissible to eat without removing the ants from it. If any ant goes down the throat with it, it is like the sin of eating of a dead animal. Some children and even adults eat wild-figs with its moths and think that eating of these moths prevents eye-sore. This is prohibited and sin like eating of dead.

7—The slaughtered flesh to be permissible should remain under the supervision or observance of a Muslim till cooked and served for eating.

8—A hen which takes excretion as its food, it desired to be slaughtered, should be kept shut for three days before slaughtering. If not kept closed, then its flesh is execrable.

## Intoxicants

1—All kinds of wines are prohibited and unclean. Taree (juice of date trees) is also in the same order. The use of wine even as medicine is prohibited. Even the external use of a medicine mixed with wine is not permissible.

2—Other intoxicants like opium, saffron etc. may be used as medicine internally or externally, is permissible in such quantity which does not intoxicate.

3—Vinegar prepared by palm-juice or wine is permissible.

4—Some women give opium to children to make them sleep. This is strictly prohibited.

# CLOTHES AND PURDAH (COVER)

1—It is not permissible for women to wear very fine and thin clothes i.e. muslin etc. as it is to go naked. It has been reported in the traditions that on the Day of Judgement many women will be naked. It is more awful if the shirt and scarf of a woman are very fine and thin.

2—It is not permissible for women to put on male shoes or dress like men. Such women have been cursed by the Holy Prophet (SAW).

3—It is permissible for women to wear ornaments but not too many. One who did not love these in this world, she will get much to wear in the hereafter. Wearing of jingling ornaments is not permissible. Rings of metals other than gold or silver are not permissible for women.

4—Women have been required and directed to keep their body covered from head to foot. No part of her body should be exposed before a *na-mehram* (non-permitted person). However, it is permissible for old women to keep their face, hands and feet below the ankle uncovered and no other part of the body. It is also not permissible to touch any part of her body with that of a *na-mehram*. The hair which come out in comb while dressing the head and clipped nails should not be thrown at such a place where a *na-mehram* may see it. If he sees them and knows that these are of such and such woman, then she will be a sinner.

5—It is not permissible for a young woman to open her face before a *na-mehram*.

6—It is not a sin if the head, chest, arms and calf are uncovered before a woman's *mehram*, but abdomen, back and thigh should not be exposed even before a *mehram* (permitted person).

7—The exposing of a woman's body from navel upto the thighs even before woman is not permissible.

8—In case of necessity i.e. an ulcer in the thigh, only the affected part may be exposed before a doctor or compounder for its operation or dressing.

9—The parts of the body, the covering of which is essential, should not be exposed even before women. The Holy Prophet (SAW) has said that curse of Allah be upon those women who show or see the essential parts of other women.

10—Athiest or unbelieving women such as milkmaids, vegetable sellers. sweepress etc. who frequently visit houses, injunction about them is the same as for *na-mehram*, that is, the parts of the body which should remain covered in the presence of a *na-mehram*, should also remain covered before such women. Only face, hands and feet upto ankles may remain uncovered before such women.

11—There is no restriction for husband and wife between themselves. They can see each other's private parts but not without necessity.

12—For a woman to remain in seclusion with a *na-mehram* or to sit with him, is not permissible.

13—Women are not permitted to appear unveiled even before their spiritual preceptor. He is also a *na-mehram* like husband's brother, sister's husband, sister-in-law's husband, uncle's son etc. Purdah should be observed by women before all *na-mehrams*.

14—Some women and grown up girls get bangles worn by male bangle merchants, it is immodesty. The merchant holds the hands of women. This should not be done as it is improper and matter of great shame.

15—An adopted boy is also *na-mehram* as he cannot become a son. Women of the house hold should treat him like a *na-mehram* when he is grown up.

16—One should not walk with one shoe on. Start wearing clothes and shoes from the right side and take them off from the left side.

17—After wearing clothes recite :

$$\text{اَلْحَمْدُ لِلَّهِ الَّذِى كَسَانِى هٰذَا وَرَزَقَنِيهِ مِنْ غَيْرِ حَوْلٍ مِنِّى وَلَا قُوَّةٍ}$$

18—Do not wear such dress which may not cover the essential parts of the body.

# MISCELLANEOUS INSTRUCTIONS

1—It is appreciable to take bath at least once a week and clean the body by removing or shaving the hair of pelvis and of arm-pits. If it is not possible to bathe every week due to paucity of water or some unavoidable reason, then one should bathe at least every fort-night or utmost in forty days. Beyond forty days it is not permissible to remain unclean and it would be a sin.

2—It is not permissible to burn any living being in fire such as wasps or bugs. But if it is inevitable and there is no other way then to burn wasps and pouring of boiling water on cots and beds is allowed to get rid of bugs.

3—It is not permitted to bet on anything but if it is one sided, then allowed.

4—If the persons are talking in low tone or whispering, then do not go near them and it is a sin to eavesdrop them. It has been reported in the Traditions that anyone who eavesdrops to someone's talk and they dislike it, then on the Day of Judgement molten lead will be poured into his ears.

5—It is a major sin to tell others what the husband and wife had between them in privacy. It has been reported in the Traditions that wrath of Allah and curse will be upon those persons who reveal such private things to others.

6—To joke with anyone in such a way which is not liked by him or embarrass him, is not permissible.

7—To curse oneself or desire death in times of difficulty or adverse circumstances, is not proper.

## MISCELLANEOUS INSTRUCTIONS

8—When children are of ten years of age, then boys should not be allowed to lie with mother or sisters on the same bed nor girls with father or brother.

9—After sneezing one should say *Alhamdolillah* and when he said it then it is essential for those who hear to say *yarhamakallah* (may Allah favour you with His Mercy) and if not said the hearers will be sinners. In reply to *yarhamakallah* the sneezer may say, *yaghferullaho lana walakum* (may Allah forgive me and you). It is better but not essential for the sneezer to say so.

10—If several persons heard *Alhamdolillah* after sneeze, then it is not essential for all to respond it with *yarhamakallah*. If only one does, it is sufficient, but if none said then all will be sinners.

11—If anyone sneezes continuously for several times and says *Alhamdolillah* each time, then it will be essential to respond it for three times only and not thereafter.

12—If anyone pronounces or hears the sacred name of the Holy Prophet (SAW) it becomes essential for him to send *Darood Sharif* (greetings) to him. It would be a sin if not done.

13—It is not proper and permissible to cut some of the hair of a child from the centre of his head. The entire head should be shaved or kept unshaven.

14—It is Sunna for women to say *Assalam-o-Alaikum* and shake hands. This habit should be propagated and popularised among them.

15—If one is guest somewhere, then do not give anything from the food etc. to any beggar. It is a sin to do so without the permission of the host.

16—One should not be proud of one's dress and should not walk in an unmannerly way.

17—One should not lie on his or her belly.

18—If after some ceremony or gathering any unclaimed article is found, it is prohibited to take it. It should be picked up with the intention to find its owner and give it to him.

19—It is not a sin to pick up an unclaimed article but it is essential to find its owner and restore it to him.

20—If anyone picked up an unclaimed article then it becomes essential for him to find out its owner and restore it to him. It would be a sin if he dropped it there again or brought it to his home and did not try to find out its owner.

21—If after all possible efforts and publicity one is disappointed in finding the owner of a lost thing, then he should give it to some poor man and should not keep it himself. But if he himself is so poor then he may keep it for his own use.

22—If some pet bird like pigeon etc. comes to one's house by chance and he catches it, then it is essential for him to find its owner and restore it to him. It is prohibited for him to keep it.

23—It is prohibited to pick up fruits from a garden and eat them without the permission of the owner.

24—The same rule applies to anything or a treasure in a house or jungle. It is not permissible to keep it with oneself. If after all efforts no owner is found, it should be given in charity.

# SALUTATION
## (SALAAM)

1—Muslims should greet one another with *Assalam-o-Alaikum* meaning "Peace be on you" and its reply should be *Wa-alaikum-assalam* meaning "Peace be on you also." All other methods are absurd.

2—One who takes the initiative in offering salute gets greater reward.

3—If anyone brings salam from any other, it should be replied thus: "Alaihim wa-laikumassalam," that is, "Peace be on you and him also."

4—If out of a group of persons one salutes, then it is from all of them. Similarly if anyone from a gathering has replied it is also from all of them.

5—It is forbidden to salute with the motion of hand or head or bowing. But if anyone is at a distance and salutes, then it is permissible to reply by raising hand but words of salam should also be uttered with the motion of hand.

6—Muslim children studying in non-Muslim schools, should not salute in their (non-Muslim) fashion but strictly in Islamic way. If a teacher or class-mate is non-believer, then he should be greeted with "Assalamo-Ala-Manittaba'al Huda" that is, "Peace be on him who performed allegiance." Words of salutation of non-believers should not be uttered in any way.

# WAQF—ENDOWMENT

1—It is an act of great credit and merit if one endows his or her property such as house or a garden or village or land etc. for benefit of poor, needy and indigent declaring that all the income from the property or its produce will be spent for the benefit and amelioration of the poor ; or the house is reserved for poor people to live and it will not be put to any other use. All the good and noble acts of a person end with his death, but endowment is such act that its credit will continue till the property lasts and so long as poor people are benefited by it. Its credit will continue to be recorded in the record of the donor.

2—If anyone donates any of his property, it should be given in the charge of a good, pious and honest man to look after it and to see that its income is spent for the specific purpose.

3—Anything which has been donated does not remain of the donor but belongs to Allah and it is not proper to sell it or transfer it to anyone nor can anyone interfere in it. It shall now be used exclusively for the purpose for which it has been donated and not for any other purpose.

4—It is not proper to bring into one's own use anything of a mosque, like bricks, lime, wood etc. however useless they may become. They should be sold and the money spent on the mosque.

5—Such condition in a Waqf is permissible that so long as the donor is alive all or any part of the income will be taken by him and after his death the entire income will be spent in the specific charitable businesses. Or that a certain portion of the income shall be given to his heirs and the remaining part shall be spent in the charitable cause for which it has been donated.

**About Dreams**

1—If anyone sees a dreadful dream and wakes up after it, then he should spit thrice towards his left side and recite thrice :

$$\text{أَعُوذُ بِاللهِ مِنَ الشَّيْطَانِ الرَّجِيمِ}$$

*"A'oozo-billahe-minash shaitanirrajim."*

and change his side on the bed. By the grace of Allah no harm will come, and should not say about it to anyone.

2—If you want to tell your dream, then describe it to a wise man who is your well-wisher.

3—Do not coin a false dream. It is a great sin.

## RIGHTS AND DUTIES

**Parents**

1—Never tease and trouble the parents though there may be excesses from them.

2—Respect them in words and deeds.

3—Obey their all permissible orders and instructions.

4—If they are in need, help them with money and serve them even if they are non-believers.

5—When they are dead, pray to Allah for their absolution and for His Mercy upon them.

6—Treat their friends with respect and behave properly with them.

7—If any debt is due towards them, get it settled and fulfil their Will, if any.

8—Do not weep over their death in such manner which is forbidden by *Sharia*. Such weeping pains their souls.

9—The rights of grand-father, grand-mother, maternal grand-father and mother etc are also the same as that of parents. In the same way uncle, father's mother and sister etc. have their rights and these have been stressed in the Traditions.

**Wet-Nurse**

10—She should be respected and due regards should be paid to her. If she is in need and one has the means, she should be helped with money also.

**Step-Mother**

11—She is a friend of father and father's friends should be treated with kindness and beneficence. So a step mother should also be respected and treated like one's own mother.

**Elder Brother**

12—According to the Traditions elder brother is like father in his position. So a younger brother is like a son and both have the same rights and duties between them as father and son. Similar is the case of elder and younger sister.

### Relatives

13—If one's relatives are poor or invalid and have no means of livelihood, then they should be helped according to one's own means. They should be visited occasionally and one should not severe relations with them even if they give some harm.

### In-Laws

14—Relation and genealogy has been mentioned by Allah in the Holy Quran which shows that mother and father-in-law, brother-in-law, son-in-law and daughter-in-law etc. have also their rights and they should be preferred over others in matter of treatment.

### General Muslims

15—(a) A Muslim should forgive another Muslim. (b) He should be treated with kindness. (c) Cover his faults and defects. (d) His excuse should be accepted. (e) Remove his difficulties. (f) Be his well-wisher always. (g) Endure his love. (h) Keep his promise and pledge. (i) Take care of him in illness and pray in his death. (i) Accept his gift and invitation. (k) Return his good acts with good in need and protect his family. (m) Do not disappoint him. (n) Return greetings and behave properly with him. (o) Protect him from oppression and check him from oppressing. (p) Do not disgrace him. (q) Do not envy him nor disbelieve him. (r) If two Muslims quarrel, get them resolved. (s) Do not back bite or speak ill of a Muslim. (t) Do not harm him in any way.

### Neighbours

16—(a) Treat him with concession and good acts. (b) Respect and protect the honour of his wife and children. (c) Send gifts to him occasionally and particularly when he is hungry and in need. (d) Do not quarrel with him on petty matters, (e) A co-traveller also has the same rights as a neighbour.

### Orphans and Poor

17—An orphan, poor, widow, aged, sick and invalid persons, helpless travellers have also their rights and they should be helped with money etc. One should try to keep them happy and solve their problems. Their requests for help in need should not be rejected when one has the means.

### All Human Beings

18—All are creatures of Allah whether Muslims or non-believers. They also have their rights.

(a) They should not be ill-treated or punished without fault. (b) Do not abuse them or use indecent language with them. (c) If anyone of them is found hungry or in trouble or in illness, he should be fed and treated medically. (e) There should be no excess even in legitimate punishment with them.

### Animals

19—Animals and birds should not be ill-treated. It is tyranny to bring out young ones of birds from their nests or to cage them. Animals which are permissible for consumption should also not be killed for mere pleasures. Domestic animals should be properly fed and cared for. They should not be made to work more than their strength. Animals should be slaughtered with very sharp weapons and very quickly.

## ABOUT WILL

1—If one says that after his death so much of his wealth or property be given to such and such persons or be given for such business etc. then it is Will, whether he says this in health or illness and whether he dies in his illnes or recovers from it. If he gives something himself or remits some debt then it is proper to do so in health and in such illness from which he recovers and if he dies in illness it would be a Will.

2—If recompensation for prayers, fasts, *Zakat* or oath is due towards anyone and he has sufficient money or property then it is necessary and essential for him to make his Will. It is also essential to make a Will in case someone's debt is due on him or someone's deposit is kept with him and it would be a sin not to do so. If such a rich person has some poor relatives who are not entitled to inherit him according to Islamic Law and he makes some provision for such relatives it would be appreciable. For the rest it is optional to make or not to make a Will.

3—After one's death first of all the expenses of his property and then his liabilities and debts should be settled out of the remaining property. If his entire property is utilised in settling his debts then it should be done and let his heirs be deprived of their share because it is essential to discharge the bebts. Debts should be cleared whether a Will has been made or not. But it is better to make a Will about debts. Besides debts one can make a Will but it cannot exceed one-third of the property left by the deceased. If the Will can be met out of one-third, it is not essential for the heirs to spend more. If the Will cannot be met out of one-third then only such part of the Will should be met as can be discharged with one-third and rest of the Will should be left over.

4—It is not essential to make Will in respect of those heirs who are entitled to shares in legacy such as parents, husband, wife, sons and daughters etc. Will is, however, permissible for such relatives who are not entitled to share in the legacy or any out-sider.

5—No doubt it is allowed to make a Will for one-third of the property but it is better to make a Will for less than one-third. If the person is not rich enough he should not make a Will and leave everything for the heirs so that they may live conveniently. It is also meritable to leave sufficient for the heirs. But it is essential to make a Will for recompensation of prayer, fast etc. It would be a sin not to do so.

6—If anyone has no heirs, he can make a Will for his entire property.

7—Will by a minor is not proper and admissible.

8—If after having made a Will a person goes back on it and declares it to be unreliable, then the Will becomes invalid.

9—One had remitted his debt on someone during his illness and he died in the same illness, then the debt will not be remitted as he had no right to do so in that illness. If he did, then more than one-third will be remitted. In the same way the custom that the wife forgoes her claim of her *Mehr* on the death of her husband is also not justified. The *Mehr* of also amounts to bebt.

10—It is proper and permissible to entertain guests or give as charity and *sadqa* etc. out of the property left by the deceased. There is a custom of distributing foodgrains to the poor after the death and before burial of a person. It is strictly forbidden. It carries no credit for the dead and on the other hand it is a sin. The heirs after distributing the legacy according to their shares can do any such thing permitted by *Shariah* out of their shares.

# GIFT
## (HIBA)

1—If someone gave anything to anyone and he accepted it or did not say anything and the thing was left in his hand, then it becomes his property and no longer remains of the giver. This is called *Hiba* (gift) in Islamic Law. There are several conditions for *Hiba* to be valid :

   (*a*) Handing over of the thing by one and taking by the other. Possession by the other is essential. If someone gave some clothes locked in a box but did not give its key, then the gift is not complete unless the key is also given.

   (*b*) The donor should be a major. If a minor gives anything, the gift will not be proper and it is not permissible for anyone to take a thing from a minor.

2—If anyone did not give whole thing but just half or one-third or one-fourth of it, then the nature of the thing will be judged whether it can be of any use after its division. If it cannot be of any use after division, it is permissible to give without dividing it and if the other takes it in possession then it will become a joint property. But if the thing can be divided and can be of use after division, then it is not proper to give it without dividing it such as house etc.

3—If two persons purchased a thing jointly i.e. house, garden or cloth length, then unless it is divided amongst them, it will not be proper for one to give his share to someone else in any shape.

4—If someone gave his house as gift to anyone, he should give its possession after vacating it.

5—If anything was kept as deposit with someone and the

same was given to the custodian by the depositor as gift then in this case mere acceptance by the custodian is sufficient and possession is not essential as it is already in his possession.

## Gift to Children

1—There is a custom of giving things to children on certain occasions and functions. As a matter of fact they are not intended to be given to them but to their parents or guardians. But if one gives something specially to the child then it becomes the property of that child. If a child does not take its possession or is unable to do so, then its possession is taken by his father and grand-father or some guardian, then the child will become its owner. In the presence of father or grand-father, it is not proper for mother etc. to take possession of the thing.

2—If anything is given to one's children, it should be distributed equally among them. The share of boys and girls should also be equall otherwise the gift will be objectionable.

3—The thing which is the property of a minor, it should be used for his benefit alone. It is not proper and permissible for the parents to use it for themselves or other children.

4—In the same way the parents are not allowed to give child's property on loan to others.

## To Take Back the Gift

1—It is a great sin to take back a gift. But if anyone takes back a thing and the person to whom it was given also agrees to return it, then the donor will again become its owner. But there are certain circumstances in which there is no authority to take a gift after giving it. For instance someone gave a goat to anyone who fed and reared it well, then its taking back is not proper. Similarly some land was given to someone and he built a house over it or planted a garden over it, then no right of taking it back remains. In the case of a goat it may be taken back but not its kids.

2—In all the conditions when taking back is permitted the consent of the other is essential but it is a sin even then.

**Rent And Wages**

1—If a house is taken on rent for a month and its possession is also taken, then at the end of the month the payment of its rent is essential whether it was occupied or kept vacant.

2—If the tailor stitched some clothes, a dyer dyed the clothes or a washerman washed some one's clothes, then they have a right not to deliver the goods to the owner until they are paid their wages or charges. It is not proper to take those things by force. But a labourer who was engaged to bring some food-grains, cannot detain it for payment of his charges as the condition of the commodity has not been changed and it was changed in the former instance of tailor etc.

3—If a person was engaged on the specific condition that he himself would tailor, dye or wash the clothes, then he cannot get it done by others.

## TRANSACTION ON INTEREST

1—Transaction on interest is very sinful and it has been greatly condemned by the Holy Quran and the Traditions of the Holy Prophet (SAW). To refrain from such transaction has been greatly stressed. The Holy Prophet (SAW). has cursed both—one who takes interest and one who pays and also who arranges it between the parties along with the writer of the bond and its witnesses etc. He has said that the lender and the payer of interest are equally sinners. Muslims should save themselves and refrain from interest.

2—There are four kinds of commodities for which transactions are done :—
  (i) Gold and silver and articles made of them.
  (ii) The things which are sold by weight i.e. grain, iron, copper, cotton etc.
  (iii) Things sold by measurement, like cloth, and
  (iv) Things sold by number or count.

3—There are different methods and systems of purchasing gold and silver. One system is to exchange silver with silver and gold with gold. That is silver is purchased with rupee coins and gold with gold coins i.e. the same commodity is on both sides. In such case two considerations are essential the first being that the commodity of both sides should be equal and the other is that the bargain should be struck on the spot and nothing should be left in arrear. Anything against these would be interest. If one purchased silver with one rupee, it should be equal to the weight of the coin, more or less than that would be interest.

4—The other method is that the commodity on both the sides is not the same. One party has gold and the other silver

# TRANSACTION ON INTEREST 351

Then it is not necessary that both commodities should be equal in weight. but whatever quantity of silver for a rupee and whatever quantity of gold for a gold coin is available is permitted but the transaction should be executed on the spot and it is also essential that there should be no deferred payment or purchase.

5—The things which are sold by weight as grain etc. in their exchange also the two considerations are essential, that is, it should be executed on the spot and possession should be taken.

6—If two such commodities of different kind are exchanged, then it is not essential for both to be equal in weight.

## SALE THROUGH ADVANCE MONEY
### (BAI-US-SALAM)

1—If after harvesting anyone gave certain amount of money to the cultivator on the understanding that at a certain time he will take so much of wheat at such and such rate, then the transaction is in order. But for such transaction to be permissible, there are several conditions:

(*a*) *Quality* of the commodity should be clearly settled before purchase. If at the time of purchase or giving money only it was said that wheat or some other commodties be given for the money without specifying quality, then it is not permissible.

(*b*) *Rate* should also be settled before giving money, If one said that the seller may give at the market rate, it is not permissible.

(*c*) *Quality* of the commodity should also be specified.

(*d*) *Fixation of time*—The time or date of delivery should also be settled, whether it would be taken immediately or after some time.

(*e*) *Place of Delivery* should also be decided at the time of bargain, whether it would be taken immediately on the spot or delivered at his house, should be made clear, if not done the transaction would not be proper.

(*f*) *Searcity of commodity* — One important condition of sale on money to be in order is that from the time of settlement of bargain the commodity in question is available in the market till delivery. If it is not available or can be procured from anywhere else with much difficulty, then the sale will become ineffective.

## Transaction on Loan

1—It is permissible to take on loan such things the like of which you can give i.e. eggs, grain etc. It is not permissible to take on loan a thing like which one cannot give.

2—If anyone took ten kg. of wheat on loan when the rate of wheat was 75 paise per kg. and then it became cheaper and was being sold at seventy paise per kg. but he will have to return ten kg. of wheat whether the rate is cheaper or dearer at the time of returning the wheat.

3—If at the time of giving back, the quality of wheat is better than that taken on loan, then it is permissible as it is not interest, and also because it was not a condition that better quality will be taken at the time of its return.

4—If anyone took some money etc. on loan for one month or a fortnight and the creditor agreed to this promise, even then it is not permissible. If the creditor needs his money etc earlier than the promised period and demands, then it should be paid to him on his demand.

5—It is permissible to take on loan bread or cooked food.

# TO BE SURETY
## (ZAMANAT)

1—In our day-to-day life we stand surety for our friends and relatives. This entails great responsibility and should be understood properly.

If Naim owed some money of someone and Saleem took the responsibility for its payment. If Naim defaults and the creditor accepts the surety of Saleem, then it becomes Saleem's responsibility to repay the amount. If Naim defaults to pay the amount on the appointed day or time, then Saleem will have to pay it and the creditor has a right to demand the amount from him. So long as Naim does not pay or get it remitted by the creditor ; Saleem shall continue to remain responsible for the repayment of the amount. But if the creditor did not accept Saleem's surety and did not trust him, then Saleem is not responsible for the payment.

2—The surety of a minor is of no account.

3—The loan due towards one can be shifted to another person i.e. Naim owes some money of Saleem and Kalim owes some money of Naim. Saleem demands his money from Naim and Naim shifts it towards Kalim. It is permissible. Now Saleem can demand his money from Kalim.

### To Appoint Agent or Representative

1—A person can perform a job himself or can get it done through someone else. According to Islamic Law such a person is called *Vakil*—agent or representative.

2—The person who appoints an agent is called the principal. Any act done by the representative shall be deemed to have been done by the principal and it shall be binding upon him.

3—The principal has the right to dismiss his representative

or to cancel his authority to act on his behalf at any time even without assigning any reason for the same.

## Mudarbat To Join Together in Business—Definition :—

If anyone gives his money to another for business on the condition that they will share the profit between themselves. This is called *Mudarbat* and is permissible with certain conditions. If it conforms to these conditions then it would be in order otherwise bad and not permissible. The conditions are :

    a. The amount to be given for business should be determined and handed over to the other person. If the amount is not determined or not given to the person for business after its determination, then the transaction is not valid.

    b. The exact share of profit of the parties should also be determined before hand and if not settled and the person advancing the money merely says that the profit will be divided between them, then the transaction is bad.

    c. No definite amount should be fixed by the financer as his share but it should be as half-and-half or one-third or two-third or one-fourth etc.

    d. Any loss in the business shall be borne by the person who advances money.

    e. So long as the money is with the other person and he has not purchased any goods with it, the financer can withdraw the money from him. But if he has purchased goods then he cannot demand the money.

## Keeping Deposit—*Amanat*

1—Keeping of *Amanat* is a great responsibility according to *Shari'ah*. If anyone deposits something with someone and he accepts it, then it becomes essential for him to keep it safe and protected. If it is lost due to negligence or is stolen or burnt due to the house being set on fire, then the depositor cannot claim its compensation. Even if the keeper had promised to compensate it in case of loss also, the depositor is not entitled to any compensation.

2—If anyone while going away asked someone else to keep his articles with him and he agreed to it or did not say anything and the man left leaving the article with him, then it has become a deposit (*amanat*). But if the man clearly refused to accept it and even then the man left the article with him then it is not a deposit. But if the person took up the article after the other person has left and kept it, then it became a deposit.

3—The condition—that is—one who keeps the deposit with him—may keep the deposit in his own custody or with some of his relatives who live in the same house and with whom he can keep his own deposits and is trust-worthy. But it should not be kept with an unreliable person because in case of its being lost he will have to give its compensation. It is not proper to keep it with any other person without the permission of the owner.

4—If the custodian forgot the deposit and it was lost, then he is responsible to compensate the article.

5—If fire breaks out in the house of the custodian, then the deposit may be kept with someone else. But it should be immediately taken back when the cause is removed. It is also permissible to entrust the deposits to someone else at the time of dying if no relative or member of the family is present.

6—If anyone has deposited some cash with someone, then it is essential to keep the same cash—coin or notes etc.—in safe custody. It is not permissible even to mix this amount with one's own money or to spend it. It is wrong to presume that all money is the same and spend it thinking that the amount will be paid when demanded. The deposit may be used if permitted by the owner. But in such case it would become a debt. If the same money is kept and somehow it is lost, then the custodian will not be liable to pay the compensation. But if the money was spent with the permission of the depositor, then it shall have to be paid in every case.

7—If anyone deposited Rs. 100/- with someone and the custodian with the permission of the depositor mixed these Rs. 100/- with his own hundred rupees, then this amount of

Rs. 200/- became a joint property. If these are stolen then both will suffer and the custodian shall have to pay nothing to the depositor.

8—If anyone deposited milch animal with someone, then it is not permissible to use its milk without the permission of the owner. If it is used without his permission, then its price shall have to be given to the owner.

9—The same is true about ornaments, clothes and other domestic goods. These also should not be used.

10—If someone gave some money as deposit to a person and while keeping the money in his pocket or purse it fell down and the custodian believed that he has kept it in his pocket or purse, then no compensation will be due on him.

11—Whenever the depositor demands his deposit back, it is essential to be returned immediately. It should not be delayed without any legitimate cause as it is unjustified and improper. If the depositor agrees to take it after some time, then it is permissible.

### Articles Taken on Loan

Articles taken on loan for temporary use also amount to deposit and are covered by the same injunctions. These should also be kept safely. It is a common practice that clothes, ornaments or utensils etc. are taken for temporary use on the understanding that the same will be returned when not needed. These are also deposits. If in spite of all precautions, such article is lost, then the owner is not entitled to any compensation even if the depositor had promised to compensate in case of loss. But if it was lost due to carelessness, then compensation is essential. Such article should also be returned when demanded.

### Bad Contracts

1—If while taking a house on rent the period for which it is being taken was not specified or no rent was fixed or on the condition to repair it at his own expenses, then in all such cases the contract is bad and not proper.

2—If a house was given on the understanding that no rent

will be charged but the responsibility of its repairs etc. will be of the occupier, then it is permissible as it is a concession.

3—If a house was taken on the understanding that Rs. 10/- will be paid as its rent every month, then the contract is for one month only and the owner will have a right to get it vacated after one month. If the occupier remained in it for the next month also then the contract will be deemed to have been renewed for the next month also and thus it will remain to be renewed every month till the occupier lives in it. But if the time was also specified that the house will be occupied for so many months, then the contract will be good for that period and the owner will have no right to get it vacated before the expiry of that period.

4—If anyone engaged a *Hafiz* (one who has learnt the Holy Quran by heart) to recite the Holy Quran at the grave of his relative daily for a certain period, then it is not a contract. It is bad and there will be no credit for the recitation also.

## Partnership

1—A man dies and leaves some property behind, then it belongs to all of his heirs as joint property of all. It cannot be used by anyone before division or can be used with the consent of all. To use it or earn profit out of the joint property without the consent of other heirs, would be a sin.

2—Two persons purchased some utensils jointly. To use them or sell them without the consent of the other is not permissible.

3—Two persons purchased different fruits jointly. These cannot be divided in the absence of any partner. If done and consumed by one partner, it would be a sin. But if foodgrain like wheat was purchased, it can be divided in the absence of the partner.

4—It is not proper to fix percentage of profit in partnership business, such as, to say that out of the profit Rs. 50/- will be one's share and the rest of the other. If it is settled that the profit shall be shared half-and-half or 2/3 of one and 1/3 of the other, it is permissible.

5—The profit and loss in partnership shall be borne by each partner according to the shares already settled. If joint property is lost then the loss shall be borne by the partners and not by one alone.

6—Partnership between two different artists i.e. tailor and a dyer is also permissible if they agree that each will accept whatever work come to him and the charges received will be distributed among themselves half and half or one-third and two-third etc.

7—If one of them accepts a job, then it becomes the responsibility of the other also, that is, if the tailor took a job to stitch some clothes, then the customer can demand his clothes from the dyer also and can pay the charges to either of them.

8—In such partnership it is not necessary to mix up the articles of each. Just verbal offer and acceptance is sufficient to justify the partnership.

**Compensation of Loss**—*Tawan*

1—If some clothes are given to a tailor, dyer or washerman for job, then the thing is an *Amanat* (deposit) with him and he is responsible for its safe custody. But if the things are lost inspite of his best care, it is not proper and right to take compensation from him. But if the man spoils the clothes that they are torn or burnt then it is permissible and justified to take compensation. If the cloth is lost and it is not known how it is lost then also it is right to take compensation but not if his house was burgled.

2—If a labourer was engaged in the bazar to carry oil etc. and it fell from him, then compensation may be charged from him.

3—It is not proper to charge *Tawan* (compensation) from a permanent domestic servant in case of some accidental loss from him.

4—It is not proper to take compensation from a nurse kept for a child in case if some ornament of the child is lost due to her carelessness.

### Cancellation of Contract

1—If a house was taken on rent and it began to leak or its substantial part fell down, or it became inhabitable due to some defect, then it is permissible to cancel the contract. But if the entire house falls down, then the contract is cancelled automatically and it is not necessary to take the consent of the owner.

2—The contract is automatically rescinded if either the tenant or the owner dies.

3—If there is a legitimate and valid excuse to cancel the contract, then it is permissible to cancel it i.e. a conveyance is engaged to go anywhere, but the intention is changed, then it is permissible to break the contract.

4—There is a practice that some advance is paid as earnest money after settling hire of some conveyance and full hire is paid when it is actually used and the advance is deducted. But if the conveyance is not used then the advance is forfeited. This is not justified and permissible. The advance money should be returned and not kept.

### Taking Anything Without Permission

1—It is a major sin to take anything forcibly from anyone or to take without permission or to take in one's absence. Some women and men are in the habit of taking things belonging to their husbands or wives or other members of the family without their permission. It is not proper. The injunction about such things is that if they have not been consumed they should be returned as they are. If consumed then it is essential to replace the same from market and if it cannot be replaced its price should be paid.

2—If an article of domestic use i.e. a cot, was taken and it was damaged or spoiled, then its compensation should be paid.

3—It is not permissible to invest another person's money in business without his permission. If done, then it is not permissible to take the profit earned on that money. The actual amount should be returned to the owner and the earned profit should be given to the poor and the needy.

4—If a stray goat or cow comes to one's house, then it is forbidden to milk that animal, if done, then its price have to be paid to the owner.

5—If the husband brings some cloth etc. then the wife should not conceal anything from it without the permission of the husband.

6—Even petty things should not be taken without permission. If taken, it should either be replaced or get it remitted by the owner.

### Sharing Joint Property

1—If two persons jointly purchase wheat or some other commodity from the market, then its division in the presence of both is not essential. It is permissible for one partner to divide it correctly and exactly in the absence of the other and take his share. When the shares are separated he can use it in any way he likes.

2—This is true and applies to all things and commodities which are similar and not different.

3—But if articles are different and were purchased jointly, then their division should be done in the presence of the partners. These cannot be divided and consumed by one partner in the absence of the other.

4—The commodity was purchased and was not divided between the partners and somehow it was lost, then the loss would be of both the partners.

### Mortgage

1—When money is taken as loan from anyone, then it is permissible to keep (mortgage) something of value with the lender as guarantee and to be taken back when loan is repaid. But taking or giving of interest is strictly forbidden.

2—When a thing has been mortgaged, the mortgager has no right to demand back the article till the debt has been discharged.

3—If a thing has been mortgaged with someone, it is not permissible for him to use it in any way or earn profit out of it or take fruit or grains of the pledged garden or land or house. Such profit will amount to interest and it is forbidden.

4—If an animal like goat or cow is mortgaged with anyone, then it is not permissible for him to take its milk or kids as they belong to the owner. The milk should be sold and the amount kept aside. When the debt is settled, the animal should be returned along with the kids etc. and the price of the milk after deducting the charges of the animal's feeding should also be returned.

5—After part payment of the loan the mortgaged article cannot be demanded back. It can only be taken when full amount has been paid.

6—If an article worth Rs. 200/- was mortgaged for Rs. 150 with someone and the same was lost somehow. Now neither the lender can claim his money nor the mortgagor can claim the article. But if the value of the article was less than the amount taken on loan and it was lost, then the mortgagor shall have to pay the difference to the lender.

# BAD AND NON-PERMISSIBLE HOBBIES

## 1—Dance

There are two types of dances which are held at the time of marriage or other ceremonies or for mere pleasure without any occasion. One type is in which professional singing and dancing girls are engaged and they dance usually in gatherings of males only. The other type is in which a house-wife or professional dancer dances among the females with movements of different parts of the body. Now-a-days another type has developed due to cinema and T.V. in which boys and girls dance together on the tunes of film songs and cassettes. All such dances are against ethical norms of Islam and strictly forbidden.

Adultery is of different kinds — actual, of eyes, ears, tongue, heart, hand etc. and in such dances men are prone to commit and they do commit one or the other type of adultery. The evils and mischief of dances are self-evident. Men look and gaze at naked or semi-naked parts of an alien woman, it is an adultery of the eyes. They listen to her voice, it is an adultery of the ears. They talk and make jokes with her, it is an adultery of the tongue. Their hearts are attracted towards her, it is an adultery of the heart. Some are so shameless who even touch her, this is an adultery of the hand. They sometimes advance towards her and even dance with her, this is an adultery of the feet. Some even indulge in sexual inter-course with her, which is actual adultery and fornication.

Same is the case of dancing by family girls and boys. It is not permitted even without instruments and drums. Such dances are also accompanied by all the evils already mentioned. House-wives and girls memorise film and love songs and they sing and dance on their tunes. Their voice is heard by *namehram* and sometimes they are also seen by men. Such young girls and women are often led astray and they become corrupt. Hence such dances are sinful, obscene and immoral.

It has been clearly stated in the Holy Traditions that just as adultery is a major sin, in the same way the actions of gazing, hearing, touching etc. are all sins. The committing of a sin publicly is a major and worst sin according to *Shari'ah*.

It has been reported in a Tradition that when obscenity, immodesty and shamelessness become so common in any community that people begin to commit them publicly, then be sure that epidemics will spread in that community to such an extent as would not have occurred before. Now imagine, how great sinners are those, who arrange or take part in such obscenities. It spreads like an epidemic, when one after the other arrange such functions and it becomes a common practice. So long as such sinful activity started by one continues, its sin also continues to be recorded against him even after his death. The use of musical instruments is also prohibited and a sin in itself.

The Holy Prophet (SAW) has said that Allah has ordered him to destroy all the musical instruments. What a great sin is it to spread the evil for which the Holy Prophet (SAW) has been ordered by Allah to break and destroy it.

Some people regard it as a mark of respect and dignity. Boasting on sin and to think its avoidance as insulting, strikes at the very root of faith and losing of faith is a major sin. So it it the duty of every Muslim to refrain from things forbidden by *Shari'ah* just as they have anything offensive to their nature. May Allah protect us all from this evil. *Ameen.*

### 2—Pet Dogs and Photographs

The Holy Prophet (SAW) has said that Angels of Peace and Mercy (*Rahmat*) do not come to the house in which there is a dog or a picture and that severest punishment will be given to those who make pictures.

The Holy Prophet (SAW) has also said that a dog may

be kept for guarding the house, cattle, field or for hunting purposes only. But if anyone keeps a dog for any other purpose other than these, he will lose one carat daily from his credit earned by him by virtuous and religious acts. According to another tradition one carat before Allah is equal to mount Uhad. Thus according to the Traditions to draw or keep pictures or to have a pet dog is unlawful and forbidden and should be avoided. Similarly making of dolls or purchasing them from the market is also forbidden. Children should not be given dolls. When these acts are sin, every Muslim should refrain from them.

### 3—Fire-Works

The use of fire-works on festivities is also objectionable and not permitted. It is a sheer waste of money and the Holy Quran has condemned such persons as brethren of Satan who indulge in such waste of money. In a verse it is said that Allah loveth not the wasters and extravagant, that is, He detests them.

Secondly, the fireplay carries risk of being burnt and of the property catch fire risking others life and property as well. Hence it is not permitted by *Shari'ah*.

### 4—Playing Cards and Chess etc.

Playing of chess has been strictly prohibited in the Traditions and playing of cards etc. also come in the same category. Persons are so absorbed in such games that they totally forget all of their religious and worldly duties. Such acts are evil and sinful. Same is true of kite flying or other games played with stakes or gambling. Muslims should not indulge in such evil practices nor should waste their money and time in it invoking the wrath of Allah.

# SOME USAGES CUSTOMS AND CEREMONIES
## APPARENTLY INNOCENT AND PERMISSIBLE

Most of the usages commonly practised from birth to death are such that even sensible persons are misled to believe them permissible and not sinful because they are not accompanied by any music or dance. Men and women simply get together, eat and enjoy feast on such occasions. Hence it is thought that there is nothing illegal or against *Shari'ah* in them. The main reason of this wrong notion is that they have become common usages and their evils are not easily comprehended. In fact such evils are not so intricate or hidden and most persons are disgusted with them, but follow these practices as custom or as a fashion or for the sake of name and fame only. These evils should be abolished and eradicated from the Muslim Society. Some of such customs and evils are described here :

### 1 — Child Birth

The following customs are considered necessary and essential in family life :

(a) The first child should be born at his father's place and child-bearing bride is sent to her husband's house near the time of delivery without considering the inconvenience or discomfort of the expectant mother. It is considered so necessary that it cannot be postponed in any circumstances. Sometimes it endangers the lives of both—the mother and the child in womb. This amounts to creation of a new *Shari'ah* as it also carries the belief that its omission will be inauspicious. This is like assigning partners to Allah (*Shirk*). Traditions say that omen is nothing but a sin.

(b) Some grain or coins is put in a seive under the cot

## SOME USAGES CUSTOMS AND CEREMONIES 367

of the would-be mother just before delivery in the name of reliever of troubles. This is also *Shirk* as alone Allah can cause pain or pleasure.

(c) Some place a sword or knife near the confined woman as a measure of her safety. This is also *Shirk*.

(d) After a child is born relative females give some coins to the nurse as a custom. For this purpose relative women are invited and they must pay the money willingly or unwillingly. If anyone does not attend or give the coins then it becomes a lifelong complaint. The only motive behind such contributions might have been show of dignity and fame. About such show, Tradition says, "One who dons the robe of fame will be given the robe of humility on the Day of Judgement".

(e) It is also held for the sake of false vanity and it has been reported in Traditions that Holy Prophet (SAW) has prohibited acceptance of such invitations in which food is served for self-assertion, name and vanity.

(f) The other evil custom is that it is considered as a loan. Loan can be given only when one can spare, but here it has to be given whether one can spare or not. Hence it is not permissible.

(g) It is also customary to distribute sweets when *Adhan* is called in the ears of the child. It is also baseless.

(h) Members of the family are given some gifts even at the cost of borrowing money on interest. It is a sin.

(i) Attendants are also given something in the name of 'milk-wash' and it is also considered obligatory.

(j) Barber is sent to the house of bride to convey the information of the birth of the child and he is given money and clothes etc. as reward.

(k) At the end of forty days confinement of the mother, relatives gather in a ceremony and they are served with rice and milk.

(l) During the days of confinement, the mother is not

allowed to offer prayer, while according to *Shari'ah* as soon as the bleeding stops the mother should take bath or make *Tayammum* and offer prayers. Tradition says that one who omits prayer deliberately and without any legitimate cause, will lose his faith and such a person will go to Hell.

(m) Besides these ceremonious gifts—clothes etc. are prepared at the house of father of the bride and sent to bride-groom's house. When these are sent, women and relatives gather to see these things and are served with meals. If these are not sent, it is considered to be against traditions and an act of indifference.

(n) The clothes, bedding, shoes etc. of the child's mother are given to the nurse as a right and with this custom in view the bride is made to wear old and worn out clothes etc.

(o) The confined mother is considered to be unclean and women avoid to sit near her or eat in utensils used by her.

(p) The husband is not allowed to see his wife during her confinement and if he goes near her, it is considered highly objectionable.

(q) The baby is placed in a winnower or basket and is dragged about as an omen for his long life. This is superstition and against the faith.

(r) It is considered essential to give three baths to the bride on three specific occasions, while religion ordains that as soon as bleeding stops the bride should bathe and start offering prayers. But the custom of three baths has been made obligatory although it has nothing to do with Islam. All of the abovementioned Customs and Traditions are superstitious, anti-religion and transgression and should not be practised.

## 2—*Aqiqa* Ceremony (Shaving of New-Born's Head)

1—Relatives and friends gather on the occasion of shaving the head of new-born child and they give some money and it is considered to be the right of the barber. This giving of money is considered to be a must. While according to *Shari'ah* the only thing to be done is that on the seventh day of the birth of the child two goats for male and one goat for female child are sacrificed and their raw or cooked meat is distributed. The head of the new born baby is shaved and silver equal in weight to the hair is given in charity and saffron is also applied to the shaved head. That's all and all other customs and practices are absurdities.

2—On this occasion sisters also take their 'right.' It is an imitation of the non-believers. Sometimes it causes great inconvenience to the giver. Those who give, they do so as a matter of hypocrisy and self-pride which is not permissible.

3—There is also a wrong belief that the goat should be sacrificed just at the moment when the barber puts his razor on the head of the child. According to *Shari'ah* it is equally good whether the goat is sacrificed some time before or after the shaving of head.

4—It is absurd to think that the head and legs of the sacrificed goat are the right of the barber and the nurse respectively.

5—At some places breaking of the bones of the sacrificed goat is considered bad and they are buried. This is without any justification. Unfortunately it is all done in the name of religion.

### 3 – Circumcision—Khatna

1—On the occasion of *Khatna*, relatives and friends are invited which is against *Sunna*. Once a companion of the Holy Prophet (SAW) was invited to such ceremony but he refused to go there, saying that during the life-time of the Holy Prophet (SAW) no one was invited on such occasions. Hence it is against *Sunna*.

2—Sweets and meals are also offered on this occasion which involves substantial expenditure. Sometimes due to lack of means, the circumcision is delayed to the extent that the boy becomes matured. It is forbidden to see the private part of men or women and in such case the private part of a man is exposed before the gathering which is a sin.

3—Some cash and clothes are sent from the house of maternal grand-father which is called *Bhaat*. It is a custom of Hindus as their daughters have no share in their legacy and they had introduced such customs to compensate them. Hence it is irreligious.

4—There is also the custom of arranging music or dance on such occasions. It is against *Shar'iah*.

## 4—*Bismillah* (Beginning of Child's Learning)

1—*Bismillah* is also one of the customs which is observed with great regularity and pomp and show.

2—The notion of fixing the age of four years, four months and four days is quite absurd. But it is observed with such strictness that ignorant people regard it as a part of religion which is not correct.

3—Sweets are distributed or feast is arranged on this occasion compulsorily which is very bad and not permissible.

4—According to *Shari'ah* it is required that when a child begins to speak he should be taught to recite *Kalima* and then *Bismillah* can be taught when education is started and as thankfulness to Allah some charity according to one's means may be given to the poor and needy.

5—Similar ceremony is also held on completing the reading of Holy Quran and many undue and unnecessary things done for the sake of name and fame only. These are all mere customs having no ground in *Shari'ah*.

## 5—Participation in Ceremonies

Sometimes women go to visit a patient or to congratulate on some occasion just for the sake of pleasure. It is not permitted. They may go out occasionally to visit their parents or their *Mehram* relatives.

Women should not go out aimlessly without the permission of their husbands even in ceremonies of pleasure or sorrow.

Sometimes husbands are pressed for new clothes by the women to participate in ceremonies even if he is not in a position to purchase. Obviously it is done for the sake of show and self-praise which is forbidden according to Traditions.

In such gatherings women indulge in unnecessary talks, back-biting or complaint against others. It is all strictly prohibited, non-permissible and sinful.

## 6—Engagement—*Mangni*

In *mangni* (engagement) ceremony a barber comes from bridegroom's house to the bride's and cooked rice with sugar is given to him. This is considered as important as a religious duty and is observed irrespective of the consideration whether the bride's people have the means or not. If it is not done even the engagement is broken. Hence loan is taken on interest. Stern warnings have come in Traditions against such loans.

The barber is also given a suit of clothes and some cash. When the barber returns, the suit and cash is shown to ladies of the bride-groom's house-hold and is also sent in each house of the clan. This amounts to hypocrisy which has been clearly prohibited in the Holy Quran and the Traditions.

After some time some sweets, ring, handkerchief and some money is sent from the bride's side as a mark of approval of the engagement. This also amounts to waste of money and hypocrisy. The barber who brings these things is rewarded and the sweets are distributed and sometimes more is added to it by the bride-groom's side for the sake of name.

Sometimes a man comes from the side of the bridegroom and puts dry fruits etc. in the lap of the would-be bride and a rupee in her hand. This is full of evils. An alien man comes inside the house and in presence of women puts the things in the lap of the would-be bride. It is quite improper and impermissible.

## 7—Marriage Customs

On the occasion of marriages customs and usages are observed very strictly in their full measure. It is nothing but sheer waste and it ruins not only this world but also faith and religion. The customs and ceremonies are :—

1—When the date of marriage is announced all male

members of the community are invited. The letter of date is written on a red paper and is tied with a red cord and raw sugar is sent with it. It is nothing but confrontation with religion.

2—When the barber takes this letter to the bride-groom's house, he is served with a tray of boiled rice with ghee and sugar. Then the males of the bride-groom's side gather to write the reply of the letter and it is given to the barber with a costly suit of clothes and substantial money also. Sometimes loan is taken for this purpose.

3—Whe the barber returns to the bride's house his suit and money is shown in all the houses of the community. It is all hypocrisy.

4—When the letter of date of marriage has been sent, the would-be bride is confined and secluded in a room whatever may be the season or weather. A perfumed mixture (*Ubtan*) is rubbed on her body and sweets are distributed. At some places to apply this perfumed mixture seven married women are invited as an omen and charm and it amounts to assigning partners to Allah (*Shirk*).

5—The girl is not allowed to come out of that place and it is also accompanied with a lot of absurdities. All these are satanic and against *Shari'ah*.

6—In the same way from the same date the bride-groom's body is also rubbed with perfumed mixture.

7—Then there are the problems of bridal robes and dowry. In the earlier days bridal clothes were meant to be a gift for the bride from the side of the bride-groom and dowry meant a provision for the children. Now it has assumed the form of an evil custom.

8—Bridal clothes and dowry is now-a-days pre-arranged and are announced and the intention behind all this is nothing but name and fame only. Very often the parties are indebted to fulfil the demands of these customs and usages.

9—A day before the marriage bride-groom's barber brings myrtle and the bride's barber carries the bridal robe for the bride-groom. The barbers are rewarded by both the parties,

10—On the day of marriage the bride-groom is given a bath and dressed with bridal robes. On this occasion also some absurd usages are observed which are not permissible as they have been adopted from the non-Muslims. Traditions say that 'one who imitates another community is of the same community.'

11—When the marriage party starts it is accompanied by musical bands and fire-works. Sometimes more people are taken in the party than invited to the feast. To go uninvited anywhere is prohibited and it has been stated in Traditions that one who goes to a feast uninvited is a thief and returns as a robber.

12—During the marriage ceremonies reward is given to the barber etc. at every step. No doubt it is good to reward the workers, but to give it at different stages is nothing but hypocrisy.

13—Frivolities before *Nikah* take so much time that the *Nikah* is delayed unnecessarily. *Nikah* is the only proper ceremony according to *Shari'ah* but at some places the *Qadi* or their deputies are quite ignorant of the rules of *Nikah* and as such sometimes *Nikah* is not performed properly due to which the couple remains in a state of adultery for their whole life. Great care should be taken to get learned persons for performing *Nikah*.

14—After *Nikah* the bride-groom is called inside the house of the bride to perform certain customs alien to Islam and immodest jokes are cut by young girls. Sometimes the bridegroom is also accompained by his friends. This is all against Islamic teachings.

15—When meal is served to the marriage party the barber comes to wash the hands of the bridegrooms party. He is given reward. After the feast the bride groom's party also gives some money for the menials of the bride's house-hold. It is also nothing but a show of wealth.

16—At the end of marriage feast the articles of bride's dowry are displayed before all and the list of ornaments is also announced. Some do not show the articles but give the list of dowry. In both cases it is a matter of show and hypocrisy.

17—At the time of departure of the bride, the father and other relatives come inside and keep their hands on her head as blessings. Even some start weeping. In some places the bride-groom is required to pick up the bride in his arms and put her in the conveyance. This is done in the presence of all which is obviously against modesty.

18—When the bride's conveyance moves, coins are showered over it as an omen and they think that it will make her immune from evils and ill-luck.

19—When the bride reaches the bride-groom's house a goat's kid is brought and passed over the heads of the couple and given back to the herdsman with a few coins thinking it to be its price and *Sadqa*. It is totally absurd and against *Shari'ah*.

20—When the bride's face is uncovered, the relative women and friends give her some cash and it is collected by the woman who accompanies the bride. When the women have seen her face a child is brought and put in the bride's lap as an omen to have children. This is transgression and *Shirk* as in spite of this charm many women remain childless.

21—After the privacy between the husband and wife next morning the bed sheet of the couple is examined by the women. Then the bride is sent to her home clothed with ceremonial dress with some sweets etc. The bride-groom also goes with her. When the bride-groom enters the house of the bride his sisters-in-law steal his shoes and charge money to return it. In this ceremony much immodesty and shamelessness is practised.

22—There is a practice that the bride should pass the 15th of Sha'aban or the month of Muharram at her father's house. There is no religious sanction behind it.

23—In addition to the irreligious usages some dates or months are considered to be inauspicious for marriages etc. This belief is against *Shari'ah*.

The customs and usages described above are accompanied by sins as under :

(a) There is unnecessary waste of money.
(b) These involve sense of hypocrisy, pride, pomp and show.
(c) There is undue rigidity in their observance.
(d) There is invitation of unbelievers.
(e) These entail borrowing on interest.
(f) Disregard of purdah.
(g) Exacting of rewards by force.
(h) There is risk of assigning partners to Allah (*Shirk*) and perversion of faith.
(i) In their observance even offering of prayers is omitted.
(j) Collaboration with sin.
(k) Persistence on sin is in these usages and also to regard anything good which has been clearly denounced and prohibited by the Holy Quran and the Traditions. It destroys faith.

In the Holy Traditions the Holy Prophet (SAW) has said that whosoever does anything for show, Allah will show his limitations and whosoever does anything so that others may bear it, Allah will publicise his lapses on the Day of Judgement. The Holy Prophet (SAW) has denounced both who give and take interest, both are equally sinners.

In another Tradition the Holy Prophet (SAW) has said: "May Allah curse one who sees and also one who exposes herself before him. A man's looking at an alien woman or a woman's looking at an alien man are both sinful."

The Holy Prophet (SAW) has said that Allah hates three persons and one of them is one who being a Muslim follows the customs and usages of non-believers. There is great honour and fame in obeying the laws of Allah.

When men of means and resources will do some thing, poor men will also do the same for the sake of their name. Hence it is the duty of rich persons to give up and abolish such customs.

Engagement can be declared verbally and there is no need of sending a barber with a letter.

After marriage, *Walima* (feast) is *Sunna* but it should be with a sincere heart and intention without any tinge of show or pride. *Walima* with an intent of show has been denounced by Holy Prophet as a worst kind of meal. So no man of faith should participate in such functions and ceremonies. Allah's displeasure is more and terrible than regard for the pleasure of men and clans.

### 8—Excessive Mehr

There is a custom of fixing excessive and exorbitant *Mehr* (dowry). It is against *Sunna*. It is reported that Hadrat Umar warned against demanding and fixing excessive *Mehr* (dower money) for "if it were a matter of honour in this world and piety of credit before Allah, the Holy Prophet (SAW) deserved it most, but I do not know whether the Holy Prophet (SAW) had married any of his wives on more than twelve Auqia of dowry."

Some people have the wrong notion that excessive *Mehr* is fixed so that the husband may not divorce the wife for fear of payment of dower money. This is quite absurd because one who wants to divorce, will do it whatever be its consequences. Those who do not divorce for fear of payment of *Mehr*, create a very unbearable situation, that is, they neither divorce nor maintain the wife and keep her in suspense. As a matter of fact excessive *Mehr* is fixed merely for the sake of pride and show. It is *Sunna* to fix the *Mehr* according to the *Mehr* of the daughters and consorts of the Holy Prophet (SAW). But if anyone wants to fix it higher than that, it should be according to the status and means of the person. May Allah give guidance to all Muslims to follow His orders and Traditions of the Holy Prophet (SAW). *Aameen*.

### 9—Prayer for the Dead—*Fateha*

It is a way of sending credit to the dead. Its reality according to religious law is that if one does an act of virtue and its credit is wished to be transferred to the dead and he prays to Allah that its credit be transferred to such and such dead person. This is called *Fateha*.

For instance if anyone gave some food, money, cloth etc. as

charity in the name of Allah and prayed that its credit may be transferred to any of his dead relatives. Or one may recite the whole or part of the Holy Quran and transfer its credit to some dead person, the credit is transferred by the grace of Allah.

But ignorant and innovators have added complications and absurdities to it. For offering *Fateha* a portion of the floor is plastered with mud on which some food or sweet-meat is placed. Some people put some leaves of betel also with it. Then a person recites some verses of the Holy Quran and transfers its credit to the dead name by name. Ignorant people believe that credit cannot be transferred without observing this process and without it the food is not given to anyone. Some believe that only recitation of *Fateha* is a credit which may be transferred and there is no need of giving food in charity. Under this belief in the *Fateha* given for the Holy Prophet (SAW) or some saint, the food or sweets is taken by one himself or distributed among his friends and relatives. It seems that the belief is that thus two credits of *Fateha* will be transferred. This is quite wrong as in fact it is nothing in itself which reaches the dead but the credit of it. The thing should be given to the poor and the needy and its credit will be gained only when it has been given to the poor and not before that. Hence this custom is quite meaningless.

It is quite wrong to believe that thing in itself reaches the dead. This is utter ignorance.

The restriction of offering *Fateha* on Thursdays is quite absurd and innovation. All days are equal before Allah. This restriction has given birth to another evil that people believe that the souls of the dead visit their houses on Thursdays. It is sinful to think so.

There is another wrong notion that *Fateha* of each is offered separately as this is for Allah, this is for Prophet (SAW) and this is for Hadrat Fatima etc. which means that only so much is given to Allah which is in His name and the rest is for others. It is like assigning partners to Allah.

There is another restriction invented by ignorant persons that in the *Fateha* of Hadrat Fatima, food is covered and no *na-mehram* can see it or eat it. This is a major sin.

Some people believe that saints are relievers of ills and calamities and their *Fateha* is done to gain benefits or desires to be fulfilled. This belief is *Shirk* (like assigning partners to Allah).

Some people cover tombs of saints with sheets to seek fulfilment of their desires and needs. It is strictly forbidden.

In sickness some people give meat to kites and crows to recover from illness. There is no religious sanction for this belief in *Shari'ah*.

There is another obnoxious custom that some food is placed on the road-crossing. This is the custom of non-believers and it amounts to *Shirk*.

Some women go to mosques with some sweets or food and place it in arch or the pulpit and sometimes they go singing accompained by drums. This is all absurd and not permissible.

All these methods and customs of charity should be given up and simple method as described in the beginning should be adopted. Whatever can be spared may be given to the poor and needy in the name of Allah and He being pleased will remove the trouble and the calamity with His Mercy. Charity should not be made an object of show or pride.

## 10—After-Death Ceremonies

Bad customs have also been introduced in matters of death and funeral. Bathing and shrouding of the dead is delayed unnecessarily. The Holy Prophet (SAW) has stressed that there should be no delay in shrouding and burial of the dead.

There is a custom of sending some grains with the funeral to be given in charity at the grave. Often clothes, Holy Quran of the dead are given away in charity. A man's property on his death descends to his heirs and all of them become joint owners of it and it is not lawful to give anything out of it. The property should first be divided, then each of them can give out of his share as charity if he desires.

There is also a custom of arranging cooked food on certain fixed dates and is distributed among the relatives and friends and some of it is given to the poor also. These dates are called 10th, 20th and 40th day ceremonies of the death. In some cases loan is taken to perform these ceremonies. This is not right and there is no credit in it for the dead, on the other hand it is a sin.

Sometimes these are performed out of the property of the deceased in which there is share of orphans also. Orphan's property cannot be spent in anyway.

Similarly there is a belief that on certain specific days like Thursdays and 15th of Sha'aban the souls of the dead visit their homes. This is all baseless.

There is also the custom of weeping jointly with the members of the family of the deceased. They weep with lamentations and beating their faces and chests. All this has been strictly forbidden by the Holy Prophet (SAW). This does not console the bereaved family but refreshes their grief.

Relatives or friends coming from distance stay with the bereaved family and thus burden the family.

In case of a widow, she has to suffer the pangs of the death of her husband repeatedly. Relatives collect again when her period of *Iddat* expires and all the expenses of the ceremony are borne out of the property of the deceased. The proper thing is that relatives should come for a short while and console the widow and there should be no serving of food etc.

It is a custom on the occasion of death that food is sent to the bereaved family by near relatives. This is appreciable as they cannot arrange to cook their food being overwhelmed with grief. But an evil practice has been introduced in it that the food is sent in large quantity and all those who had come for condolence also eat that food. This should be stopped and all others should take their food at their houses.

Some people appoint a *Hafiz* i.e. those who have learnt the Holy Quran by heart, to recite Holy Quran at the grave and transfer its credit to the deceased. The *Hafiz* is also paid for that. All this recitation and expenditure goes waste as the recitation is done on greed and not for the pleasure of Allah.

If the recitation is done voluntarily and just for the pleasure for Allah and then its credit is transferred to the deceased, it will certainly reach him and this way is good and appreciable. But no specific date, day or time should be fixed for it.

## 11 – Ceremonies of Ramadan

Some bad practices have also been attached with the holy month of Ramadan. Some women call a *Hafiz* inside the house and offer *Tarawih* prayers in congregation behind him with recitation of Holy Quran. If the *Hafiz* is a *Mehram* and women are of the same house and the *Hafiz* has offered his *Fard* (obligatory) prayer in the mosque and only leads the *Tarawih* prayer only, then there is no harm.

But generally the *Hafiz* is a *Na-Mehram* and although arrangement of purdah is made but it is not proper as women begin to talk with the *Hafiz* during the recitation.

Some *Hafizs* recite the Holy Quran with intonation and in a very sweet voice that it attracts the heart of the listeners (women).

Women of the locality assemble for this congregation daily. They are not permitted to go out of houses without urgent need and according to *Shari'ah* offering of *Tarawih* in congregation is not essential for women.

Another custom is that on the 14th day of Ramadan special dishes of food are prepared and it is considered to be creditable. There is no religious sanction behind it and should be given up.

When a child keeps his first fast, elaborate arrangements are made for it and it is observed as an essential ceremony even by poor persons. They take money on loan for this ceremony. To think a thing essential which is not enjoined by *Shari'ah* is a sin and it should be given up.

## 12—Eid Ceremony

On the occasion *Eid-ul-Fitr* cooking of makaroni or vermicelli is considered to be necessary and essential, but there is no such provision in *Shari'ah*. It may be prepared but do not think it to be creditable. If one has the means he can send sweet etc as *Hadya* to relatives and friends. Children are given cash but it is preferable not to give them cash. It may be given in other shape.

### 13—Sermons and Ceremonies of Rabi-ul-Awwal

On the occasion of 12th Rabi-ul-awwal or during this month gatherings are held of men and women separately and sermons on the birth of the Holy Prophet (SAW) are arranged. Poems are recited. There are certain evils in it :—

  (a) If the sermon is delivered by a woman then her voice goes outside and *Na-Mehrams* hear her voice. This is not permissible.

  (b) If the sermon is delivered by a man and he recites poem with intonation, as is the practice now-a-days, then it is not permissible for women to hear it.

  (c) Some people believe that the Holy Prophet (SAW) comes to such gatherings and they stand up when the account of birth is described and it is considered necessary but it has no sanction in the *Shari'ah* and to believe in it is a sin.

  (d) Sweets or food is distributed in such gatherings and it is believed to be essential and its omission is considered to bring displeasure of the Holy Prophet (SAW). It is wrong and senseless to be so particular about such things.

  (e) Even if one's belief is not perverted and he observes such thing with rigidity, then it would be a precedent for ignorant people and there is risk of their being misguided. Anything which does not have religious sanction should be avoided.

  (f) If it is desired to read the life of Holy Prophet (SAW), then some authentic book may be read. If credit is to be transferred to the soul of the Holy Prophet, then something may be given to the poor at some other time.

### 14—Shab-e-Barat and Muharram

  (a) The day and night of 15th of Sha'aban is of great veneration and blessing. The Holy Prophet (SAW) has enjoined and induced to remain and keep fast in the day. On this night he (SAW) used to visit grave-yards and pray for the salvation of the dead. So it is *Sunna* to transfer some credit (*Fateha*) to the dead either by reciting the Holy Quran or by feeding the poor or giving them some cash or simply by praying.

Besides this, all usages and customs are baseless and absurd. The preparing of sweet dishes and offering *Fateha* over them is practised with great regularity which has no religious sanction.

(b) The ceremonies and customs of Muharram are also in the same category. The tenth of Muharam is observed with great rigidity. The reality about this day according to religion is that the Holy Prophet (SAW) has said that whosoever on this day feeds his family well, shall have abundance throughout the year. When so much food is prepared at home, some of it may be given to the poor also in the name of Allah. More than this is full of evils. There is the custom of distributing *Sharbat* believing that they are transferring credit to the Martyrs of Karbala. As already described, nothing reaches the dead but only its credit. Then why should one stick to the observance of *Sharbat*, anything can be given to the poor. To think that the *Sharbat* will quench the thirst of the martyrs is nothing but perverted belief and it is a sin according to *Shari'ah*.

(c) Some people read the account of martyrdom of Hadrat Imam Husain and his companions. Some of these accounts are based upon wrong reports, so their reading is not permissible. But if even the correct account is read collecting together with an intent to weep and lament over the calamity, it is also not permissible.

To give up wearing coloured clothes and ornaments in Muharram and adopt mourning attitude and to clothe children in some particular robes or to make them 'beggars' of Husain, are all innovations and sins.

### 15—Ziarat of Sacred Relics

At some places the robe or hair of the Holy Prophet (SAW) or some saint have been preserved and on some particular occasions people gather to have a glimpse of them. Women also go to such gatherings. Everywhere the robes or the hair are not genuine or authentic and even if these are genuine, gathering of people is not proper. The evils of such gatherings has already been described. There is no harm if these things are seen individually without assigning any particular benefit to them and also nothing against religion should be done.

The touch-stone of such things is that whatever has not been permitted by religious laws should not be considered essential or creditable. If considered as essential, it would be a sin. To think anything as inauspicious as a sin and to invent anything and believe in it is also a sin. To pray to anyone other than Allah is *Shirk* and sin. May Allah save us all from these wrong notions and sins. *Aameen.*

### 16—Widow's *Nikah*

Among the absurd customs and usages, there is the custom in which a widow's second marriage is considered to be evil and a matter of insult. It is more prevalent among rich and the so-called respectable families. According to common-sense and Islamic Law the second *Nikah* of a widow is just like the first *Nikah*. If any widow takes courage and observing the order of Allah and the Holy Prophet (SAW) gets herself married, she is looked down upon and is considered to be mean. She is disgraced, taunted and laughed at. It is infidelity to think it so. It is to be remembered that all the consorts of the Holy Prophet (SAW), except Hadrat Aishya Siddiqa, were not virgins. May Allah forgive, can these be considered unrespectable ? Can anyone be dishonoured by an act which is done according to the order of Allah and His Holy Prophet (SAW) ? If we will continue to think the second marriage of a widow as an evil, our faith (*Iman*) will not be proper. We should get rid of all these absurd notions and evils. Widows should be induced for second marriage. The Traditions have reported the Holy Prophet (SAW) have said, "whosoever will spread my given up *Sunna* again among the people, he will be rewarded with recompense of hundred martyrs." The propagation and inducement for the second marriage of widows amounts to renewal of the *Sunna*.

# ETIQUETTE OF DEVOTIONAL PRACTICES

## Ablution (*Wudu*) and Cleanliness

1—*Wudu* should be performed well and carefully even if it seems inconvenient at sometimes.

2—Fresh ablution carries great credit.

3—Do not face Ka'aba or turn your back towards it while easing or passing urine.

4—Save yourself from the drops of urine. Carelessness in this regard leads to punishment in the grave.

5—Do not urinate in a hole. It may be the residence of some animal or ants. It is also possible that a snake or scorpion may come out of it and may attack you.

6—Do not urinate in bath-room or at the place where you take bath.

7—On waking up from sleep do not put your hands in water without washing them properly.

8—Do not talk while easing or urinating.

9—Do not use the water heated in the sun as it is injurious for health and may cause white-leprosy.

## Prayers

1—Offer prayers at the appointed times and with sincere intent. Perform bowing (*Ruku*) and prostrations (*Sajdas*) properly and with sincere concentration.

2—When a child is of seven years, parents should induce and press him to offer prayers and force them when they are ten years of age.

3—Do not offer prayer on a printed or decorated cloth or place where attention may be diverted towards its flowers and decorations.

4—There should be some obstruction (*Surat*) in front of the person offering prayer. If nothing else is available some stick or any high thing may be put opposite the right or left eye-brow in front.

5—After offering *Fard* (obligatory) prayer, it is better to move a little from that place for offering *Sunna* and *Nafl* prayer.

6—Do not look hither and thither or upwards while offering prayer. Suppress yawning as far as possible.

7—If there is urgency, first ease yourself and then offer prayer.

8—Offer as many *Nafls* as you can perform conveniently.

9—If you recollect some calamity recite :

Inna-lillah-e-wa-inna-ilaihe-raje'oon

"All of us are for Allah and we all are to return to Him."

10—Recite the same *Kalima* even on the least trouble, difficulty or loss. You will be rewarded credit for it.

### Zakat—Charity—Fasts

1—As far as possible *Zakat* should be given to such needy person who do not go about begging but remain patiently and respectably at homes.

2—Do not be ashamed of giving something small or little in quantity as charity. One should give whatever he can spare to give.

3—Do not presume that after giving *Zakat*, there is no need of giving charity. Whenever deemed necessary charity should be given as much as possible.

4—Giving of charity to relatives has double credit—one for the charity and the other for helping them.

5—Be considerate towards poor neighbours.

6—Do not give so much charity out of your husband's or wife's property which may embarrass or put him or her to difficulty.

7—It is not proper to talk absurd or use obscene language or quarrel while fasting. Back biting is still greater sin.

8—When the husband is at home, wife should not keep a

*Nafl* fast without his permission.

9—During the last ten days of Ramadan devotional exercises should be increased.

### Recitation of Holy Quran

1—Do not give up the habit of reciting of Holy Quran even if you are unable to recite it properly. Go on reciting as in that case the reward is double—one for recitation and the other for learning it.

2—If you have learnt or memorized the Holy Quran, do not let it be forgotten as it is a major sin to forget it after learning. So continue reciting it regularly.

3—The Holy Quran should be recited attentively and with fear of Allah.

4—Do not swear by the Holy Quran or anything else except Allah.

5—If anyone asks you to recite some verse or part of Holy Quran to see how you recite, it is natural that you will recite very correctly and carefully. Remember that Allah has enjoined to recite Holy Quran and He sees how you do it. So we should be more careful and attentive while reciting the Holy Quran. While reciting the Holy Quran we should bear in mind that Allah is seeing and listening our recitation. In this way our recitation of the Holy Quran will be correct and clear and shall be attentive also.

6—If one cannot recite the Holy Quran easily, it should not be given up in disgust. One should go on reciting. This will be doubly rewarded.

### Some Prayers—*Dua*

1—While praying (*Dua*) or seeking blessings of Allah, do so with zeal, eagerness, humiliation and sincerity. Never ask for anything of sin. If there is delay in the acceptance of your prayer (*Dua*) do not give it up being disappointed. Believe that it will be granted because Allah alone knows the appropriate time of granting our prayers.

2—Do not curse yourself, your children or property even in anger because that may be time of granting our wishes and prayers.

3—In gatherings also remember Allah and the Holy Prophet (SAW) otherwise those gatherings may be the cause of some trouble.

4—If unfortunately some sin is committed, then do not delay to repent and seek forgiveness of Allah.

5—While going to sleep recite :

اَللّٰهُمَّ بِاسْمِكَ اَمُوْتُ وَاَحْیٰی

On waking up recite :

اَلْحَمْدُ لِلّٰهِ الَّذِیْ اَحْیَانَا بَعْدَ مَا اَمَاتَنَا وَ اِلَیْهِ النُّشُوْرُ ۰

6—Recite in the morning :

اَللّٰهُمَّ بِكَ اَصْبَحْنَا وَ بِكَ اَمْسَیْنَا وَ بِكَ نَحْیٰی وَ بِكَ نَمُوْتُ وَ اِلَیْكَ النُّشُوْرُ ۰

and in the evening say :

اَللّٰهُمَّ بِكَ اَمْسَیْنَا وَ بِكَ اَصْبَحْنَا وَ بِكَ نَحْیٰی وَ بِكَ نَمُوْتُ وَ اِلَیْكَ النُّشُوْرُ

7—Recite after meals :

اَلْحَمْدُ لِلّٰهِ الَّذِیْ اَطْعَمَنَا وَ سَقَانَا وَ جَعَلَنَا مِنَ الْمُسْلِمِیْنَ وَ كَفَانَا وَ اٰوَانَا

ETIQUETTE OF DEVOTIONAL PRACTICES

8—After offering Fajr and Maghrib prayers recite this *dua* seven times :

اَللّٰهُمَّ اَجِرْنِیْ مِنَ النَّارِ

and thrice :

بِسْمِ اللهِ الَّذِیْ لَا یَضُرُّ مَعَ اسْمِهٖ شَیْءٌ فِی الْاَرْضِ وَلَا فِی السَّمَآءِ وَھُوَ السَّمِیْعُ الْعَلِیْمُ ۵

9—While sitting in a conveyance recite :

سُبْحَانَ الَّذِیْ سَخَّرَ لَنَا ھٰذَا وَ مَا کُنَّا لَهٗ مُقْرِنِیْنَ وَ اِنَّا اِلٰی رَبِّنَا لَمُنْقَلِبُوْنَ ۵

10—After eating at someone's house recite :

اَللّٰهُمَّ بَارِكْ لَهُمْ فِیْمَا رَزَقْتَهُمْ وَاغْفِرْ لَهُمْ وَارْحَمْهُمْ

11—On seeing a new moon recite :

اَللّٰهُمَّ اَھِلَّهٗ عَلَیْنَا بِالْاَمْنِ وَ الْاِیْمَانِ وَ السَّلَامَةِ وَالْاِسْلَامِ رَبِّیْ وَ رَبُّكَ اللهُ ۔

12—On seeing someone in misery recite :

اَلْحَمْدُ لِلّٰهِ الَّذِیْ عَافَانِیْ مِمَّا ابْتَلَاكَ بِهٖ وَ فَضَّلَنِیْ عَلٰی کَثِیْرٍ مِّمَّنْ خَلَقَ تَفْضِیْلًا ظ

13—While bidding fare-well to someone say :

یَسْتَوْدِعُ اللهُ دِیْنَكُمْ وَ اَمَانَتَكُمْ وَخَوَایْمَ اَعْمَالِکُمْ ۔

14—While congratulating the newly weds say :

بَارَكَ اللهُ لَکُمَا وَبَارَكَ عَلَیْکُمَا وَجَمَعَ بَیْنَکُمَا فِیْ خَیْرٍ ط

15—When any calamity befalls say :

$$\text{يَا حَىُّ يَا قَيُّومُ بِرَحْمَتِكَ أَسْتَغِيثُ}$$

16—After every prayer and while going to bed recite thrice :

$$\text{أَسْتَغْفِرُ اللهَ الَّذِى لَا اِلٰهَ اِلَّا هُوَالْحَىُّ الْقَيُّومُ وَأَتُوبُ اِلَيْهِ}$$

and once :

$$\text{لَا اِلٰهَ اِلَّا اللهُ وَحْدَهُ لَا شَرِيْكَ لَهُ لَهُ الْمُلْكُ وَلَهُ الْحَمْدُ}$$

$$\text{وَهُوَ عَلٰى كُلِّ شَىْءٍ قَدِيْرٌ}$$

Thirty-three time as each :

$$\text{اَلْحَمْدُ لِلّٰهِ} \qquad \text{سُبْحَانَ اللهِ}$$

(*Alhamdolillah*)　　(*Subhanallah*)

and thirty-four times :

$$\text{اللهُ أَكْبَرُ}$$

(*Allah-o-Akbar*)

17—Recite *Surah Yasin* once in the morning. *Sura Waqia* after *Maghrib* and *Surah Mulk* after *Isha* prayers. On Fridays recite *Surah Kahaf* once.

18—Recite Holy Quran daily as much as possible.

## CORRECT DEALINGS

1—One should not be greedy and do not covet money so much that there may be no discrimination between permissible and prohibited. One should not waste what Allah has given, but it should be spent wisely and economically.

2—If anyone is in distress and is forced by his circumstances to sell something, then undue advantage of his misery should not be taken. He should be helped and the article be purchased at reasonable price.

3—If any person indebted to you is poor, he should not be harassed. Give him some time to repay or if possible remit some or whole of the debt.

4—If you are indebted to anyone and you are in a position to repay, it is very unjust to delay.

5—Do not borrow or take loan as far as possible. If forced by circumstances to take, be particular about its repayment. If the creditor uses harsh language, do not be angry or retaliate.

6—Do not tease anyone by concealing his things even in joke.

7—Do not delay the payment of wages of the labourer or workmen from whom you have taken any work.

8—At the time of famine some persons sell their children. It is prohibited to purchase them and make them slaves. Such people should be helped.

9—There is much credit even for small virtuous acts i e. you gave some salt for anyone's food, it is as creditable as you have fed one person.

10—It is highly creditable to quench the thirst of a thirsty person. It is like liberating a slave where water is plenty and like giving life to a dead where water is scarce.

11—If you are indebted to anyone or have anyone's deposit (*amanat*) with you, then let it be known to members of your family and others, in case you die, the same may be discharged and it does not remain due on you.

12—It is a great sin to keep a dog or a cat caged so that the same may be distressed with hunger and thirst.

13—While talking, do not exaggerate. Be clear and concise in your conversation.

14—Suppress your anger as far as possible.

15—Seek forgiveness from others before your death.

16—Cover the defects of others. Do not publicise it.

**Eating and Drinking**

Stomach is the root-cause of most of the evils and vices. Do not be habitual of delicious food. Do not over-eat. Avoid prohibited and unlawful income. These have many benefits. The heart remains pure and love for Allah remains in it.

Secondly the heart remains soft and affiable on account of which praying and remembering Allah is relished.

Thirdly the 'self' does not become rebellious.

Fourthly the self is put to some inconvenience and this recalls Divine punishment and one is induced to refrain from sins.

Fifthly there is lesser inclination towards sins and the world.

Sixthly the mind and heart remain clean and relieved and one is inclined towards prayers and worship.

Lastly such a person feels compassion for the hungry and poor and has sympathy for everyone.

1—Begin eating with *Bismillah*. Eat with right hand and from the part of the dish nearest to you.

2—Do not leave some part of the food in the plate.

3—If a morsel slips from the hand and falls, clean it and eat it.

4—If you have eaten some bad smelling thing like raw onion or garlic, then wash and clean your mouth properly afterwards and particularly before going for prayers or some gathering.

5—After eating offer thanks to Allah and recite the prayer already mentioned.

6—Wash your hands properly before and after meals.

7—Do not eat in haste.

8—Entertain your guests. Eating jointly leads to abundance. Accompany the guest upto exit. It is *Sunna*.

9—Do not drink water while standing or in one draught. Drink with three breaths.

### Safe-guard of Tongue and Good Manners

1—Do not speak without thinking. When you are quite sure that whatever you are going to say is not unreasonable, then speak otherwise not.

2—Do not call anybody as dishonest or curse, anyone to go to hell because if he is not so, it will return to you.

3—If anyone accuses you or uses indecent language so you can say only that much in reply. If exceeded than that, it would be a sin.

4—Do not talk double facedly.

5—Do not talk ill of anyone nor listen to such talk.

6—Never tell a lie or praise anyone in flattery. Do not praise anyone too much even behind his back.

7—Do not back-bite. If it is not true it would be a slander which is a sin.

8—Do not dispute with anyone and try to holster up your word.

9—Do not laugh too much. It destroys the glare of face and hardens the heart.

10—If you have talked ill of anybody, get it excused by him. If he is dead, pray for his salvation.

11—Do not make a false promise.

12—Do not cut such jokes by which another person may be disgraced.

13—Do not brag about your possession or art.

14—Do not repeat hear-say. It is generally false.

15—Do not talk haltingly nor exaggerate or lengthen your talk. Speak only so much as is needed.

16—Do not appreciate or be attentive towards one's singing.

17—Do not laugh at anyone's bad face or imitate bad actions.

18—If you learn about anyone's defect or fault, cover it and do not propagate it.

19—If one seeks your advice, give him the best which is most reasonable to you.

20—It is wrong to taunt a sinner. However, something may be said as an advice.

21—Do not lie upon your belly.

22—Do not sit at any place by pushing others.

23—If anyone comes to meet you, then move a little to make room for him. It would be a sign of respect for him.

24—Do not try to sit at a prominent place in a gathering but take your seat wherever available.

25—While sneezing put your handkerchief or palm to the mouth and sneeze softly.

**Talkativeness**

Self-exultation and talkativeness leads a number of absurdities and sins, such as, false-hood, back-biting, abuse, aspersions, self-praise, useless arguments, flattery of rich persons etc.

The only way to avoid and saving one's self from all these evils and sins is to restrain and check the tongue and its way is not to speak abruptly. It should first be weighed whether it is reasonable, just and proper, creditable or sinful. If the self urges to say such thing, suppress it because it is easier to check it than the punishment of Hell.

The other way of guarding the tongue is not to meet anyone unless it is inevitable. In this way the mouth will remain shut.

**Anger**

While in anger, one loses his sense of wit and wisdom and unbecoming words are spoken by him. Every effort should be made to check and suppress anger. The best way of controlling the anger is to ask the person who is object of anger, to go away and if it is not possible then one who is in anger should himself leave that place — and should think that he himself is more guilty before Allah than that person who is the object of anger. The way we seek Allah's forgiveness for our faults, in the same way we should also forgive other's faults.

The other way of checking and suppressing anger is that one should say, *Aa'oozo-billahe-Minash Shaitanirrjim* that is, "seek Allah's protection from the vicious Satan" and drink water or make ablution and the anger will pass away. Vindictiveness is generated by anger and when anger is controlled and suppressed, vindictiveness, too, will vanquish. Traditions say that a man asked the Holy Prophet (SAW) to tell him something which may lead him to Paradise. The Prophet (SAW) replied, "Do not show anger and Paradise is for you."

**Envy**

Holy Tradition says : "Virtues are eaten away by envy as the fire consumes wood." To feel jealous and sad on seeing anyone flourishing and in prosperity and to be pleased when he is in distress or trouble, it is called envy. It is a great vice and sin. Such a person's life passes in misery and bitterness. It is unpleasant in this world and hereafter. Every effort should be made to get rid of this evil and its remedy is to realise the fact that envy is painful and injurious to one's own-self and it does not harm at all the person envied.

The great loss of an envious person is that his virtues and good acts go waste, because to envy is like finding faults with Allah as to why He gave prosperity to that person and not to him. Thus envy is, Allah forbid, confrontation with Allah and the greatness of such a sin is obvious. The apparent loss of envy is that envious person always remains in grief and it is of no loss to the other because anyone's prosperity will not decrease by it. On the other hand the virtues of the envious person are transferred to the person envied. May Allah protect us all from this vice. *Aameen.*

**Love of Worldly Wealth**

The greed of wealth is such an obnoxious evil that when it sets one's heart, the love of Allah does not enter into it. A greedy person is ever in search of acquiring and hoarding wealth and money. He gets no time to remember Allah. The thought of ornaments, clothes, utensils and good house always haunt him. What amenities should be provided and how to acquire them ? When a person is absorbed and engaged throughout the day and night in such thoughts, how can he find time to remember and worship Allah. Another evil of love of worldly wealth is that such a person does not want to die because he fears that all the comforts will end with death. Some feel much pain at the time of death and Allah forbid, he becomes hostile to Allah thinking that He will deprive him of his wealth. This condition is very bad as such a person dies on disbelief. Another evil of greed of wealth is when a person falls a prey to collecting and amassing wealth, he loses all sense of right and wrong, lawful and unlawful ; permissible and prohibited and cannot discriminate false-hood and fraud. His only intent and motive of life becomes the acquisition of wealth from whatever means it may be. The Holy Traditions says :

"Love of worldly wealth is the root of all sins." It is such a bad habit and motive that every Muslim should try to refrain from this evil and cast off its love from his heart.

The remedy to get rid of this evil is to remember death frequently and excessively and should realise that one has to leave the world one day, then why should we develop attachment for such a thing.

Another remedy is that one should not have a wide circle of acquaintances and unnecessary association and contacts with many persons.

Do not collect and amass worldly wealth, money and property and do not expand business beyond your limits.

Avoid extravagance as it increases greed of money and other evils.

Make a habit of simple living and use coarse food and

clothes.

Associate more with poor people and less with rich people. Read and remember the lives of saints and holy people who abandoned the world.

All precious and things of attachment should be given in charity or sold.

With such measures, by the Grace of Allah, the greed of world and its wealth will be removed from the heart and also the ambition and desire of acquiring wealth, etc. will vanish automatically.

**Miserliness**

A miser cannot perform such obligatory duties as *Zakat*, Sacrifice (*Qurbani*), helping the poor and needy etc. because of his nature, and it is a sin. From worldly point of view also the miser is looked down upon and not respected. Such a person is a loser in terms of religion and the world both.

The remedy of this evil is to remove the love of wealth and money from heart, and when there is no love of worldly wealth, one cannot be a miser.

Another remedy is that whatever is more than one's need may be given to the poor and needy by forcing the 'self' and bearing the strain which it may cause. This should be continued to be practised till one gets rid of evil. But all this would be possible only when one understands and realises the religious and worldly loss of the evil of miserliness.

**The Desire for Name and Fame**

When a man desires name, fame and exaltation for himself, he is sure to be jealous and envious of the popularity and praise of others and is pleased to hear ill and disgrace of others. This is a major sin to wish ill of others. There is another evil in it that sometimes popularity or fame is gained by unfair and dishonest means i.e. one spends extravagantly in marriages and other ceremonies just for the sake of name and the money is collected by unfair means, such as, bribery, smuggling etc. or on loan with interest. The worldly loss of this evil is that such a person makes many enemies who are jealous and ever remain in search of an opportunity to defame and humiliate him.

A remedy to get rid of this evil is to realise and believe that the praised and those who praise shall not live in this world for ever. All have to die and after some time no one will remember. Then why should one desire a baseless and temporary thing. It is sheer foolishness.

Another remedy is that one should do such a thing which must not be against *Shari'ah* but he may be humiliated in public eye on account of that act. The result of it would be that his bad manners shall be reformed.

**Pride and Boastfulness**

To boast and be proud means to think oneself superior than others in matters of learning, piety, devotion in religion, pedigree, wealth, property, and wisdom etc. and to regard others as low and inferiors. It is a major sin. The Tradition says: "Any one who has even an iota of pride will not enter Heaven."

Even in this world such a person is hated and not liked by others and they remain hostile towards him. He is respected outwardly or in fear only.

Such a person does not listen to good advice from others and on the other hand tries to harm those who advise him. This is another evil.

The remedy to get rid of pride and boastfulness is to realise the fact and one's own reality that he is born from earth and few dirty drops of semen. All the qualities and graces have been given by Allah and He may take away everything whenever He likes. Then what is there to be proud of ! Remember the Greatness of Allah. This will make one to look down upon one's own sense of superiority. One should respect the person whom he considered inferior and meet him with all humility in himself. If done so it would remove pride and boastfulness from the mind and heart.

If one does not possess the courage to do all this, then he should, at least, make it a point to take the initiative in offering Salam to the person whom he considered inferior or low. By the Grace of Allah thus will also create humility in one's 'self'. Offering of *Nafl* prayers frequently is also an effective remedy of removing this evil from one's mind and heart.

**Conceit**

If one has the complex of self-importance or struts on wearing good clothes etc. it is an evil and vice even if he does not look down upon others. The Tradition says : "This habit disrupts *Iman* (faith). Such a person does not care to correct himself, because of self conceit he never looks to his own defects.

Its remedy is that one should recall and scrutinize one's defects and shortcomings and judge his actions and habits and understand that any good in him has been given by Allah and it is not his own achievement and should be thankful to Allah and pray that he may not be deprived of whatever virtues he has.

**Hypocrisy or Pretence in Good Acts**

Hypocrisy and false profession or pretence is of several kinds. Sometimes it is declared in word i.e. I have recited so much Holy Quran or kept a fast or woke up at night for prayer etc. Sometimes it is indirect. Often an act is done publicly to show others and sometimes it is done boastfully, such as one recites the Holy Quran regularly but in the presence of others does it ostentatiously. Sometimes it is done by gestures such as, one sits down with eyes closed and head bent to show that he is very Allah fearing and is engaged in devotion or that he kept awake in the night offering prayers and is now dozing. Whatever be its form, it is evil and on the Day of Judgement such persons instead of being rewarded shall be punished by Allah. The Holy Prophet (SAW) has said that if one did any act for publicity or show, Allah will show him his shortcomings on the Day of Judgement.

The remedies of the shortcomings described above, will not be effective if practised once or twice. These should be made a routine in life and should be practised for long period.

Only then one can expect to get rid of the evils.

Another remedy of all the evils that one has in self is that when any bad or sinful act is committed, one should punish himself for that by fixing an amount according to his means to be given to the poor each time such an act is committed. Another way of punishing oneself is not to take food for one or two times. By the Grace of Allah, he will get rid of the evils. The other ways of getting rid of evils and vices are as under :

### (i)—Repentance

Repentance is such a good thing which begets and secures forgiveness for all sins. Anyone who ponders about himself will find that one after another sin is committed by him. Hence repentance is necessary at all times. Its method is that one should remember and recall the warnings against sins which have been mentioned in the Holy Quran and the Traditions and should repent over it with words of penitence and remorse. All the missed prayers and fasts should be performed. If anyone else's rights have been neglected or violated, forgiveness should be obtained from those persons or fulfil those responsibilities. One should also pray and seek forgiveness from Allah.

### (ii)—Fear of Allah

Allah says that you should fear Him and this fear is such a thing which prevents men from sins and evils. One should always remember the punishment which Allah gives and should continue to repent over one's sins and vices.

### (iii)—Hope from Allah

Allah says that men should never be despaired of His Mercy and 'hope' is such a fine thing which encourages virtue and strengthens the heart for penitence. So one should always think and remember Allah's Mercy.

### (iv)—Patience

To remain steadfast in matters of religion and faith and not to allow the 'self' to do anything contrary to religion, is patience in the real sense. There are many occasions of observing patience. If one is living in comfort and peace and Allah has given him health, wealth, honour, children etc then in such case patience means not to forget Allah and not to treat the poor with humiliation. He should not be proud of his position but should be lenient and helpful to the poor. The other occasion is when at times of prayer and devotion, 'self' is inclined towards ease and laziness or it is inclined towards miserliness and avoids giving of *Zakat* and charity.

On such occasions three kinds of patience are required to be observed : The first is, keep intent and motive pure before offering prayer and it should be selfless and only for pleasure of Allah. Secondly there should be no laziness and slothness in prayer and it should be performed at its proper and due time. Thirdly not to mention to others about his prayers and devotion.

Another occasion for patience is at the time of sins and it is to restrain and check the self from committing sin.

An occasion for patience is when someone abuses, accuses and gives him harm and trouble. At such time the patience is not to retaliate but to keep quiet and bear it patiently.

At the time of illness, some calamity or death of some relative, the patience is to control the tongue and not to utter any word against the *Shari'ah* or to cry or lament.

The best way of observing patience on all occasions is to recall the reward of such occasions and to believe that everything is for his good and realise that impatience will not change the fate, then why should one lose the credit of patience.

### V—Thankfulness

One should be pleased with the bounties of Allah as it creates His love in the heart and this love gives birth to the urge that Allah is so Merciful that He showers unlimited bounties upon us, we too should worship Him with all sincerity and devotion. This is a major sin to disobey Him. This is the gist and essence of Thankfulness to Allah.

There are unlimited bounties of Allah upon His being at every moment and even if there is some calamity, it is also for the good and is a blessing. To bear it patiently is creditable and also it reforms the self and sometimes a good return for the same is also given in one's life. When there are bounties and blessings of Allah at every moment the heart must remain filled with joy and love of Allah and there should be no failing and deviation in carrying out His commands.

Every Muslim knows and believes that there can be no gain or loss without the Will of Allah. So it is necessary that whatever one does, he should not depend and rely on his own efforts and ways but should expect and depend upon Allah for success and do not depend upon anyone or fear anyone else. One should realise that no one can do anything for him without the Will of Allah. This is called trust in Allah and reliance on Him. The way of acquiring this trust is that one should think and remember very much Allah's Power and Wisdom and the helplessness of human beings.

The attraction of one's heart towards Allah and to enjoy hearing about Him and seeing His Deeds, is love of Allah. To acquire love of Allah one should remember his name frequently and repeat His qualities and ponder over His love for His creatures.

When it is known and is an admitted fact that whatever is done by Allah it is for the good then one should remain satisfied with everything without complaining and grumbling.

In all our acts of faith there should be no worldly intent, or hypocrisy. One should think well before doing anything and get rid if there is tinge of worldly gain in it.

It should be kept in mind at all times that Allah knows everything—open or secret. If there is any evil act or thought, then Allah may punish for the same either in this world or in hereafter. At the time of prayer it should be realised that Allah is watching, then the prayers should be offered properly. If one continues to think in this way, by the Grace of Allah, nothing contrary to Allah's pleasure will be done by him,

## RULES FOR GUIDANCE OF MUSLIMS

1—Every Muslim should acquire knowledge of religious laws either through books or from learned men.

2—Abstain from all sins and vices.

3—One should repent immediately if some sin or wrong act is committed.

4—One should not usurp the right and dues of others. Do not harm anyone with hand or words and do not speak ill of others.

5—One should not covet wealth, fame, good food and clothes.

6—If one is censured on some fault, the gilt should be accepted immediately and repented without discussion or argument.

7—One should not travel without urgent need as many careless acts are committed during a journey and good acts are omitted.

8—Never laugh or talk too much and particularly with *Na-Mehram* persons.

9—One should not quarrel with anyone.

10—The observance of *Shari'ah* should always be kept in mind.

11—One should not be lazy and slothful in prayers.

12—Keep mostly in seclusion and while meeting others observe humility. One should not associate much with rich people.

13—Avoid and keep away from irreligious company.

14—Never try to find faults of others or be suspicious of others. One should try to look into one's own shortcomings and reform oneself.

15—Prayers should be offered properly with regularity at the appointed times.

16—One should not be negligent in remembering Allah in mind or by words, and if relished then Allah be thanked.

17—One should talk gently and regulate everything in his life.

18—If any sorrow or grief comes it should be taken as from Allah and should not worry about it. But should believe that it should be rewarded.

19—Whole time should not be spent in worldly affairs, but Allah should be kept in mind.

20—As far as possible be helpful to others, be it materially or in matters of faith.

21—One should be moderate in taking food, that is, it should neither be too little as to be harmful for health, nor too much as to produce slothness in matters of prayers.

22—Never be greedy or expect some benefit from anyone else except Allah.

23—Always take pains in search of Allah.

24—Always thank Allah for His bounties — large or small — and should not be disappointed at one's own poverty or starvation.

25—The errors and faults of the subordinates should be forgiven.

26—Cover the shortcomings of others and avoid its publicity. But if anyone wants to injure or harm someone, then he may be informed.

27—One should serve guests, travellers, the poor, the learned (Ulemas) and the saints.

28—Always keep good company.

29—Always have fear of Allah in mind.

30—Always remember death.

31—One should scrutinize his daily works and dealings at some time. Allah be thanked for good and virtuous acts and sins and vices should be repented.

32—Never tell a lie.
33—Never attend a gathering which is contrary to *Shari'ah*.
34—Practise humility, shyness and tolerance.
35—One should never be proud of one's own merits and qualities and always pray to Allah to be kept on right path and guidance.

# REWARD AND PUNISHMENT
## SOME HOLY TRADITIONS

1. **Purity of Motive**
   (a) A person asked the Holy Prophet (SAW) what was *Iman* (faith). The Holy Prophet (SAW) replied, "Purity of motive". It means that everything should be done for the sake of Allah.
   (b) The Holy Prophet (SAW) said, "All acts are judged by motive or intent". It means if an act is done with good intent, then the good act will be rewarded.
2. **Fame and Show**
   (a) The Holy Prophet (SAW) has said that if anyone did anything to be heard by others or for show, then Allah will describe or show his defects on the Day of Judgement.
   (b) The Holy Prophet (SAW) has said that even a slightest show is like assigning partners to Allah.
3. **To follow the Holy Quran and Traditions**
   The Holy Prophet (SAW) has said that when disruption or deterioration spreads in his *ummat* (community), the person who holds on and sticks to his Traditions, shall have the reward equal to one hundred martyrs and further said that he (SAW) was leaving such a thing behind that if they (Muslims) will hold it, they will never go astray—one is the Holy Quran and the other his Traditions.
4. **To initiate Virtue or Evil**
   The Holy Prophet (SAW) has said that whosoever lays foundation of a good path and people follow it, then the founder will get his credit for the virtue and also credit

equal to those who follow it without any decrease in their credit. Similarly one who introduces an evil, he will be a sinner and the sins equal to those who follow will also go to his account without any decrease in their sins. For instance anyone gave up all evil customs in the marriage of his child and others also follow him, the initiator will get credit for that also.

5. **Religious Knowledge**

The Holy Prophet (SAW) is reported to have said that whomsoever Allah wants to favour. He gives him the understanding of religion, that is such a person becomes fond of seeking and learning religious laws and injunctions.

6. **Concealing of Religious Knowledge**

   (a) The Holy Prophet (SAW) has said that 'if anyone is asked about some religious matter and he does not tell but conceals it, then on the Day of Judgement he will be given a bridle of fire'. So if anyone asks about some religious injunction and one knows it well, he should not hesitate or refuse but explain it clearly.

   (b) The Holy Prophet (SAW) has said knowledge is a burden on the learned proportionate to the amount of knowledge, except for one who acts according to it. It means that one should never act against the religious injunctions or *Shari'ah* just to please oneself or his friends.

7. **Precaution against Urine**

The Holy Prophet (SAW) has warned to be very careful about urine because mostly the punishment of grave will be due to carelessness about urine.

8. **About Ablution and Bath**

   (a) The Holy Prophet (SAW) has been reported to have said that conditions in which the 'self' feels inconvenienced; careful and proper washing in ablution and bath washes away the sins. The inconvenience is felt on account of laziness or cold.

(b) The Holy Prophet (SAW) has said that offering two *Raka'ats* of prayer after cleaning the teeth with *Miswak* is more creditable than offering seventy *Raka'ats* without it.

(c) The Holy Prophet (SAW) saw some people who made ablution but their heels were still dry upon seeing this he (SAW) said 'that punishment of heels is very severe in the Hell'. Hence rings, bangels etc. should be moved thoroughly so that water may pass under them properly. Sometimes in winter season the skin of feet is hardened and so they should be washed well. Some men and women wash just the front of the face and not upto the lobe of the ear, this is not proper.

9. **Place of Prayer for Women**

The Holy Prophet (SAW) has said 'that the best mosque for women is the inner part of their house'. It shows that going of women to the mosques is not good and it should be noted that nothing is more important than prayer and women are not allowed to go out even for prayers, then how bad it would be for them to go out of houses uselessly just for meeting others or for the sake of evil customs.

10. **Punctuality in Prayers**

(a) The Holy Prophet (SAW) has said that the example of five times' prayer is such as if one has a canal flowing at his door and he bathes in it five times daily.

It means that such a person will have no filth or uncleanliness on his body, in the same way all the sins are washed away by five times' prayer.

(b) The Holy Prophet (SAW) has been reported to have said that the first thing to be accounted on the Day of Judgment will be prayer.

11. **Praying in Early Period**

The Holy Prophet (SAW) has said that Allah is pleased if the prayer is offered in its early time.

## REWARD AND PUNISHMENT

**12. Careless Offering of Prayers**

(a) The Holy Prophet (SAW) has said that one who does not offer prayers in time, or does his ablution improperly, or does not put his heart and attention in the prayer, and does not offer *Ruku* (Bowing) and *Sajdas* properly, then such a prayer becomes dark and black and it curses the person that Allah may destroy him as he has destroyed it (prayer). When the prayer reaches its assigned place where Allah wishes, it is wrapped like an old cloth and struck against the face of the person who offered it.

(b) The Holy Prophet (SAW) has advised that while offering prayer one should not look upward lest his eye-sight may be taken away.

(c) The Holy Prophet (SAW) has said that whosoever while in prayer looks hither and thither, then Allah will turn back his prayer, that is, it is not accepted.

(d) The Holy Prophet(SAW)has said "that if a person passes before a person saying his prayers, knew that how sinful it is, he would have preferred to stand waiting for forty years instead of passing before anyone praying". But if there is anything raised high equal to arm's length before the person praying, then it is permissible to pass before him.

(e) The Holy Prophet (SAW) has said that anyone who gives up praying, Allah will be very angry with him when he will appear before him on the Day of Judgement.

**13. Debt and the Debtor**

(a) The Holy Prophet (SAW) has said that on the night of *Me'raj* he saw it written on the gate of Paradise that credit for charity is ten times and credit for giving on loan is eighteen times.

(b) The Holy Prophet (SAW) has said that treating the debtor leniently till the time of repayment of loan will be rewarded as if the creditor has been giving that much money in charity every day. But when the creditor allows time after the promised time for repayment, then he will be rewarded as if he has been giving double of that amount in charity everyday.

## 14. Recitation of the Holy Quran

The Holy Prophet (SAW) has said that "whosoever recites a single letter of the Holy Quran, he gets one virtue for that and the reward for one virtue is its ten times, and He does not consider *Alif-lam-Meem* to be one letter, but '*Alif*' is one, '*Lam*' another and '*Meem*' the third". So the reward is thirty times on these letters.

## 15. To Curse Oneself

The Holy Prophet (SAW) has strictly prohibited to curse oneself, his children, servants, or his wealth and property, because that may be the time of granting of prayers and Allah may accept whatever one has said at that time.

## 16. Ill-gotten Income

(a) The Holy Prophet (SAW) has said that the blood and flesh prospered and nourished on ill-gotten income will not go to Heaven. It is just fit for Hell.

(b) The Holy Prophet (SAW) has been reported to have said that if anyone purchased some cloth worth ten dirhams in which one dirham is from illegal income, then so long as the cloth will remain on his body, Allah will not accept his prayers. (A dirham is a little more than onequarter of a rupee).

## 17. Cheating

The Holy Prophet (SAW) has said that whosoever of our community cheats or commits a fraud, is not of us.

## 18. To Borrow

(a) The Holy Prophet (SAW) has said that if anyone dies without discharging his debt, then it will be met with his virtues on the Day of Judgement.

(b) The Holy Prophet (SAW) has said that debt is of two kinds—one is that the debtor dies but had the intent to repay. About it Allah says that He will help him.

# REWARD AND PUNISHMENT

The other kind is that the debtor dies and had no intention to repay the debt, then it will met out of his virtues on the Day of Judgement.

### 19. To Defer the Due

The Holy Prophet (SAW) has said that it is most unjust to defer or put off the discharging of any claim when one has the means.

### 20. Interest

The Holy Prophet (SAW) has cursed both—one who takes interest and the one who pays.

### 21. Unlawful Possession of Land

The Holy Prophet (SAW) has said that whosoever unjustly grabs or encroaches upon another's land, he will be yoked with all the seven earths round his neck.

### 22. Prompt Payment of Labour

(a) The Holy Prophet (SAW) has said that the labourer should be paid his wages before his sweat dries.

(b) Allah says He Himself would prefer claim against three persons one of those will be the person who engaged someone for work and did not pay his wages after completion of the job.

### 23. About the Death of Children

The Holy Prophet (SAW) has said that if three children of a Muslim couple die, then Allah with His Grace and Mercy will send the parents to Heaven. Someone asked if two children die; the Holy Prophet (SAW) said that the same reward is for them also. Then one of the companions asked if only one child dies, the Holy Prophet (SAW) replied that even for one the reward is the same. Then Holy Prophet (SAW) said swearing by Allah in whose hands his life is "that even a miscarried child will drag its mother towards Heaven by its navel cord if the mother had the intent of credit." It means that if the mother had borne the loss of child with patience in the hope of credit.

### 24. Women's Use of Perfume and Fine Clothes

(a) The Holy Prophet (SAW) has said that if a woman having perfumed herself passes by a stranger, then she is wicked. A woman should not use perfume where her husband's brothers, cousins, etc. come frequently.

(b) The Holy Prophet (SAW) has said that some women wear clothes in name only, while in fact they remain naked. Such women will not be allowed to enter Heaven or smell its fragrance.

(c) The Holy Prophet (SAW) has cursed those women who dress like men. Now-a-days women have started dressing themselves like men. Such women should bear in mind the punishment for this vice.

(d) The Holy Prophet (SAW) has said that whosoever wears clothes for the sake of show, dignity or fame, Allah will dress such a man with clothes of humility and disgrace on the Day of Judgement and will throw him in Hell.

### 25. Injustice

The Holy Prophet (SAW) asked his companions if they knew who was poor. They replied that one who has no wealth or property is poor. The Holy Prophet (SAW) said that in his *Ummat* (community) the poorest person is one who will come on the Day of Judgement with prayers (*Namaz*), fasts, *Zakat* etc. to his credit, but at the same time he would have abused or back-bited someone or misappropriated anyone's property or beat or killed anyone. Then the reward of his virtues will be transferred to those persons. If his virtues are exhausted before the claims of others have been met, then the sins of those persons will be transferred to him and as a result he will be thrown into Hell.

### 26. To Be Kind and Merciful

The Holy Prophet (SAW) has been reported to have said that one who is not merciful to human beings, Allah, will not be merciful to him.

### 27. Propagation of Virtue

The Holy Prophet (SAW) has said that if anyone sees an irreligious act being done, he should stop it by hand, but if not possible he should stop it by mouth and if even that is not possible, then he should regard it as evil in his mind and this is the last stage of *Iman* (faith).

**28. Covering of Faults**

The Holy Prophet (SAW) has said that one who covers the fault of his Muslim brother, Allah will cover his faults on the Day of Judgement and one who exposes or publicises the faults of his Muslim brother, Allah will expose his faults to the extent that he will be humiliated even in his house.

**29. To be Pleased on Someone's Loss**

The Holy Prophet (SAW) has prohibited to be pleased on the trouble of a Muslim because Allah will have Mercy on the troubled man and invoke the other in trouble.

**30. Taunting on One's Sins**

The Holy Prophet (SAW) has said that if anyone taunts his Muslim brother on his sin, then such a man will not die till he himself has committed that sin. It means that it is very bad to remind one's sin or taunt him when he has already repented for the same. But if he has not repented, then it is permissible to admonish him as an advice.

**31. Committing of Minor Sins**

The Holy Prophet (SAW) has advised Hadrat Aiyesha Siddiqa to refrain from minor sins even as Allah has deputed an inquisitor for these also. That is, an angel keeps record of these sins also and these will be accounted for on the Day of Judgement and punishment will be awarded for the same.

**32. Parents' Pleasure**

The Holy Prophet (SAW) has said that pleasure of Allah is in the pleasure of parents and their displeasure is the displeasure of Allah.

**33. Ill-Treatment with Relatives**

The Holy Prophet (SAW) has said that on every Friday night the deeds and prayers of people are presetned before Allah and the actions and prayers of the person are not approved who has ill-treated his relatives.

**34. To Look After Orphans**

(a) The Holy Prophet (SAW) has said that "one who looks after orphans and he (SAW) will be found in Paradise so"—he spread his first and middle fingers and pointed towards them.

(b) The Holy Prophet (SAW) has also said that one who passes his hand over the head of an orphan just for the pleasure of Allah, then he will be rewarded with as many virtues as the number of hair of the orphan are covered by his palm.

### 35. Treatment with Neighbours

The Holy Prophet (SAW) has said that one who troubles his neighbour, will trouble him (SAW) and Allah and one who quarrelled with his neighbour, he quarrelled with him (SAW) and Allah. It means that troubling and quarrelling with neighbours on petty matters is very bad.

### 36. Helping a Muslim

The Holy Prophet (SAW) has said that one who helps a Muslim brother, Allah helps him.

### 37. Modesty and Immodesty

The Holy Prophet (SAW) has said that modesty is a matter of faith and faith (*Iman*) leads to Heaven, while immodesty is evil nature and evil nature leads to Hell. But one should never be shy in matters of religion.

### 38. Politeness and Impoliteness

(a) The Holy Prophet (SAW) has said that politeness melts away sins as water melts salt, while impoliteness spoils prayer and worship as vinegar spoils honey.

(b) The Holy Prophet (SAW) also said that dearest and nearest to him (SAW) on the Day of Judgement will be one who has good manners and politeness and the most annoying and farthest from him will be one who is devoid of politeness and has bad manners.

### 39. Mildness and Rudeness

(a) The Holy Prophet (SAW) has said that Allah favours mildness and bestows such boons on it that rudeness will never get.

(b) The Holy Prophet (SAW) has said that one who is deprived of mildness, is deprived of all virtues.

## REWARD AND PUNISHMENT

**40. To Peep in Anyone's House**

The Holy Prophet (SAW) has said that no one should peep in any one's house without permission and if did so, it means as if he actually entered the house.

**41. Eaves-Dropping**

The Holy Prophet (SAW) said that one who eavesdrops some conversation and they resent it, then on the Day of Judgement melted lead will be poured into the ears of such person.

**42. Anger**

A man requested the Holy Prophet (SAW) to teach him something which may lead him to Heaven. The Holy Prophet (SAW) told him never to be angry and he will go to Heaven.

**43. To Stop Talking**

The Holy Prophet (SAW) said that it was not permissible for a Muslim to stop speaking with any Muslim brother for more than three days and if did so and died in this condition, he will go to Hell.

**44. To Curse and Call Unbeliever**

(a) The Holy Prophet (SAW) said that whosoever called a Muslim a non-believer has committed a sin which is like murder.

(b) The Holy Prophet (SAW) also said that to curse a Muslim is also like murdering.

(c) The Holy Prophet (SAW) further said that when one curses anyone, the curse first goes towards the sky and finds its doors closed, then it returns to the earth which is also closed. It then wanders hither and thither and when finds no access anywhere, it goes to the cursed person. If that person deserves it, the curse sticks to him otherwise it comes back to the person who has cursed.

**45. To Frighten a Muslim**

(a) The Holy Holy Prophet (SAW) said that it is not permissible for a Muslim to frighten any other Muslim.

(b) The Prophet (SAW) further said that if any Muslim stares at anyone to frighten him, then he will be frightened by Allah on the Day of Judgement.

### 46. To Accept a Muslim's Apology

The Holy Prophet (SAW) said that if a Muslim apologises to another Muslim and he does not accept it, then such a person will not be allowed to come to him (SAW) on *Kausar* tank. It means that if someone commits a fault and then apologises, the apology must be accepted.

### 47. Back-Biting

The Holy Prophet (SAW) said that anyone who will eat flesh of his dead brother in this world, that is, will indulge in back-biting ; Allah will put before him flesh of dead body on the Day of Judgement and will ask him to eat it in the same manner as he had eaten the flesh of the living. So this man will cry and gesticulate but will be forced to eat it.

### 48. Slander

(a) The Holy Prophet (SAW) said that one who speaks ill of someone will not go to Heaven.

(b) The Holy Prophet (SAW) said that whosoever accuses Muslim of anything which he had not done, then Allah will send him to such a place where blood and pus of the residents of Hell is collected till he withdraws his accusation and repents.

### 49. To Talk Less

(a) The Holy Prophet (SAW) said that one who keeps silent, remains safe from many troubles.

(b) The Holy Prophet (SAW) further said that except in remembering Allah one should not talk much, because talking much hardens the heart and a person with hard heart is farthest from Allah.

### 50. Humility

The Holy Prophet (SAW) said that one who observes humility, Allah raises his position and one who is proud, Allah will break his neck, that is, he will be humiliated and disgraced.

### 51. Pride

The Holy Prophet (SAW) said that such a person who has even an iota of pride in his mind, will not go to Heaven.

## REWARD AND PUNISHMENT

### 52. Truth and Falsehood

The Holy Prophet (SAW) advised people to be particular about speaking the truth as it leads to the path of virtue; and truth and virtue both lead to Heaven. Avoid telling a lie as falsehood leads to vice and they both lead to Hell.

### 53. Double Facedness

The Holy Prophet (SAW) said that anyone who has two faces here, shall have two tongues of fire on the Day of Judgement. Having two faces means to say one thing to one and another thing to the other to please them.

### 54. Swearing

(a) The Holy Prophet (SAW) said that one who swore by anyone other than Allah, has committed *Kufr* (infidelity) or assigned partners to Allah (*Shirk*).

(b) The Holy Prophet (SAW) said that if anyone swears by saying that he may not have faith (*Iman*), if he is telling a lie, then if he has told a lie, he will become what he has said and even if he spoke the truth, his faith will not remain sound.

Such oaths are prohibited and if one utters such oath, he should immediately recite *Kalima*.

### 55. To Remove Offensive Things from Path

The Holy Prophet (SAW) said that a person found a thorny twig on his way and he removed it. This action was highly appreciated by Allah and He forgave his sins. It shows that throwing of offensive things on the path is very bad.

### 56. Promise and Trust

The Holy Prophet (SAW) said that one who is not trustworthy is without faith (*Iman*) and one who does not keep his promise is irreligious.

### 57. Sooth-Saying

The Holy Prophet (SAW) said that if anyone goes to a soothsayer and asks about something and believes in whatever the sooth-sayer says, his forty days' prayers (*Namaz*) will not be accepted.

## 58. Pet Dogs and Pictures

The Holy Prophet (SAW) said that Angels of Mercy do not enter the house where there are pictures and pet dogs.

## 59. Lying on the Belly

(a) The Holy Prophet (SAW) passed by a man who was lying on his belly, he (SAW) touched him with his foot and said that Allah does not like lying like this.

(b) The Holy Prophet (SAW) has prohibited to sit partly in sun and partly in shadow.

## 60. Omen and Charms

(a) The Holy Prophet (SAW) has said that superstition is *Shirk* (assigning partners to Allah).

(b) He (SAW) further said that believing in charms is also *Shirk*.

## 61. Greed of the World

(a) The Holy Prophet (SAW) said that avoidance of greed of the world gives peace of mind and body.

(b) The Holy Prophet (SAW) further said that if two ferocious wolves are let loose on a flock of goats and they freely devour the goats, then the destruction caused by the wolves will be less than the harm caused to one's faith (*Iman*) by greed of wealth and his desire for name and fame.

## 62. To Remember Death

The Holy Prophet (SAW) stressed upon people to remember the thing very much which cuts off all worldly pleasures, that is, death.

## 63. Value of Time and Patience in Trouble

(a) The Holy Prophet (SAW) said that if you get morning do not plan for the evening and vice-versa. Utilise your health before illness and enjoy the fruit of life before death. It means that health and life are boons of Allah and these should be utilised for some good work and virtue.

(b) The Holy Prophet (SAW) further said that if a Muslim is subjected to some grief, illness or some anxiety, Allah forgives the sins of the sufferer.

**64. Visiting a Sick**

The Holy Prophet (SAW) said that if a Muslim goes to visit a sick Muslim in the morning, seventy thousand angels pray for such person till evening and if he visits in the evening the angels pray till morning.

**65. About Dead**

The Holy Prophet (SAW) said that one who gives bath to a dead he becomes so purified from sins as if he was born just then. One who shrouds the dead Allah will award him with Heavenly robes and one who consoles a bereaved, Allah will clothe him with robe of piety and will bless his soul. He who comforts a person in distrces, Allah will award him with two dresses of Paradise that the whole world will not be equal to their value.

**66. Crying with Lamentation**

The Holy Prophet (SAW) has cursed those women who lament loudly and those who join or listen it.

**67. Orphan's Property**

The Holy Prophet (SAW) said that on the Day of Judgement some people will rise from their grave in such condition that flames of fire will be coming out of their mouths. Someone asked him (SAW) who will be these persons ? The Holy Prophet (SAW) replied, "Do you not know that Allah has said in the Holy Quran that those who unjustly eat the property of orphans are filling their bellies with fire ?" Unjust means that they have no legal right to be benefited from the orphan's property according to *Shari'ah*.

**68. Qiyamat or Dooms Day**

(a) The Holy Prophet (SAW) has said that on the Day of Judgement no one will be allowed to move from his place so long as four facts are not asked from them":
Firstly how the life was spent by one.
Secondly how much one acted according to the acquired religious knowledge.

Thirdly, how the wealth was acquired and how it was spent.

Fourthly, how one utilised oneself, that is whether everything was done according to *Shari'ah* or according to 'self'.

(b) The Holy Prophet (SAW) said that on the Day of Judgement all rights and dues shall have to be fulfilled.

## 69. To Remember Paradise and Hell

The Holy Prophet (SAW) said in a sermon "that two things are very important and should not be forgotten—Paradise and Hell". Saying this he wept so much that his beard was wet with tears and then said, "I swear in the name of Allah in Whose hands my life is, the facts of *Akhirat* (the end) which I know, if you come to know about them, you will run away to the jungle and will throw dust on your heads."

# QAYAMAT—DOOMS-DAY

**Some Signs**

Before actual happening of *Qayamat*, people will begin to regard Allah's property as their own. *Zakat* as a burden or fine, appropriate trusts as their own and husbands will obey their wives in anti-*Shari'ah* acts. They will disobey the mother and consider father as alien and would regard friends as their own. Religious knowledge will be acquired to earn money. Leadership and administration will be in the hands of worthless people who will be mischievious, greedy and ill mannered.

Responsibilities will be entrusted to unfit persons. Wine will be used commonly and openly. Musicians and dancers will become very popular. Musical instruments will be in abundance and in the *Ummat*, successors will abuse and condemn their predecessors.

The Holy Prophet (SAW) said that at such time one may expect such calamities as red dust-storm, the disappearance of some people in the earth, raining of stones from the sky, changing of appearances (faces) i.e. men will become dogs and pigs and many such calamities may follow in quick successions as if the string of a rosary has broken and the beads are falling rapidly.

Some more signs have been reported, such as, learning of religion will decline, lie will become an art, regard of trust (*amanat*) will disappear, modesty and shame will vanish, infidels will dominate every where. When all the abovementioned signs will have appeared, the *Nasara* (Christians) will dominate the world and will become its rulers.

Just at this time a man will be born in the clan of Abu

Sufian in Syria and he will kill a large number of Syeds and shall rule Syria and Egypt.

During this period there will be a battle between the Muslim ruler of Rome and Christians, but there will be compromise with one party of Christians. The enemy Christian party shall invade Constantinople and will conquer it and its king will go to Syria leaving his country. There will be great battle between the enemy Christian party and the Muslims joined by the Christian party in peace with Muslim. The Muslim army will be victorious.

But one day all of a sudden a man from the friend party of Christians will cry out that the victory was gained by the blessings of Cross and the Muslims will cry that it was due to the blessings of Islam. The difference will take a serious turn and there will be battle between the two in which the Muslim king will be killed and Syria also will go under the Christian domination. The surviving Muslims will migrate to Medina and the Christian rule will extend upto Khyber, a place near Medina.

In such circumstances the Muslims will become anxious to find out *Imam Mehdi* to be relieved of all these calamities. At this time *Imam Mehdi* will be in Medina but apprehending that people will press him to take over the administration will go to Mecca. Some pretenders will also come claiming themselves to be *Imam Mehdi*. In short, *Imam Mehdi* while engaged in *Tawaf* of Ka'aba will be recognised by some pious men between *Hajar-e-Aswad* and *Maqam-e-Ibrahim*. He will be pressed by these pious men to take their pledge (*Baiyat*) as their ruler. During the course of pledge a voice will come from the sky which will be heard by all those present that "This is Caliph of Allah, *Imam Medhi*."

After the appearance of *Imam Mehdi* most prominent signs of the Last Day will begin to appear. With the spread of the news of pledge, the Muslim army of Medina will come to Mecca and the devotees of Syria, Iraq, Yemen and many other Arab armies will join him. A man from Khurasan will march

It is certain that you will give up taking delicious dishes because life is very dear to you. No doubt sins are very tasteful and virtues are insipid, but Allah, the greatest of all physicians, has indicated the harms of these and benefits of the other—the loss is Hell and benefit is Paradise—then how strange and unfortunate it is that for the sake of life, the instructions of the physician are followed but in matters of faith the injunctions of Allah are discarded and no courage is shown to give up sins. How foolish you are not to value the ever-lasting bliss of Paradise".

Tell your Nafs, "The world is a journey and no comfort is possible in a journey and one has to face troubles and inconveniences in it. But a traveller endures all these in the hope of complete rest and comfort on reaching home. But if the traveller being harrassed of these difficulties makes some inn to be his home and collects all stuffs of comfort then he may not be able to see his home for ever. In the same way so long as one has to live in this world, all troubles and inconveniences are to be endured as next world is our real home. If one desires comforts in this world, it would be very difficult to get it at home".

So one should not covet the comforts and pleasures of this world, but the betterment and good of the next world. All difficulties and troubles should be borne willingly. So with such persuasions the self (*Nafs*) should be brought to the right path and thus should be practised everyday. It must be clearly understood and remembered that if you will not try for your own good, who else will be so sympathetic to you.

# NIKAH OF THE CONSORTS AND DAUGHTERS OF THE HOLY PROPHET

## Nikah of Hadrat Fatima

First of all Hadrat Abu Bakr and then Hadrat Umar (peace be upon them) requested the Holy Prophet (SAW) for his daughter Hadrat Fatima to be given in marriage. The Prophet (SAW) declined the proposal as Hadrat Fatima was too young for marriage at that time. Then Hadrat Ali himself came to the Holy Prophet (SAW) and very modestly asked for the hand of Hadrat Fatima in marriage. Immediately it was revealed to him (SAW) through 'Wahi' (Divine Inspiration) by Allah to accept the proposal of Hadrat Ali. The Holy Prophet accepted the proposal accordingly.

It shows that in proposals of betrothals all the unnecessary ceremonies which are observed now a-days are quite useless and against Sunna. Simply verbal proposal and acceptance is sufficient. At that time the age of Hadrat Fatima was $15\frac{1}{2}$ years and Hadrat Ali was twenty-one years old. This also shows that when the boy and the girl reach that age, marriage should not be delayed and also there must be some proportion in their ages, that is the bridegroom should be older than the bride.

At the time of *Nikah* the Prophet (SAW) said, "O' Anas go and call Abu Bakr, Umar, Usman, Talha, Zubair and some members of the Ansar Community". This proves that to call some important persons or near ones at the time of *Nikah* is not objectionable. The chief motive of such a gathering is that the news of the performance of *Nikah* should be spread properly among the community. But there should be no pomp and show to such gatherings.

When all the Companions arrived, the Holy Prophet (SAW)

## NIKAH OF THE CONSORTS AND DAUGHTERS

recited the Sermon (*Khutba*) and performed the *Nikah*. Four hundred *mithqals* of silver was fixed as dowry. It shows that to fix large amount of money as *Mehr* is against *Sunna*. The *Mehr* of Hadrat Fatima is proper and also a blessing. Then the Prophet (SAW) took some dry dates in a dish and distributed the same among those present. Thereafter Hadrat Fatima was sent to Hadrat Ali's house with Hadrat Umme Aiman. The ceremony was quite simple. There was no pomp and show and this was the marriage of the daughter of the king of both the worlds.

Then the Holy Prophet (SAW) went to their (Hadrat Ali's) house and asked Hadrat Fatima to bring some water and he (SAW) poured his gargling in the cup and asked Hadrat Fatima to stand before him and sprinkling the water over her chest and head prayed, "O' Allah, I entrust you the children of these both to Your Protection from the cursed Satan". Then the Prophet (SAW) asked her to turn her back towards him and sprinkled the water between her shoulders and again recited the same prayer (*Dua*).

Then the Holy Prophet (SAW) asked Hadrat Ali to bring some water and did the same thing as he had done with Hadrat Fatima, but did not sprinkle the water on his back. (It is advisable and proper to perform this act after calling the bride and the bride-groom together. It is an act of blessing). Then the Holy Prophet (SAW) said to them, "Now both of you go to your home with the blessing of Allah."

In another report it has been said that after the performance of *Nikah* and departure of Hadrat Fatima, the Holy Prophet (SAW) went to the house of Hadrat Ali after *Isha* prayer. He took some water and poured his saliva in it and recited Surah *Qul-aoodho-berabbil-falaq* and *Qul-aoodho-berobbinas* and prayed. Then he (SAW) ordered Hadrat Ali and Hadrat Fatima to drink from the water and make ablution with it. Then he (SAW) prayed for their purity, for love between them, increase in their children and good-luck and then asked them to go and rest. (If the house of son-in-law is near, then to follow this act is cause of blessing).

Hadrat Fatima's dowry consisted of two sheets of cloth, two quilts filled with the bark of lind tree, four beds, two armulets of silver, one blanket, one pillow, one bowl, one water skin, one hand-mill, one water container and one cot.

Muslims should be careful about three things in giving dowry :
1. Do not give far beyond your means.
2. Only most necessary things of daily use should be given.
3. There should be no intention of show because it is a favour to the children and not a matter of name or fame.

After the marriage Hadrat Ali arranged the feast of *Walima* which consisted of bread of about eight seers of barley, some dates and *maleeda* (pounded meal cakes mixed with butter and sugar). The *Walima* according to *Sunna* is that it must be very simple without any tinge of show. Whatever is possible and within one's means may be offered to important and related persons.

### Dowry (Mehr) of Consorts of the Holy Prophet

The dowry (*Mehr*) of Hadrat Khadija was about five hundred dirhams or camels of that value for which Abu Lahb took the responsibility. The dowry of Hadrat Umme Salma was something of daily use of the value of about four hundred dinars which were paid by the king of Abyssinia. The dowry of Hadrat Sauda was also four hundred dirhams.

In Hadrat Umme Salma's *Walima* food prepared with barley was served. In Hadrat Zainab's *Walima* goat-meat and bread were served. In Hadrat Safia's *Walima* mutton the companions of the Holy Prophet had was collected and served. In Hadrat Aiyesha's *Walima*, a cup of milk which was sent by Hadrat Saad Bin Ubada was served.

### About Women

Allah has said that those women who devote themselves to Islam : offer prayers and observe fasts regularly ; distinguish between good and sinful acts; keep their faith intact, that is, do not let anything against the Holy Quran and Traditions take root in their minds and hearts; live obediently and do not brag; give *Zakat* and charity; protect their honour and chastity; remember Allah very much in heart and by words; for such women Allah has reserved great reward and His Forgiveness.

Allah has said that women of good disposition possess such qualities, that they obey their husbands and even in their absence protect their respect, honour and chastity.

The Holy Prophet(SAW)has said that blessed be the women who wake up in the later part of the night to offer *Tahajju*d prayer and also make their husbands wake-up for the same.

The Prophet (SAW) said that a woman who dies unmarried (virgin) or during delivery of a child or during the maternity period, will get the status of a martyr. He (SAW) further said that a woman whose three children die and she bears the shock and loss patiently with an intent for credit, shall be sent to Paradise. A woman asked the Holy Prophet (SAW) if only two children die. The Prophet (SAW) replied that credit is the same even for two.

The Holy Prophet (SAW) said that the best treasure is an obedient wife having good disposition so that her husband is pleased to see her and she obeys him.

The Holy Prophet (SAW) said that the women of Quraish are better than other women in two respects firstly because they love children and secondly they guard the property of their husbands.

It shows that these two qualities should be in women. The Holy Prophet (SAW) advised men to marry virgins because they are soft in conversation, modest and not out-spoken and they are pleased with little amount for expenses.

It shows that modesty and patience are good qualities and women should possess them. But it does not mean that men should not marry widows. On the other hand the Holy Prophet (SAW) has blessed and prayed in favour of those men who marry widows. The Holy Prophet (SAW) is reported to have said that a woman who has offered five times' prayers regularly, kept fasts in *Ramadan* and has guarded her modesty and chastity, she may enter Paradise from any of the doors of Paradise which she likes.

The Holy Prophet (SAW) has said that if a woman dies in such condition that her husband was pleased with her, she will go to Paradise.

A person told the Holy Prophet (SAW) that such and such woman offers *Nafl* prayers abundantly, keeps fast and gives *Zakat* and charity, but taunts and hurts her neighbours with her tongue. The Holy Prophet (SAW) replied that she will go to Hell. Then the person said that there was another woman who is not very particular about *Nafl* prayers, fasts or charity, but does not harm her neighbours with her tongue. He (SAW) replied that she will go to Paradise.

The Holy Prophet (SAW) said to women that they should be pleased when anyone of them conceives from her husband and he is pleased with her then she gets as much credit as for a fast in the name of Allah kept by one, when she is in throes of labour she gets such repose which has been kept secret from the beings of Heavens and earth. When she delivers the child and every draught of her milk that the child sucks is rewarded by a virtue. If she remains awake in the night for the sake of the child she is rewarded as if seventy slaves were freed by her.

The Holy Prophet (SAW) said that when a woman spends from the wealth of her husband in charity and she does not destroy the home but spends reasonably and within permissible limits, then the woman and her husband both get credit for that.

It shows that a woman should spend reasonably out of the income of her husband and also she should not think that she will not get any reward for spending in charity out of the income of her husband.

The Holy Prophet (SAW) said to women that "their *Jihad* was *Haj*." *Jihad* is the most difficult worship and women are entitled to get its reward by performing *Haj* only which is not so difficult as compared to *Jihad*.

The Holy Prophet (SAW) performed *Haj* with all of his consorts and then advised them to remain confined to their houses i.e. should not go on journey without legitimate cause.

The Holy Prophet (SAW) said that Allah likes that woman who obeys and loves her husband and protects herself from other men.

The Holy Prophet (SAW) said that women are part of men i.e. Hadrat Hawwa (Eve) was created from the left rib of Hadrat Adam and instructions for both (men and women) are the same.

The Holy Prophet (SAW) said to men that "they get reward equal to *Sadqa* by doing works of their wives." It is a great inducement to men and matter of repose for women.

The Holy Prophet SAW) said that the best of all the women is one who pleases her husband when he looks towards her, obeys him when given some order and does not oppose him by displeasing him out of her 'self' and wealth.

The Holy Prophet (SAW) said that the vice of an immoral woman is equal to the vices of one thousand immoral men while the virtue of a pious woman is equal to the credit of worship by seventy *Aulia* (saints).

The Holy Prophet (SAW) said that performing the domestic chores by a woman equals have to those engaged in Jihad.

The Holy Prophet (SAW) said that out of your wives she is the best who is pure in her chastity and loves her husband.

Hadrat Asma daughter of Yazid Ansari has reported that she appeared before the Holy Prophet (SAW) on behalf of the women and submitted that because of Juma prayer, congregation, visiting a sick, funeral prayer, Haj, Umra and Jihad men have gained superiority over the women. He (SAW) replied, "Go and inform the women that their decoration for their husbands, to discharge the husband's rights, to seek their husband's pleasure and to follow the wish of their husbands are equal to these acts of men."

The Prophet (SAW) said that a woman from the time of

being pregnant upto delivery and suckling of the baby remains in such condition in matter of credit as one who has been appointed to guard the boundaries of Islam and always remains prepared for Jihad. If she dies during this period, she will get reward equal to a martyr.

The Holy Prophet (SAW) said to women to remember that virtuous and pious ones of the women will go to Heaven before pious men and when their husbands will go to Heaven, these women will be bathed and perfumed and handed over to their husbands.

The Holy Prophet (SAW) said to men, "Among you the best are those who are good to their wives."

The Holy Prophet (SAW) said, "In respect of women accept my advise : Treat them well, because woman has been born out of a rib and do not expect complete uprightness and soundness from them and be patient upon their strong headedness."

The Holy Prophet (SAW) advised men not to treat their wives as slaves.

**Defects of Women**

Allah has said in the Holy Quran (to men) "that if it appears that your wives do not obey you, first advise them. If they do not listen, give up sleeping and sitting with them. If even then they do not listen or obey, then beat them (lightly). they begin to obey thereafter, then do not try to find excuses to harrass them."

Allah has ordained women not to walk with thumping steps so that the jingling of their ornaments be heard by men. Muslim women are strictly forbidden the use of such garments which are worn for display or effect. Such women have been cursed who wear such clothes which reveal their body. Also cursed are the women who walk with a swinging gait.

The Holy Prophet (SAW) said to women that he has seen women in Hell in large number. The women asked why. He (SAW) replied, "Because you are habitual of cursing everything, show thanklessness to your husbands and scowl the things given by them."

In the presence of Holy Prophet a woman cursed fever. He (SAW) prohibited to curse fever as it is a cause of forgiveness of sins.

The Holy Prophet (SAW) said that if a woman who weeps with lamentation does not repent. She will be raised on the Day of Judgement in such state that her body will be oiled with a shirt of solution which catches fire immediately and her entire body will be itching, that is, she will be subjected to two punishments—she will scratch her entire body on account of itching and burnt with the fire of Hell.

The Holy Prophet (SAW) said that women should not look down upon the thing sent by her neighbour as a gift, however invaluable it may be.

The Holy Prophet (SAW) said that a woman was punished by Allah for keeping a cat tied without giving it anything to eat or drink and did not let it go till it died.

The Holy Prophet (SAW) said that some men and women worship Allah for sixty years, then at the time of death become entitled to Hell by making a will against the injunctions of Islam. That is, they deprive their lawful heirs and give their legacy to others by Will or by distributing unfairly among the heirs.

The Holy Prophet (SAW) has said that a woman who harms her husband in the world then the *Hoor* (Heavenly being) who is to be awarded to the husband in the Hereafter curses that woman and says that he is like a guest with you (woman) and will come to us very soon.

Muslim women should avoid all these evil deeds and save themselves from the wrath of Allah and punishment in the other world.

# FOR PLEASANT LIFE

## 1—Behaviour with the Masses

Generally people are of three kinds. One of them are those who are relatives, friends and companions. The second are those who are mere acquaintances. The third are those who are not even acquaintances. So the way of dealing with each category is also different.

So far as the first category is concerned, see if they possess the following five qualities. If they have these, there is no harm in becoming familiar and establishing friendship with them:

Firstly, see that he is wise, because friendship with a foolish person cannot be maintained.

Secondly, his habits, nature and manners should be good. He should not be selfish in friendship, should not lose temper and should not feel offended on petty matters.

Thirdly, he should be a practising Muslim because nominal Muslim does not pay his due to Allah, how can he be depended as faithful. The next evil is that when you see him committing sins and un-Islamic acts again and again and you ignore them due to your friendship, you will gradually forget to hate sins and there is strong possibility of your committing those sins yourself.

Fourthly he should not be greedy and coveting worldly wealth, because association with greedy person may also increase your greed. He will always talk of worldly wealth and entangle you sooner or later in this greed. One, who has no greed and is content with what he has, always talks of transitoriness of the world and this helps eradicating whatever greed one has in his mind.

Fifthly, he should not be in the habit of telling a lie because a liar cannot be trusted.

Before cultivating any friendship with anyone one should take care to look for the abovementioned five qualities. When satisfied with him and having become friends, one should fulfil the following rights and duties of friendship :

As and when possible help your friend in need and if you have the means, help him with money also.

Do not give out his secrets or propagate his weaknesses and shortcomings.

If anyone speaks ill of him, do not tell him about it.

Be attentive to him when he says anything.

If you find some wrong in him, tell him very politely about it.

Forgive or ignore if he commits some fault and always pray to Allah for his good and betterment.

The second category of persons, who are neither friends nor acquainted, one has to be very cautious about them as they profess friendship and goodwill verbally, but in reality they plan to ruin you. Such persons always seek opportunities to defame and disgrace.

The persons of the third category who are not acquainted even, are neither friends nor foes. If they are not good, they not bad also. Mostly such persons are not feared.

So it is advisable that as far as possible do not acquire acquaintance with anyone because in that case there is greater possibility of being harmed. Do not covet worldly things in their way and nor disrupt your faith for their sake. Do not pay attention towards their talk about worldly things or notions. Do not mix with them. Do not except anything from them or ask for any help. If their talk is immoral and you are confident they will listen to your advice, then tell them about it in a lenient way.

Do not be inimical to those who keep enemity with you because it would lead to greater evil which may not be able to bear, and it may ruin this world and the next one also. If anyone respects you or praises you and shows affection towards you, then be cautious and be not deceived by trusting him immediately; because there are people whose outer and inner self is not the same and you cannot judge at the first monent whether he is sincere to you or not.

If anyone back-bites or speaks ill of you, you should not be angry with him or wonder at his critical behaviour, because, to be fair, you, too can be a prey of the same habit. So first judge about yourself before being angry with anyone else.

To sum up, you should not expect any good from anyone —neither any honour nor any affection for you in anyone's heart. This 'expectation' is the greatest enemy. When you will expect anything from anyone, you will have no disappointment and also you will not feel sorry for any treatment by anyone. So far as you are concerned, do good to others without expecting any return or recognition for the same. If anyone does some good to you, thank Allah and pray for that person. But if any harm or loss comes from anyone, take it as a punishment for some of your sins or wrongs and express repentance to Allah and do not be angry with that person. Do not look to the good or evil of other persons, look towards Allah and devote yourself of His obedience and remembrance. May Allah bless us all to do so. *Aameen.*

## 2—Fear of Allah and Cleanliness of Heart

Allah says that you should fear Him as fear prevents men from evils. One should always remember Allah and repent for evils and wrong actions. One should not lose hope in Allah's Mercy, because hope in Him encourages virtues and fortifies the heart for penitence. So one should always remember and think of Allah's Mercy. Be delighted with Allah's favours and thereby foster His favours are innumerable and if there is some trouble then it is for our benefit and it is a favour also because in trouble we turn towards Allah and seek His help. It is the faith of every Muslim that there is no favour or trouble without the Will of Allah. This trust or faith in Allah, that is, one should always remember and realise the Power and Wisdom of Allah and the smallness and insignificance of human beings.

When we know that whatever Allah does, is for our benefit, we should be satisfied and contended with everything and should not complain or show embarrassment over it. Whatever is done in obedience of Allah there should be no thought of worldly gain, and if there is the least trace of worldly gain, it should be cleared from the mind and heart.

It should always be kept in our minds that Allah is aware of all what we say and what is in our minds. Nothing can escape from Him. If any evil is done, it is at the discretion of Allah to punish us either in this world or in the next.

Hadrat Abu Huraira has reported the Holy Prophet (SAW) to have said that Allah certainly does not see your body or face but your hearts. So when you obey Allah outwardly without full attention and devotion of heart, such acts will not be accepted by Allah. All such acts should be accompanied by sincerity of heart as has been said in the Holy Quran and the Traditions. So if any prayer, charity or devotional act is performed just for the sake of show or name, it will not be taken into account. One who is not free from inner ailments, cannot perform even the essentials of religion.

Hadrat N'oman bin Bashir has reported the Holy Prophet (SAW) to have said, "There is a part in the body and it is just a piece of flesh. If it is right, the whole body is right and if it is spoiled, the whole body is spoiled. Beware, that part is heart." It means that the correct functioning of the body and obedience to Allah depends upon the purity of heart. Thus correction and purification of heart becomes incumbent on every Muslim to be true in obedience to Allah. The Holy Prophet (SAW) has said that offering two *Raka'ats* of prayer with purity of heart is better than whole night's prayer offered with an indifferent heart. This emphasis on the purity of heart means that in any action it is quality that matters and not quantity.

## REMEMBERING DEATH

The Holy Prophet (SAW) is said to have asked the Muslims to remember death very frequently as recalling the death keeps one away from sins. It creates disgust with this world and fear of awful punishment in the next world for sins. The world is condemned beacuse it makes one forget Allah.

It has been reported in the Holy Traditions that, one who visits the graves of his parents every Friday, his sins will be forgiven and he will be recorded as obedient to his parents. But it is prohibited to go round the graves or kiss them, whether they are of Prophets or Saints. On visiting the graves one should recite :

*Assalamo-alaikum ya-ah-lal-qubure-e-minal momineena-wal-muslimina-yaghferullaha-lano—Walakum-wa-antum-Salafna wa nahno bilsar*—That, "Peace be on you O' grave dwellers, on all believers from all the Muslims. You have gone ahead of us and we to follow" and turning back towards Ka'aba and facing the grave one should recite Holy Quran as much as one remembers.

It is reported in the Traditions that one who passes by graves should recite *Sura Ikhlas* eleven times and transfer its reward to all the dead or recite *Sura Ikhlas*, *Sura Takathur*, *Alhamd* and *Sura Yaseen* and that Allah may forgive their sins and send blessings to them. The person reciting these will also get credit for reciting them. May we all be able to do good. *Aameen.*

## A'AMAL-E-QURANI

Sickness is treated with medicines, in the same way it is treated with "A'amal-e-Qurani". It is better to resort to these than to consult sooth-sayers or take omens etc. Such evil practices spoil faith and are sinful. So some very effective Quranic A'amal are given below:—

**For Head and Tooth-Ache**

Spreading clean dust or a clean plank write with a nail the Arabic letters—"Abjad, Hawwaz, Hutti" "and first press the nail on 'Alif' (and the person suffering should press that part with his finger) and recite Alhamd once, then ask him about the pain. If it is still there, then press 'Ba' (next letter of the first word) and recite Alhamd. In this way go on pressing the next letter. By the Grace of Allah before the end of all the letters, the pain will vanish.

**For All Kinds of Pains**

Recite this verse thrice with *Bismillah,* blow on the affected part or blow it on some oil and massage the affected part with it.

وَبِالْحَقِّ أَنْزَلْنَاهُ وَبِالْحَقِّ نَزَلَ ط وَمَا أَرْسَلْنَاكَ اِلاَّ مُبَشِّراً

وَنَذِيراً ٥

**For Weakness of Mind**

After each *Fard* prayer recite *Ya-Qawiyun* eleven times keeping your hand over the head.

**For Weak Eye-Sight**

After each *Fard* prayer recite *Ya-Nooro* eleven times and puffing on the tips of fingers of both hands pass them over the eyes.

## For Stammering

After *Fajr* prayer keeping a clean pebble in the mouth recite this verse twenty-one times :

$$رَبِّ اشْرَحْ لِى صَدْرِى وَيَسِّرْ لِى أَمْرِى وَاحْلُلْ عُقْدَةً مِنْ لِّسَانِى يَفْقَهُوا قَوْلِى$$

## For Depression of Heart

Write the following verse with *Bismillah* on a piece of paper and wear it round the neck with a long cord so that the amulet may be hanging on the heart :

$$اَلَّذِيْنَ اٰمَنُوْا وَتَطْمَئِنُّ قُلُوْبُهُمْ بِذِكْرِ اللهِ ط اَلاَ بِذِكْرِ اللهِ تَطْمَئِنُّ الْقُلُوْبُ ط$$

## For Stomach-Ache

Recite the following verse on water and give the patient to drink :

$$لَا فِيْهَا غَوْلٌ وَّلَا هُمْ عَنْهَا يُنْزَفُوْنَ ط$$

## For Cholera and Plague

During these epidemics before eating or drinking anything recite *Sura Inna Anzalna* thrice over it.

## For Spleen

Write this verse with *Bismillah* on a piece of paper and tie it over the spleen :

$$ذٰلِكَ تَخْفِيْفٌ مِّنْ رَّبِّكُمْ وَرَحْمَةٌ ط$$

## For Fever

If it is without cold, then write this verse and tie round the neck :

$$قُلْنَا يَا نَارُ كُوْنِيْ بَرْدًا وَّسَلَامًا عَلٰى اِبْرَاهِيْمَ$$

If the fever is with cold, then write this verse :

## A'AMAL-E-QURANI

بِسْمِ اللهِ مُجْرٖىهَا وَمُرْسٰىهَا اِنَّ رَبِّىْ لَغَفُوْرٌ رَّحِيْمٌ ط

### For Boils and Ulcers

Take a clod of earth and after reciting the following prayer (*Dua*) spit thrice over it and after sprinkling some water over the clod rub it on the affected part for a few times in a day :

اِنَّهُمْ يَكِيْدُوْنَ كَيْدًا o وَّاَكِيْدُ كَيْدًا o فَمَهِّلِ الْكٰفِرِيْنَ اَمْهِلْهُمْ رُوَيْدًا o

### For Snake and Wasp Bite

Dissolve some salt in a little water and rub it on the affected part reciting and puffing *Sura Qul* on it.

### For Dog-Bite

Write the following verse on forty pieces of bread or biscuit and give these to patient to eat :

بِسْمِ اللهِ بِتُرْبَةِ اَرْضِنَا بِرِيْقَةِ بَعْضِنَا الْمُشْفٰى سَقِيْمَنَا بِاِذْنِ رَبِّنَا

### For A Son

A woman who always gives birth to a girl, during the beginning of her next pregnancy, her husband or some woman should make seventy circles with finger on her belly and each time should recite *Ya Mateeno*. By the Grace of Allah she will give birth to a boy.

### For Small-Pox

Take seven blue thread strings and recite *Surah Rahman* and when he reaches the verse *Fabi-aiyy-e-ala-e* he should puff at the string and tie a knot in the string. By the end of the *Sura* there will be thirty-one knots and then put the string round the neck of the child. If it is done before the Smallpox, then it will protect the child and if tied after appearing of the disease, then the patient will not suffer much.

### For Removal of Poverty

After *Isha* prayers recite *Darood Sharif* eleven times before and after and in between say *Ya Moeezo* eleven hundred times. Or recite *Darood Sharif* seven times before and after reciting *Ya Wahabo* for fourteen times.

### For Removal of Difficulties

For twelve days recite the following prayer (*Dua*) twelve thousand times each day :

*Ya Badi'ul-Ajaib Bil-Khair Ya Badee'*

Howsoever difficult the task may be, it will be achieved by the Grace of Allah.

### God's Help for Good Acts

Recite *Al-Baseero* one hundred times after Juma prayers. It cleans the heart and Allah helps one for doing good acts or recite abundantly *Al-Qaiyuum* or *Ya Hayyo Ya-Qayyuum*.

### To Get Pleasure of Allah

Recite *Al-Afwo* abundantly. It redeems sins.

### To Get Rid of Difficulties

Recite regularly the following verse and by the Mercy of Allah all of the difficulties will be removed ;

*Hasbo nallaho wa n'emal wakeel*

Or recite *As-Sameeo* five hundred times on Thursday after Chasht prayer.

Or recite *Ayatul Kursi* seventy times on Friday sitting in seculsion after *Asr* prayer.

Or recite *Al-Wakeelo* abundantly. It is useful for every need.

**THE END**